EGYPTOLOGY TODAY

Egyptology Today examines how modern scholars study all aspects of ancient Egypt, one of the greatest of all ancient civilizations. In essays by archaeologists, curators, scholars, and conservators who are actively involved in research or applied aspects of Egyptology, this book looks at the techniques and methods used to increase our understanding of a distant culture that was as old to the Greeks and Romans as their cultures are to us. Topics range from how tombs and other monuments are discovered, excavated, recorded, and preserved to the study of Egyptian history, art, artifacts, and texts. Each chapter shows how modern Egyptology approaches, learns about, and strives to preserve the ancient remains of one of the most fascinating cultures in human history.

Richard H. Wilkinson is professor of Egyptian archaeology at the University of Arizona. As Director of the University of Arizona Egyptian Expedition, he has conducted archaeological projects in Egypt's Valley of the Kings for twenty years and is currently excavating the memorial temple of Queen Tausert in western Thebes. He is the author of many articles and reviews as well as seven previous books, most recently *The Complete Gods and Goddesses of Ancient Egypt* and *Egyptian Scarabs*.

EGYPTOLOGY TODAY

Edited by

Richard H. Wilkinson
University of Arizona

CAMBRIDGE
UNIVERSITY PRESS

CAMBRIDGE UNIVERSITY PRESS
Cambridge, New York, Melbourne, Madrid, Cape Town, Singapore, São Paulo, Delhi

Cambridge University Press
32 Avenue of the Americas, New York, NY 10013-2473, USA

www.cambridge.org
Information on this title: www.cambridge.org/9780521863643

First published 2008

Printed in the United States of America

A catalog record for this publication is available from the British Library.

Library of Congress Cataloging in Publication Data
Wilkinson, Richard H.
Egyptology today / edited by Richard H. Wilkinson.
p.   cm.
Includes bibliographical references and index.
ISBN 978-0-521-86364-3 hardback
ISBN 978-0-521-68226-8 (pbk.)
1. Egyptology.   2. Egypt – Antiquities.   I. Title.
DT60.W768   2007
932.0072–dc22   2007018738

ISBN   978-0-521-86364-3 hardback
ISBN   978-0-521-68226-8 paperback

CONTENTS

PART I
METHODS: PATHS TO THE PAST

PART II
MONUMENTS: STRUCTURES FOR THIS LIFE AND THE NEXT

Contents

LIST OF ILLUSTRATIONS

BRIEF BIOGRAPHIES OF CONTRIBUTORS

JAMES P. ALLEN
Wilbour Professor of Egyptology and Chair, Department of Egyptology and Ancient Western Asian Studies, Brown University
Allen, J. P., *Middle Egyptian: An Introduction to the Language and Culture of Hieroglyphs*. Cambridge, 2000.

A. ROSALIE DAVID, OBE
Professor of Biomedical Egyptology and Director of the KNH Center, University of Manchester
David, A. R., ed. *Egyptian Mummies and Modern Science*. Cambridge, forthcoming.

PETER F. DORMAN
Professor of Egyptology and Chairman, Department of Near Eastern Languages and Civilizations, Oriental Institute, University of Chicago
Dorman, P., *Faces in Clay: Technique, Imagery, and Allusion in a Corpus of Ceramic Sculpture from Ancient Egypt*. Mainz, 2002.

ANN L. FOSTER
Fellow, The American Research Center in Egypt
A. L. Foster is currently working with J. L. Foster on the publication of the literary ostraca from the collection of the Oriental Institute of the University of Chicago.

JOHN L. FOSTER
Research Associate, The Oriental Institute of the University of Chicago
Foster, J. L., *Ancient Egyptian Literature: An Anthology*. Austin, 2001.

RITA E. FREED
John F. Cogan and Mary L. Cornille Chair, Art of the Ancient World, Museum of Fine Arts, Boston, and Adjunct Professor of Art at Wellesley College
Freed, Rita E., Yvonne J. Markowitz, and Sue H. D'Auria. *Pharaohs of the Sun: Akhenaten, Nefertiti, Tutankhamen*. Boston, 1999.

SUSANNE GÄNSICKE
Conservator, Museum of Fine Arts, Boston
Gänsicke, S., and Timothy Kendall, "A Fresh Look at the Cylinder Sheaths from Nuri, Sudan," *Nubian Studies 1998. Proceedings of the Ninth Conference of the International Society of Nubian Studies, August 21–26, 1998, Boston, Massachusetts*, 24–33. Boston, 2004.

MICHAEL JONES
Associate Director, Egyptian Antiquities Conservation Project, American Research Center in Egypt, Cairo
Jones, M., "The Church of St. Antony: The Architecture." In Elizabeth S. Bolman, ed., *Monastic Visions, Wall Paintings in the Monastery of St. Antony at the Red Sea*. New Haven, CT, and London, 2002.

ARIELLE P. KOZLOFF
Former Curator, The Cleveland Museum of Art
Kozloff, A., and B. Bryan. *Egypt's Dazzling Sun: Amenhotep III and His World*. Cleveland, 1992.

RONALD J. LEPROHON
Professor of Egyptology, Department of Near and Middle Eastern Civilizations, University of Toronto
R. Leprohon. *Stelae 1. The Early Dynastic Period to the Late Middle Kingdom*. Corpus Antiquitatum Aegyptiacarum. Fasc. 2. Boston Museum of Fine Arts. Mainz, 1985.
R. Leprohon. *Stelae 2. The New Kingdom to the Coptic Period*. Corpus Antiquitatum Aegyptiacarum. Fasc. 3. Boston Museum of Fine Arts. Mainz, 1991.

SARAH H. PARCAK
Assistant Professor, University of Alabama–Birmingham
Parcak, S., "Satellite Remote Sensing Methods for Monitoring Archaeological Tell Sites in the Middle East," *Journal of Field Archaeology* (forthcoming): 41 pp.

DONALD B. REDFORD, FRSC
Professor of Classics and Ancient Mediterranean Studies, The Pennsylvania State University
Redford, D. B. *Egypt, Canaan and Israel in Ancient Times*. Princeton, NJ, 1992.

KENT R. WEEKS
Professor Emeritus, the American University in Cairo and Director of the Theban Mapping Project
Weeks, K. R. *The Atlas of the Valley of the Kings*. Cairo, 2000.

Acknowledgments

THE EDITOR:

The editor would like to acknowledge with gratitude the work of the contributors to this volume and the kind help of his wife, Anna, whose patience and encouragement were invaluable. Thanks are also due to Cambridge University Press Publishing Director Beatrice Rehl, Aptara Inc. Production Manager Mary Paden, and everyone involved in the volume's production.

S. GANSICKE:

Thanks are due to Arthur Beale, Michele Derrick, Lisa Ellis, Abigail Hykin, Dawn Kimbrell, Richard Newman, Deborah Schorsch, and Timothy Kendall for advice, for discussions, and for providing resources or scientific analysis.

A. KOZLOFF:

This author would like to thank the following people for having added their thoughts to this discussion: Lawrence Berman, Vivian Davies, Élisabeth Delange, Renée Dreyfus, Rita Freed, Thomas Hardwick, Zahi Hawass, Christine Lilyquist, Maarten Raven, Regine Schultz, Neal Spencer, Nigel Strudwick, Mary Suzor, and John Taylor. She is also grateful to the Muses for having brought her to work with Sherman Lee, Jack Cooney, Evan Turner, and the outstanding staff of the Cleveland Museum of Art.

S. PARCAK:

I would like to thank Richard Wilkinson for inviting me to contribute to this volume, Peter Piccione for sharing the results of his Luxor project, and Greg Mumford for his editorial assistance.

INTRODUCTION

THE PAST IN THE PRESENT

Egyptology Today

Richard H. Wilkinson

The civilization of ancient Egypt was one of the greatest of the past, often inspiring awe and respect in other ancient societies such as those of the Greeks and Romans, whose cultures were themselves highly developed for their time. Today, ancient Egypt still continues to fascinate us through its many achievements. Depictions of the pyramids, temples, obelisks, colossi, and tombs of the Nile Valley are recognized by people around the world and Egyptology – the study of all aspects of ancient Egypt – has developed into a focused and thriving branch of our study of the past.

BEYOND TUTANKHAMUN AND INDIANA JONES

Probably no other area of historical study has been so typecast in the popular image it has developed, however. It is undeniable that both extraordinary real events such as the discovery of the tomb of Tutankhamun and fictional figures such as Hollywood's adventurer-archaeologist Indiana Jones have colored popular perception of the study of ancient Egypt. Regardless of whether the events and figures entrenched in popular culture fit any part of Egyptology as it is actually practiced as a modern scientific discipline, a large percentage of the general public remains enamored of the very idea of the search for and study of tombs, temples, mummies, and priceless artifacts.

Nevertheless, and Hollywood creations aside, many people are fascinated by aspects of real Egyptology that go beyond treasures and discoveries, and exhibitions of Egyptian art, studies of the ancient culture's kings and queens, and efforts to record, save, or restore its threatened monuments all attract genuine interest. A fairly constant flow of television documentaries (the poor, but often more honest, relatives of Hollywood movies) dealing with such subjects attests to this fact.

Despite the great popularity of Egyptology and the wealth of books on ancient Egypt in the popular press, however, until the present volume there has been no single-volume introduction covering the present state of Egyptology as a modern field of study. This book fills that need by showing what Egyptology actually is as a modern discipline – what it does, what it knows, and where it is going or trying to go. It is an introduction to Egyptology written by practicing Egyptologists – all of whom have different careers and interests, backgrounds, training, and types of experience in the field, yet who share common goals.

BEYOND SPECIALIZATION

In the formative period of Egyptology, beginning with the early nineteenth century decipherment of the hieroglyphic script, most Egyptologists functioned like today's medical general practitioners – knowing something about everything in their field – even if they had some particular interest in art, history, archaeology, language, or some combination of these subjects. In a second stage of the discipline's history, especially in the early twentieth century, increasing specialization often resulted in scholars who knew and worked with only a narrow slice of this immensely broad field, which, it must be remembered, has as its subject virtually every aspect of a whole civilization over thousands of years. Whether concentrating on linguistic, historical, art historical, or archaeological aspects, these scholars sometimes had relatively little interaction with colleagues in other areas of the field. In recent years the stress on this kind of deep knowledge of some narrow aspect of Egyptology has been mitigated to some extent because of the realities of the job market and also the needs of the discipline itself.

Today, it is not uncommon to find Egyptologists who have broader training or who possess specific knowledge in related areas such as archaeology and geology, art history and conservation, or history and social sciences. This broader yet not entirely unspecialized training has also been enhanced by an increasing stress on interdisciplinary approaches and by cooperation in the everyday practice of Egyptology – whether on dig sites, in laboratories, or in museum galleries. This ever-increasing trend toward cooperation between Egyptologists and other specialists – both within the field and from related disciplines – has had a significant impact on Egyptology. It is seen, for example, in the fact that the archaeological excavation of an ancient site that does not utilize specialists when and where they are needed now draws immediate and justifiable criticism *within* the field. Egyptology is no longer a gentleman's pastime or the realm of the lone adventurer, as it may have been for many in its early years. The field has changed considerably as a discipline – not only in the last century, or the last thirty years, but it has also made some great advances in the application of modern techniques and approaches in even the last decade. Today's Egyptology demands a much wider level of scholarly interaction and cooperation, and while it may not yet be perfect in this regard, this stress on interaction or the avowed need for it may be seen in every one of the following chapters.

EGYPTOLOGY TODAY

The chapters of this book have been organized into four themes, each of which looks at modern Egyptology not only as a distinct discipline but also as one that interacts with many other areas of knowledge.

Part I, "Approaches: Paths to the Ancient Past," examines some of Egyptology's major lines of evidence in terms of the relationships between the modern discipline and the underlying fields of archaeology, history, and science. Despite its specific geographic and chronological focus, Egyptology remains a part of these broader areas of knowledge, or implements them in its goal of discovering and interpreting ancient Egypt. So the discipline is perhaps best understood by first considering its relationship with these three larger fields of study. Other areas of humanistic study or social and physical sciences could certainly also be said to provide "paths to the past" for Egyptology, but many of these areas are considered in the following chapters in the contexts of their specific areas of application.

Part II, "Monuments: Structures for This Life and the Next," looks at the most visible remains of Egyptian civilization and how Egyptologists approach them. By surveying the manner in which pyramids, temples, tombs, palaces, dwellings, and other structures are now mapped, studied, documented, and conserved, this section covers a number of areas of the discipline, as well as looking at how Egyptology is approaching some of the very real problems that face some of its most important primary material – the monumental legacy of ancient Egypt.

Part III, "Art and Artifacts: Objects as Subject," continues the survey by examining Egyptology's study of smaller-scale objects – artifacts ranging from items of everyday life to some of the finest works of art (even though they may not have originally been viewed as art) produced in the ancient world. The chapters within this section deal with many issues regarding the analysis, handling, display, and conservation of this material evidence, as well as discussing questions of current importance, such as the worldwide trade in antiquities and aspects of their repatriation to Egypt.

Part IV, "Texts: The Words of Gods and Men," looks at a final area of primary evidence for ancient Egypt – the linguistic and literary. The first chapter deals with our current understanding of the Egyptian language and some of the recent approaches that have led to increased understanding of how it worked and of the ancient texts written in the hieroglyphic script. The second chapter covers the study of ancient Egypt's rich and amazingly varied literature, including the earliest examples of a number of literary genres, while the third chapter provides a focused examination of current study of the mythological and religious texts that represent an important aspect of ancient Egyptian civilization and an invaluable "window" into the ancient Egyptian's worldview.

Thus, the following chapters survey Egyptology as the fascinating discipline it is – a discipline incorporating the study of many types of evidence for one of the richest cultures to have developed in ancient history. The essays are not, however, merely paeans of accomplishment, but deal frankly, where necessary, with the ongoing growing pains of a discipline that, although two hundred years old, is still developing. These are the successes, challenges, motives, and materials of *Egyptology Today*.

PART I

METHODS

Paths to the Past

CHAPTER 1

ARCHAEOLOGY AND EGYPTOLOGY

Kent R. Weeks

Around 1250 BC, the High Priest of Ptah at Memphis, Khaemwese, fourth-born son of Ramesses II, cleared and repaired nearly a dozen pyramids and temples at Giza and Saqqara. Even in his day, they were ruins over a thousand years old, and he restored them, he said, because he "so greatly loved antiquity" that he could not bear to see them "falling into decay." Modern scholars have called Khaemwese the world's first archaeologist. Certainly, he was an enthusiastic supporter of archaeological preservation: he believed that by protecting religious buildings he honored Egypt's ancestors and ensured that contemporary religious practices would remain true to older – and therefore purer – forms of worship.[1]

Unfortunately, protecting ancient monuments has rarely been most people's goal: from antiquity onward, most saw them as buildings to be ignored or plundered. If a monument was accessible, it probably served as a village quarry, its stone blocks used to make new buildings, its crumbling brick walls used to fertilize fields. Nearby tombs were used as animal pens or storerooms. Even more detrimental, ancient sites were seen as treasure chests. Since antiquity, people knew that tombs and temples contained riches, including valuable herbs and spices, *objêts d'art*, expensive woods and cloth, papyri, and, best of all, gold. Stories of their great riches had become so common that by the eighth century AD, handbooks excitedly (and fictitiously) described how men became wealthy by robbing sites, even telling readers which sites to dig.[2]

And dig they did, even in remote corners of the country. For twenty-five centuries, until the twentieth century AD, the monuments of ancient Egypt were plundered, their treasures melted down, hacked apart, ground up, carted away, and sold. Few people showed any interest in recording or protecting antiquities.

One of the few who seemed to care was Al-Idrisi, an Arab scholar in the thirteenth century AD who published detailed descriptions of monuments at Giza. He measured their stones (and noticed that some were reused in later structures), described the clay plaster on their walls (he identified its composition and source), and analyzed the debris that buried their walls (he was one of the first to trace the stratigraphic history of an ancient site). Al-Idrisi also offered theories about the monument's functions. It would be many centuries before Europeans published comparable studies.[3]

There were several reasons for the lag in Europe's Egyptological scholarship. First, few Europeans read Arabic, and sources such as Al-Idrisi were unknown on the continent. Second, before the decipherment of hieroglyphs in 1822, the only readily available information on Egypt came from Biblical commentaries and classical writers. Classical visitors to Egypt, including Herodotus, Diodorus Siculus, Horapollo, and Pliny the Elder, described some of the things they saw on visits to Alexandria and, occasionally, up the Nile beyond Giza and Memphis, but their descriptions were cursory and often fanciful. Postclassical travelers were interested in how Egypt might shed light on the Bible, not in Egypt itself, and that emphasis skewed what they wrote about and how they explained it. Third, until the seventeenth century, few Europeans visited Egypt. The only monuments they saw firsthand were the few obelisks carted back to Europe by the Romans.[4]

But, in spite of these limitations, stories about Egypt by European travelers were growing increasingly popular, and writers who had never been to Egypt simply invented tales that would sell books. They claimed to have seen one-headed, one-legged beings in the desert behind the pyramids and argued that Egyptians were semi-divine geniuses, intermediate between men and gods. They proclaimed that Egyptian culture was more advanced than anything Europe had ever produced, and that its science, engineering, art, and architecture reached levels ordinary mortals would never again achieve.

Egypt's natural environment was no less wondrous than the cultural. Writers reported frogs spontaneously generating in the black silts of the Nile Valley and told of women who had become pregnant simply by drinking the Nile's water. Egypt, they believed, was the Garden of Eden – literally, the most perfect place on earth.[5]

Accurate or not, such stories gained wide popularity in Europe, and people's appetite for things Egyptian was further whetted by the growth of museum collections in the eighteenth century. Thousands were now able to see Egyptian objects, and what they saw – mummies, statues with human bodies and animal heads, indecipherable hieroglyphs – seemed to confirm even the wildest ideas. Egyptology would not become an academic discipline until the nineteenth century, but by the 1600s and 1700s, ancient Egypt occupied a prominent place in the European imagination – romanticized, adored, imitated, and exaggerated. These early fantasies about Egypt had long-lasting consequences for its study. For example, many respected historians argued that, although all other ancient civilizations developed along similar paths, Egypt was an exception to the rules and should be excluded from any cross-cultural studies. (Arnold Toynbee argued this case in his famous *A Study of History*.) Such ideas delayed our understanding of how Egyptian civilization arose and prolonged the idea that it had appeared full-grown in the Nile Valley, with no indigenous antecedents.

The basis for such views began to change after the decipherment of hieroglyphics by Champollion in 1822, but only slowly. European scholars now clamored for accurate copies of hieroglyphic texts, and epigraphic expeditions duly set out from Europe to record Egypt's monuments. Great projects, such as those of the French (resulting in the *Description de l'Egypte*), Carl Lepsius (the *Denkmäler aus Aegypten*), and John Gardner Wilkinson (*Manners and Customs of the Ancient Egyptians*), produced copies of texts and drawings of monuments, and offered interpretations on which much of nineteenth-century Egyptology was founded. Once hieroglyphic texts began to be translated and published, Europe's picture of Egypt began to be transformed. Accurate descriptions began to replace fanciful ones, and Egypt's culture was seen to have a human origin, not a semi-divine one. (See Sidebar 1.1 for some key contributors to the growth of Egyptology.)

These early epigraphic works are still of great value, because so many of the monuments they recorded are gone. Explorers sometimes carted away whole tombs and temple walls. Egyptian peasants, moreover, ransacked sites, searching for objects to sell to the increasing numbers of tourists. Poor excavation techniques also destroyed sites. Egyptian epigraphy and architectural history were improving their methods in the nineteenth century, but Egyptian archaeology was not. Even the most incompetent digs could produce treasure, and excavators still saw little to be gained by adopting more meticulous methods. Egyptian sites were archaeological cornucopias, they believed: there would always be more to find.

For example, in the 1830s, Howard Vyse was using gunpowder to locate the entrances of Giza pyramids and drilling holes in the body of the Sphinx to see if it was hollow. Excavators would hire hundreds of unsupervised workmen to clear sand from monuments. The sites they dug were usually stone temples or tombs, monuments known to have inscribed and decorated walls and fine-quality artifacts. Sites in the desert were preferred because they were easier to dig, less likely to have been plundered, and better preserved than sites in the wet mud of cultivated fields. An excavator might cursorily map a few stone walls during his work, but mud-brick walls were hacked away. Broken or undecorated objects were discarded, and only objects judged attractive enough for museum displays were saved. No record was made of where objects were found or of the features associated with them. Excavators published superficial information about their work, or they published nothing at all.

There were a few exceptions. In the 1850s, the Scotsman Alexander Henry Rhind dug in the Valley of the Kings and at Giza and meticulously recorded what he found, even describing fragments his colleagues would simply have thrown away. Rhind, who had dug early sites in Scotland before coming to Egypt, was one of the first to point out the dating potential of stratified deposits. He was one of the first to recognize the existence of a predynastic culture in Egypt, in several graves he cleared near Giza. He pleaded with his colleagues to leave ancient buildings intact and take away only copies of their inscriptions. He was also one of the first to urge that photography be used to record monuments, a practice that Maxime du Camp had begun in 1849. Finally, Rhind insisted that excavators should publish what they uncovered, promptly and completely. His pleas fell on deaf ears.[6]

SIDEBAR 1.1:
Fifteen Archaeologists Who Increased Our Knowledge of Egypt and Helped to Improve the Quality of Archaeological Research

(For bibliography, see Dawson and Uphill 1972.)

1. Giovanni Battista Belzoni (1772–1823). Italian, uncovered the entrance to the Giza pyramid of Chephren and the Valley of the Kings tomb of Seti I and made many other discoveries.
2. Auguste Ferdinand Mariette (1821–1881) – see text.
3. Alexander Henry Rhind (1833–1863) – see text.
4. Gaston Camille Maspero (1846–1916) – see text.
5. William Matthew Flinders Petrie (1853–1942) – see text.
6. James Edward Quibell (1867–1935). British student of Petrie, excavated in the Valley of the Kings and extensively at Saqqara.
7. George Andrew Reisner (1867–1942) – see text.
8. Hermann Junker (1877–1962). German-Austrian priest, excavated various sites, including predynastic Merimde and, most importantly, Giza, where 15 years' work resulted in a masterful 12-volume study of its mastaba tombs.
9. Herbert Eustis Winlock (1884–1950). American, worked for the Metropolitan Museum of Art at several sites, especially the Deir el-Bahari cirque; considered one of the finest archaeologists of his day; his discoveries were among the century's most important.
10. Howard Carter (1873–1939). English discoverer of the tomb of Tutankhamun; meticulous record-keeper, artist.
11. Selim Hassan (1886–1961). First Egyptian professor of Egyptology at Cairo University; excavated at many sites, but best known for his work at Giza which he published in over 12 volumes.
12. Walter Bryan Emery (1903–1971). English, worked extensively in Nubia and in Early Dynastic remains at Saqqara.
13. Margaret Benson (1865–1916). The first woman to be granted a concession to dig in Egypt, at the Temple of Mut in the Karnak complex.
14. Gertrude Caton-Thompson (1888–1985). English archaeologist best known for her excavations of the prehistoric Fayum.
15. Jean-Philippe Lauer (1902–2001). French archaeologist and architect who for over 70 years dug and studied Early Dynastic and Old Kingdom remains at Saqqara.

Despite these efforts, it was another man (whose atrociously bad digging techniques destroyed as much evidence as they recovered) who was responsible for changes that eventually brought an end to the destructive archaeological practices that Rhind railed against. August Mariette, a young assistant at the Louvre in Paris, had been sent to Egypt to purchase Coptic manuscripts, but instead used his grant money to excavate at Saqqara, uncovering there the great labyrinthine burial place of sacred Apis bulls called the Serapaeum. This highly publicized discovery was followed by others at Thebes, Abydos, Edfou, and dozen of other sites. By 1858, Mariette's reputation as an Egyptologist was unequalled, and the ruler of Egypt, Ismail Pasha, appointed him Conservator of Egyptian Monuments, forerunner of the Supreme Council for Antiquities. Indeed, one of Mariette's first acts was to establish the Egyptian Museum in Cairo.

At his death in 1881, Mariette was succeeded as Conservator by another Frenchman, Gaston Maspero, a professor of Egyptology who had come to Egypt in 1880. He served until 1886 and again from 1899 until 1914. Maspero made several important archaeological finds, among them the cache of royal mummies at Dayr el-Bahari and several major buildings at the great site of Karnak. But his reputation today rests principally on three other accomplishments. He founded the great *Catalogue générale* of the Egyptian Museum, a catalog that has grown to over eighty volumes and is still in progress, and he established a journal, the *Annales du Service des Antiquitiés de l'Egypte*, which is still the official record of Egyptian archaeological work. Third, Maspero and Mariette together took the first effective steps to stop the looting and protect archaeological sites in Egypt by establishing new rules for excavations and clamping down on thievery.[7]

It was also in the 1880s that an Englishman changed forever the way archaeological work in Egypt was carried out. William Matthew Flinders Petrie had come to Egypt as a young man to survey the Great Pyramid and prove correct a theory about its measurements that his father had supported. Instead, his precise work proved the theory wrong, and the meticulous report he published so impressed Amelia Edwards, founder of Britain's recently established Egypt Exploration Fund, that she offered to support his future work.

Petrie was self-taught, and he came to have very precise ideas about how best to conduct archaeological excavations and analyze their data (see Fig. 1.1). Compared to other excavations at the time, his work was so detailed that his colleagues dismissed it as a waste of time and money. Unlike his contemporaries, who still saved only museum-quality finds and rarely published their data, Petrie argued that even broken and uninscribed objects should be preserved for analysis, the context in which objects were found should be recorded, and sites should be mapped and photographed. He trained his workmen, developing a permanent staff that he employed for decades, rewarding good excavation technique with money and praise. Over nearly six decades, Petrie excavated and published more important archaeological discoveries than any archaeologist before or since. He worked at major sites, such as Giza and Thebes, but he also excavated minor cemeteries and mud-brick hovels – the kinds of sites other excavators had ignored because they were difficult to dig and considered unimportant.

Petrie's work was revolutionary. Although few of his colleagues adopted his methods, his students did, and future Egyptology benefited. Petrie showed that archaeological data could be every bit as informative as hieroglyphic texts. He showed the value of noting the archaeological context of finds; this would later lead to the use of grids and squares to divide a site into well-controlled excavation units. He was aware of the importance of stratigraphy as a chronological tool; by methodically tracking architectural details of badly preserved remains, he explained how royal tomb architecture had evolved in earliest Egypt. He developed a brilliant system for tracing the chronology of tombs and their contents by plotting the changing attributes of their pottery (seriation and sequence dating). It is a tribute to Petrie that even now, a century after sequence dating first appeared, it is still being followed. Four times in the past century (in 1939 by Petrie himself, in the 1960s by Walter Federn, 1957 by Werner Kaiser, and 1982 by Barry Kemp), the process has been re-examined, but only minor revisions have been found necessary. Petrie's work greatly changed archaeology, not only in Egypt but also throughout western Asia, and after his death, in 1942, he came to be called, with only some exaggeration, the "Father of Modern Archaeology."[8]

One Egyptologist in particular stands out as a worthy successor to Petrie, and he, too, pushed Egyptian archaeology away from its pot-hunting past toward a more intellectually disciplined future. George Andrew Reisner was a highly respected Egyptologist who dug at many Egyptian sites. Supported by Phoebe Hearst and the University of California, Reisner worked at Deir el-Ballas and Naga ed-Deir, Middle Egyptian sites with extensive predynastic cemeteries, and at several major sites in Egyptian and Sudanese Nubia. But his principal work was at Giza, where he served as director of the Harvard University–Boston Museum of Fine Arts Giza Expedition. Reisner's work at Giza was brilliant – careful, precise, and meticulous, with a heavy emphasis on thorough record-keeping. Like Petrie, he trained his Egyptian workmen well: they kept their own field notes and took photographs as they worked. Even today, it is unusual to find projects that keep such detailed records or teach their local staff proper archaeological methodology.

Reisner's work resulted in several masterful publications, *Mycerinus* (1931), *The Development of the Egyptian Tomb* (1936), *A History of the Giza Necropolis* (1942), and *The Tomb of Hetep-heres* (1955), all of them massive works of the highest scholarly quality. If Reisner can be faulted for anything, it was his decision to delay publishing his extensive work in Giza's Great Western Cemetery until all its tombs had been excavated. He wanted to wait and prepare a multivolume, chronologically ordered synthesis of the data. Unfortunately, Reisner died before that could be done, and his boxes of notes are only now being assembled and published. But the data are all there, in his notes and those of his workmen, and sixty years after his death, Reisner's Giza is being accurately reconstructed from those remarkable records by a number of scholars.[9]

Both Petrie and Reisner devoted considerable time to studying and recording the pottery from their excavations, something few other archaeologists at the time bothered to do. We now know that potsherds can reveal important information about trade, economy, diet, agriculture, economy, technology, and chronology. But a century ago, decorated, whole vessels were objects for museum display, nothing more, and potsherds were annoying bits of rubbish. Archaeologists have called this the "art-historical" phase of ceramic study, the first of three phases into which it is divided. These phases are worth looking at more closely, because they mirror the way other specialties in Egyptian archaeology have grown.[10]

In Egyptology, the art-historical phase lasted well into the twentieth century. Excavators were slow to move from it into the second, or typological, phase, because typology involved examining not just whole vessels, but thousands, even millions, of potsherds, from a single

FIGURE 1.1. *Excavating in Egypt: Professor Petrie at Thebes*. Watercolor by Henry Wallis. Photo: UCL Art Collections, University College London.

Egyptian site, and then arranging them into categories based on such attributes as fabric, shape, and surface treatment. It was a tiresome, time-consuming undertaking, but worth the effort: for example, the seriation techniques devised by Petrie were one result, and Reisner's work at Kerma (in Nubia) and Giza was another.

In the third, contextual, phase, vessel shapes, decoration, fabric, and other attributes were found useful to trace trade routes and cultural interconnections and to identify changes in ceramic technology. Contextual studies also helped to refine pottery typologies. The contextual phase is especially well illustrated by work done in the Nubian Salvage Campaign of the 1960s, when anthropologically trained archaeologists worked on sites that offered no decipherable written records, and in recent studies of predynastic Egyptian pottery.

The contextual study of Egyptian ceramics today is a complex specialty that has become a standard part of nearly every archaeological project. Excavation teams include at least one person specialized in pottery analysis, and every sherd found in an excavation today is cleaned, catalogued, and analyzed (Fig. 1.2). Egyptological conferences have developed standards for describing fabrics and wares and the clays and silts from which they came. Ethnographic studies have helped explain ceramic manufacturing, and numerous chemical and physical tests have further refined our ceramic data.

FIGURE 1.2. Susan Weeks examining pottery from KV-5 in the Valley of the Kings. Photo: Theban Mapping Project.

Put simply, over the past century, studies of Egyptian ceramics have moved toward the study of increasingly smaller units: from the connoisseurship of whole vessels in phase 1 to the typology of sherds in phase 2 to the microscopic study of clays, temper, surface treatment, firing temperatures, pigments, and fabrics in phase 3. This increasing emphasis on component parts and attributes is true of nearly all aspects of Egyptian archaeology. It is no longer a discipline populated by theologians, philologists, and historians who speak only in broad generalities, as they did a century ago. Instead, Egyptologists and the specialists they employ pore over archaeological minutiae – animal bones, plant remains, pollen samples, mud bricks, stone tools, basketry fragments – to extract every possible

FIGURE 1.3. Using surveying equipment in the Valley of the Kings. Photo: Theban Mapping Project.

bit of information. The data they produce can be of unexpected value. A few years ago, botanists identified several species of weeds among the grains and flowers ancient priests had placed in Tutankhamun's tomb and from them helped reconstruct New Kingdom farming practices.[11]

Today, the task of an archaeological project director – in addition to the never-ending job of fund-raising – is to synthesize the masses of technical data his team produces and translate them into a meaningful picture of life in ancient Egypt. His team will be a large one. Take, for example, two archaeological projects that have been working in Egypt over this past decade. The Giza Plateau Mapping Project is excavating an Old Kingdom workmen's village beside the pyramids. The Theban Mapping Project is clearing a tomb, KV 5, in the Valley of the Kings and designing management plans for the entire Theban West Bank. Between them, they have employed over thirty different specialists. These included land surveyors (Fig. 1.3), architects, cartographers, photographers, conservators, forensic anthropologists (Fig 1.4), x-ray technicians, archaeobotanists, archaeozoologists, palynologists (who study pollen), geologists, mineralogists, hydrologists, artists, art historians, ceramic specialists, soil experts, stratigraphy experts, hot-air balloon pilots (Fig. 1.5), aerial photographers (Fig. 1.6), satellite imaging technicians, electrical, mining, and structural engineers, chemists, computer programmers, draftsmen, graphic designers, cultural resource managers, statisticians, philologists, epigraphers, geophysicists, stone technology experts, and Egyptologists (Fig. 1.6).[12]

FIGURE 1.4. Balloon at Deir El Bahri. Photo: Theban Mapping Project.

The kind of information that such an eclectic group of archaeological team members can provide is illustrated by recent work at Giza. The Giza Plateau project is excavating a village in which 8–10,000 men employed in building the Great Pyramid lived over 4,500 years ago. Meticulous digging has so far recovered over 175,000 animal bones and bone fragments. About 10 percent have so far been identified by species, and of those, most are domesticated sheep and goats (75 percent), cattle (15 percent), and pigs (5 percent). The bones came mostly from young, male animals.

What can archaeozoologists learn from these statistics? They can see that a well-planned system was in place to supply meat for this large workforce and that meat was more common in the diet of workmen than formerly thought. They note that such a large number of animals could not have all been raised locally, but had to come from many different places in Egypt, meaning that the animals would have been driven in herds to the Giza village for slaughter. Sheep and goats are especially suitable for herding and for cost-effectively providing high-grade protein to a population. Therefore, they are the most common domestic animals found here. Cattle are more expensive, but a single animal can feed a larger number of people than a sheep or goat, and therefore their number in the site is smaller. Pigs are difficult to herd, and those slaughtered at Giza probably came only from nearby farms. Thus, they are fewer in number. Young animals are better able to make long drives, and they provide better quality meat than older animals when they arrive. Finally, it would have made better

FIGURE 1.5. Aerial view of temple excavation, Thebes West Bank. Photo: Theban Mapping Project.

economic sense to kill male animals rather than females, because females could continue to bear more offspring.

Giza project specialists are now exploring the kinds of bureaucratic and economic structures needed to manage these complex activities. How did officials supervise raising animals far from Giza and arrange for the on-time delivery of the necessary numbers? How did they organize slaughterhouses and kitchens to kill and cook the animals and orchestrate meal preparation for thousands of people every day for several years? The Giza project is studying the site's bakeries and fish-processing facilities, both for the technical information they provide, and for what they, too, reveal about the labor force. This is truly Egyptian archaeology at a hitherto undreamed-of level, helping to reconstruct the well-organized and complex social and economic systems that made possible the building of a pharaoh's pyramid.[13]

In other studies of Old Kingdom sites, stone vessels have been analyzed to determine from which quarries their raw material came, data that allow us to plot shipping routes and economic patterns.[14] A chronologically ordered study of Egyptian bread molds showed that a dramatic change in mold shape occurred at the end of the Old Kingdom, and archaeologists are now seeking its cause: was it an economic decision, or perhaps a technological one introduced by a new group of craftsmen?[15] An examination of how grave goods distribute themselves in graves in large cemeteries, by location, grave size, the sex of the tomb-owner, and their association with other funerary features, is shedding light on hierarchically ordered, stratified, and gender-based aspects of Egyptian society.[16]

Despite such advances, it cannot be denied that archaeological excavation is a destructive process. Once dug, a site can never be put back together, and archaeologists now realize that excavations must be conducted wisely and with care, or sites should not be dug at all. How does a modern Egyptologist decide which site to excavate, and how does he (or, increasingly, she) go about doing so?

Until a few decades ago, a site was chosen because it was thought to contain nice objects. That probably meant it was a cemetery, whose tombs would contain funerary furniture and decorated walls. Less frequently, excavators chose to dig temples, because they promised statuary and texts. Least likely to be dug were habitation sites, especially ones in the Nile floodplain, because they were difficult to excavate and provided little beyond animal bones, mud brick, and potsherds. Today, sites are more often chosen because they are likely to provide information about a specific subject, often a social or cultural one. For example, archaeologists have asked what can this site tell us about social stratification, the role of women, the structure of the labor force, diet, health and mortality, trade, urbanism, technological change, the rise of central government, or the life of Egyptian soldiers in Nubia?

Egyptologists no longer excavate sites completely, because that would deprive later generations, who will be armed with different – and better – excavation techniques, and who seek answers to different questions, the chance to learn from them. Instead, we are likely to dig only a statistically significant sample of a site, or a part of a site that holds the most promise of answering our questions.

The site we select will not be one in Upper Egypt, unless it is part of an already established and continuing project, or unless the site is seriously threatened. That is because the Supreme Council for Antiquities (the SCA) recently banned new excavations in Upper Egypt, arguing that threats to archaeological sites in the Nile Delta had become so great that excavations there had to be encouraged. Delta sites were largely ignored by earlier excavators, who lacked the training needed to dig in the Nile floodplain and who had little interest in the kinds of artifacts likely to be found there.

FIGURE 1.6. Kent Weeks examines human skull from KV-5. Photo: Theban Mapping Project.

Today, archaeologists are likely to select one of those long-neglected Delta sites, even choosing a simple mud-brick village instead of a cemetery or temple complex. Workmen dig slowly to expose walls of sodden mud-brick buried in wet mud. Team members pore over undecorated potsherds, animal bones, and plant remains. Rather than employing hundreds of untrained, unsupervised workmen to haul away hundreds of cubic meters of sand, skilled specialists work with a handful of trusted and experienced workmen, perhaps spending several weeks scraping away a single centimeter of silt in a square only 10 meters wide. Detailed plans showing the precise location of every object and every feature are drawn, hundreds of photographs taken, drawings prepared, and extensive notes written down. Statistics are collected to show how different pottery attributes change in frequency within the site. Fragments of a woven reed basket, a splinter of wood, and a scrap of bread found beside an ancient oven, are all prepared for analysis in on-site laboratories. Today's archaeologists work very much like crime scene investigators, and no evidence is too inconsequential.

It must be admitted, however, that many of the techniques adopted by archaeologists working elsewhere in the world have been slow to make their way into Egyptological research. Some of them, such as chemical and physical techniques of dating, are too imprecise, giving dates rounded to a century or even a millennium, while Egyptologists require dates accurate to within a decade or less. Others are too expensive. But many are unfamiliar to Egyptologists. Egyptian archeology is still an isolated specialization in academia, and few of those who dig Egyptian sites have taken part in excavations in other countries or studied the archaeological methodology or interpretive theory used elsewhere in the world.

Gradually, however, new techniques are making their way into Egyptology, and they will undoubtedly have a positive effect on its results – if Egypt's archaeological sites survive long enough to benefit from them. Most sites are seriously threatened today by pollution, rising ground water, incursions of agricultural land and modern developments, and vandalism. Only in the past two or three decades has greater emphasis finally – and belatedly – been given to site conservation and protection. Indeed, Egypt's SCA now requires that every expedition include a significant conservation/site protection component.

The SCA issues a contract allowing an archaeological team to work at a site subject to several other rules as well. The team must consist of recognized experts in their various fields, the director must be a professional Egyptologist, and the project must be sponsored by a recognized academic institution or museum. A conservation program must be a part of the work, and the project must agree to leave the site in safe and sound condition at the end of the work. The project's goals are reviewed by the SCA's Permanent Committee, a group of about 15 Egyptian scholars, and if they approve, a one-year contract, called a concession, will be awarded, renewable only if the project has worked in an acceptable manner and regularly published its results. In the field, the project will be assigned an inspector from the SCA who is responsible for overseeing the work and making sure that all government rules are followed. The SCA provides none of the funds for such work – that is the project's responsibility – but neither does it charge for the necessary permits. Increasingly, the SCA encourages foreign expeditions to include Egyptian Egyptology students on its staff and to include a training component for them in its work. Final reports must now be published in Arabic as well as in the project's chosen language, so that junior-level members of the SCA staff and Egyptian students can be kept informed of current work.

The Egyptian government took control of its country's monuments only in 1952, after the revolution that deposed King Farouk and ousted the British and French delegations that controlled much of the Egyptian bureaucracy. Before then, the Egyptian Antiquities Service (later, the Egyptian Antiquities Organization; still later, the SCA) was directed by the French. Courses in Egyptology were rare in Egyptian schools, in part because Europeans feared a rise in nationalism and in part because they wanted to retain control of the country's antiquities. There was no full Egyptology program in Egypt's national universities until after World War II. Today, many students graduate from the nation's Egyptology department, but most then work as tourist guides, because their salary is significantly higher than that of an antiquities inspector. Only in the past few years have courses in archaeological methods been offered to Egyptian Egyptology students, and several foreign missions have recently established archaeological field schools in Egypt. But there are still only a few Egyptian-run and staffed excavations. Instead, as has been the case for over two centuries, most archaeological work in Egypt is conducted by foreign missions.

On average, perhaps 90 foreign expeditions dig in Egypt each year. They work in the Delta and the Nile Valley, the eastern and western deserts, the oases, the Sinai, along the

---

SIDEBAR 1.2:
*Six Current Projects That Demonstrate Recent Advances
in Archaeological Research*

1. Workmen's village at Giza: www.aeraweb.org
2. The Valley of the Kings and the Theban Necropolis: www.thebanmappingproject.com
3. Hierakonpolis: www.hierakonpolis.org
4. Tell el-Amarna: www.mcdonald.cam.ac.uk
5. Dakhleh Oasis: www.arts.monash.edu.au/archaeology/excavations
6. Tell el-Daba'a (Bietak 1996).

Mediterranean and Red Sea coasts, and at underwater sites. The missions come from nearly all European countries, the United States, Canada, Australia, and Japan. Some countries have well-established archaeological institutes that sponsor several projects every year. Among the principal ones are the French Institute (established in 1880), the Egypt Exploration Society (1882), the German Archaeological Institute (1907), and the American Research Center in Egypt (1948). Others represent the Swiss, Dutch, Austrian, Italian, Polish, and Japanese. The American University in Cairo, which offers a degree in Egyptology, also conducts several projects annually.

Most excavations working in Egypt today produce highly technical reports. Accounts of excavations in the nineteenth century, such as those of Giovanni Belzoni, who worked in the Valley of the Kings, read more like adventure stories than scientific studies. Today's reports lack the sweeping generalizations and broad histories that characterized earlier work, in part because the data modern projects collect are beyond the scope of one person to synthesize. As with most branches of learning, Egyptology, too, has become a collection of microspecialties, and scholars who can claim both wide-ranging and deep knowledge of their field are long gone. In one way, this is a promising development, for it brings unrivaled detail to our knowledge of ancient Egypt. But it has also left most Egyptologists unwilling, and even unable, to write the kinds of syntheses that were popular a century ago.

For those who revel in the details of ancient Egypt, however, and want to know not just *what* happened but *how* and *why*, this is truly an exciting time. New techniques of excavation and analysis are shedding light on aspects of Egyptian culture that were hitherto unknowable. The recent emphasis on habitation sites instead of cemeteries has transformed our view of Egyptian society, making the lives of illiterate peasants nearly as accessible as the lives of the nobility. Prehistoric and Early Dynastic sites are receiving overdue attention and disproving the nineteenth-century notion that changes in Egyptian culture were the result of biological changes in its human population. With these new approaches and interpretive tools, the study of ancient Egypt is on the threshold of a new age. (For some examples, see Sidebar 1.2.) And there are still thousands of archaeological sites waiting to be studied, if – and this is the challenge – they are not destroyed before that can be done.

NOTES

1. Fisher 2001; Gomaa 1973.
2. Greener 1967.
3. El-Daly 2005.
4. Iversen 1968–72; Habachi 1977; Curl 1982.
5. Iversen 1993.
6. Wortham 1971.
7. Reid 2003.
8. Drower 1985; James 1982.
9. Reisner's notes are available online at www.gizapyramids.org.
10. Orton et al. 1993; Wenke 1997.
11. De Vartavan 2002.
12. For reports and bibliography see www.aeraweb.org and www.thebanmappingproject.com.
13. See the Giza project Web site at www.gizapyramids.org.
14. Aston 1994.
15. Jacquet-Gordon 1981.
16. Wenke 1997; Bard 1994; Meskell 1999.

CHAPTER 2

HISTORY AND EGYPTOLOGY

Donald B. Redford

The historiographical genre has always been somewhat poorly represented in Egyptological writing,[1] being overshadowed by the perceived need to write about art objects first and foremost.[2] Whereas elsewhere historical scholarship often delves into deconstruction or postmodern or neo-Marxist approaches, Egyptology continues to be absorbed at a basic level (with notable exceptions!) with presenting and interpreting the primary evidence. Because the vast majority of items from archaeological (or museum) excavations fall within the ambit of the art historian or historian of "religion," any historian wishing (rightly) to use this material must be drawn away for varying periods of time into the realms of aesthetics, anthropology, and theology. These might prove stimulating exercises, but the results will always constitute only a prolegomena. We are still a long way from that period of "short returns" in which we can enjoy the luxury of sitting back, mulling over the existing evidence, sorting it, assessing it, and building it into the foundations of a definitive history.

But a moment's reflection shows that the qualification of the last word in the preceding paragraph is questionable at best. No history can, at any stage, be "definitive," and an indefinite article must always accompany "history of. . . ." Time and again a history course on Ancient Egypt, begun with confidence, will suffer emendation or enjoy amplification four months later at its conclusion, thanks to new archaeological discoveries made in the interim. Perhaps it is the prospect of being forever condemned to provisional statements that deters the would-be historian from attempting a formal "history" of Egypt. How much safer (and more lucrative) again to visit those popular areas of "appreciation" of a King Tut, or a Ramesses the Great, or the "great women" of Ancient Egypt, or to produce a picture book of objets d'art (most of which we have seen many times before), with a banal text written over the weekend. And because Egypt continues to be the haunt of armies of foreign tourists, the market demands brief, popular "introductions" masquerading as histories.

But the serious student of history who feels constrained, in spite of the drawbacks, actually to write history will face the next hurdle: what sort of history to write? The choice of philosophical stance, mode, format, emphasis, and interpretation is more exigent for an Egyptologist than for, say, a classical historian. The latter has fallen heir to a long, uninterrupted tradition of periodization and interpretation, the defiance of which almost automatically marginalizes his work or disqualifies it. The perspective is dictated and the stance imposed by the self-consciousness of a Europe that valued its own classical roots in a very narrowly conceived form. In Greece the "Dark Age" and the Archaic Period must be denigrated, or at least seen through the prism of latent glory, as periods in which humanity had not yet "arrived," but was groaning and travailing after the fulfillment of the Age of Pericles. The Hellenistic Period must be grudgingly tolerated, but only if the absence of democratic institutions is pointed out. In Rome the Republic represented in its pristine form all that was good and intellectually advanced, and tears were to be shed over, and lessons learned from, the transition to an unspeakable, retrogressive tyranny, which we can largely gloss over. And anyway, the traditional compass obliges us to end with Constantine.

The historian of Ancient Egypt is not hampered by such a dominant tradition of long standing. His domain is a recent creation: 200 years ago it did not exist (Sharpe's history by today's standard is a misnomer). The evidence continues to accumulate on all fronts, and the unspoken wisdom is that it is premature to write a history of Egypt. Already in the mid-nineteenth century those histories that followed the decipherment and the text-collecting expeditions of Champollion, Rosselini, and Lepsius were little more than lists of available evidence.[3] Such "catalogs" continued to pass themselves off as "histories" – some would say of necessity – right up to the third quarter of the twentieth century.

One can, however, sense the inauguration of a traditional approach that, if allowed to grow, will be as confining as the classical. To some extent it is tied in with the "periodization" that we have been saddled with since Manetho and that continues to distort the picture.[4] "Old," "Middle," "Late," and "Intermediate" are hopelessly judgmental and characterize the eras in question – much less do they delimit real époques! – not at all.

STRUCTURE VERSUS NARRATIVE

A common tendency in history writing arises subconsciously out of a natural human distaste for "open-endedness." The myriad of disparate facts must find their meaningful place in a seamless sequence that reaches denouement and resolution as though it were played out in cosmic theatricals. This "suprahistorical perspective . . . compose(s) the finally reduced diversity of time into a totality fully closed upon itself . . . and implies the end of time, a completed development."[5] This conceit that we are the ones on whom "the end of the age" has come, that what has happened until now is pre-eminently meaningful in contrast to what will come after us, is perfectly natural and one wonders whether it should be resisted. Should we not – can we do other? – round out our histories with our moment, our perspective, ourselves? We would be foolish not to recognize that this exercise is inherently fraudulent, and dishonest into the bargain not to tell the reader so. But historiography involves essentially and finally a *narrative* as Stone has stressed,[6] and that narrative will suffer if it does not attempt the "view from the mountaintop." Although the narrative will be informed by a plot and enjoy a resolution and "rounding off," there need not be a happy ending, nor even any nod in the direction of "progress" or its absence.[7]

In the ongoing debate between structural and narrative historians the latter have often been accused of being reductionist,[8] a criticism that ignores a necessary prolegomena to all history. An in-depth analysis of structure *must* precede any attempt to launch into narrative, and this prolegomena may well dwarf in size the history proper. This analysis must be followed, however, by a history in literary form, a story arising from an intuitive imagination, at once an artistic creation and a distillation of the facts – a "significant narrative," a "real sensual delight."[9] The question of what *kind* of history to write does not often plague Egyptologists. They are little concerned with theory or the debate between the traditional, academic approach of the 1960s and the postmodern world.[10] The tendencies and categories that have appeared in the last 40 years, by the very restrictions of the Egyptian evidence, have only partly made an appearance in Egyptology. Social history, it is true, is substantially served by the plethora of works on Deir el-Medina and the labor force, while the ever-burgeoning list of word-studies might fall under the category of "micro-history." "Women's history" too is well represented in Egyptological literature. But it is striking the number of themes and genres reviewed in the recent past[11] that have failed to put in an appearance in our discipline. Moreover two categories usually spurned by high-minded historians, viz. popular history and biography,[12] are thriving in writings on ancient Egypt. The question of the relative weight, in historiography, to assign to "large, impersonal forces," as contrasted with the "big man" in history, can only to a limited degree be discerned in our history writings.[13]

The concerns of Egyptological historians continue to be dictated by the peculiarities of their evidence, its nature, distribution, and spottiness. The preoccupation with art history and the dominance of the curator are inevitable facts that set Egyptology apart from studies on the Near East, Greece, and Rome. The ongoing archaeological program of excavations, which shows no sign of diminishing, renders historical statements provisional in many cases and fosters the distortion of historiographical works into interim reports, popularizing and sensationalizing "discoveries."[14] This has had the deleterious effect of diverting the energy of scholars into pandering to a public whose fleeting attention must be captured by gimmickry. The result is that publishers and producers, who know how to use gimmicks, feel free to dictate, rewrite, distort, and generally manhandle a scholar's work, telling him what to say, how to say it, where to stand, and what posture to adopt. The final result may well be slick, but it is done in the image of the producer.

THE USE OF TEXTUAL EVIDENCE

The writing of Egyptian history has suffered, and probably will continue to suffer, from an extreme paucity of written sources. The demise of the pharaonic state and the concomitant obsolescence and disintegration of aging files, along with the ravages perpetrated by the malevolent Bagoas and by fanatical Christians on temple libraries and sculpture, has robbed us of the kind of sources our Assyriological colleagues have in abundance. *They* can write, say, an economic history of Mesopotamia from which few can dissent; we cannot do the same for Egypt. We have been robbed, not only of the corpus of written records and thoughts, but even of the very mind-set of the ancients, that "general system of the formation and transformation of statements" that Foucault called "the Archive."[15]

Several consequences have followed from this lamentable situation. One is the tendency to treat an historian's ingenious hypothesis that has won a consensus of acceptance, not as the mere suggestion once proffered, but now as proven fact. Anyone who continues to doubt is branded as daringly unconventional, or declared guilty by association with an outmoded viewpoint. One can protest, not simply that the textual evidence does not exist – that should be obvious – but that the *a priori* reasoning may be fallacious. Examples are easy to cite, ranging from hypotheses on state formation, to the nature of the collapse (too daring perhaps?) of the Old Kingdom, the advent of the 15th Dynasty, and the identity and seat of rule of the 23rd. A second tendency can be detected, sometimes as a counterblast to the first, in the practice of debunking. A long-held view is now deemed to have been hallowed only by time and is denigrated without the presentation of any new evidence. All too often the debunking becomes part of a polemic.

One practice that has increased over the past quarter century is the introduction of methods of another discipline into Egyptology, along with use of its arcane rules and models. This has proven remarkably illuminating in the region of economics and economic history,[16] less so elsewhere. A problem arises when people with only limited training in the external discipline use it, as it were, in an act of prestidigitation, knowing that few in their audience can master the *recherché* vocabulary. That each discipline necessarily employs a specialized jargon may be true, but the danger is that novices from the outside will employ it as an obscurantist argot to enhance their own image.[17]

One discipline whose arrival has proven of immense benefit to Egyptology is anthropology.[18] When this began to influence our discipline the results had a purifying and enriching affect. The technical lexicon of the newcomers and their novel methods in treating evidence long known opened doors we never knew were there! The palsied hand of the philologist was restrained and then replaced by the thrusts of a fist that knew not the "word," only the "artifact."

In more recent times, however, the picture has darkened, and this can trace to the hegemonic position anthropology has achieved, especially in committee. Guidelines for grant applications now apprise us of the fact that "empirical social scientific research" will not be funded, and "archaeological surveys to determine the feasibility of excavation" will not be countenanced. Consideration will be shown to those projects that center upon "problem solving"; projects designed to cover broad swaths in order to "fill in the gaps" will be rejected. These guidelines were clearly devised by anthropologists familiar with only one area of investigation (where further large-scale archaeology is unnecessary) and the specific methodology devised to address its problems. They should not apply to the archaeological "situation" of large parts of Asia and Africa, where far too little work has been done even to identify "problem" areas wherein "problem solving" – what a loose, imprecise term! – might be expected to work. In Egypt we still know too little of the archaeological and historical landscape to identify tidy and self-contained problems that can be addressed by techniques anthropology offers. We need extensive surveys, broad-brush archaeology, identification of the "gaps" – we can scarcely fill them in before we know where they are! – judicious planning, and collaboration.

One defect inherent in the "problem-solving" mind-set can be detected in the hierarchical ranking of different types of evidence and the virtual rejection of texts. To illustrate the point I wish to draw upon personal experience.[19] In our excavations in East Karnak we encountered in building Phases C and B (seventh to fourth centuries BC) a peculiar architectural feature that defied explanation. This was a mud-brick structure, roughly 8 meters square, containing many small rooms of varying size. Because no room communicated by doorway with its neighbor, it was assumed that the original entry had been from above and that the "rooms" had probably been used for storage. When flotation of the contents of the units failed to reveal any organic material, a further assumption was made, that the "rooms" had been intended for "dry storage." Extended excavation, however, revealed that this "storehouse" had been set in a *domestic* context: gate and courtyard before, and facilities for food preparation, sleeping, and bathing behind. Because of the date of these remains it occurred to me that help in identifying the elusive feature might be forthcoming from Demotic house documents; and sure enough the layout of our East Karnak houses was generally reflected in the property descriptions. But just where, in the sequence of architectural elements, our putative "storage unit" was located, the texts spoke of a *tp-rd*, "podium staircase," and a *ryt hryt*, an "upper part." Clearly our storehouse had in reality been a casemate structure to support a multistoried unit. No set of doctrinaire guidelines set forth by grant committees would have been at all helpful in this exercise in interpretation: only broad area excavation coupled with novel and unexpected sources of evidence could have solved the problem.

ORALITY STUDIES

In a culture in which significant discourse from and about the organs of state and discourse of a didactic, aesthetic, and sapient nature are carried on and transmitted mouth to ear, it behooves the investigator to think in terms of the "word." An approach to this body of material first and foremost from the direction of orality studies makes better sense than invoking literary theory to the exclusion of all else. This unwarranted classification of Egyptian compositions under the rubric "literature" leads, in the extreme, to the curious conclusion that they were intended, not for "performance" (see below), but for the predilection of a small, *reading* elite! But orality and literacy are not distinct phenomena: they interact with each other, as Finnegan, Rydberg-Cox, and others have shown.[20]

Nonetheless we would know nothing of this word-discourse were it not for the fact that some of it was written down. Clearly this results from pedagogical practices in some cases; but the ubiquity of the tag *mi gmyt m sš* "as found in writing"[21] points to the strength of a *written* tradition paralleling the oral. Therefore the circumstances of inscription constitute a fair field of investigation.

The phenomenon of a gifted orator, speaking *ex tempore* to a crowd, is well represented in life situations in Ancient Egypt.[22] Composition and performance are accomplished at the same time and share an immediacy because of the "live audience." The qualities of eloquence characterizing a *mdwty*, "elocutionist, speaker, raconteur," were striven for at all levels of society.[23] And if the speech was deemed technically excellent, and/or its content of importance, custom promoted the practice of transcribing it to dictation.[24] If the piece must be committed to memory, at least in its broad thematic structure, there were those in every society who could do so by "processing chunks of acoustical data" in a "mental lexicon" and skilful use of mnemonic devices;[25] but at that point the written copy became an aide-mémoire. The notional form is made explicit: cf. "[. . .] written as a verbal transcription" (lit. "writing of words": *Urk.* I, 67:14); "I have come today with Ptah; I sit among the Two Enneads. The Horizon-magnates are brought to them, and a writing brought of what I said, given to them as their aide-mémoire" (*sḥ3.sn*: CT VII, 231n-q).

But the composer of a piece of discourse may very well choose to pronounce it aloud, in private, and write his own words in advance of public dissemination. This prior writing down of a piece turns the creation into a literary text *parlando* which, in spite of the fact that the act of composition allowed reflection in the privacy of the study, was nonetheless intended for oral delivery. *Parlando* composition may, to a limited extent, rob the text of the spontaneity of the orator – he lacks the gauge of audience reception and reaction – but it does allow a more sophisticated "post-oral" style.[26] Thus oral composition and oral transmission do not eliminate written composition and transmission: they exist side by side, and the written tradition, conceived in an "oralizing" mode, can be as memorable as extempore creation (cf. Chester Beatty iv, vs.2.5ff).

Whether created extempore or written in advance, all pieces of narrative, liturgical, lyrical, magical, or "historical" composition were intended for *performance*. "Voiced texts live only in, and solely for, oral performance . . . and their audience knows them only as oral poems."[27] This sometimes, or perhaps in most cases, involved some kind of music or prosodic meter,[28] but in any event the *sine qua non* was speaker and audience.[29] The phrase "every scribe who will read (audibly) and every person who will listen" conjures up the life situation of visits to the necropolis in commemoration of the ancestors in which a literate individual functioned as a resource person for the community.[30] There is every reason to believe that the same situation obtained in the case of the formal, "historical" texts, that is, relief scenes with their captions, séance stelae, building inscriptions, encomia, and toponym lists, which historians draw on for the history they write. These sources often derive from the *obiter dicta* of the monarch or his representative, taken down "hansard" fashion, and carved on prominent surfaces from which they could be "read out" to gawking spectators.

Whether truly orally composed, or voiced from prepared texts, records and belletristics of the type adumbrated above, by virtue of the fact that they are presented before a live audience, demand an investigation of audience reception. Both performance and reception take place immediately, and speaker/singer and audience interact intimately. Thirty-five years ago the present writer was privileged to be a member of the audience at the performance of an orally composed "epic" at a dinner party in Gurneh. The host was wooing one of the guests and in her honor he had hired an ancient bard who came with two young acolytes in tow, equipped with tambourines. The bard certainly possessed an innate skill, an implicit "memory expertise."[31] The composition took shape before our eyes and ears and was roughly modeled on what the bard conceived to be the personal relationships of the guests. Sections were lengthened or cut short depending on our perceived interest or ennui; and at one point every guest had to rise and dance with the bard. When the latter tired or became thirsty, the "chorus" of acolytes would repeat a set refrain for as long as it took him to refresh himself. (Images of the Egyptian *Harfner* came immediately to mind!) In all, the bard passed from factual truth in his own statements to a twilight world of nontruth and fantasy.[32] Often the bond between performer and audience became so strong that the bard came to evince amity or aversion to various members of the audience, depending on their own assumed roles. In this the performer showed careful attention to his *own* reception by the listeners.[33] Awareness that performance is necessary for pieces of discourse provides a key to understanding as well as a corrective. It gives a context to the whole gamut of writing from recording through belletristics to *Maerchen*, lyric, and high-flown encomia. It also demonstrates the inadequacy of certain models with which we have long been burdened. One of the most pernicious is the notion of the intellectual genius of individual literati, *writing* in that code-medium, and cross-fertilizing each other solely through *intertextuality*. In fact it is not the text that is fundamental here but, at the mechanical level, the stock of *oral* formulaic sound-bytes and the register of ethnopoetics and immanent art, the infinity of modalities (phonetic, societal, personal) – all of them oral – that govern a performance.[34]

Interplay between speaker and audience is crucial to reception, as Louden showed in relation to the *Odyssey*.[35] Audiences show ambivalence in the degree of acceptance they evince toward speech content[36] and reserve an independence of judgment no matter who is the author/speaker, even if it be the king himself. The protestations that there is no "misstatement" (*iw-ms*) or "exaggeration" (*cbc*) in a piece of discourse signal the speaker's rebuttal to the audience's explicit or suspected skepticism.

Consonant with the ubiquitous markers of orality, cognitive research has thrown up another phenomenon well represented in ancient Egyptian discourse. This is the *Script*,

Schema, or "Memory Organization Package,"[37] a predictable sequence of episodes, organized and stored in auditory memory according to the personal experience of everyday life, shared by the community at large.[38] Scripts constitute sets of narrated acts in causal sequence, generalized *topoi* that nonetheless allow individual variation.[39] Auditory or gestural markers immediately and subconsciously apprise the audience of the script in question and automatically unlock whole event patterns and modalities. In Egypt scripts related to the ideology of kingship are central to the discourse (even though their true significance has been hopelessly skewed by the application of the meaningless term *Koenigsnovelle*).[40] The major schemata with their marker-tags may be listed as follows:

1. "One came to tell His Majesty . . ." (arrival of messenger)
2. The King in Council: divine versus terrestrial conceit
3. "The King raged thereat like a southern panther . . ."
4. The trope of the "great slaughter [*ḫȝyt ꜥȝt*]" and the might of the king on the battlefield
5. Sleepless king crafting policy
6. "Beneficent king [*nsw mnḫ*]"
7. The king's Progress ("West and East banks in joy . . .")
8. Royal séance ("the king appears . . . courtiers ushered in . . .")
9. Divine revelation to the king (oracle or a "dream of the night")

These do not constitute a single genre, nor are the modalities identical. In each case the designation, sometimes the very phrase translated, would have "tagged" the script for the audience and triggered expectations triggered by their collective auditory memory.

Scripts pictured, in painting, relief, or sculpture, become points of reference no less than auditory markers.[41] But they permit greater latitude of interpretation. Though often glossed by text, the latter inevitably loses out to the grandeur of the picture, and over time is apt to be ignored, especially in the absence of a reader. The hieratic and limited number of poses the royal person adopts in this kind of figurative discourse stems, not from a prior requirement to solemnize his image, but from a practical attempt to avoid misinterpretation by the viewer. A wide variety of poses would introduce ambiguity and obscure the message. Nevertheless the freedom the viewer enjoys when text or speaker are secondary or not present will foster etiology or iconatrophy. Both Herodotus and Manetho reflect such popular "readings."[42]

IDEOLOGICAL FOUNDATIONS

The ideology of the incipient state in Egypt is revealed, not only through iconographic symbolism, but also in roots that penetrate into the realms of oral tradition and archaeological metrology. The period in question currently acts like a magnet on researchers coming from all ranges of the spectrum: cultural anthropology, history of religions, political systems analysis, script invention and evolution – all with a welter of subdisciplines in tow. The result is a kaleidoscope of interpretive works, some worth reading, on the subject of the advent of complex society and state formation.[43] A new door has opened with the increasing awareness of the role played by the Uruk "world system" in the formation of the Egyptian state.[44] Conversely, theories of indigenous development that postulate processes entirely internal or confined to northeast Africa and the deserts are becoming less and less convincing.

It might stimulate discussion to state that, in order to understand the context wherein Egyptian society developed complexity, one must address the problem of class hierarchy and its relationship to production. In this regard the problem arises of the gravitation of sociopolitical power into the hands of a bloc of power-wielders often termed the "elite."[45] We seem to be stuck with this word, although it is an unfortunate choice, as it inevitably conjures up the vision of a group of aesthetes, an intelligentsia whose views transcend politics, who spurn the tastes of the great unwashed, and who view the universe from the vantage point of god on high.[46] Even on the definition of A. L. Rouse ("an elite is a group with standards"), it is difficult to see the usefulness of this notion in elucidating the social hierarchy of ancient Egypt. That a bloc of power-wielders did exist no one can doubt; but that it defined itself on the basis of its relationship to "high culture" is doubtful.[47]

The incipient Egyptian state created a system in which two ideas strove in tension: ancestral rights held through inheritance, and empowerment of an individual isolated in time and space. At the head of society such an individual was positioned, not as a representative of the power bloc, but as a colossus of a wholly different order, rising far above all else. Closer in character to a "big man" system than a chiefdom, the Pharaonic monarchy imposed a mask, a persona, and a role on the incumbent that almost completely concealed a true self, or so at least it seemed. The concept early crystallized into a rigid and enduring framework comprising a series of expectations: championing good and order against evil and disorder; promulgating good "doctrine" [sb3yt] and "laws" [hpw]; refurbishing temples and increasing their endowments; maintaining the good life for the people by distribution of royal largesse; showing physical prowess and daring on the battlefield; and guarding the frontiers and placing the "fear of Horus" in the hearts of foreigners. The paragon of leadership thus created engages in acts, in the discourse describing him, that rapidly become predictable and cliché-ridden, and for that reason tend to be taken for granted by the reader/listener. The necessity for slavish adherence to the ideal and the repetitive description in the discourse invites mediocrity in formulation and presentation, with a consequent loss of interest in the audience. The latter, or at least their modern equivalent, begin, in fact, to cast judgments of denial, declaring that the kingly role can seldom be fulfilled and never corresponds to reality. Such tropes as king in council disregarding sage advice, king succumbing to rages, king on battlefield all alone performing feats of military prowess, king facing innumerable enemies, king masquerading as the font of wise doctrine, king disposing of largesse to Egypt and the world – all these stereotypes are wholly and always divorced from historical fact, and it is naïve even to consider using them to reconstruct the event.

This hyperskepticism, *en tant que tel*, is in itself naïve and simplistic. Whenever pharaonic deeds are seen through the eyes of contemporary Asiatics and Greeks, the Pharaohs are found in actual fact to be playing the role to the hilt! Ramesses II's encapsulated description of the battle of Kadesh,[48] clearly inviting Hattusilis's honest concurrence, mirrors the reliefs and hieroglyphic texts. Nektanebo I's pompous statements on the Luxor sphinxes regarding his careful preparations and protection of Egypt[49] coincide with Greek descriptions (Diodorus xv.42.1–3). That Pharaoh is chief celebrant of the cultus and thus enmeshed in a web of ritual demands (the ubiquitous message of the temples) is confirmed by Hecataeus. Nektanebo II falls into a rage at being met by a ragtag army of artisans (Plutarch *Aegesilaus* xxxviii.1), as had Piankhy according to his stela. Tachos recklessly disregards his advisors' counsel and invades Asia (Diodorus xv.92.3). Nektanebo II, in the center of the line leads the charge against the enemy, easily overthrowing them (Plutarch *Aegesilaus* xxxix.4). A "Psammetichos" sends grain abroad to alleviate famine (Plutarch *Pericles* xxxvii.4). The pharaonic mantle is so heavy and the part to be played so demanding that the personality of each king is warped, beaten, and molded to the role willy-nilly: Pharaoh in fact and in life loses his individuality and *becomes* the Horus-king, not superficially but in essence and action.

"PROPAGANDA" AND ADMONITION

Much of the discourse, whether figurative, oral, or written, that the historian takes as grist for his mill has been dubbed "propaganda" and treated under that rubric.[50] Its derivation from the *Congregatio de propaganda fidei*, that is, an organization proselytizing for the faith, indicates clearly that "through systematic dissemination of doctrines" (Shorter Oxford English Dictionary) this type of communication belongs, as a coarser component, to the category of "persuasion" discourse. But the latter, even if the threat of force is not precluded, is applicable as a term only if the audience enjoys freedom of option: to accept or reject. The final aim of the propagandist may well be ultimately to restrict that freedom, but at the moment of his preaching one can only infer that his hearers are uncommitted.[51] No ancient Egyptian enjoyed the luxury of being free of commitment: he was locked into a system and proselytizing was needless.

A more appropriate term is political discourse. In this "argot of the power-wielders," lexical meaning becomes technical and often far removed from what is commonly accepted. The purpose of this political "Newspeak" is to direct the thinking of the masses, withhold precise information from them, and occasionally deceive them. The constellation of words and phrases that today accompanies and defines the notion of "terrorism" provides a case in point,[52] as does the rhetoric surrounding the metaphor of putting on soldiers' suits and declaring "war on . . ." every conceivable "evil" from minor social irritants to world enemies. In ancient Egyptian such words as *shtp* "to pacify," *nrw* "fear, dread," *swsh t3s* "to extend the frontiers," *ph* "to attack," and the like were powerful referents, markers at the mere pronunciation of which a whole horizon of meaning opened out (cf. the function of "Script" markers, reviewed above).

In most cases propaganda and persuasion rhetoric prove themselves to be inappropriate terms. The majority of the discourse the historian must deal with falls under the rubric of "doctrine" (sb3yt) and takes the form of a didactic piece, an expression of chastening thoughts. The tone is paternal or avuncular. "Let me say something important! I'll make you listen and understand the matter of eternity! . . . The (way to) pass a lifetime in peace! Adore the king in your innermost being, worship H.M. in your hearts," and so forth.[53] For the king's power "traverses the sea, the Asiatics live in fear of him; his terror encircles Pwenet and the shores of the Hau-nebu. God binds for him. He who does not oppose him will go to heaven; he who does not curse him will rest in his tomb."[54] And so a system, whether benign or oppressive, will be accepted as occupying a high moral plane and corresponding to ma'at through being internalized by constant repetition, insistence, and threat.[55]

THE RELEVANCE OF EGYPTIAN HISTORY

Apart from a handful of academics who earn their daily bread by writing and teaching Egyptian history, students at large often puzzle over what use this recherché knowledge will be to them. Is there any value, theoretical or practical, in studying "this stuff" (especially now that Lady Thatcher has dismissed the discipline)? The answer usually is "yes" when parts of that history impinge on the Bible and the Judaeo-Christian confession: then devotees display a vital interest in the most recherché aspects of that history, an interest that all too often descends into apologetics and ends up on the loony fringe. Even secular attempts to show "relevance" and "timeliness" succumb to ludicrous prejudice and presupposition. In fact, attempts to interpret the past in the sense of ordering it into a rational shape frequently, and especially in the era of deconstruction, become a species of "game-playing."[56]

Ancient Egyptian society, economy, and political structure are as far removed from us moderns and our world as China of the warring states period, or the Inca Empire. Ancient Egypt represents a past that is dead; it is not about to resurrect itself and clobber us.[57] The issues plaguing Pharaoh in antiquity are not our issues today. What useful models does ancient Egypt afford? What vital interest is served by ancient Egyptian wisdom and knowhow? What specific political lessons can Pharaoh teach us? Facetious answers could, of course, be given, but the huge gap in time and ethos separating us from Egypt of antiquity is all too real.

And yet we press on, and I can think of two reasons. The late professor Gilbert Bagnani told me once about an incident from his schooldays, in which he complained to the master about the senseless course in the logic of the mediaeval Schoolmen that he was forced to take. What good will this course be to me later on in life, complained Bagnani; their work is defunct, erroneous, and useless. The master nodded. Yes, he said, you are right, it will be of no practical use. But you should be ashamed of being ignorant of a way of thinking that dominated your ancestors' minds for centuries. And to that, Bagnani remarked, there is no answer.

The only negotiable course for a writer of history is one that takes its rise from a contradiction. This is Hauser's "paradox of historicity and timelessness." History has no meaning and we cannot conceive of its components; and yet, in the words of Marx, it exists "as aesthetic satisfaction . . . as a norm, as an unattainable paragon."[58] It lives, enshrined in narrative, as a guide to the unknown and a key to unlock its beauty.[59]

NOTES

1. A quarter century ago the present writer contributed a piece on historiography to a collection of works edited by Kent Weeks (Redford 1979). The present chapter might be considered an "update" were it not for the fact that so much has happened in the interim that it seems better to begin *de novo* with little reference to that earlier assessment. To paraphrase the late J. M. Roberts, the general editor of the *New Oxford History of England*, one might construe the purpose of the present chapter, *mutatis mutandis*, as to address "the present state of historical knowledge about ancient Egypt, drawing attention to areas of dispute, and to matters on which final judgment is at present difficult (or perhaps impossible)." This might prove a salutary exercise if undertaken by uncommitted pens, but the danger is that it could easily result in a bland (and essentially meaningless) *mélange* of views characterized by a lack of resolution. Since the fair adumbration of views is always difficult, the bewildered reader is often left in a situation in which "you pays your money and you takes your choice."

2. See Hoffmeier 1992 and Redford 2003.

3. Brugsch 1859; Brugsch 1877; Birch 1879; Wiedemann 1884.

4. Spiegel 1950; Malek 1997; Foxhall 2000.

5. Foucault 1980: 152.

6. Stone 1987.

7. Eagleton 2003: 179.

8. Burke 1992: 235–6.

9. For "significant narrative": Breisach 1994: 333–5; "sensual delight": Willett 1964.

10. Thomas 2006.

11. Burke 1992.

12. Tillyard 2006.

13. Assmann 1996.

14. Purkiss 2006.

15. Foucault 1972.

16. See, for example, Janssen 1975; Menu 1998; Warburton 1997; Grimal and Menu 1998.

17. Eagleton 1996: 207.

18. Lustig 1997.

19. What follows is to be published in the final volume of the *Akhenaten Temple Project* V. *The Excavations of the Gm-p3-itn.*

20. Finnegan 1977; Rydberg-Cox 2003.

21. See Redford 2000: 166, and, for the written tradition paralleling the oral, Brunner-Traut 1979.

22. Derchain 1989.

23. Doxey 1998: 52–8.

24. Redford 2000: 215–17.
25. Evans 1991: 129; Zevit 1992; Redford 2000: 206–7.
26. Friedrich 2000.
27. Foley 2004:20; and see Bauman 1977; Minchin 2001: 17; Hearon 2004; Yamagata 2005.
28. Reichl 2000.
29. Hadot 1995: 413.
30. Cairo 20017; *Urk.* IV, 368: 3, 965–6; Helck 1975: 42; Shubert 2006.
31. Rubin 1995.
32. Richardson 1996.
33. Doherty 1991.
34. For oral "sound-bytes" see Vanseveren 1998; for performance-governing aspects, Foley 2004: 32–3.
35. Louden 1997.
36. Rabinowitz 1977.
37. Tannen 1979.
38. Shank-Abelson 1977; Bower et al. 1979.
39. Minchin 2001.
40. See on this, most recently, Loprieno 1996; Hofmann 2004.
41. Gaballa 1977; Tefnin 1981.
42. On etiology and iconatrophy see Vansina 1985: 10; Poucet 1994: 177. On Herodotus and Manetho reflecting popular "readings," Kaiser 1967; Lloyd 1975–88; Redford 1986; Lloyd 1988.
43. Cf. among others van den Brink 2002; Castillos 2002; Gundlach and Seipel 1999; Hendrickx *et al.* 2004; Moorey 1995; Rice 1991; Spencer 1996; Trigger 1993; Wilkinson 2001.
44. Algaze 2005; Mark 1997; Rothman 2001.
45. On class hierarchy: Eagleton 1989: 6; cf. 15. On "elite": Cohen 1981; Porter 2004.
46. Eagleton 1996: 207; and Eagleton 2000: 38–44, 77, 125.
47. Eagleton 1990: 342–5.
48. KBo I, 15+19; Edel 1994 ad loc.
49. Hegazy 1982.
50. Williams 1964; Otto 1977; Bleiberg 1985–6; Grimal 1986; Simpson 1996.
51. Burke 1971: 267; Gadamer 1977: 11.
52. Chomsky 1999: 662–5.
53. Posener 1976: 56–9.
54. Helck 1984: 55–6.
55. Chomsky 2001: 165, cf. 167.
56. See Felling 1999: 351 and Sim 1999: 31.
57. Said 1993: 3.
58. Quoted in Hauser 1985: 255.
59. Momigliano 1990: 37.

CHAPTER 3

MEDICAL SCIENCE AND EGYPTOLOGY

A. Rosalie David

The wealth of evidence that survives from ancient Egypt includes texts, sites, monuments, artifacts, plants, and human remains. In particular, inscriptional translations and scholarly interpretations of the art and architecture have provided the basis for our understanding of this civilisation. However, art and literature can provide a distorted or propagandist viewpoint that does not tell the whole story.

Human remains, on the other hand, represent an important and unbiased resource for analytical studies on disease, living conditions, medicinal treatments, genetics, and mummification techniques. In principle, scientific evidence should produce more accurate insight into ancient lives, and although researchers must always be aware of the pitfalls associated with some methodologies and the possibility of misinterpreting the data, nevertheless biomedical Egyptology can make a significant contribution to this subject.

MUMMIFICATION: AN OVERVIEW

A mummy is a body in which natural or artificial preservation of the tissues has prevented putrefaction. Although they occur in several countries, the term "mummy" was originally used to describe artificially preserved bodies from Egypt. The word comes from the Arabic *mumia*, meaning "pitch" or "bitumen," and was first applied to Egyptian bodies because of their blackened, bituminous appearance. Both natural (unintentional) and artificial (intentional) mummies occur in Egypt.

Environmental factors produced the natural mummies: a combination of the sun's heat and the dry sand in the earliest graves on the edge of the desert desiccated the body tissues and arrested decomposition. The introduction of a different type of elite tomb (c. 3400 BCE) that no longer provided the conditions that would preserve the body may have prompted the Egyptians to develop an artificial method of mummification. Experimentation led to a procedure that involved evisceration of the body (the viscera were eventually either returned to the body or stored in special containers), followed by dehydration of the bodily tissues and viscera by means of natron (a mixture of sodium carbonate and bicarbonate found in natural deposits). Resin was another substance used in the procedure.

Intentional mummification, originally introduced for royalty and the elite and then made available to the wealthy, was still in use in the Christian era, but most people continued to be interred in simple graves, where environmental conditions resulted in natural mummification. However, since museums and collectors have usually acquired artificial mummies, these have become the focus of most modern scientific studies, and consequently this has produced a disproportionate emphasis on the health status of the upper classes.

In addition to human mummies, the Egyptians also mummified many animals, believing them to be manifestations of various gods. These have survived in large numbers, and also provide a major – but less exploited – resource for analytical study.

RESEARCH RESOURCES
Mummies: A Finite Resource

Scientific studies can add information about disease, lifestyle, genetics, and funerary customs, as well as the process of deterioration in mummies, which can be the result of inadequate storage, environmental factors, physical damage, or earlier inappropriate conservation attempts. These conditions can be arrested or rectified by various means, but the impact such treatments may have on the preservation of the scientific evidence must be carefully considered.

The International Ancient Egyptian Mummy Tissue Bank

Established at Manchester to support an epidemiological study on schistosomiasis, this unique bank currently holds nearly 2,000 samples from Egyptian mummies held in collections outside Egypt. Since the samples represent a range of periods and social groups, the Bank has considerable potential for palaeoepidemiological and other disease studies in Egypt and elsewhere, as well as research on diet, genetics, and mummification techniques. The Bank lends small quantities of tissue for such projects, providing material for analytical work that would otherwise depend on direct access to mummies. By limiting the need to probe mummies for samples, the Bank is contributing to the conservation of a finite resource.

The Medical Papyri

Twelve extant papyri provide the basis for current knowledge of the ancient Egyptian medical system, but these must surely represent only a fraction of the medical documentation that once existed. Based on the observation of patients and the experience of anatomy derived from mummification, the papyri describe various body systems (sometimes inaccurately), specific diseases and injuries, and a range of pharmaceutical prescriptions which appear to include both "rational" and "magical" treatments. The papyri and data from investigations on human remains are important complementary and comparative resources.

EARLY INVESTIGATIONS

From the Renaissance onwards, museums, learned societies, and wealthy individuals acquired mummies for their collections. The earliest unwrappings of mummies in Europe date to the sixteenth century. Many of these frivolous social events have left no academic record, but a few investigators adopted a multidisciplinary, scientific approach and published their results. Most notable unwrappings were performed in London by the surgeon T. J. Pettigrew (1791–1865) and the physician A. B. Granville (1783–1872). A significant autopsy was also carried out by members of the Leeds Philosophical and Literary Society in 1825.

In 1908, M. A. Murray revived palaeopathological studies in Britain when her team autopsied and studied two mummies at the University of Manchester (see Fig. 3.1). Meanwhile, in Egypt, new discoveries led to major investigations. Two caches of royal mummies had been discovered at Thebes in 1871 and 1898, and after transportation to Cairo, these were unwrapped and became the basis for G. E. Smith's pioneering work on mummification techniques.

The Archaeological Survey of Nubia, established as a heritage rescue operation when the first Aswan dam was built in the early twentieth century, retrieved some 6,000 ancient bodies which became the focus of an important study by G. E. Smith, W. R. Dawson, and F. W. Jones.

MODERN DIAGNOSTIC AND INVESTIGATIVE TECHNIQUES
Autopsy of Mummies

Early investigators of mummies were limited to unwrapping and dissecting the body (autopsy), followed by a visual and physical examination of its general state and condition (morbid anatomy). Autopsies can provide more detailed information than less destructive techniques and enable researchers to take samples for further analyses. Therefore, several autopsies involving multidisciplinary teams were performed in the 1970s and 1980s, and these have formed the basis for extensive studies.

FIGURE 3.1. Dr. Margaret Murray and team unwrapping a mummy at the University of Manchester (1908). Photo: The Manchester Museum, The University of Manchester.

Some Important Studies

Cockburn's team autopsied several mummies. These included DIA I (1971) (Detroit Institute of Art); a series from the Pennsylvania University Museum, PUM I (1972), PUM II (1973), and PUM III and PUM IV (both 1979); and ROM I (1974) (Royal Ontario Museum, Toronto).

Meanwhile, in Britain, a mummy was autopsied in 1975 at the University of Manchester, as part of the Manchester Egyptian Mummy Research Project (see Figs. 3.2 and 3.3). The team's aim was to develop a methodology for examining mummified remains which would provide new evidence about disease, diet, living conditions, and funerary customs. The first scientific autopsy performed in Britain since 1908, this used an extensive range of techniques to obtain maximum information from the mummy. The Manchester methodology was then applied to a mummy in the City of Bristol Museum (UK), autopsied in 1982. Other similar projects included the autopsies of a mummy at Lyon and of three incomplete human mummies, as well as some heads and animals, as part of the Munich Mummy Project.

Results, Limitations, and Potential

Such modern autopsies, and subsequent studies, have aroused widespread scientific and public interest, demonstrating how mummies are a unique resource for studying disease.

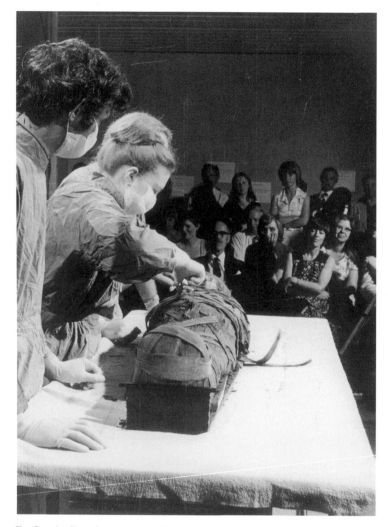

FIGURE 3.2. Dr. Rosalie David commences the unwrapping and autopsy of Mummy No. 1770 at the University of Manchester (1975). Photo: The University of Manchester.

Decisions to autopsy these bodies were usually taken on the basis that the mummy was in a poor state of preservation anyway.

Nevertheless, autopsy is a destructive, irreversible procedure. Since the 1980s, ethical considerations about the status of all human remains and the fact that mummies are a finite, valuable resource for studying an ancient culture have prompted investigators to develop other, minimally destructive techniques.

FIGURE 3.3. Painted cartonnage slippers revealed during the unwrapping of Mummy 1770 at the University of Manchester (1975). Photo: The University of Manchester.

Radiology

Radiology provides a minimally destructive method of examination and can retrieve information about each individual's cultural and archaeological context, as well as specific evidence of disease and injury.

There were important developments in this field in the 1970s. Until then, most mummies had been X-rayed on site, with mobile compact equipment attached to a local electricity supply, but this method had its limitations. In 1973, the Manchester Project introduced a new standardized procedure: the human and animal mummified remains were briefly transferred from the University's museum to the medical school and teaching hospital, where they could be X-rayed under controlled conditions, using state-of-the-art equipment.

Techniques included fluoroscopy (the visualisation of transmitted X-rays on a television screen) and tomography (which provides X-rays of a section or slice of tissue in a plane). The former procedure allows the investigator to assess the contents of the mummy, while the latter gives additional information about specific areas of the mummy.

A continuing programme at Manchester has also used computed tomography (CT). This technique, developed in Britain, creates a three-dimensional image and presents information about the patient that conventional procedures may not provide. CT was first successfully applied to a mummy in 1976, when images of the brain of the mummy (ROM I) of Nakht, a young weaver, were produced in Toronto. The intact brain had been removed when the mummy was autopsied. Now, CT is a standard procedure in most radiological investigations of mummies.

Some Important Studies

The discovery of X-rays in 1896 was rapidly applied to Egyptology. W. Konig radiographed the mummies of a child and a cat in Frankfurt, Germany, and Thurstan Holland X-rayed a mummified bird in 1897–8, but W. M. F. Petrie was the first Egyptologist to recognize the potential of the technology to archaeology and use it to study ancient human remains.

In 1904, G. E. Smith and H. Carter pioneered the use of radiography for the royal mummies. The recently excavated and unwrapped mummy of Tuthmosis IV was transported by horse-drawn cab to private X-ray facilities in Cairo, and the radiographic study helped Egyptologists to estimate the king's age at death. One of the earliest comprehensive surveys of mummies was carried out in the 1930s on the Egyptian and Peruvian mummies in the Chicago Field Museum, while in the 1960s, P. H. K.Gray X-rayed some 200 mummies in museums across Europe and Britain. Between 1966 and 1971, a radiographic survey of the royal mummies was carried out by J. E. Harris and K. R. Weeks at the Cairo Museum.

Since the 1970s, radiology has played an important role in many multidisciplinary studies of mummies, including the investigation of the mummy of Ramses II, which was transported to Paris in 1976, where it underwent radiography and xeroradiography but not CT.

Recent surveys include the study of the collection at the National Museum of Leiden which developed out of an earlier project. At the British Museum, the application of CT scanning to mummies has been taken a step further: the use of a software toolset allows the viewer to 'tour' inside the mummy and perform a 'virtual unwrapping.' This new technology has revealed evidence not found in previous radiographic studies of the mummy.

So far, most studies on animal mummies have been limited to radiological surveys. These have produced some interesting results, demonstrating that the contents of the mummy are not always compatible with its exterior. Some contain an animal of a different species, eggs, single bones, feathers, or sticks, and some are empty.

Results, Limitations, and Potential

Radiological investigations can provide archaeological, sociological, and biomedical evidence about mummies. Skeletal maturity and development can be evaluated, based on the ossification of the bone (bony development) in each skeleton. For identification of sex, X-rays can provide the sole evidence or confirm inscriptional information on associated coffins. The presence of disease and trauma in the skeleton and any remaining soft tissue can also be demonstrated radiographically.

Sometimes, however, the radiological evidence can be misinterpreted. For example, the intervertebral disc opacification observed radiographically in mummies was first attributed to *Ochronosis*. However, a later review of 64 mummies, which indicated an unexpected frequency of this rare condition, concluded that the disk opacification must be due to an effect of the mummification procedure rather than disease, a conclusion confirmed by later scientific studies.[1]

Generally, X-rays provide a range of information that can help to identify the historical date of each mummy. Radiography can also enhance knowledge about the mummification procedure, demonstrating the presence of natron or resin, and visceral packages in the thoracic and abdominal cavities. X-rays show the positioning of the arms, presence of jewellery and other artifacts, and embalmers' restorations (subcutaneous packing to imitate bodily contours or false eyes or prosthetic limbs). They will reveal any attempt at excerebration and indicate which method has been used. This technique has also revealed 'false mummies': sometimes, these were fakes sold to gullible tourists or attempts by the ancient embalmers to deceive their client's family if the corpse had been lost or damaged.

As a virtually nondestructive technique, radiography has been chosen as the main method for modern investigative studies on the royal mummies. For example, radiological data have been used to determine the age at death of individual rulers. However, the application of North American and European radiological standards to define bone age in ancient Egyptians has posed problems because there are differences in skeletal maturity in the ancient and modern populations, due to genetic and nutritional influences. Because of this, some of the radiological results from the mummies do not agree with the lengths of reigns indicated by the historical and archaeological evidence.

Answers to specific questions have also been sought. In the 1960s, R. G. Harrison led a multidisciplinary survey of the mummies of Tutankhamun, the two foetuses found in his tomb, and the body from Tomb 55 (generally presumed to be that of Smenkhkare, Tutankhamun's supposed brother). Theories about kinship, disease, and the cause of Tutankhamun's death were largely based on the radiological data. In 2005, the latest study – a CT scan of Tutankhamun's mummy – was undertaken by a team from the Supreme Council of Antiquities, led by Z. Hawass. The initial report comments on the king's age at death, disease in the mummy, and refutes previous speculation that he may have been murdered, suggesting an alternative cause of death.

Radiology, as a virtually nondestructive technique, plays a key role in mummy studies and should be the first step undertaken in examining a mummy. However, it has its limitations: it is expensive, and suitable equipment and expertise may not be readily available. Also, it cannot provide all the answers: much of the information preserved in a mummy can only be accessed by means of other techniques, some of which are minimally intrusive.

As well as biomedical and archaeological evidence, radiography also provides important data for dental studies, endoscopy, and scientific facial reconstruction.

Palaeo-odontology

Studies on human remains, samples of ancient bread, and inscriptional evidence provide the basis for knowledge of the Egyptians' dental status, diet, and dental practitioners.

Human remains available for dental study include dry skulls and mummified heads (separated or attached to the body). Collections of dry skulls present a valuable opportunity to handle and visually examine this material, providing direct experience of pathological and nonpathological conditions that can then be used to interpret the radiographic data obtained from wrapped and mummified heads.

This is especially important because, in many cases, the radiographic results can be impaired, even if specialised equipment, such as the orthopantomograph (which gives a panoramic view of the teeth), is used. This is because dental details can often be obscured by the funerary face mask enclosed within the wrappings, or the hard facial tissue around the mouth.

However, in one mummy, it was possible to take direct intraoral radiographs of the individual sections of the mouth and then produce a survey that was as complete as any obtained for a modern patient. This was because the mouth of the mummy was open (with the tongue protruding), providing excellent access to the teeth.

Some Important Studies

Some multidisciplinary projects on individual mummies have included dental studies, and surveys of the dentitions of population groups have also been undertaken. For example, the annual expeditions since 1965 from the University of Michigan have examined the elite mummies of the Old Kingdom at Giza (c. 2800 BCE), and the priests and nobles of the New Kingdom at Luxor (c. 1250 BCE). From 1966 to 1971, the Universities of Michigan and Alexandria supported a project to examine and study the dentitions of most of the royal mummies in the Egyptian Museum in Cairo.

Another study investigated oral health and disease in contemporary Egyptian and Nubian populations, providing comparative data for work on ancient material. From 1966, when the High Dam at Aswan was under construction, a rescue operation that surveyed some

5,000 ancient Nubian bodies was also involved in radiographing over 1,000 skulls as the basis for palaeo-odontological studies. More recently, some 500 skulls from the Duckworth Collection in Cambridge (UK) and the Natural History Museum, London, have been studied for evidence of severe dental pathology and how this was affected by the diet.

Results, Limitations, and Potential

In many cases, information about dental disease and general oral pathology can be gleaned from the teeth and the well-preserved, desiccated soft tissue that supports the teeth.

Also, bread from the tombs has been examined microscopically, revealing that the flour was contaminated with windblown sand and many impurities, including debris from the storehouses and quernstone particles. Regular consumption of gritty bread – a main component of the diet – caused attrition (wear) of the cusps (biting surfaces) of the teeth.

Attrition, the most common dental ailment in pharaonic times, could lead to exposure of the tooth pulp, which might then become infected and develop into a septic cyst, which sometimes resulted in death. This sequence of events is clearly demonstrated in the mummy of Djedmaatesankh in the Royal Ontario Museum, Toronto, where CT scans have revealed a large cyst in the bone of her upper left jaw.

In some mummies, there is also evidence of caries (tooth decay). This condition was not widespread in pharaonic times, but the incidence increases in mummies of the Graeco-Roman Period (c. 332 BCE–fifth century CE), perhaps as a result of dietary changes.

As well as providing data about dental pathology, diet, and nutrition, the teeth – as the most indestructible of human remains – are a valuable resource for studies on age determination.

The Medical Papyri contain some prescriptions for dental treatment, and texts also suggest that some medical practitioners held the title of dentist, although there is a continuing debate about the existence of any specialized profession that was proficient in dental procedures.

Endoscopy

Endoscopy is a virtually nondestructive means of obtaining tissue, bone, and other samples from inside a mummy. An endoscope is a narrow tube that incorporates a light source at the probing end. Initially, flexible (medical) endoscopes were employed in mummy research, but the rigid (industrial) version is generally more successful, since mummified tissue is usually hard and inflexible. Artificial openings resulting from the mummification process, natural orifices, and small damage holes in the skin provide means of entry for the endoscope.

A small retrieval forceps is attached to the probing end of the endoscope to take the required biopsy samples. Wherever possible, this is facilitated by using a radiographic screen or monitor to visualize the exact position of the endoscope inside the mummy, thus maximising the possibility of sampling specific tissue from an identified site for predefined investigations.

Some Important Studies

The introduction of endoscopy in the 1970s replaced the destructive methodology of unwrapping and autopsying mummies. Early experiments included the endoscopy of three mummies in Cairo in 1975 and its use in conjunction with radiography to pinpoint specific areas for sampling.

From the 1980s, the Manchester Mummy Project adopted and developed the technique as a regular procedure in its investigations and identified disease in biopsy samples obtained this way (see Fig. 3.4). When a mummy from Leeds (UK), originally autopsied in 1824, was re-examined by the Manchester team in 1991, they combined autopsy techniques with endoscopy to gain new information.

Results, Limitations, and Potential

As well as supplying samples for studies on disease and genetics, endoscopy is a means of exploring the mummification procedure itself. It can reveal the state of the tissue and the method of preservation, confirm if the viscera have been removed from the thoracic and abdominal cavities and if brain removal has been attempted, and pinpoint any artifacts or insect remains still present inside the mummy.

However, endoscopy provides only partial access inside the mummy and can never produce as much evidence as a full autopsy. Essentially, however, it is the modern alternative to autopsy, offering a minimally destructive means of acquiring samples for further investigation while preserving the integrity of the mummy as a valuable and irreplaceable resource for future studies.

Palaeopathology

The concept of palaeopathology, which studies the occurrence of disease in ancient populations, was pioneered by the bacteriologist M. A. Ruffer in the early twentieth century. It draws on many disciplines, including anthropology, archaeology, palaeontology, and palaeohistology.

Generally, researchers who work on skeletal remains (often the only evidence that survives from ancient societies) can only identify those diseases that are evident from the bones. However, in mummified remains, the preserved tissues provide an additional resource for disease identification.

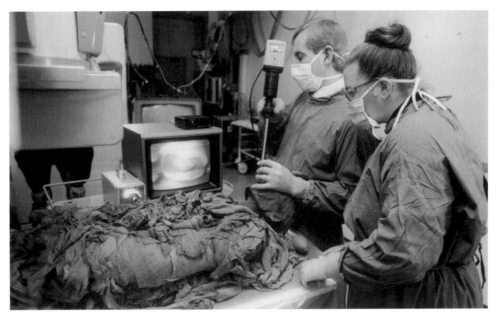

FIGURE 3.4. Dr. Rosalie David and team member Ken Wildsmith use an endoscope to examine a mummy at the University of Manchester. Photo: The University of Manchester.

For modern patients, pathology uses various techniques to identify and study disease processes; two of these – morbid anatomy (the naked-eye study of the body) and histopathology (the study of changes in the tissue caused by disease) – have been successfully adapted to investigate mummies.

Techniques available to the histopathologist include histology (which uses light microscopy to show the microscopic structure of tissue and any changes caused by disease), electron microscopy (where greater magnification of the sample provides much better resolution of its detailed structure), and immunohistochemistry (where specialized stains increase the likelihood of identifying cell constituents in tissue).

The application of histological techniques to ancient tissue is known as palaeohistology. To achieve success, the technique requires an interim procedure: the material must first be rehydrated and fixed, and then, as with modern tissue, it is frozen and cut in sections which are stained with dyes, in preparation for microscopic examination.

Some Important Studies

Palaeohistology was pioneered by Fouquet in 1889. Ruffer developed this further by inventing an agent (Ruffer solution) for rehydrating ancient tissue, and this still forms the basis of modern studies. Latterly, several scientists, including Sandison and Tapp, have introduced advances in rehydrating and processing ancient material. Also, since the 1960s, the contributions of electron microscopy and immunohistochemistry have ensured that studies in this field continue to produce significant results.

Palaeohistological techniques greatly enhance the opportunity of identifying disease in mummies. For example, tissue analyses undertaken by Cockburn's team on samples from the PUM and ROM mummies revealed a range of diseases; many were parasitic infestations, or anthracosis and silicosis, which had all been caused by environmental factors.

Using histology and electron microscopy, the Manchester team identified two hydatid cysts in brain and lung tissue, and also possibly part of a liver fluke (*Fasciola hepatica*), as well as worm and cyst remains (tentatively identified as the genus *Strongyloides*) in intestinal tissue. Analytical electron microscopy (AEM) demonstrated that dense crystalline particles found in lung tissue were silica, indicating that the person had suffered from the disease *sand pneumoconiosis*.

Results, Limitations, and Potential

In addition to disease studies, these techniques can contribute to knowledge in other areas. For example, analytical studies have revealed structural components of tissues, such as cell membranes, nuclear tissue, and chromatin, in skin samples, and in 1967, transmission electron microscopy (TEM) was used for the first time to examine the ultrastructure of skin and muscle tissue taken from an ancient Egyptian head.

Electron microscopy studies have been used to determine the presence of heavy metals in bone and mummified tissue, and scanning electron microscopy (SEM), which examines the surface of solid objects, has proved to be an effective method of identifying insect remains found in mummies. Since a mummified body and its wrappings can be host to a variety of insects that arrived before, during, and after mummification, this research has added useful data about patterns of insect attack. TEM and SEM have also been employed to examine the surface, structure, and diseases of hair samples from mummies.

In addition, mummification procedures have been investigated: there have been studies on the preservation of skin and on the chemical constituents of mummified tissue, which have indicated that the method of using natron correlates with the quality of the tissue preservation. Studies on the eye have demonstrated that it is possible to recover the remnants of the globes of the eyes from a rehydrated mummified head.

The main limitation of these techniques is that there is no way of ensuring that the samples taken from mummies will contain evidence that is significant. In many instances, microscopic examination of a sample will reveal only bandage fragments or dust, but nothing of histological interest.

Immunological Techniques

Radiographic and direct microscopic examination of tissue samples can be effective diagnostic tools for identifying many diseases in mummies. However, radiography is dependent on having access to expensive equipment, usually only available in a hospital department, and successful microscopic examination requires particular types of tissue which contain the remains of parasites or their eggs or other histological evidence of disease.

Immunological techniques, however, are relatively cheap and can be applied to large numbers of samples; even when viscera (where evidence of disease is often found) are not available, these methods can be used for small samples of bone or other tissue. In 1989, Deelder led the first project to successfully apply ELISA (enzyme-linked immunosorbent assay) to mummified remains, a procedure that can detect the presence of circulating anodic antigen (CAA) in the sample.

When working with living tissue, scientists will try to detect a disease by looking for its antibody, but antibodies probably do not survive in ancient tissue. However, in several studies, immunocytochemistry (which can detect the presence of any remaining antigen that was part of either the causative worm or egg associated with a particular disease) has proved to be an effective diagnostic tool.

Some Important Studies

In 1995, the Manchester Mummy Project began a collaborative study with American and Egyptian scientists to construct a comparative epidemiologic profile of schistosomiasis in ancient and modern Egypt. To provide sufficient statistical data for this research, the International Ancient Egyptian Mummy Tissue Bank was established at Manchester. Immunocytochemistry was adopted and developed as the best method of detecting this disease in large numbers of samples.

Results, Limitations, and Potential

In previous studies on individual mummies or groups of mummies, immunocytochemistry showed that schistosoma antigens could survive after thousands of years, and the Manchester research reinforced this conclusion. Of the fifty mummies investigated in this project, 30 percent were shown to be infected with the disease.

In order to confirm the results produced by immunocytochemistry, ELISA and DNA studies have been undertaken on the same material. Also, for the first time, DNA has been identified in a schistosome parasite and some eggs found in these samples, enabling researchers to compare this ancient DNA with modern examples. Eventually, such studies may contribute to knowledge of the evolution and development of this parasite over thousands of years and help to determine why it has been so successful in avoiding destruction by the immune system of its human host.

Immunocytochemistry, which has demonstrated its effectiveness as a method of detecting schistosomiasis in mummified remains, can be developed as a diagnostic tool for some other diseases. In particular, it has considerable potential for future epidemiological studies, but these will require a resource such as the Ancient Egyptian Mummy Tissue Bank.

Researchers are also pursuing the detection of other diseases, including tuberculosis and leprosy. Additionally, in studies on a range of mummies from all periods, the *Para*SightTM-F test has identified the antigen produced by *Plasmodium falciparum*, indicating that these people were infected with malaria when they died.

DNA Analysis and Palaeoserology

In the 1980s, S. Paabo became the first scientist to isolate genetic material from ancient human remains. Later, polymerase chain reaction (PCR), which is also known as "gene amplification," provided a quicker and better method of processing ancient DNA (aDNA) samples.

Before Paabo's success, palaeoserology (the study of blood groups in ancient human remains) offered some possibility of tracing kinship patterns and population movements. Various experiments since the 1930s culminated in some limited successes with techniques such as the serological micromethod (SMM) and the inhibition agglutination test (IAT). However, palaeoserology always presented considerable technical difficulties and never produced entirely convincing results, and it has now been superseded by DNA analysis.

Results, Limitations, and Potential

Only a small sample of bone or tissue is required for DNA analysis, but ancient genetic material poses many problems. This is mainly because aDNA, which survives only in small amounts, is very often damaged, contaminated, or badly preserved. Additional factors that can contribute to its deteriorated state include the agents used in mummification and the handling, storage, and conservation methods applied to the mummy.

Studies usually focus on mitochondrial aDNA because it poses fewer problems than nuclear aDNA. However, in all mummy research, in order to limit the possibility of modern contamination, it is essential that very strict protocols are observed in selecting, sampling, and processing the material.

Despite the difficulties, aDNA analysis presents considerable opportunities. Potentially, a wealth of material is available for study, including mummies from newly excavated sites and those in museum collections. Already, identifying the genetic profiles of mummies can sometimes confirm individual sex and familial relationships. Ultimately, genetic markers in ancient populations may help to determine the origins, migration patterns, and composition of ancient societies.

There is also the possibility of gaining more information about infectious and parasitic diseases. Parasitic aDNA in a schistosome and eggs has already been identified by Manchester researchers, and future studies on fungal, viral, and bacterial aDNA could make a further significant contribution, confirming the presence of some infectious diseases that currently elude detection.

However, there are pitfalls associated with these techniques. For example, an attempt to obtain viral aDNA from baboon mummies (part of a project to investigate the AIDS virus) was unsuccessful because of a reaction between the natron used for mummification and the gypsum in which the embalmers had packed the mummies.

Instrumental Methods of Analysis

Many investigations have attempted to detect disease in mummies, but there have also been studies on the structure and quality of the linen wrappings and the therapeutic and cosmetic substances and plants found in mummies and associated funerary goods. Mass spectrometric protocols are increasingly used for this type of research.

Some Important Studies

Some early investigations employed thin layer and gas–liquid chromatography to isolate and characterize substances such as resin, galbanum, and beeswax that impregnated mummy bandages, and others have explored the use of resin in mummification and funerary procedures. Research in Manchester is currently using the evidence of plant remains associated with mummies to examine ancient trade routes.

Analytical studies can sometimes confirm ancient literary accounts. Herodotus and Diodorus Siculus stated that the body cavities of mummies were cleansed with palm wine, and it is probable that traces have now been identified in a minute sample of bladder tissue from a mummy.

These techniques have also been employed in multidisciplinary studies of ancient Egyptian therapeutic treatments and the use of narcotics. Some projects have involved analytical methods to explore the possibility that the Egyptians used drug substances for medicinal, religious, or social reasons.

Radioimmunoassay and gas chromatography–mass spectrometry (GCMS) were used by scientists in Munich to investigate a group of mummies. They reported the presence of cocaine, hashish, and nicotine in samples of hair, skin, and bone, but this raised questions since the earliest mummy investigated dated to c. 1000 BCE, and there are no known sources of nicotine or cocaine in Egypt or the Old World at this date.

These discoveries raised the intriguing possibility that there may have been some previously unrecognised early contact between the Old and New Worlds. However, comparative studies in Manchester on different mummies have revealed no evidence of these drugs, and continuing research focuses on problems posed by these techniques, especially any association that may be demonstrated between sample contamination and false results.

Another study has re-examined the theory that opium was imported into Egypt from Cyprus as early as the New Kingdom (c. 1450 BCE), in special juglets that, it is claimed, resemble the inverted head of an opium poppy. However, the residues from selected juglets, analysed in Manchester by means of liquid chromatography and GCMS, have failed to reveal the presence of opium or any of its alkaloids.

In wall scenes in Egyptian tombs, guests at banquets are depicted either smelling lotus flowers or drinking from lotus-shaped cups that perhaps contained wine steeped in lotus flowers. Egyptologists regarded these as straightforward art representations, symbolising the beauty and religious significance of the lotus for the Egyptians, but one study has proposed that the blue lotus may contain potent narcotic alkaloids in its flowers and rhizomes, which the Egyptians possibly used to induce euphoria.

However, new analytical studies to establish the true status of the lotus indicate that, although it was probably not used for this purpose, the Egyptians may have been aware of this plant's potential for inducing sleep and reducing pain.

A new project entitled *Pharmacy in Ancient Egypt*, which is based in Manchester, is combining historical and analytical methodologies to investigate ancient Egyptian medical prescriptions. An international, multidisciplinary team has unprecedented access to material that includes literary evidence from the Medical Papyri, ancient and modern plant specimens, and samples of mummified tissue. Using DNA techniques and mass spectrometric methods, the aims are to identify any traces of pharmaceutical remedies in the mummies and to assess the accuracy and therapeutic effectiveness of these treatments.

Limitations and Potential

Although these techniques offer considerable possibilities, it is evident from the examples cited above that some analyses, for a variety of reasons, may produce results which are at variance with the historical evidence. Researchers should be aware that scientific analyses may, in certain circumstances, be misleading, and a conservative evaluation of all the data is always necessary.

Scientific Facial Reconstruction

Techniques developed for forensic human identification have been adapted successfully for reconstructing the faces of ancient Egyptians from skeletal or mummified remains.

The earliest reconstructions were built up in clay or wax on a cast of the skull. However, because Egyptian heads are usually wrapped in bandages or covered in skin tissue, affording no direct access to the skull, it has been necessary to develop other methods. The digital data provided by CT can now be used to produce a detailed polystyrene replica of the skull, forming the basis for a reconstruction. Also, groundbreaking methods involving computerised 3D modelling and stereolithography add a new dimension to this work.

Some Important Studies

Many multidisciplinary mummy teams have produced or commissioned a scientific facial reconstruction as part of their project. This can provide a dramatic visual aid in a museum display describing the research carried out on a particular mummy. It can also contribute to an overall scientific study by illustrating disease or trauma and any marked familial characteristics.

Studies can also address a particular historical question. For example, during the Roman Period in Egypt, panel portraits were placed over the faces of some mummies, and it has been argued that these may have been true individual likenesses, painted in the owner's lifetime. A recent project used four mummies to compare the face shown on each panel portrait with a corresponding facial reconstruction, based on digital data obtained from CT scans of the head. This study has revealed some surprising information about the accuracy of the portraits.

Some Limitations

The accuracy of the scientific reconstructions has sometimes been questioned: do they really represent true likenesses of individuals from antiquity? However, the credibility of this methodology is confirmed by its forensic application: when an individual in a modern forensic case is finally identified, there is a good opportunity to assess the accuracy of the facial reconstruction, and this lends support to the results achieved with ancient heads.

FUTURE POSSIBILITIES

Since the 1970s, the subdiscipline of biomedical Egyptology, based on the analytical investigation of mummies and associated material, has added a new dimension to the study of ancient Egypt. It can provide information not available from other sources and confirm or correct theories and interpretations based on literary or archaeological evidence.

Future Egyptologists will need to be aware of its potential and limitations, and appropriate opportunities should be introduced for those who wish to pursue a career in this field.[2] Specialised training and research opportunities now exist at the KNH Centre for Biomedical Egyptology, established at the University of Manchester in 2003, which are enhanced by a formal agreement agreed between Manchester and bioanthropologists at the National Research Centre in Egypt, to promote cooperation in research and joint training programmes.

Egypt offers unique opportunities for comparative epidemiological studies across the millennia. Disease evidence is provided not only by analyses of ancient mummified tissue and skeletal remains, but also by contemporary health studies of a people who, for the most part, can trace their descent from the country's original population.

This special set of circumstances presents a rare opportunity to make a scientific assessment and comparison of disease data over some 7,000 years. Eventually, it should be possible to contribute this knowledge to a broader study of the universal history of disease.

NOTES

1. Isherwood et al. (1979): 37.
2. Aufderheide (2003): xiii.

PART II

MONUMENTS

Structures for This Life and the Next

CHAPTER 4

SITE SURVEY IN EGYPTOLOGY

Sarah H. Parcak

In recent years, the question of how much remains to be uncovered in the archaeology of ancient Egypt has become increasingly pertinent.[1] Locating a large, well-preserved structure like Edfu Temple is highly improbable, but detailed excavations of diverse contexts offer similar payoffs in reconstructing ancient Egypt's past. Settlement archaeology, in particular, has received far greater attention in recent decades, especially at the sites of Elephantine, Tell el-Amarna, and Tell ed-Da'ba. It has also demonstrated just how much new information can be gained from either mound ("tell") sites with a long history of archaeological investigation or sites largely buried beneath modern fields. With trace element and neutron activation analyses, the smallest potsherd or flint bladelet can contribute invaluable information to reconstructing past lifeways. In museums across the globe and in excavation storehouses, many hundreds of thousands of ancient Egyptian artifacts require further study, especially those from earlier excavations. Perhaps the question is not so much how much information remains to be recovered from Egypt itself, but how much can be done with what has already been found.

This question is important since we have reached a crossroads in Egyptian archaeology: modern development is increasingly and irrevocably altering ancient Egypt's landscape and is changing the way archaeology is practiced in Egypt. Many sites are threatened by agricultural and urban development, while the inscribed faces of numerous temples and tombs are exfoliating through rising water tables and increased salinity. These factors have made it even more essential to record as much as possible about known sites before they are irretrievably lost over the next 20 years and to explore ways in which new sites and features can be located using cost- and time-efficient methods. The development of such a surveying methodology will affect how future surveys are conducted in Egypt and will help the Egyptian government to locate, map, and safeguard archaeological surface sites

Robbers' Trench

FIGURE 4.1. Image of the site of Tell Fagi, visited during the 2003 Delta survey. Note the robber's trench running through the center section of the site. Photo: S. Parcak.

endangered by urban expansion and cultivation. A broad range of survey techniques can address these issues. Subsurface, ground, aerial, and satellite survey methods have had high success rates in mapping sites, recording new features on known sites, and locating previously unknown sites. In the face of exponentially increasing site loss due to population increase, looting, and urban expansion, technical survey will form the basis for future archaeological exploration in Egypt (Fig. 4.1).

Archaeological site survey has not played as pivotal a role within Egyptology as it has in the broader field of Near Eastern archaeology. In Iraq and Syria, for example, surveys have revealed thousands of archaeological sites. The majority of extant tell sites in Egypt remain little known, poorly recorded, and buried beneath modern fields or towns, making it seemingly impossible to realize the total number of sites. To assess ancient Egyptian settlement patterns in a particular region, it is often necessary to use records over 100 years old for data on landscapes that have now largely disappeared. It is telling that the most comprehensive survey of ancient Egyptian sites took place in 1798 with the Napoleonic survey. Aside from desert surveys, most surveys in Egypt have focused primarily on epigraphic, architectural, and art-historical remains. Excavation work often provides broader contextual information for one or more portions of a single site, but lacks regional data, while inter-site surveys yield a lesser picture for individual sites, but cover a broad area. Although the two approaches complement one another effectively, at this point Egypt still needs a comprehensive inter-site survey.

FIGURE 4.2. Cemetery of the town of Nazlet Mahmoud, found during the 2004 Middle Egypt survey season. There is a tell measuring 8 m × 200 m × 500 m beneath the cemetery. Photo: S. Parcak.

A variety of tools are available for surveying, including magnetometry and resistivity. These have helped archaeologists to detect subsurface ancient structures, including tombs, temple enclosure walls, houses, and palaces, and have even helped to map entire cities. As described by Greg Mumford and colleagues in 2004, magnetometry surveys at Tell Tebilla revealed the outline of various rectilinear complexes, later found by excavation to be mud-brick mastaba tombs. In 1999, Helmut Becker and Jorge Fassbinder discussed the use of magnetometry at Pi-Ramesses, which revealed the outlines of many structures beneath agricultural fields. Many other projects in Egypt have used or are adopting magnetometry and resistivity surveys.

The focus of this article, however, will be on the application of more broadscale surveying tools, in particular satellite remote sensing and differential GPS surveys. Magnetometry and resistivity are best used once archaeologists have located archaeological sites in order to detect and trace subsurface structures before excavating or mapping them. Unfortunately, many of Egypt's undiscovered tell sites lie beyond the abilities of the aforementioned analytical methods. Most likely lie beneath modern towns and cemeteries (Fig. 4.2) or have been sufficiently denuded or buried by a site to make a detailed beneath-ground survey unfeasible.

Though many towns contain sufficiently wide and unpaved streets to accommodate such investigations, modern debris, such as metal, would mask most subsurface readings. Also, these tools are best applied to small areas and would require prohibitive labor costs and time for large-scale coverage. In contrast, a number of the free-standing *tells* in the Delta would benefit from magnetometry and resistivity surveys as well as coring and excavation. At this stage, is it more crucial to locate as many sites as possible before they are destroyed, in order to facilitate future ground-based surveying? Of note, most sites are never completely "destroyed," bur remain below ground level, as shown by work at Pi-Ramesses and Tell ed-Da'ba. Hence, should archaeologists focus more on known sites? Ideally one should cover both approaches or, failing funds and personnel, try to record as much as possible before things vanish completely.

Satellite remote sensing offers a way to assess broad areas prior to ground reconnaissance. With the advent of high-resolution imagery such as Quickbird (60 centimeters pixel resolution), available free through Google Earth, basic remote sensing is a tool available to all Egyptologists, regardless of their expertise in the physical sciences. Satellite images have seen limited use in Egypt, yet the results are encouraging, revealing numerous new sites and features, such as the remote sensing work conducted by the author in Middle Egypt and the Delta and other studies in the Western Desert and the Memphite pyramid region. Satellite remote sensing offers only a way to minimize foot survey work across Egypt's vast flood plain: once sites are discovered, they need to be mapped accurately on the ground. Differential GPS survey has allowed archaeologists Helen Fenwick and Peter Piccione to map Tell el-Amarna and the tombs of the nobles in Luxor, respectively, obtaining a high degree of accuracy. Hence, combining satellite and surface survey allows sites to be detected and mapped quickly and accurately.

Landscape survey in Egyptology has changed significantly over time. The 1798 Napoleonic Survey achieved a reasonable degree of accuracy, and the Napoleonic Survey's description of sites remains reliable and often the sole remaining evidence to this date. The presence of engineers, surveyors, architects, and artists represents, somewhat ironically, a degree of multidisciplinary scientific inquiry to which Egyptologists are now returning. Such early surveys also provided maps useful for showing landscapes subsequently altered by the Aswan High Dam and other projects. In the formative years of the Egyptian Antiquities Service, inspectors undertook surveys within their inspectorates, such as Georges Daressy's Delta surveys in 1912, describing sites in varying detail. These inspectors noted major site features, site dimensions, and suggested occupation dates apparent from surface material culture. In the 1920s and 1930s, expeditions to remote desert sites such as the Gilf Kebir recorded inscriptions and material culture. This time also saw the introduction of aerial photography to Egyptology, with the work of Reginald Engelbach in 1929. Beginning at this point, Bertha Porter and Rosalind Moss's bibliographic topographical catalog of inscribed materials represented an advance in publishing in one series all known information from specific sites. It was, in effect, a major survey of inscribed ancient Egyptian material culture and still represents the starting point for most Egyptological endeavors. However, random foot surveys remained the main process for locating sites and lacked a uniform approach to recording.

The 1960s brought anthropological approaches to Egyptology with the construction of the Aswan High Dam. Countless sites would soon be underwater beneath Lake Nasser, so UNESCO appealed to archaeologists across the globe to survey and excavate sites in Northern Sudan (Nubia). Archaeologists worked under significant time constraints. Their site survey methodology included aerial photography to locate and map sites, recording as much as possible before the water levels rose. Post–Aswan High Dam site recovery, a shift to settlement archaeology began in Egyptology with archaeologists such as Barry Kemp, David O'Connor, and Manfred Bietak.

Survey in modern Egyptology is complex, involving diverse situations and approaches. It has three primary forms: epigraphic surveys, inter-site surveys, and intra-site surveys. Epigraphic surveys have focused upon many areas throughout Egypt, including the Western Desert, Eastern Desert, and Sinai. Inter-site surveys are the least developed in terms of methodology, especially when compared with regional survey methodologies in other parts of the world. With cost and time factors in relation to expansive and difficult geographical areas, it is difficult to visit more than a few sites at any given time. Most ancient Egyptian sites (i.e., Prehistoric to Islamic Periods) remain partially explored, undiscovered, or destroyed or are not equated with ancient toponyms. Currently, we do not know the extent of settlements and sites in the Nile Valley, while surveys in the Delta have shown just how little we know about the extent of settlements there.

In Egypt's remote regions, a growing problem with popular survey publications is that looters use them for site maps and GPS locational data, especially for desert regions where few ghaffirs are available to protect sites. This problem is hard to resolve. For example, in the 2002 study of Eastern Desert rock art by Michael Morrow and Margaret Morrow, the authors published GPS points and satellite images showing the location of inscriptions.

Survey in Egyptology must not only be equated with broad-scale landscape types, but should be connected to the type of archaeological remains one is examining, especially with epigraphic survey. The detailed recording of temple inscriptions advocated by the Chicago House method, described in this publication by Peter Dorman, has yielded exceptional results for over 80 years. Equally important are the epigraphic surveying methods in use by John and Debbie Darnell, who have recorded over 2,000 inscriptions in Egypt's Western Desert as part of their Theban Desert Road Survey Project, published in 2004. These inscriptions contribute much toward our understanding of Egypt's earliest writing systems, First Intermediate Period–Second Intermediate Period military routes, and later periods. The Darnells' work is unique in incorporating intensive archaeological survey, ceramic analysis, and epigraphic survey, augmenting our understanding of Egyptian activity in the Western Desert.

Intra-site survey forms the third type of archaeological reconnaissance in Egypt. Much as different types of material culture form the basis for choosing a specific survey method, individual sites determine the best techniques to apply, especially within Egypt's diverse landscape types. Two primary types of settlement sites exist in Egypt: desert occupation sites such as Tell el-Amarna and tell sites within or beside Egypt's flood plain regions (e.g., Mendes). Barry Kemp and Salvatore Garfi carried out an extensive survey of Tell el-Amarna in 1977, producing detailed maps of excavated uninvestigated parts of the city. David Jeffreys is utilizing coring and GPS mapping to reconstruct the past landscape history of the Memphis region. Alexandria yields a different landscape type, as a significant section of Ptolemaic Alexandria lies beneath the sea. The application of detailed grids of submerged artifact scatters follows broader surface survey and site mapping techniques. Larry Pavlish has applied diverse site transect surveys and sampling techniques at Mendes, publishing his findings in 2003.

Surveying multiple sites on a regional basis is growing within Egyptology and is needed to document sites quickly. The EES Delta Survey Project, led by Jeffrey Spencer, has collected data on over 600 known archaeological sites from the Delta over the past 20 years. Information about site location, size, date range, and published information is available on the project Web site, which is continuously updated from ongoing field checking by project members and additional archaeological projects.[2] The Egyptian Antiquities Information Service (EAIS) Geographic Information System (GIS) has recently begun compiling a database covering all of Egypt's known sites on a governate-by-governate basis. The EAIS employs archaeologists, Egyptologists, lawyers, and computing specialists and is scrutinizing land ownership issues in order to prioritize high risk sites for immediate registration and protection. Using a standardized form, bibliographic, archaeological, and related information is collected for each site, placed in a GIS database, available online.[3] The first volume, published in 2005 and edited by Naguib Amin, details the archaeological sites of Sharqiyya province in a fashion similar to the EES Delta survey. The EAIS has completed recording sites from Sharqiyya, Daqueliyah, and North Sinai and is currently concentrating on South Sinai, Luxor, and Minya provinces. This broadly defined survey plan has already begun to save some of Egypt's most threatened known sites.

Although the earliest expeditions to Egypt adopted survey work, why Egyptologists have since mostly neglected regional survey work is an important question to consider. As David Jeffreys reiterated in 2003, Egyptology is biased toward monuments, artifacts, and funerary archaeology. This focus on sites with high yields of historical and architectural information has avoided settlement studies that analyze site formation and destruction processes. Manfred Bietak reminded the Egyptological community in 1979 that very little is known about settlements in Egypt in comparison to other regions in the Near East.

In Susan Alcock and John Cherry's 2004 book, advances in surveying methodologies are discussed in a number of case studies throughout the Mediterranean. Egypt is conspicuous through its absence.[4] Nor is Egypt mentioned in Tony Wilkinson's 2005 book *Ancient Near Eastern Landscapes*. Is this because survey work in Egypt is less prominent and is outdated methodologically compared with work being conducted elsewhere, or is Egyptology perceived as a field only interested in recording monumental remains? Both points are partially true. In Egypt, in particular in the flood plain, studying settlement patterns via inter-site survey has received much less attention than site-specific excavation. The numerous tombs, temples, and other significant sites have long held the primary attraction for most Egyptologists, and still do, despite increasing threats of destruction and looting of archaeological sites. Zahi Hawass, Secretary General of the Supreme Council for Antiquities, has recognized this problem and has called upon Egyptologists to help record and excavate the relatively less well investigated sites in the Delta and threatened desert regions.

Today, Egypt's landscape is dynamic, with rapidly expanding towns and agricultural development on desert regions. Satellite images of Egyptian towns and fields from 2002 reveal immense settlement growth and agricultural expansion into the desert in comparison with maps from the 1920s. These factors, including the earlier exploitation of *sebbakh*, or fertilizer from archaeological sites, have leveled innumerable archaeological sites. In many cases, modern settlements and diverse industrial complexes have covered ancient sites, capping and preserving the earliest levels, but also preventing most excavation work. With the increasing loss of archaeological remains and sites each year, conventional foot-based survey methods are simply insufficient to locate and document ancient settlements and their environs before they are irretrievably covered or destroyed.

In light of such modern site destruction, the location of Egypt's ancient unknown sites is crucial for archaeologists interested in carrying out detailed surveys. How many and what kinds of cities, villages, and hamlets did the ancient Egyptians occupy over a roughly 3000-year time period? This is a question that Egyptologists will never be able to address fully. Too many sites either are too deeply buried beneath the flood plain's surface or have been lost to the shifting Nile river course or land development through time. In his 1976 work, Karl Butzer provided the most comprehensive overview of pharaonic settlements for all of Egypt, charting the number of known towns in each nome (province). He does not provide dated occupation sequences for each site and only lists an average of 8.4 sites per nome. For Lower Egypt he lists nine sites, including the pyramid fields and Memphis. Many of his historical sites remain unidentified geographically. He acknowledges the lack of macrosettlement pattern studies, and his study and the following thirty years underscore how little we still know about ancient Egypt's overall settlement patterns.

Aside from settlement pattern studies, defining a given "site" in the context of its broader function in ancient Egypt is relatively easier than describing its specific changing roles. An archaeologist can only begin to describe a site fully and accurately if its historical, geographical, and overall contexts are known. Once archaeologists have examined a site's material culture remains, it can be placed in local, regional, national, and international contexts and any changes throughout time. Compiling a full catalog of site typologies and changes through time is indispensable for settlement pattern and socioeconomic, political, and cultural studies in Egypt. In establishing such survey objectives, differing site types require the application of appropriate survey techniques. For instance, archaeological sites range from simple localized pot sherd scatters to rock-cut sites more than 20 meters in height.

Ultimately one deals with only a small percentage of the remaining evidence within each site and time period, while the number of "missing" below-ground sites is high in the flood plain due to shifting Nile courses and silt deposition over the millennia.

Defining an area as a "site" is more complicated than one might assume, when a range of temporal, spatial, and contextual factors are considered. Earlier occupation levels located below the surface or excavation levels are still part of a site, even though there may be gaps in occupation during certain periods. Landscape changes over time, such as the Delta's northern expansion, affect how we perceive sites and settlement patterns. Penny Wilson's discovery of Neolithic period material at Sais, issued in 2005, shows the potential of earlier occupation remains at Delta sites and demonstrates that earlier layers are not necessarily beyond reach.

Although a vertical sequence of occupation is unquestionably part of one site throughout time, what about horizontal boundaries? Many past settlements had an immediate hinterland with field systems, irrigation, canals, field shelters, stables, minor structures, and access routes. Given the density of human settlement and the importance of agricultural land and waterways in ancient Egypt, defining a single "site" is closely connected to its immediate ancient landscape and how the individual site interacted with its associated hinterland. The 2005 coring work of Judith Bunbury and Angus Graham at Karnak revealed that in the Middle Kingdom, Karnak temple was actually built on an island. This connects the archaeological importance of the site with its placement in the ancient landscape. Another example is the work of Jim Hoffmeier and Stephen Moshier at Tell el-Borg in North Sinai, described in 2006, and the relationship of this and other New Kingdom forts to a paleolagoon in what is currently a desert plain. Having a holistic view of archaeological landscapes in Egypt versus specific sites supports how sites are explored and recorded.

The former annual Nile inundation and silt deposition, alongside other processes of human and natural destruction, have altered and obscured the ancient landscape sequence. Calculating the density for surface and above-ground sites would show the averages of site preservation per period though both ancient and modern multivariate processes. Consider the site of Tell Tarha in the northeast Delta, newly discovered through the remote sensing analysis of this author. Only 2 meters × 75 meters × 100 meters of the site survives above ground. If its overall preserved area, and hence importance, is considered, it would appear rather insignificant. However, dense sherds scatters, artifacts, and mud-brick remains are visible for over a kilometer in the fields surrounding the site's core, with sherds spanning the Old Kingdom–Roman Period. Thus, Tell Tarha probably originally represented a major Delta settlement. Without further investigation, however, one can only hypothesize the significance of Tell Tarha in regional administration and international trade.

Past archaeological excavations play a significant role in determining the overall percentage of what remains to be discovered in Egypt. Early excavations, though widescale in extent, ignored or did not analyze or publish the majority of what most archaeological expeditions process today, such as pot sherds, bones, seeds, small finds, and industrial debitage. How much can we say early excavations truly omitted? Sifting or even excavating past archaeological refuse dumps is an important part of many expeditions today. With many early excavations missing or neglecting what is now considered significant material, and numerous findings remaining unstudied in museum and storehouse collections, our reconstruction of ancient Egypt relies upon even less evidence. If the 2007 satellite remote sensing results of this author are any indication, there are thousands of sites awaiting discovery in the Nile Valley and Delta flood plains. Taking these data into account, it can be suggested that far less than 1 percent of ancient Egyptian sites have been uncovered in the Nile flood plain regions. Estimating site sizes and total excavated areas of sites, based on the EES Delta survey, gives a figure of less than 0.001 percent of the overall ancient occupation area of the Delta as being excavated.[5]

Uncovering new material at known sites is different from locating entirely new sites, but reveals a significant point: if archaeologists have focused on a small portion of well-known sites, then Ancient Egypt's *total* landscape is just beginning to be uncovered. The percentage of known archaeological material in Egypt is significantly smaller than the sample of excavated material in the Delta, especially considering how many unidentified sites likely exist beneath the Nile Valley. For instance, in Middle Egypt, the total number of known ancient Egyptian surface sites is very small in comparison to the total number of sites that would have made up the landscape in all periods. Many of the known sites, such as Tuna el-Gebel and Tell el-Amarna, actually lie on the edge of the flood plain or in the adjacent desert. Satellite remote sensing by this writer, however, suggests that the "new" surface sites found in Middle Egypt contain sufficient material to occupy archaeological survey teams for at least a decade. The surface remains are Late Roman through Byzantine Period (ca. 400–800 AD), while initial deep coring at various sites suggests earlier phases of occupation. Locating buried landscapes from all periods of pharaonic history is much more difficult, but could reveal much about prevailing economic, social, political, and environmental conditions through time, as they have done for other fields, in particular European archaeology. Developing and establishing tools, such as remote sensing, detailed mapping, and coring, are the primary means through which Egypt's past landscapes can be reconstructed and provide an additional impetus for broadening the scale of surveying work.

As documented by William Lawrence and his colleagues in 2002, Egypt's tremendous population growth and urban expansion, illustrated through remote sensing, threaten to take over a large percentage of agricultural lands, many of which contain Egypt's archaeological remains. If Egypt's rate of urban expansion remains unchecked, all of the Delta's agricultural lands are theoretically at risk of disappearing in 70 years, including free-standing tells in modern fields. The author's own survey and satellite remote sensing work showed many towns and villages expanding between 10 and 200 percent in the past 30 years, obscuring many archaeological sites once visible in satellite images from the late 1960s. Tell sites often represent open stretches of land ideal for constructing schools, water plants, cemeteries, or expansion zones for adjacent modern towns. For example, during this writer's 2004 Middle Egypt survey season, only three freestanding tells survived out of 70 surface sites. Tells may be visible from a fair distance, depending on their size and height, but if they are often obscured by modern construction and vegetation, they require other locational aids, such as satellite remote sensing, detailed topographic maps, and published documentation.

More traditional archaeological surveys and settlement pattern analyses have covered the ancient Near East, including Israel, Jordan, Syria, Iraq, and Turkey. Robert Adam's survey and settlement pattern analysis approach in 1981, which proved to be a seminal contribution to Near Eastern archaeology, is sorely needed in Egypt. Surveys in Syria and Jordon have relied heavily on Corona high-resolution satellite photography, a U.S.-based satellite program started during the height of the Cold War. This is not surprising, with the long history of aerial photography in Jordan, starting with Antoine Poidebard in 1923. Both Jason Ur in 2003 and Tony Wilkinson in 2002 have shown how Corona imagery can detect ancient roadways and site features not otherwise visible at ground level.

The earliest application of remote sensing in Egyptology came with Royal Air Force (RAF) aerial photographs of well-known sites in the 1920s and 1930s, including the pyramids of Giza and temples in Luxor by Reginald Englebach in 1929. In 1995, Rog Palmer discussed how, aside from archaeological site detection, aerial photos can be used to highlight crop marks, ditches, house foundations, ancient field boundaries, and roads.[6] For example, oblique air photos taken by the RAF in 1932 above the flood plain near Tell el-Amarna revealed a number of suggestive crop marks.[7] A large number of aerial photographs of Egypt and the Middle East from the 1930s are housed in government archive centers, including the Smithsonian Institute in Green Park, Maryland, the Joint Air Reconnaissance Intelligence Center archives in Brampton, UK, and German Web sites dealing with World War I. These images provide useful comparative material, especially in conjunction with maps from the early 1900s. Aerial photographs appear in Jean Vercoutter's 1976 publication detailing UNESCO's salvage work during the 1960s. Maps recently made available from the Cairo map center have utilized photogrammetric cartography for the 1992 1:50,000 series, compiling information about Egypt's topographic features from aerial photographs.[8]

Royal Air Force photographs and kite and balloon photography should augment crop mark analysis and archaeological site location in Egypt. At a number of archaeological sites, such as Mendes and several sites in Middle Egypt, this author has observed identical crop types growing at different heights in suggestive patterns. By observing the architecture exposed in tell sections, one can see higher crops following ancient walls. Richard Knisley-Marpole, adopting kite photography at Kharga Oasis in 2001, and Gwil Owen, using balloon photography at Tell el-Amarna in 1993, have had great success with tracing ancient features. Until RAF and other aerial photographs become easier to obtain for Egypt, kites and balloons represent the easiest way to obtain aerial pictures of sites.

Viewing the landscape through aerial photographs reveals only a small part of what satellites can detect from space. Many types of multispectral satellites, each with specific spatial and spectral resolutions, circle the globe collecting data reflected from the earth's surface. In use by a wide range of scientific fields, satellites can offer much to archaeological surveys, but, like any scientific instrument, must be used with caution. Satellite instrumentation acts like an aerial resistivity survey: it can isolate areas that appear as anomalies via spectral signatures. Satellite instrumentation cannot, however, detect sites or parts of sites that are buried under more than a meter of silt.[9] These image data can detect surface archaeological sites that are invisible to human eyes, which are limited to the visible part of electromagnetic spectrum. Satellite instrumentation also gives a broad-scale view of the landscape, illuminating surface features that would remain hidden at ground level. Though satellite instrumentation cannot elucidate the complex nature of settlement sites, it helps to highlight the complex nature of the landscape surrounding sites and can yield spectral signatures for many new surface sites that have otherwise evaded ground-based surveys.

A major problem in remote sensing research projects is the frequent lack of follow-up ground-truthing or coring, which is crucial to verify analysis indicating potential archaeological sites and features. In addition, a well-organized methodology is needed to bridge computer analysis of image data in the laboratory and subsequent ground surveys. Devising an appropriate ground-truthing data collection form, flexible for supplementary data, and a reasonable season itinerary is important to the project's success. Remote sensing surveys are different from traditional archaeological surveys in that the data analysis has already located a series of potential archaeological sites and their exact coordinates. How and what to record on the ground are additional issues because they require greater uniformity and approach, especially to compare survey data between different sites and surveys.

Archaeologists have employed many types of satellites for their research across the globe over the past 30 years, selecting different imagery according to geographical coverage and resolution. Satellite images have been able to locate ancient cities, road systems, environmental features connected to settlement patterns, and numerous subsurface features. Archaeologists have not yet developed a comprehensive methodology for using satellite remote sensing in archaeology, but this is partly due to the wide range of satellite imagery available for archaeological research. Satellite resolution also ranges greatly from 1 kilometer to 0.6 meters Costs can vary from thousands of dollars for Quickbird imagery (with a 0.6 meter resolution) to free data for Landsat (15- to 30-meter resolution) and limited SPOT imagery (5- to 20-meter resolution). Different satellites may cover varying portions of Egypt, such as the SIR-C RADAR mission, which covers only a small percentage of Egypt's landscape.

The earliest use of satellite imagery in Egyptology, described by Fred Wendorf and his colleagues in 1988, used SIR A/B RADAR imagery to map "radar rivers" in the Western Desert. After locating paleochannels deep in the desert, Wendorf and his team followed the rivers and mapped ancient Neolithic sites along ancient river edges. Another desert-based remote sensing project took place along the pyramid fields, conducted by Sayshura Yochimura and his team in 1997. The Japanese team identified potential buried sites using SPOT satellite imagery and field-checked the results, with a 38 percent success rate. A more recent study, released in 2005, led by Miroslav Barta and Vladimir Bruna, has employed Quickbird imagery to map the region surrounding Abusir. This project shows how Quickbird imagery is essential for the overall visualization of the ancient landscape (Figs. 4.3, 4.4).

The author applied a broader approach using satellite remote sensing in the northeast Delta and Middle Egypt, locating 87 previously unknown archaeological sites in two survey

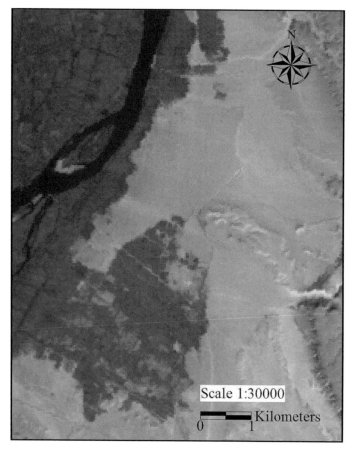

FIGURE 4.3. Part of 2002 Landsat satellite image of the central city part of Tell el-Amarna, with a 30-m pixel resolution. Photo: Courtesy of S. Parcak.

seasons (Fig. 4.5). The northeast Delta survey covered a 40 km × 50 km region surrounding the Late Period site of Tell Tebilla. The Middle Egypt survey project focused on a 15 km × 30 km region located within Akhenaten's boundary stele on the West Bank from Tell el-Amarna. After each survey area's boundaries were established, all known archaeological sites were tallied using published regional surveys and modern maps from the U.S. Army Survey of Egypt. The EES Delta survey proved to be an invaluable tool for the Delta. By correlating known ancient sites with potential ancient site signatures in the satellite image data, specific satellite remote sensing techniques could be applied to detecting unknown archaeological sites within each survey region.

Following the evaluation of remote sensing techniques used by specialists concentrating on Egypt's flood plain or regions similar to this, the next step included selecting appropriate satellite images for their geographic coverage, resolution, and cost. The most appropriate

FIGURE 4.4. Part of a 2005 Quickbird satellite image of the same area with a 0.6-m resolution. Note the clarity of the Quickbird satellite image. Both images are at a scale of 1:30,000. Photo: Courtesy of S. Parcak.

images included Landsat, SPOT, Quickbird, and Corona data. Correlating the perimeters of known archaeological sites with their exact locations in satellite images assisted in determining what techniques could best identify other previously unidentified sites. Differentiation of tell material from modern towns and villages above or beside ancient sites is a continuing problem in Near Eastern archaeology and also caused difficulties in the Delta and Middle Egypt survey regions. This differentiation is often problematic because many buildings are constructed out of mud-brick, or have mud-brick installations on their roofs, thus blurring the distinctions between potential archaeological sites and modern materials. By fine-tuning

FIGURE 4.5. The 2003 Delta survey region (Area A) and the 2004 Middle Egypt survey region (Area B). The location of the sites of Tell Fagi and Tell Tebilla are noted. Photo: Courtesy of S. Parcak.

a technique to identify a high percentage of known ancient sites in satellite image data, it was possible to isolate potential new sites within the same survey region.

Each survey region permitted slightly different techniques to identify both known and previously unknown tell sites. The application of various classification methods, which group together related satellite imagery pixels, to Landsat 2002 satellite image data did not isolate ancient spectral signatures in the Delta but proved successful in Middle Egypt. Instead, principal components analysis (PCA), another classification method, identified 90 percent of the known archaeological sites in the Delta survey region, namely 119 sites. Forty-four potential new sites appeared using PCA in the Landsat imagery, with a 93 percent success rate. Corona imagery from 1972 confirmed that these signatures represented tell sites. It became apparent that the very nature of ancient site formation processes in Egypt lent itself to detection from satellite imagery. Despite varied urban expansion across tells, where sufficient portions of the original tell earth remain exposed, tell soil can be detected with satellite remote sensing, which can measure the higher moisture rate absorbed by tell earth. In 2003, this author visited 62 Delta sites spanning known, little-known, and previously unknown tell sites in order to confirm the remote sensing results. Twenty sites represented previously unknown tells in an area otherwise intensively surveyed by traditional techniques and described by Manfred Bietak in 1975, Edwin Van den Brink in 1987, and Marek Chlodnicki and colleagues in 1992, During the 2003 survey the project team mapped, photographed, and described each site, collecting surface material culture for dating analysis.

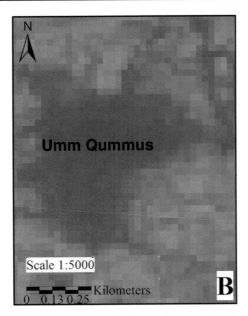

FIGURE 4.6. The town of Umm Qummus, visited during the 2004 Middle Egypt survey – part of a 2002 Landsat satellite image in the visual part of the electromagnetic spectrum. Photo: Courtesy of S. Parcak.

Although the Delta survey area (2000 sq. km) proved too large for a single survey season, a future project, called R.E.S.C.U.E. (remote sensing and coring of uncharted Egyptian sites), aims to continue work here, applying detailed mapping and coring to each new site. The initial Delta survey produced a preliminary settlement pattern sequence, from ca. 3000 BC to 200 AD. Using Corona imagery, the project located the foundations of a Dynasty 30 temple enclosure wall, measuring 235 meters East–West and 280 meters North–South, excavated in the 2003 season and described by Greg Mumford in 2004.

The 2004 Middle Egypt survey design was augmented based on the preceding survey. Unlike the Delta, which already had a number of articles and reports from previous survey projects, the 1798–1801 Napoleonic Expedition represented the most recent and comprehensive published survey in Middle Egypt, noting 13 sites. The 2004 remote sensing analysis measured spectral signatures for the area's best-known tell site, el-Ashmunein, for comparative purposes. Unsupervised classification identified 70 possible tell sites using 2002 Landsat imagery, with a 95 percent confirmation from 1972 Corona images (Figs. 4.6, 4.7). Subsequent ground survey work verified that 69 (98 percent) of the 70 signatures were ancient tell sites, 37 of which represented previously unknown sites. Only one of the 70 tell sites proved inaccessible. The material culture found at the 69 sites ranged in date from 100 to 1000 AD.

Determining whether the Middle Egypt sites had earlier occupation levels formed the impetus for the 2005 (West Bank) and 2006 (East Bank) coring seasons. The initial coring

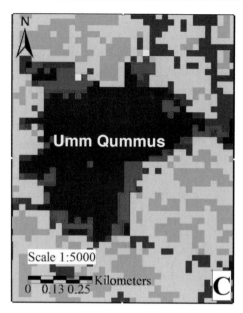

FIGURE 4.7. The town of Umm Qummus, using an "unsupervised classification" system. The gray pixels within the boundaries of the city are representative of archaeological material. Photo: Courtesy of S. Parcak.

season, described by the author in 2005, found Late Roman–Byzantine Period (ca. AD 400–800) material culture to a depth of 5 meters at ten sites. The further coring at Tell el-Amarna in 2006 suggested that the eastward-shifting Nile had washed away a sizable section of the Dynasty 18 city, with later Nile silt deposits accumulating in the Late Roman Period. In modern fields to the west of the preserved city, only deep foundations near the Great Temple yielded Amarna Period material culture. Both coring seasons suggested Nile silt deposition of 3 millimeters a year in southern Egypt in contrast to Karl Butzer's 1976 figure of 1 millimeter a year for the Delta, where silt deposits would naturally be lower. The author integrated the coring program, survey work, and remote sensing results to generate a landscape history of the Amarna region during the Late Roman–Byzantine Period, showing how the Nile has shifted between 400 and 1,000 meters to the east in the past 1600 years.

The proposed surveying and coring model presented here suggests using regional site survey data to glean information about site placement, function, and changes through time in relation to past landscapes. Reconstructing regional patterns allow insights into single-site trends (e.g., differential site sizes and fluctuations) that may otherwise be detected only through excavation seasons. Site placement also allows us to examine environmental trends, correlating dated sites and locations to suggest potential previous Nile river channels, which can later be confirmed through coring. Similar approaches can be used to suggest past trade routes, regional centers, and other aspects linking past landscapes.

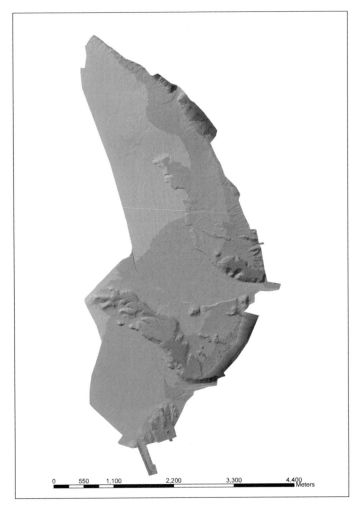

FIGURE 4.8. Differential GPS-generated map of the Tell el-Amarna region (created by Helen Fenwick). Image courtesy of Helen Fenwick, Barry Kemp, Patricia Spencer, and the Egypt Exploration Society.

The comprehensive mapping of archaeological sites is an integral part of surveying efforts. Three-dimensional differential GPS technology offers one way to map large areas of diverse sites and their immediate hinterlands in Egypt quickly. As described by Helen Fenwick in 2005, the removal of intentional error by the U.S. military in 2000 enabled the locational accuracy of GPS units and receiving satellites to increase from 100 meters to 25 meters (95 percent of the time). Using a differential GPS with two receivers improves the accuracy of mapping to an even greater degree. For example, the author used differential GPS mapping at Tell Ahmar in Middle Egypt in 2004, taking 1,000 points in a single day and mapping the extant site, measuring 500 meters × 1000 meters × 15 meters in size. The receivers require an open space, which can be difficult on some tell sites covered partially by trees or buildings that can obstruct radio signals. The final topographic map is generated using ArcView GIS software.

At Tell el-Amarna, Fenwick has integrated detailed foot survey work with a Leica 500 series differential GPS (Fig. 4.8). In a 2005 article, she described how she took over 80,000 points to map an area of 15 sq. km to the east of the main city. She mapped a road network 2–11 meter wide not visible from the air. Inhabitants of el-Amarna apparently used these roads for foot patrols, while additional functions are being explored in future. Fenwick's study has also produced a highly detailed map of her survey area and uncovered additional archaeological features, such as several cemeteries. Her work shows the necessity of continuing ground surveys in conjunction with differential GPS technology at both new and well-explored sites, such as Amarna.

Peter Piccione has undertaken additional work with differential GPS technology on the West Bank in Luxor. He has recorded hundreds of nobles' tombs to produce an up-to-date, accurate, and comprehensive map of areas largely built over and looted. Piccione's highly detailed maps and survey data will allow archaeologists and Egyptologists to assess fully the distribution patterns of different time periods, social classes, reuse, and related spatial aspects for the Theban necropolis. This work is connected to his ongoing research project "The On-Line Geographical Information System for the Theban Necropolis." By connecting Quickbird satellite imagery with differential GPS technology, Piccione and his colleagues have created a searchable online GIS.[10] This work is also important for creating site protection plans in the face of ongoing development in Luxor.

The aforementioned problems of increasing population, urban sprawl, and looting in Egypt have necessitated the development of a more efficient and cost-effective methodology for surveying and recording both known and new sites. Multifaceted issues drive archaeological project designs and their implementation, and archaeological work in Egypt is no exception. Egyptology will always need to balance its focus on inscribed monuments versus settlement remains. Many inscribed rock faces, tombs, and temples are equally endangered as archaeological sites: each year, more and more information is lost to salinization, pollution, looting, or destruction from urban development. By looking at the broader landscape and hinterlands surrounding known archaeological sites, more detailed surveys can contextualize individual isolated sites and monuments within their broader settlement network and past environment. Satellite imagery and aerial photography is best used together to identify new archaeological sites and features, as well as to track overall site destruction patterns today. The EAIS's recording and evaluation of Egypt's known sites on a governate-by-governate basis is indispensable, but Egypt's unknown sites also need attention. Once new sites are located, a form of archaeological triage must be implemented. Each new site should be mapped using a differential GPS, photographed, described, and explored, with possible test trenches and cores to gain an overview of the occupational sequence. More time can be spent investigating sites that appear to have promising remains. Too many of Egypt's sites are lost each year to warrant more detailed excavation at already known and protected sites: time is simply running out for the archaeology of Egypt's flood plain settlements and many desert sites.

The current training of future Egyptologists forms a key factor in how Egyptology will evolve. Bietak emphasized this very point in 1979 and described how new generations should be trained in salvage work, gathering information to be used by future scholars before it is lost. Students of Egyptian archaeology not only should be trained in modern archaeological methods, including the use of technology such as satellite remote sensing, but also must be aware of the large-scale problems affecting Egypt's archaeological heritage. Providing Egyptology students with more training in archaeology and related technology and incorporating more interdisciplinary approaches will better prepare the overall field for dealing with Egypt's changing landscapes and combating its diminishing heritage.

Understanding the mechanics behind ancient landscape changes affects how models can be best designed to study settlement patterns in Egyptology. The addition of new sites to the known archaeological record in Egypt would help to address diverse historical and geomorphological questions, especially settlement pattern studies, which have been limited by a paucity of archaeological and environmental evidence in the Nile Valley. At present, little is known about changing settlement patterns and landscapes through time in Egypt, simply because too few widescale surveys, settlement pattern studies, and intensive drill-core projects have been implemented. Additional issues in Egyptian archaeology include how people have interacted with their environments and natural resources over time and how this has affected site growth, collapse, and abandonment. Important historical issues such as the growth of the ancient Egyptian state, the evolution and collapse of the Old Kingdom, and the impact of foreign incursions are understood mostly in terms of the known textual and archaeological evidence. Landscape evolution studies and broader settlement patterns on a local and regional scale will greatly augment how these trends are understood.

Egypt is only one of many countries that must balance the needs of its current and future population against the preservation of fragile ecosystems and relic landscapes, including archaeological sites. Too often ancient landscapes and their remains are sacrificed to modern local, municipal, provincial, and national needs. Before a community can foster local archaeological resources for potential tourism, albeit mainly limited to monumental remains, archaeological sites, or parts of sites, are destroyed to facilitate new fields, schools, roads, or other projects.

Modern survey techniques form only one of a number of resources available to archaeologists to record sites before they disappear through modernization. Archaeologists need the means to record not only Egypt's cultural heritage, but also our global heritage, before this and future generations lose irreplaceable archaeological and historical data. We have already lost an incalculable amount of information through the natural, biased preservation of the archaeological record, let alone widely varying continuous destruction by human and other agencies. Although the resources do not exist to excavate and record everything in time, most existing surface sites can be located through the extant satellite image and ground survey data. The high yield gains from what survives of the archaeological record make such thorough survey work worthwhile. Ultimately, the choice lies with individual institutions, archaeologists, Egyptologists, their research designs, antiquities organizations, and funding agencies. These are decisions, however, that will have profound effects on the future of diverse archaeological disciplines and the overall future of Egyptology and the broader global archaeological heritage.

NOTES

1. I would like to thank Peter Piccione for sharing the results of his Luxor project.
2. See www.ees.ac.uk/deltasurvey for more information.
3. See www.eais.org.eg.
4. A possible answer might be that people do not consider Egypt to be a "true" Mediterranean country.
5. Can one estimate the average proportion examined from this 1 percent of sites? Out of 649 known Delta sites, based largely on the EES Delta survey, 150 sites are dated, and 215 have published dimensions. Applying a minimum size of 4 m × 300 m × 300 m (the size of a medium-small village in modern Egypt) to the remaining unmeasured sites yields an average area of 360,000 m^3. Out of the 150 dated sites, excavations have been conducted on only 53. In an average excavation season, incorporating the early mass-clearance of some major Delta sites, an expedition might investigate nine 10 m × 10 m squares to a depth of 3 m, for a total area of 2,700 m^3. Many of the 53 excavated sites only had data from one or two seasons, while long-standing excavations at such sites as Qantir and Mendes have witnessed a minimum of ten seasons, with an estimated excavated area of 1,431,000 m^3. If one estimates the minimum total area of all the known sites in the Delta (233,640,000 m^3), less than 0.001% of the overall ancient occupation area of the Delta has been excavated. The figure is probably much smaller, owing to the low estimate for unknown site dimensions, but emphasizes just how little archaeologists have uncovered from flood plain tell sites.
6. Differences in vegetation height, type, and color often indicate subsurface structures.
7. As viewed by the author. This method has great potential for Egyptian archaeology, as it could possibly show the presence of large numbers of buried ancient structures beneath the flood plain.
8. A number of the maps do not match up when placed side by side, suggesting that the majority of the photographs did not undergo georeferencing or correction of the distortion in the aerial photographs.
9. Such as SIR-C radar imagery, which only works in the desert, picking up features meters below the current ground surface. It would not work in the flood plain because the moisture would create too much backscatter.
10. Visit www.cofc.edu/olgis/.

CHAPTER 5

EPIGRAPHY AND RECORDING

Peter F. Dorman

In its broadest sense, epigraphy comprises a multiplicity of techniques that have as their primary goal the precise documentation of inscriptions of all sorts painted on or engraved into stone or other durable surfaces, as well as their critical editing, translation, analysis, and publication. While epigraphy is applicable to all cultures and historical time periods, it holds a special role within Egyptological studies, since the majority of the extant monumental inscriptions of pharaonic times are accompanied by pictorial representations that implicitly reflect the intimate relationship in ancient Egypt between art and writing. The interpretation of texts on formal monuments, therefore, often involves the interplay between text and representation: the content of such inscriptions cannot be separated entirely from their fundamental, if often implicit, association with formal conventions of Egyptian art and architecture. The interdependency of art and writing – and the pervasive influence of the latter on the former – is an ever-present undercurrent of Egyptian epigraphic methodology.

THE CONTEXT OF MONUMENTAL INSCRIPTIONS

The earliest examples of writing in the Nile valley appear toward the end of the fourth millennium BC and consist primarily of very brief notations, usually composed of one or two signs, that seem to denote either the contents of a storage container or the ownership of property, initially painted with a brush or scratched into the surface of a vessel.[1] Within a matter of several generations, however, these rather simplistic marks of economic require-ment had been elaborated into a conventionalized corpus of detailed hieroglyphic signs suitable for public display on early emblems of tribal prestige and rulership, such as the Scor-pion Macehead and the Narmer Palette, which pre-date the historical onset of Dynasty 1 and presage the appearance of a more complex writing system by Dynasty 3.[2] The early manifestation of writing as a mark of elite status and its employment on commemorative objects of stone created an indelible bond between formal art and Egyptian writing that was to last until the end of pharaonic civilization.[3] To be sure, a more cursive form of the writing system, hieratic, was soon developed for everyday purposes, and for different writing materials such as papyrus, at the same time that the hieroglyphic corpus of signs was formalized and codified as appropriate for the monumental context.[4] In future centuries these two modes of writing were to acquire – in differing degrees – separate orthographies, scribal conventions, and even literary devices and formulas suitable for their differing uses in a highly complex social order.

It is the monumental texts and, for the most part, the hieroglyphic writing system that primarily concern practitioners of epigraphy. In this regard it is necessary to recall that although writing may have developed in response to particular economic needs, public display was initially limited to royalty and the highest levels of society for use on objects of prestige.[5] Literacy thereafter was always limited to a relatively minute sliver of society and pursued as a vocation by a scribal class trained essentially for two purposes: administration and business on the one hand and draftsmanship on the other.[6] While all scribes (sš.w) learned the basics of writing cursive texts, it was a more restricted number – elite draftsmen (sš.w-ḳd) – who were schooled in the complexities of drafting monumental decoration, invariably accompanied by hieroglyphic inscriptions.

The individual hieroglyphic signs represent a range of miniature depictions drawn from the Nilotic environment comprising human beings, plants and animals, features of the natural world, religious insignia, and objects from the realm of craftsmanship. Most of the signs have a specific orientation, in that they are rendered in profile facing right or left, and because of this characteristic, from an early time it was recognized that by reversing the orientation of the signs, hieroglyphic texts could be written in either direction, with the individual glyphs facing toward the beginning of the text. The flexibility of such a writing system was perfectly suited for the adornment of elite commemorative objects and, later on, of architectural forms such as doorways, lintels, and grave stelae. In yet more elaborate contexts, such as temple walls bearing ritual scenes, representations of kings and gods could thus be accompanied by their names and epithets, as well as by captions describing their actions or representing the words they uttered, with the orientation of such texts coinciding with that of the major figures. The hieroglyphic system also offered unlimited opportunity for variation in the spelling of words and for the grouping of signs, permitting a draftsman to arrange inscriptions either in horizontal rows or vertical columns, according to the physical space available.

Despite such options available to the monumental context, the preferred direction of writing in ancient Egypt was always from right to left. This is certain from cursive texts written in hieratic – consisting largely of business accounts, letters, religious and literary compositions, and jar dockets – in which the signs are invariably written facing toward the right-hand side. But this preference is also reflected less obviously in the monumental

FIGURE 5.1. Right-facing text on the "Second Stela" of Kamose. Luxor Museum. Photo: P. Dorman.

context, as, for example, in free-standing stelae carved with inscriptions that are unassociated with human representation or independent of a larger architectural context: when freed from such exterior constraints, hieroglyphic texts are normally carved from right to left as well (Fig. 5.1).

The proclivity for right-oriented text, consisting as it does of signs that may be considered "art in miniature," naturally offered a representational pattern for the depiction of the (right-facing) human figure, a pattern that was conscientiously imitated and quickly codified for both two- and three-dimensional art forms. That is, the typical standing human form taken from the hieroglyphic corpus was formally conceptualized as facing toward the right, with the left foot and arm placed to the fore as if advancing, and the right foot and arm to the rear. When translated into a major figure in a scene, this hieroglyphic model caused little difficulty for the artist in portraying a right-facing figure; but the reverse often posed conundrums that were imperfectly resolved in the confusion of left and right sides (Fig. 5.2). In the same way, the overwhelming predilection in Egyptian statuary for the male figure to be shown with the left foot advanced – in which the complete figure can be viewed only when seen as if advancing to the right, in accordance with the orientation of Egyptian texts – is a legacy of the formulation of the writing system at the end of the late Predynastic Period.

The earliest commemorative objects, from the Early Archaic period and the century or so directly preceding it, consist either of votive donations intended for temple dedication (such as the large cosmetic or oversize mace heads, both now grown too large for actual use) or of individual tableaus that celebrate royal achievements in distant territories, usually carved as formal graffiti in the sides of rocky hillsides. They are complete in and of themselves and follow their own internal composition, often reflecting the right-oriented preference for the hieroglyphic writing system.[7] The application of hieroglyphs to standing durable elements – such as doors and walls – came gradually, only after sacred structures came to be built mostly of stone rather than mud-brick. In such a holistic context, however, architectural symmetry trumped the established rules for the internal organization of any particular scene, and the orientation of major figures came to be dictated according to the requirements of cult activity and the topographical axis of the monument. In temple scenes the king was portrayed as if entering from the main door, gradually approaching the inner sanctum of the resident deity, with the main god(s) of the place facing him. Consequently, on opposite walls of any cultic space, the scenes on the right-hand side were organized as a reflection of those on the left-hand side in terms of their orientation: on every wall surface, the king strode ever closer to the divine sanctuary, and in each scene, the god faced outward to greet and welcome him. Decorative symmetry within a temple was thus achieved by overriding the consistent right-facing predilection of the writing system – which was itself moot when the direction of writing itself could so conveniently be inverted.

Beyond this, there is to be found a definite sacral program for Egyptian temples, a prescribed hierarchy and disposition of space that governs the content of scenes and inscriptions within a sacred milieu and that not only incorporates the formal ritual tableaus on the interior and exterior walls, but also includes seemingly peripheral elements as well, such as door jambs, lintels, architraves, and marginal spaces. Architectural context is therefore a critical factor in the methodologies used by epigraphers in analyzing monumental texts from ancient Egypt, whether complete and still standing in situ, or existing now only in small fragments.

THE ORIGINS OF EGYPTIAN EPIGRAPHY

A review of the first epigraphic missions and their techniques is illuminating both for the historical perspective and for pointing out how early some of the most essential methods of Egyptian epigraphy were initially devised and employed.

The first scientific mission charged with recording ancient Egyptian monuments arrived on the banks of the Nile as a scholarly adjunct to Napoleon Bonaparte's ill-fated attempt

FIGURE 5.2. Figure of Mereruka from his tomb at Saqqara, illustrating the confusion entailed in showing the human figure facing left. Photo: Courtesy of Emily Teeter.

to seize Egypt and deprive the English of the Suez route to India. The field notes of the scientists and artists who accompanied the French army to the Nile in 1798 were, in fact, to have a long-lasting impact on the Western world, when they were published in the *Description de l'Égypte*, a series of volumes almost as monumental as their subject matter.[8] While the *Description* was envisioned as a complete record of the varied botanical, geographical, cultural, and ancient phenomena of contemporary Egypt, it was the nine volumes devoted to pharaonic antiquities that fired the imagination of an unsuspecting Europe and laid the foundations of the field of modern Egyptology. Vistas of ruins, maps and plans of monuments, tables of hieroglyphic signs and royal cartouches, and drawings of sculpture and funerary objects accompanied the myriad copies of carved reliefs and painted walls, all arranged in geographical sequence from Aswan to Alexandria.

From an epigraphic point of view, the folio-sized antiquities plates of the *Description* are a curiosity. The audacity of the work is breath-taking, in that the French scholars were attempting a task that was on the face of it unachievable: a thorough record of ancient monuments. Moreover, the hieroglyphic script had not yet been deciphered (the key was to emerge from another discovery of Napoleon's expedition, a trilingual decree of Ptolemy V known today as the Rosetta Stone[9]), so that the texts had to be rendered purely from what the copyists perceived them to be at first sight. In many cases, the French artists recognized familiar forms of the natural and human world in miniature, but in other cases the signs seemed to be purely enigmatic objects. Because the texts could not be read, there was no way to "correct" the copies being made, or even to attempt to understand their meaning. In many instances, the French copyists were instead drawn to what they could fathom visually on the monuments – ancient Egyptians clearly engaged in recognizable activities such as warfare, agriculture, and religious ritual. The human figures were not rendered according to Egyptian canons but were assimilated to current European romantic models, with Attic musculature, articulated joints, and asymmetrical weight shifts that are virtually nonexistent in Egyptian art.

These earliest copyists often did not bother to record the hieroglyphic signs that appeared in conjunction with scenes: that is, there was no clear commitment to making a complete record, nor (understandably) an awareness that the texts might be integral to the scene. Of those signs that were copied, of course, many can be recognized, but numerous misreadings are obvious and little reliance can be placed on the overall result. But the French artists did experiment with epigraphic technique to the extent of occasionally using weighted lines ("sun" and "shadow" lines) that indicate clearly to the reader whether the relief is sunk or raised.

A great advance came with better understanding of the hieroglyphic script, which occurred two decades after the collapse of Napoleon's venture, in 1822, when Jean-François Champollion announced his decipherment in *Lettre à M. Dacier*, an initial scheme that was fully outlined in his subsequent *Précis du système hiéroglyphique*.[10] Champollion was to follow up his epic decipherment with a research expedition to Egypt in the years 1828 to 1829, but died before the magnificent publication could be completed. The plates appeared as *Monuments de l'Égypte et de la Nubie*, and were accompanied by extensive notes and commentary in *Notes descriptives*.[11] In these volumes, monuments were correctly identified in their chronological context, and representations and texts were "read" as integral parts of a whole, as they were originally intended. A splendid offshoot of the Champollion expedition was a separate publication by the Tuscan representative on his team, Ippolito Rosselini, who grouped the monuments according to their perceived character: historic, civil, and sacral.[12]

From an epigraphic perspective, the Prussian expedition to Egypt led by Karl Richard Lepsius set astonishingly high standards of copying that, even today, are worthy of emulation. The results were issued in a set of magisterial volumes, *Denkmaeler aus Aegypten und Nubien*, in which the monuments are arranged chronologically, so that the achievement of pharaonic civilization can be viewed in one continuous historical sequence.[13] Lepsius' *Denkmaeler* represents a great stride forward in accuracy and in the completeness of its recording. It remains the primary (and largely trustworthy) source for individual monuments on which no further epigraphy has been done since the 1840s, and in cases where epigraphic missions have updated the work of Lepsius, often only incremental improvements are possible.

The Prussian expedition was the last of the comprehensive surveys that were commissioned to make a record of the standing temples and tombs of the entire Nile valley. Henceforth, epigraphic missions would target individual monuments as more limited topics of inquiry. With this greater focus, recording techniques could be selected and adapted that were appropriate to a particular monument.

PRACTICAL TOOLS OF MODERN EPIGRAPHY

The task of epigraphy is essentially one of critical editing in the broadest sense (encompassing both text and representation), a process that involves a number of techniques that can complement each other to produce a definitive reading of a monument.

As noted above, however, the situation is usually made considerably more complex in the case of ancient Egypt if the inscriptions are integral to monumental decoration and are combined with scenes of some sort. Complete interpretation in such cases therefore involves more than the accurate copying of words and their translation; it entails an analysis of spacing, internal grouping, text orientation, interpretation of iconography, and association with physical context. Another complication arises through the fact that many Egyptian monumental inscriptions and reliefs are three-dimensional, executed in two styles of carved relief. The first is raised relief, in which hieroglyphic signs and all major figures protrude slightly above the flat background, each one usually elaborated with internal details and (for the human figures) subtle contours indicating the swelling of facial and bodily features; this style was preferred by ancient Egyptians for internal spaces, where light was indirect and the raised figures could be seen to advantage under dim lighting conditions (Figs. 5.3 and 5.4). The second style, sunk relief, is typified by signs and figures sunk directly below the surface of the stone, to varying depths, but often without losing any of the internal detail of raised relief; sunk relief was normally used for exterior surfaces, where direct sunlight would catch the sunk figures at almost any angle. In any case, the epigraphic challenge for Egyptian monuments has frequently been to produce an accurate record of a three-dimensional modeled surface on a two-dimensional printed page.[14]

Direct Tracing

The most straightforward method of taking a direct record is tracing an inscription or tableau, producing an accurate one-to-one scale drawing with as much detail included as is visible. Tracing works best for monuments decorated with simple incised signs cut in sunk

FIGURE 5.3. Raised relief scene from the Temple of Luxor. Photo: From the Epigraphic Survey, *Reliefs and Inscriptions at Luxor Temple*, Vol. 2: *The Façade, Portals, Upper Register Scenes, Columns, Marginalia, and Statuary in the Colonnade Hall.* OIP 116 (Chicago: University of Chicago, 1998), pl. 164. Courtesy of the Oriental Institute of the University of Chicago.

relief, or where the tracing paper – or, in current usage, a sheet of acetate – can lie flat against the surface, as on painted plaster. It is also invaluable for curved surfaces, such as columns, or for walls that are difficult of access. This seemingly ideal technique is to some extent limited, however, since it has disadvantages for three-dimensional raised relief, and even for sunk relief, whose hieroglyphic signs and figural representations may contain internal detail, features that may not be easily copied in a flat film. Direct tracing is also realistic

Drawing by Di Cerbo and Johnson

THE KING (*A*) OFFERING OINTMENT BEFORE AMUN-RE AND (*B*) OFFERING TO AMUN-RE
NORTH PORTAL, SOUTH FACE, EAST JAMB, THIRD AND FOURTH REGISTERS
(See plate 164)

FIGURE 5.4. Drawing of the scene in Fig. 5.3; the cartouches of Tutankhamun have been usurped by Horemhab, while the damage to the major figures is due to a postpharaonic iconoclastic attack. From idem, pl. 165. Courtesy of the Oriental Institute of the University of Chicago.

only for objects of relatively manageable size. But it has shown to be eminently practicable, for example, even on expansive tomb walls whose colored decoration is applied to painted plaster, walls that often measure about 2 meters high. The only real constraint in this case is the resultant severe reduction required to fit the final record onto a printed page; in such cases, fine details can easily be lost. For colossal Egyptian monuments – temples built on a pharaonic scale, in which scenes can cover hundreds of square meters of surface – other methods must be employed without sacrificing the accuracy of a one-to-one drawing.

Squeezes

One technique of obtaining a precise copy of an inscription or relief, used primarily in the nineteenth century to supplement other records, was the "squeeze," in which damp pulp was pressed against the monument in question and allowed to dry and coalesce, after which the squeeze was carefully pried away, producing an exact image – albeit in reverse – of the surface. Unfortunately, this method exposed the object to moisture, and the squeeze frequently removed paint layers and flakes of stone as well; squeezes are no longer used in the field. Although a squeeze can be molded to obtain the "positive" image of the original, as a practical scholarly tool it has limited application: the squeeze produces a copy at a one-to-one scale, it cannot be handily reproduced for dissemination to scholars at large, and it cannot easily be edited to delete extraneous features of the wall surface.

Photography

Photography is an essential component of the epigraphic method. It provides a visual image of the monument in question at a specific moment in time, affording both a conservation record and a way in which the results of epigraphic research may be compared and, to a certain extent, verified. This technique appeared very early on the epigraphic scene. An earlier experimenter in "heliography" ("sun-writing"), Nicéphore Niépce, collaborated with Louis Daguerre for many years, producing the earliest lasting images around 1824, roughly at the same time as the decipherment of hieroglyphs and the publication of the final volumes of the *Description*; it was Daguerre, after the unexpected death of Niépce, who announced the invention of photography in 1839 to the French Academy of Sciences. With the ancient ruins of Egypt very much in the forefront of popular imagination, it was immediately proposed, as one of its most useful applications, that photography would transform the laborious task of copying the inscriptions and reliefs along the Nile valley by making a perfectly accurate record of arcane inscriptions and carved reliefs without the distortions caused by the artist's hand or eye.

The potential of camera documentation was not systematically realized for some time, however, due to the problems of glass-plate negatives developed in the field and the challenges posed by shifting light conditions. Nor did publications of the nineteenth century include photographic plates on a large scale to supplement the drawings that were made by copyists. But the camera was (and remains) perfectly suited to capture the subtleties of carved relief in both direct and indirect sunlight, as well as the beauties of painted surfaces. While photographic images are indeed irreplaceable as a basic tool to capture the overall appearance of monuments, a number of internal limitations to epigraphic clarity must be pointed out.

Traditional photography depends for the most part on a sole source of light (whether natural or artificial), which inevitably casts shadows; indeed, it is the reading of shadows as much as highlights that creates the illusion of realism for the human eye. Because of this factor, it is only rarely that all pertinent details can be rendered in a single image: pictures taken from the same perspective but with light raking from opposite directions can produce very different appearances. Moreover, because ancient monuments have been inevitably damaged through the ravages of weather, human activity and reuse, and natural catastrophe, the photographic image will necessarily capture everything in its lens, not just the ancient texts and representations but also the manifold layers of destruction and abrasion, potentially creating as much confusion as clarity. The task of the epigrapher is to identify and edit out irrelevant features and to record only those that are original to the monument and pertinent to its subsequent building history.

Yet photography offers a solution to the inherent limitations of direct tracing: in addition to providing a faithful and proportional record of all details on a wall surface, a negative can be printed at any convenient scale, as a reduction or an enlargement, as an immediate aid for drawing. Appropriate scales for drawing texts and reliefs can therefore be determined ahead of time, in accordance with the detail contained on the original monument, and perfectly suited to the envisioned publication. Enlarged prints have been used as a basis for direct tracing or, in other cases, as the basis for drawings themselves, with pencil or pen being laid directly on the photographic emulsion. One of the first scholars to use photography consistently as the immediate basis for the collated drawings of an Egyptian monument was Félix Guilmant, in his publication of the royal tomb of Ramesses IX in the Valley of the Kings, almost sixty years after photography was first suggested as an epigraphic tool.[15] Further developing the potential of enlarged photographic prints as the basis for precise copies, James Henry Breasted conceptualized an epigraphic process based on scaled photography, hand copies inked on top of the photographic emulsion, and collation sheets generated from a blueprint process that are systematically verified by a team of experts. Experimentally employed during the Oriental Institute's Nubian expedition of 1905–1907, this process remains the basis of the facsimile drawings produced by the Epigraphic Survey at Chicago House in Luxor.[16] The advantages include precision of proportion, the involvement of several independent perspectives trained in text and iconography, and the production of field notes (collation sheets) that preserve a record of epigraphic observation and debate. These methodological strengths must inevitably be weighed against the investment in time, costs, and personnel that such facsimile reproductions require.

Recording Painted Surfaces

A further complexity for Egyptian epigraphy is the ubiquitous presence of color on the standing monuments of the Nile valley, which cannot be reproduced in simple line drawings and can only be suggested in black-and-white photographs. To be sure, much of the original pigmentation has been entirely lost over the centuries, but certain select monuments look almost as fresh as when they were first decorated, and thousands more contain substantial traces of paint that illuminate Egyptian procedures in drafting and painting on both relief and flat plaster. The earliest copyists in the Nile valley were struck by the color and vibrancy of Egyptian painting, and to early nineteenth-century European audiences more accustomed to the wan perfections of classical art – often washed of its pigmented brilliance and yet extolled at that time as the highest aesthetic ideal – the brilliant pharaonic palette was a revelation. The recording of pigments was a standard feature of the great epigraphic missions of the early nineteenth century, including the French Napoleonic team and the pioneering expeditions of Champollion and Lepsius; their publications were amply provided with color plates. The use of color by Egyptian artists is also a main feature of the publication of Émile Prisse d'Avennes, a meticulous recorder of Egyptian antiquities who often provided restored views of damaged monuments, and whose two-volume *Atlas* was organized according to prevailing western categories of the fine arts: architecture, painting, drawing, sculpture, and the industrial arts.[17] These early publications were content to reproduce only a close approximation of Egyptian colors, to illustrate the relative variety of pigments used in ancient times, but later epigraphers have devoted more attention to painted surfaces, recognizing that Egyptian painters did not use a consistent palette for all of pharaonic history, and employed different techniques for the application of paint. The copying of painted surfaces reached one of its apogees in the early twentieth century with the work of Norman and Nina de Garis Davies, who documented numerous tombs in western Thebes using a combination of tracing and free-hand methods in water color,[18] and with Amice Calverley and Myrtle Broome, whose documentation of the temple of Sety I at Abydos stands as a magnificent record of painted relief decoration.[19] Similarly, artists with the University of Chicago's Epigraphic Survey working on the temple of Ramesses III at Medinet Habu produced a series of colored facsimiles using a method that involved gouache applied directly over enlarged photographic prints, revealing to what extent painted details originally enlivened the carved surfaces of temple walls.[20]

To some extent color photography has now supplanted the necessity of artists working in watercolor or gouache, but to render pigments accurately in a publication, the checking of proofs must be carried out with a most critical eye, and preferably on site. Some of the most stunning color photography has been pioneered in publications of Theban tombs funded by the Deutsches Archäologisches Institut in Cairo and the Heidelberg Theban tomb project.[21] The use of color photography, however, does not pre-empt the necessity for black-and-white line drawings that reflect the critical editing process (Fig. 5.5). Moreover, the epigraphic challenges offered by painted surfaces are entirely different from those inherent in carved monuments. Certain painted features are almost impossible to render in line drawing, for example, the feathering of pigments to indicate flesh beneath a translucent pleated linen kilt, or the varying width of a brush stroke used to show the outline of a figure, laid down only after larger blocks of color have been applied. Unlike carved walls, whose preliminary drafts have been cut away in the course of their creation, painted plaster walls can reveal a

A   TT294   Roma and wife before Osiris (Sc. 7; p.18)

FIGURE 5.5. Scene of adoration, executed in painted plaster, in the tomb of Roma. Photo: From Nigel Strudwick, *The Tombs of Amenhotep, Khnummose, and Amenmose at Thebes (Nos. 294, 253, and 254),* pl. 12.

great deal about the process by which they were drafted and colored, through the occasional degradation of outer paint layers that reveals what lies beneath. A better understanding of the relevant issues – the composition of grounds and pigments, the organization of work, draftsmen's methods of laying out grids and scenes, the layering and laying on of paint, the characterization of palettes, the symbolism of various colors – not only will materially enhance the mechanical approaches to epigraphy in this area, but also can generate further research questions.[22] Many of the results of such investigations will be directly applicable to the study of carved relief as well, whose surfaces were originally painted. Nonetheless, the task of recording multicolored surfaces that may show different stages of drafting and painting remains a major challenge to field workers attempting to compile a definitive and still cost-effective publication.[23]

The careful observation of color traces can materially assist in the reconstruction of damaged or missing text. Like the conventions used for major figures and objects in a scene, the pigments employed for individual signs were codified and, to a large extent, invariable, often corresponding directly to the colors used for the major representational figures. For example, hieroglyphs representing parts of the human body – arm, hand, leg, face – were painted red to represent human (male) flesh; bird-signs were colored to imitate their typical plumage; tools and artifacts were painted to reflect the materials from which they were made. Thus, in examining a damaged surface where only traces of pigment exist – even without the clear outlines of hieroglyphs – an epigrapher with the knowledge of what colors were used for specific signs would be in a position to establish what hieroglyphs could or could not be present and could make judgments concerning text restorations on the basis of those observations.

On a more general note, it is to be observed that the Egyptian palette was not at all static: certain colors and color combinations were favored at different periods of history, so that the chronology of paint overlays may be broadly determined by the identification of characteristic pigmentation alone. Since temples in particular were often rededicated – and repainted – in successive centuries, the presence of multiple layers of paint, each one perhaps with its distinctive combination of colors, can present an insurmountable challenge for the artist in rendering the surface in a simple line drawing.

Computer Applications

The techniques summarized thus far involve mechanical processes that require extensive manual labor and are necessarily time-consuming. The relatively recent introduction of computers and software applications into the field of epigraphy, however, has held the promise of revolutionizing the traditional tasks of copying without sacrificing the accuracy of earlier methods. One early experiment involved the use of photogrammetry to record the contours of a monument, and even the outlines of deeply recessed inscriptions rendered in sunk relief.[24] Many of the uses proposed to date involve using the computer as a replacement for either the photographer or the copyist in their traditional, time-tested epigraphic roles. To be sure, advances in digital photography and the inexorable improvement of its capabilities offer attractive alternatives to the cumbersome equipment and outlay entailed by traditional photography. In place of individual negatives that must be developed in the field and then printed, digital files on a chip can be downloaded onto a computer, duplicated indefinitely, and manipulated in terms of scale, proportion, internal detail, and clarity. To be sure, pixel density and overall resolution cannot yet supplant the seamless image produced by a photographic negative, but for epigraphic purposes digital photography has proved to be practical, convenient, and cost-effective.[25] To enhance the role of copyist or artist, various graphics programs may be employed in combination with scanned photographic images to approximate the method by which enlarged prints are otherwise used as the drawing surface. In this case, the digital image and drawing surface exist as individual layers that can be separated from each other and then overlaid again as many times as needed for correction or enhancement. Such techniques are essentially refinements of traditional epigraphic roles: they are efficient in terms of facilitating the familiar mechanical processes, but cannot significantly minimize the time involved in the tasks of editing, such as the checks for accuracy, the verification of detail, and the analytic role of the Egyptologist.[26]

One as yet unrealized potential for computer applications is the production of detailed three-dimensional scans of a wall surface, which would constitute a most valuable supplement to the epigraphic method and to the final publication of a monument. Ironically, such a desideratum is simply an updated and more sophisticated version of the discredited "squeeze" of the nineteenth century, though with additional capabilities. A three-dimensional scan reproduces the wall surface itself, with all its blemishes – by itself distinctly limited as a final record. Yet by artificially casting a light source over it from different angles using a software application, an epigrapher might theoretically use the scan to perform the basic tasks of determining preliminary details of a wall surface from the comfort of an office; the confirmation of final details may be done in the field. Included as part of the final published record, a three-dimensional scan can also provide the scholar with an independent check of the reliability of the epigraphic product, since the reader can view the surface in the context of light cast from different angles, verifying all details captured in the final edited drawing. In fact, such a three-dimensional scan can be provided separately with the definitive final details, so that the two-dimensional record can appear as a three-dimensional product as well.

CHALLENGES OF EGYPTIAN EPIGRAPHY: TEXT AND ARCHITECTURE

The mechanical applications available to epigraphy must be weighed against the particular monument at hand: no single solution works best in every case. The most important considerations include the scale of the monument, the number of personnel and types of technical apparatus on hand, financial resources, time limitations, and the conception of the final publication; only then can final decisions be made regarding which recording techniques are the most appropriate. Regardless of the process chosen, the most effective epigraphy is that which is conducted in the presence of the monument itself, where the recording process may be conducted and checked against the original at all stages, and where the preliminary phases can be verified and approved by consensus through several pairs of eyes.

The goal of epigraphy, as in the editing of an ancient text, is to establish the definitive record of the original document, which comprises, for Egyptian monuments, both the text and the adjoining decorative and architectural context. Structural context may be indicated by including the presence of block lines and stone courses on walls, the levels of floors and ceilings, and the corners of rooms. Because Egyptian monumental documents – whether temples, tombs, statues, or stelae – were often exposed to human use and intervention for centuries and even millennia, they inevitably exhibit the traces of additions and restorations made by successive generations for various reasons. Field epigraphers can often explicate the history of such monumental use through the employment of simple drawing conventions.

Wall surfaces that have been carefully effaced and then recarved on a large scale usually display detectable trace lines of the original carving, on the basis of which the original scene may be reconstructed: trace lines are vital clues to the historical record. For example, the cartouches of certain kings were routinely recarved, and the intentional usurpation of cartouches may be documented through the careful discernment of layered royal names (see Figs. 5.3 and 5.4). But the motive behind this must be inferred through the relative thoroughness and distribution of the alterations, as not all usurpation can be assumed to be personally animated, but could have been ordered for a number of reasons. To be sure, various modes of intentional erasure can be undertaken within a single program of proscription that has different intents and, thus, manifestations. Certain monuments of Hatshepsut, for example, show outright effacement (on wall reliefs never intended to be reused for other purposes), or the simple usurpation of her cartouches or replacement of her entire figure (where the ritual content was to be preserved), or merely the systematic reduction and smoothing of carved relief (in places where the alterations were never completed, for which see Fig. 5.6); some show her name and figure intact (in places inaccessible to stonemasons during her dishonoring).[27] Careful epigraphy can here assist in clarifying the process of historical revision and the purpose behind it.

Similarly, the name and figure of the god Amun were attacked during the reign of Akhenaton in a campaign of iconoclastic proscription, but below the Ramesside restorations of the damage wreaked by Atonists on the figure and texts referring to Amun trace lines of the original scheme are usually discernible on the wall, as well as a distinctive difference in background color: grayish blue was preferred during the pre-Amarna period, while the Ramesside painters finished their work in white. Areas of such restoration, despite their interest, are normally never indicated in epigraphic line drawings, but – to cite just one example of epigraphic innovation – the Swiss expedition to the mortuary temple of Merneptah in western Thebes has employed a straightforward stippled convention to outline areas of Ramesside reworking, to excellent effect.[28]

Restorations were constantly made on dilapidated monuments, which were then rededicated through the actions of pious pharaohs, whose latter-day inscriptions often intrude on the original decorative scheme. During the Coptic and medieval periods, temples and tombs were reconsecrated as churches or mosques, or reused for different purposes entirely, with the result that portions of relief and text could be attacked for superstitious reasons, and religious emblems added; such damage is important to note because of its characteristic distribution, so different from pharaonic historical periods. Graffiti of devotees or travelers could be added to public areas, from the pharaonic period down to the present century, reflecting continuous human interest, access, and presence over the millennia. Egyptian monuments therefore encompass a constant record of public and private life extending back for centuries, each generation adding its own layer. The epigraphic process records all

FIGURE 5.6. A relief of Hatshepsut from the Temple of Karnak, who is shown being baptized by Horus and Thoth; the revision was halted before the alterations could be completed. Photo: P. Dorman.

these features and separates them, attempting to explain the history of the monument by a close examination of successive alterations.

What is omitted from the final record is almost as important as what is included: it is the task of the epigrapher to discern what is extraneous damage (and thus irrelevant to the monument's history) and what has been intentionally inflicted due to content or context. Areas of missing plaster, dressing marks left over from quarrying or surface dressing, areas of natural abrasion or weathering, or active salt efflorescence – though of importance to the preservation of the building – are not necessarily elements of human intervention and, insofar as they do not affect the original decoration, may be omitted in a final copy for the sake of clarity. It is this carefully edited, definitive record, compiled according to consistent and recognized standards, that provides an unassailable advantage over mere photography.

An essential challenge for the epigrapher is the same that faces the redactor of any text: comparative analysis and the task of textual reconstruction in areas of damage. For this purpose, understanding the context of an inscription is basic. For certain corpora of texts, the task of the epigrapher is immeasurably aided by the existence of projects that have undertaken to compile comparanda of similar literary (often funerary) themes. One of the earliest was Eduard Naville's *Das aegyptische Totenbuch*, providing copies of extant funerary papyri containing chapters of the Book of the Dead.[29] The mortuary compositions carved in the burial chambers of late Old Kingdom pyramids were subsequently collated

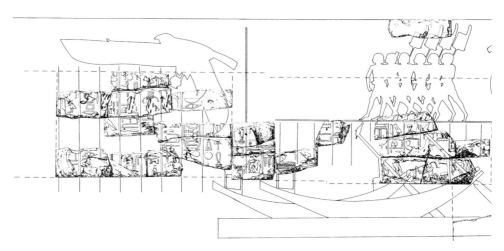

FIGURE 5.7. Architectural and decorative context can permit the large-scale restoration of missing scenes on the basis of fragments, as here with the barge of Khonsu and its towboats. Drawing: From the Epigraphic Survey, *Reliefs and Inscriptions at Luxor Temple, Vol. 1: The Festival Procession of Opet in the Colonnade Hal.* OIP 116 (Chicago: University of Chicago, 1994), detail of pl. 68. Courtesy of the Oriental Institute of the University of Chicago.

by Kurt Sethe, and parallel versions of major spells found on Middle Kingdom Coffins have appeared under the editorship of Adriaan De Buck in *The Egyptian Coffin Texts*.[30] Several funerary compositions found in the New Kingdom royal tombs have now also been compiled in a number of fundamental editions by Erik Hornung: the *Litany of Ra*, the *Book of Gates*, and the *Book of What Is in the Netherworld* (the Book of Amduat).[31] Such epigraphic projects provide enormous research impetus to scholars dealing in these areas of epigraphy.

But modern epigraphers can proceed one step beyond textual restoration. The demonstrated connection among text, figural representation, and architecture has been brilliantly utilized in several instances of epigraphic method during the past forty years, a time when research has occasionally centered on monuments that were dismantled in antiquity, and whose elements now exist in greater or lesser numbers, sometimes scattered around the world. By far the most ambitious undertaking in this regard is the reconstruction of the temples of the Aton at Karnak, of which thousands of blocks were extracted from the Ninth and Tenth Pylons and from the Hypostyle Hall between 1920 and 1965. Two independent projects, organized by the Centre d'études et du documentation des temples de Karnak and the Akhenaton Temple Project, have demonstrated the feasibility of reassembling these blocks in their original positions and recreating vast expanses of relief (both on paper and as a physical reality) that reconstruct temple scenes long lost to view. Both teams made use of data that were analyzed and sorted by computer to facilitate the classification, grouping,

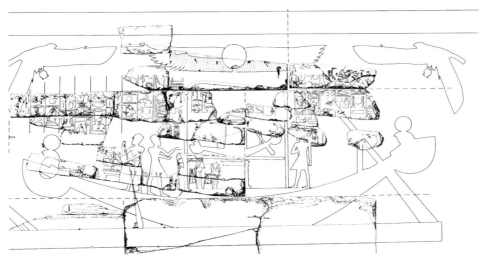

FIGURE 5.7 (*Continued*)

and joining of blocks based on decorative and textual features contained in the relief. One essential architectural parameter was the knowledge that the Aton temples were constructed from uniform-sized stones ("talatat") laid in a predictably alternating pattern of headers and footers.[32]

Similarly, the excavation of the temple of Tuthmosis III at Deir-Bahari by the Polish–Egyptian Mission, beginning in the 1960s, led to the discovery of numerous blocks, often smashed into smaller fragments due to the collapse of the cliffs above, that preserved the original decoration of the monument. Painstaking conservation on these painted fragments has resulted not only in the reconstitution of multiple registers and partial walls of relief surface, but also in clear indications as to the vanished architecture of the temple and even the original placement of the decoration within it.[33] But significant results can also be produced with only a fraction of the physical material at hand. The block yards of Luxor Temple, for example, contain stone fragments excavated in the vicinity of the temple over the past half-century, and many of them can be shown to belong to now-vanished portions of the main temple or of other structures, based on textual, paleographic, or architectural evidence.[34] Moreover, even large-scale epigraphic reconstruction is possible when a decorative paradigm may be theorized on the basis of extant traces or parallels, as in the Colonnade Hall of Luxor Temple. The preserved schema of portions of the Opet Festival on the east wall of the Colonnade can be extended into a larger framework that expands on the river and temple scenes of the Opet Festival, so that a good number of unconnected blocks and fragments may be correctly repositioned (at least on paper), to the extent that a decorative reconstruction (if not a textual one) of the missing portions of wall is largely ensured (Fig. 5.7).[35]

An important category of more recent epigraphic efforts is those dealing with graffiti, the casual inscriptions left by visitors to Egyptian temples and tombs or by travelers on rocks in the desert as a record of their journeys. These graffiti were usually incised in more or less accurately rendered hieroglyphic signs, or in a variety of cursive scripts, and in their informal commemorative character reflect the range of literacy enjoyed by various strata of Egyptian society. Scratched into the marginal areas of temple scenes, or onto roof blocks, or onto shaded boulders bordering the desert tracks where a traveler might find respite from the sun, these impromptu inscriptions can be purely textual in nature or can incorporate figural elements as well; they occasionally overlap and present challenges in reading and interpretation.[36]

To summarize, epigraphy is essentially a field technique that can be adapted to a myriad situations and a range of resources. No single method can be prescribed for every eventuality, and the final publication of inscribed texts may reasonably range from precise hand copies to virtual facsimile reproduction: each scholarly team must adapt both old and new techniques to the specific vagaries of the site. Nor is epigraphy a field method that inherently possesses a record of inexorable improvement. Some quite remarkable examples of careful copying may be found in the *Description de l'Égypte*, while even today one may find publications whose epigraphic results fall far short of standards set almost two centuries ago.

NOTES

1. Dreyer 1998.
2. Kahl 1994 and 2001: 103–34.
3. Baines 1989: 471–82.
4. The study of inscribed papyrus documents (in hieratic or other scripts) falls outside the scope of epigraphy per se; the methodologies are different and belong rather to the field of papyrology. For a general introduction, see Parkinson and Quirke 1995.
5. Baines 2004: 150–89
6. Wente 1995: 2211–22; Lesko 2001: 297–9.
7. On the context of hieroglyphic inscriptions and the importance of paleography to epigraphic observation, see Fischer 1976: 29–50.
8. *Description de l'Égypte*, 1809–22.
9. Parkinson 1999.
10. Champollion 1827–8.
11. Champollion 1835–45; Champollion 1844–89.
12. Rosselini 1832–44.
13. Lepsius 1849–1913.
14. For two useful general commentaries on epigraphic method, see Caminos 1976: 3–25; and Caminos 1987: 57–67.
15. Guilmant 1907. Other epigraphers were simultaneously employing photographs as well, in particular John Tylor at Elkab (the tombs of Paheri, Renni, and Sebeknakht and the small temple of Amenhotep III); the earliest such effort, on a more limited scale, may have been John Greene in the 1850s, for which see Bell 1996: 105.

16. Bell 1987: 43–67.
17. d'Avennes 1868–78; reprint 1991.
18. The scope of their work can best be appreciated in Davies and Gardiner 1936 and Wilkinson and Hill 1983.
19. Calverley and Gardiner 1933–58.
20. See in particular the Epigraphic Survey 1940.
21. To single out individual publications would be invidious; a number of outstanding examples may be found in the two series Ägyptologische Veröffentlichungen and Theben (Mainz, various dates).
22. On the stages of drafting, underpainting, and finishing plaster wall surfaces in Theban tombs of the 18th Dynasty, see Bryan 2001: 63–72. This symposium volume amply illustrates the scope of research opened up by the use of color on Egyptian monuments.
23. For a remarkably successful example, see Strudwick 1996. For a comparison of a drawing made by Norman de Garis Davies with a later copy, using different standards of recording the preservation of the plaster surface, see Polz 1987: 134–8.
24. Desroches-Noblecourt 1968.
25. For the rapid progress in this area, compare Seliger 1995: 85–99; Der Manuelian 1998: 97–113; Der Manuelian 2003.
26. For digitalized hieroglyphs projected in an axonometric view, see Der Manuelian and Loeben 1993: 121–55.
27. For a summary of the erasures and three views on Hatshepsut's dishonoring, see the contributions by Dorothea Arnold, Peter F. Dorman, and Ann Macy Roth on this phenomenon (Arnold 2005; Dorman 2005; Roth 2005).
28. Bickel 1997.
29. Naville 1886.
30. Sethe 1908–22; De Buck 1935–61.
31. Hornung 1975–76; Hornung 1979–90; Hornung 1987–92.
32. Smith and Redford 1976; Redford 1988; and Lauffray 1978–80: 67–89. For the epigraphic challenges posed by the Karnak talatat, see Traunecker 1987: 261–98.
33. The material is still being prepared for publication; see Lipinska 2005: 285–8.
34. Johnson 1986: 50–2.
35. Epigraphic Survey, *Reliefs and Inscriptions at Luxor*, 1994; see also Bell 1987: pl. 5.
36. Notable recent works include Cerny 1969–74; Darnell 2002; and Jacquet-Gordon 2003.

CHAPTER 6

MONUMENT AND SITE CONSERVATION

Michael Jones

Tutankhamun's famous "Restoration Stela" proclaims his intention of restoring the temples of Upper and Lower Egypt, neglected and decaying after Akhenaten's short-lived reforms.[1] As an early account of cultural heritage management in Egypt, it is remarkable how much it reflects several important concepts of conservation and preservation of cultural heritage practised in the modern world that will occur as themes throughout this chapter. Heritage survives only if it is useful, is valued, and has significance: Akhenaten suppressed the traditional cults and the temples were abandoned; Tutankhamun prompted a revival and restored the cults. In Egypt, as elsewhere, heritage conservation is often politically motivated: Tutankhamun needed the support of the traditional priesthood and wished to discredit Akhenaton. Successful stewardship addresses the buildings and their fixtures as well as their complete social and cultural environment, involving the stakeholders (including in this case employees and priests) in ensuring a future role ("monuments for eternity") with maintenance plans and requirements for sustainable development (endowments). The text also demonstrates that culture is a continuous process, with buildings and infrastructure reflecting contemporary usage.

Like many disciplines, conservation is influenced, if not guided, by fashions in academic thought, political motives, and technical advances, all predicated on contemporary notions of value and significance. Understanding these factors is essential to inform modern practices. Although Egypt's climate has contributed to the preservation of many outstanding monuments, the changes taking place today – population explosion, agricultural and industrial expansion, and tourism, all on a massive scale – are endangering their future. Therefore the terms 'cultural heritage management' (CHM) or 'cultural resource management' (CRM) are more descriptive of what we are now trying to do.[2] A series of important articles profoundly affecting the development of CHM appeared in *Antiquity* in 1993.

No amount of conservation or restoration can halt decay; it can only slow it down. Thompson's cautionary words of 1981 also warn that in the end, any monument will either disintegrate and become a ruin or be recycled. Numerous examples of ancient recycling of masonry, statues, and other monuments demonstrate how reuse has preserved material on a large scale. Tanis, founded in the Third Intermediate Period, is full of recycled earlier architecture and Middle Kingdom statuary reused by Ramesses II and later moved to its present location. The 'Red Chapel' of Hatshepsut and the bark shrines of Senusret I and Amunhotep I, now reconstructed in the Open Air Museum at Karnak, were all found reused as building material and are examples of the same process of recycling. The decorative schemes of Akhenaten's free-standing monuments have been preserved almost entirely on the thousands of blocks from his dismantled buildings found in reused contexts at numerous sites throughout Egypt. Alexandria, as it developed into a new international centre of learning, benefited from monuments transferred from Heliopolis, including obelisks, some of which were eventually taken as trophies to Rome, London, and New York, beginning in the reign of Augustus and ending in 1872.

As Pharaonic traditions melted into the culture of late Roman Christian Egypt, many of the temples found a new identity through adaptive reuse. Whatever continued in use survived. The temple precinct at Medinet Habu, where a large church was built inside the temple of Ramesses III, was occupied by the town of Djeme until the ninth or tenth century. Similarly, Luxor temple and the Roman fort that surrounded it were buried under a village built with reused blocks.[3] Sand buried many tombs and desert sites. Abandoned monuments closer to capital zones such as Memphis, Heliopolis, and Alexandria were dismantled and used as quarries for building materials. In their ruined and forsaken state the Pharaonic sites achieved equilibrium in their environment.

This was the landscape when the Napoleonic expedition arrived in 1798. The first comprehensive record of the existing conditions of Egypt, compiled by the savants who accompanied the expedition, was published in twelve volumes as the *Description de l'Égypte*. It was based on the observations of engineers and architects and not the academic interpretations of antiquarians or archaeologists and has therefore never become outdated. Egyptian monuments were suddenly fashionable, seen by Europeans as objects of study and given a new identity as curiosities. In the following decades, Egypt opened up to travellers, engineers, entrepreneurs, and collectors such as Belzoni, Salt, and Drovetti, Egyptologists such as Champollion, Rosellini, and Lepsius, and others who documented monuments but also took 'antiquities' to grace European collections as 'spoils of science' and to save them from what they saw as an uninterested or destructive population.

By the 1830s, agricultural reforms had introduced large-scale production of new crops such as cotton and sugar cane, the processing of which required fertilizers, perennial irrigation, and factories. Canals were dug, barrages were constructed to control the annual Nile flood, and at the end of the century the first Aswan dam was built. Ancient buildings, recorded in the *Description*, such as the temple of Amunhotep III at Elephantine, the portico of Philip Arhidaeus at al-Ashmunain, and the Ptolemaic temple at Armant, were put to new use and demolished for building stone. Mud-brick buildings and organic remains (*sebbakh*) of abandoned settlements provided fertiliser for the fields. Today's landscape in the Egyptian Nile Valley and Delta, and on much of the low desert along the edges of the Nile floodplain, evolved during the nineteenth and early twentieth centuries.

The same is true of the numerous historic sites throughout the country that were excavated and cleared to create access for scholars and visitors to view the architecture and mural decoration and to facilitate the extraction of portable finds. A great deal of stabilisation and repair work was done to make these large stone buildings safe. The result was that by about 1910, 'ancient Egypt' had been recast in a late-nineteenth-century construct of Pharaonic power and splendour, confirmed and exemplified by the discovery of Tutankhamun's tomb in 1922. The monuments were now visible, denuded of the palimpsest of historical debris, but exposed to other destructive forces, such as vandalism, looting, and a slow but steady degradation from the elements that was intensified by the rise of international package tourism. This last was courtesy of Thomas Cook and Son, whose steamers on the Nile began the tradition of Nile cruises, sailing from Cairo to Wadi Halfa and stopping at the sights along the way.[4]

Scholars were shocked by the destruction and degradation that had occurred since the documentation of Napoleon and Lepsius, among them Petrie and Breasted. They recognised the need for conservation to record the standing monuments before it was too late. In 1924, Breasted established the Epigraphic Survey with its headquarters at Chicago House in Luxor; its first project was the hugely ambitious documentation of Medinet Habu. The published results illustrate how, by this time, a site methodology was emerging which involved multidisciplinary approaches similar to those in use today. These combine archaeological excavation, architectural survey and building studies, epigraphic recording, and restoration, all accurately recorded, photographed, and published in full.

The huge changes to the agricultural landscape that had begun with Mohammed Ali culminated in the first Aswan Dam, completed in 1901 and raised in 1907, inspiring the first 'Nubian salvage campaign' to document the sites to be flooded. But the work focused on graves and their objects at the expense of almost everything else, including the ancient towns, and even the almost complete temples of Philae were left submerged for most of the year, thereby losing all their painted decoration.

The Aswan High Dam marks a turning point in economic development and in attitudes to monument conservation. The second Nubian salvage campaign was launched in 1960 and the multinational response led to the immense amount of archaeological excavation and recording which today provides invaluable data on a vanished resource. This time, the technology was available to move the main temples to higher ground, and with the two most important ones, Abu Simbel and Philae, care was taken that their settings should closely replicate the originals. The smaller temples were grouped together, no doubt because it facilitated both reconstruction and maintenance, but also because collectively they would be more attractive and accessible to tourists. Others now grace museums abroad, given in recognition of the support of foreign governments.[5]

Michael Jones

FIGURE 6.1. Marina al-Alamain. View of part of the Roman town from the Alexandria to Marsa Matruh highway with hotel and villa developments beside the sea. Photo: Chip Vincent, April 2006.

CONDITIONS THREATENING THE SURVIVAL OF MONUMENTS AND SITES IN EGYPT TODAY

Conservation and site management were adopted as the principal themes of the Eighth International Congress of Egyptologists, held in Cairo in 2000,[6] in response to a pressing need for Egyptologists to engage actively in the preservation of the chief resource of their subject. The main threats to Pharaonic sites and monuments are summarized under the following headings.

Population Explosion

Since the inception of the Aswan High Dam project in 1960, the population of Egypt has more than doubled. This has brought about rapid and extensive urban expansion, industrial development, and huge land reclamation schemes in the desert to increase agricultural production; all these have once again transformed the landscape. Lack of zoning and enforced planning regulations for housing, cemeteries, rubbish dumping, farming, industry, quarrying, leisure activities with stages and arenas, and car rallies means that encroachment on sites is inadequately controlled. A striking example is the Giza Pyramids, now surrounded by houses and roads on three sides. The nearby sites of Ausim, Saft el-Leben, Kafr el-Gebel, and Kafr el-Batran, which are part of the earliest urban development in the region during the Old Kingdom and Late Period, have all but vanished inside the western reaches of the Cairo suburbs. At Zagazig/Bubastis, not even the presence of monumental architecture can halt the advance. At Marina al-Alamain on the Mediterranean coast, affluence and influence have conspired to isolate the Hellenistic and Roman harbour between the main coastal highway and seaside villas for the elite (Fig. 6.1).

101

In response to the disappearance of many of the less well-documented sites, the Egyptian Antiquities Information Service was established in 2000 as a bilateral (Egyptian and Finnish) project and is a capacity-building programme integrated as an official department of the Supreme Council of Antiquities (SCA). It is a conservation measure to record archaeological sites and architectural monuments through mapping and photography and by developing a Geographical Information System (GIS) and databases. This will enable the SCA to register unlisted sites to bring them into its protection and to establish legal boundaries to safeguard designated sites from unauthorized land sales and inappropriate development.

Groundwater

Nile level texts on the western quayside at Karnak show that by the 22nd Dynasty the temple was already subject to flooding.[7] The annual summer Nile inundation saturated the entire floodplain for three months of the year and deposited a thin layer of silty clay. The valley floor rose constantly by approximately 1 meter every thousand years, so that ancient floor levels now lie several meters below the modern ground level. For example, the lower part of the Great Pyramid causeway and the valley temple floor, discovered during the Greater Cairo Wastewater Project in 1989, are roughly 14 meters above sea level. The ground level in the Cairo region had reached 18 meters when the flood was stopped by the Aswan High Dam in 1964.

Perennial irrigation for maximum agricultural production saturates the ground and impacts the ancient sites as water collects on low-lying land. High subsoil water fills old excavation trenches and creates moisture on the surface. Fertilizer residues washed into the underground water sustain and strengthen vegetation growth. Reeds and halfa grass are widespread, and even trees and bushes are now well established on some sites formerly dry. Halfa grass is prolific and has strong and deeply penetrating roots capable of prizing apart masonry and mud-brick walls both above and below ground.

Salt Damage

Limestone, sandstone, and the matrix of Nile clay contain high concentrations of salts. Water percolating through stones dissolves natural salts, and when the heat of the sun causes evaporation, the salts crystallize at the surface, destroying any decoration and destabilising the masonry. A tragic example of this is at Memphis (Mit Rahinah), where a small temple constructed under Ramesses II for Ptah, discovered in 1942 and excavated in 1955–6, now stands in a deep excavation trench where trees, reeds, and grasses grow in the moist ground. Salt efflorescence on the stone building has destroyed or severely damaged most of the fine relief carving. It was fully documented by the Egypt Exploration Society (EES) in 1984–5.[8]

Increased saturation of the ground is also linked to greater domestic consumption of water due to spreading urbanization. This affects sites near or within rapidly growing towns and

FIGURE 6.2. Medinet Habu. Entrances to the temples with adjacent tourist car and bus parking. Photo: Michael Jones, June 2005.

villages where water leaks from faulty drainage. The village of Nazilet al-Samman at the foot of the Giza Plateau and in front of the Sphinx provides a good example.[9] In response to the acute ground water problems around the Sphinx in the 1980s, a major wastewater project installed sewers to replace old leaking septic tanks. The subsoil water level dropped considerably, alleviating the threat to the heritage site. During project implementation, sections of buried archaeological remains were encountered and recorded, including the lower part of the causeway and the valley temple of the Great Pyramid and associated Old Kingdom settlement remains. The wastewater project was completed in 1992, but fifteen years later the population is much larger, the extent of urban development stretches much further, and water levels are again rising.

Air Pollution

High levels of atmospheric humidity and air pollution from industry and traffic set up a steady process of erosion on the walls of standing monuments (acid rain).[10] A constant pollution cloud is now observable along the Nile Valley, but no consistent monitoring is known, and without reliable statistics, the magnitude and impact are hard to quantify scientifically. Industrial pollution from the cement and steel plants at Tura and Helwan can be seen to affect the pyramids at Dahshur and Saqqara. Diesel engines of tour boats in Luxor, sometimes moored ten deep against the Corniche beside the Luxor Temple, are contributing to deteriorating conditions there. Tourist coaches parked in crowded car parks close to temples such as Medinet Habu keep their engines running for the air conditioners (Fig. 6.2).

Industrial Development

So far the examples chosen have been mainly from the Nile valley, but relatively untouched sites in the deserts are increasingly under threat from industrial development, especially mineral extraction. Sand and gravel quarrying to supply the massive building industry responding to the housing needs of the rapidly growing population threaten sites near the desert edges. Modern quarrying techniques used to exploit the Pharaonic quarries that produced fine building stone impact the sites far more severely than ancient methods and extract greater quantities of rock. Two examples are the Aswan granite quarries and the Gebel Qatrani/Widan al-Faras basalt quarries, both with well-preserved Old Kingdom workings and associated workers' huts and quarry causeways. In response, a joint Norwegian–Egyptian project, the Quarry Scapes Project, has been established to record endangered ancient quarries, including setting up GIS.[11] A more drastic enterprise is planned at the gold mines of the Eastern Desert, where an Australian company, Centamin Egypt Ltd., is working at Gebel Sukari, the site of extensive gold mining in the Greco-Roman period, with exceptionally well-preserved sites.[12] Egypt needs the economic benefits, but many such sites are not officially registered. Corporate influence is far more powerful than legislation protecting heritage and the environment, so that little or no regard is paid to conservation needs, not even at the level of recording and demarcation for preservation of significant areas.

Economic Development

The adverse and destructive effects of uncontrolled tourism have long been recognised and are well documented.[13] This is now one of the main threats to the survival and authenticity of many Pharaonic monuments. Tourism plays a crucial role in the Egyptian economy, with U.S.$6.4 billion in tourism revenue reported for 2005. Although the Red Sea attracts increasing numbers of tourists, 'cultural tourism' is seen as essential for development and is being assertively promoted. Unfortunately, several decades ago Egypt opted for mass package tourism that inevitably puts more pressure on the monuments, rather than 'high-end' individual and small group tourism. Few visitors return, so that quantity, not quality, is the chief objective.

The study of tourism and development has been discussed in a series of papers edited by Sharpley and Telfer in 2002 and in relation to cultural tourism in particular by McKercher and du Cros in 2002. As Naguib Amin has remarked, 'historical sites can contribute to the development of the country, but development can contribute to the disappearance of historical sites'. Until recently, however, the authorities have been remarkably unconcerned about the future of historic sites; the fact that they had survived for millennia was taken

FIGURE 6.3. Giza: Khafra Valley Temple. Tourists crowding the corridor to the pyramid causeway for a view of the Sphinx. Photo: Angela Milward Jones, March 2005.

as proof that they would last forever. Occasionally the number of visitors is restricted through specially priced and limited tickets (for example, for the interior of the Great Pyramid and the tombs of Tutankhamun and of Nefertari). Lack of enforced regulations leads to overcrowding at popular destinations. For example, at the Giza Pyramids at midday, most tourist groups have finished their tour of the Pyramids and converge on Khafra's Valley Temple because it provides a route up to a viewing platform for the 'photo-op' with the Sphinx as the backdrop. They cram into the small granite temple and up the narrow passage, wearing down the unprotected alabaster floor. It would be simple to reroute the tourists around the Valley Temple and across the Causeway, via a wooden walkway (Fig. 6.3).

THE INTERNATIONAL CHARTERS AND PRACTICAL IMPLEMENTATION

The charters are intended as a set of principles to guide and support decisions in practical conservation and management planning. They have evolved as awareness of needs has increased, and they are increasingly applied worldwide because their effectiveness is evident at well-managed sites and the reverse is visible where they are absent. The most influential charters are Athens 1931, Venice 1964, Nara 1994, and Burra 1979 revised 2000. The full texts are available on the ICOMOS Web site.[14]

It is now generally accepted that in spite of any nationalist agendas, cultural heritage possesses an intrinsic value and belongs to all humanity. Every act of conservation intervention changes existing conditions and thus influences survival and impacts the authenticity of the monument or site. The following are examples of how contemporary principles adopted in the charters can be applied in practice.

Assessing Value and Significance

Public participation in the preservation of heritage is proposed in the Burra Charter and has been adopted as fundamental for successful cultural heritage management.[15] It can, however, be a sensitive issue, and in Egypt, where 'western' concepts may not always be applicable, education, social conditions, and attitudes to authority have to be taken into account. The main stakeholders in cultural heritage in Egypt are the following:

- Government bodies including the Ministries of Tourism and Culture and the SCA, which usually make and impose decisions; as Sedky points out, 'government institutions monopolise both the strategy making and the implementation of area conservation schemes in Egypt, since they are recognised as the official and approved approach to area conservation. The political model in Egypt is a state centred one . . . the state defines the social problems and solves them'.[16]
- Tourists, tour operators, and guides, a source of ever increasing economic benefits.
- Development agencies and contractors, needed to supply the infrastructure.
- The media, giving publicity to heritage and its personalities.
- The academic community, ultimately the source that feeds information to specialist disciplines, cultural tourism, the media, and conservation implementation.

Local people, apart from souvenir vendors, security personnel, and SCA employees, are only indirectly involved and are rarely, if ever, consulted. Rashed, quoting *Al-Ahram*,[17] shows how uncomfortable their opinions can be: 'We want to ask you only one thing; why don't you take the buried Pharaohs and their tombs and remove the stones of the Karnak temple and take it to Cairo? . . . We are fed up with the temples and the pharaohs. . . . Perhaps after that one might come and inquire about our living conditions'.

A difficult factor to assess is the separation from the ancient past felt by many of the Egyptian public. An increasingly widespread belief in the 'Age of Ignorance before Islam', al-a'sr al-jibliyab qabl al-Islam, and a controversial fatwa against statues issued by the Grand Mufti of Egypt in 2006 do not encourage public interest in Pharaonic culture.[18] On the other side is the extravagant and highly inaccurate portrayal of ancient Egypt reflected in the imagery of Hollywood, which encourages most foreign visitors to feel a similar uncomfortable disconnect between such popular fantasy and the actuality of the ancient monuments today.

Efforts to encourage a more positive awareness of Pharaonic Egypt are reflected in Mrs. Mubarak's important educational initiative to promote a greater involvement for Egyptian schoolchildren in their cultural heritage, and the Egyptian Museum now has a special children's gallery. Zahi Hawass has successfully advanced public understanding of ancient Egypt through the media and documentary films.

Each of the above groups derives significant advantages from the Pharaonic heritage and influences its future. The perceived value of any site may be different for different groups. And unfortunately, as Ahmed Rashed says, 'No one party tries to understand the reasons and problems of the other', which leads to the lack of coordination between ministries directly involved in promoting heritage sites, such as the Ministry of Tourism, which has a massive impact, the Ministry of Culture, of which the SCA is a department, and the Ministry of the Environment. As yet, no formal mechanism exists that allows for coordination between the SCA, responsible for heritage sites, and the tourist industry that exploits them. As the economically and politically powerful usually have the last word, the focus tends towards the grand at the expense of the more modest and difficult-to-maintain sites. As El Iraqi, quoting the National Center for Documentation of Cultural and National Heritage, 2001, points out, 'At present only certain sites, mostly those that attract tourists are managed. Other sites, outside the tourist itineraries, as well as sites that do not consist of spectacular buildings or artistic elements, are rarely considered. . . . Management of cultural heritage sites in Egypt thus depends on the touristic value of the site and thereby its economic value'.[19]

At Matariyah, ancient Heliopolis, the solitary obelisk of Senusret I now stands in a small park, but because it is so difficult to find and there are no directional signs, it is seldom visited, although the site is officially open to the public (Fig. 6.4). The 'Apis House' at Memphis experiences another kind of isolation. Discovered and partly excavated in 1941, further excavated and reinterpreted from 1982 to 1987,[20] and again dug into by an unrecorded excavation in the 1990s, this site has been closed to visitors for several years. Its perceived lack of economic value has led to neglect and dwindling potential for conservation as vegetation forces stones apart and erosion from the weather and animals takes its toll.

By contrast, the tomb of Nefertari in Luxor was closed for decades in order not to accelerate the deterioration of its beautiful, fragile decoration, painted on plaster that was detaching from the walls because of moisture and salt action. Its conservation, sponsored by the Getty Conservation Institute and the Egyptian Antiquities Organization (EAO) from 1986 to 1992, was a successful attempt to ensure that this masterpiece would survive and was a conservation

FIGURE 6.4. Matariyah-Heliopolis. The seldom visited obelisk of Senusret I as currently displayed. Photo: Michael Jones, October 2006.

triumph. This project demonstrated two essential aspects of conservation – the reversibility of all interventions and the philosophy of minimum intervention. Visitor numbers have been restricted, so its perceived value is not so much economic, but based on its intrinsic heritage value and photogenic appeal – a powerful advertising tool. However, renewed fears concerning the effects of overvisitation on the paintings have led to closure yet again.

Recording and Documentation

Conservation through documentation is essential, although the level of recording depends on methodology, which in turn often depends on available funding and expertise and can also be influenced by perceived value. The process began with the *Description de l'Egypte*

FIGURE 6.5. Luxor Temple. Sorting, treatment, and stacking of decorated sandstone blocks on new waterproof mastabas beside the temple. Photo: Chip Vincent, January 1998.

and continued with the work of early photographers such as du Camp, Frith, and Beato (active in Egypt 1849 onwards). Standard techniques today are epigraphy, photography, surveys, and architectural and buildings archaeology, and nowadays geophysical surveys using resistivity, ground-penetrating radar, and magnetometry. Documentation should also include archive work and result in publication.

Chicago House in Luxor has pioneered a very exact method of epigraphic survey of mural decoration using photography and artists' copying. Not only is this applied to standing monuments, but also to random blocks, such as those piled up beside the Luxor Temple. These blocks were placed on waterproof benches to protect them from the groundwater; treated with poultices and chemical intervention to minimize the risk of salt damage; sorted according to subject matter, chronology, and provenance; numbered; and then recorded using the painstaking Chicago House method (Fig. 6.5). By this means whole sections of decoration have now been recovered and one group is now restored in its original position in the Tutankhamun Colonnade.

The EES Survey of Memphis, begun in 1981, is a multidisciplinary approach to the ancient ruin field combining area survey, archive work, archaeological excavation, subsoil borings, and epigraphic work on standing buildings and loose inscribed blocks. The results, published by Jeffreys, Malek, and Smith in 1984, provide a fuller understanding of the rapidly deteriorating excavated and buried remains.

Archaeology as a means of mitigating the impact of construction projects is another important conservation measure, as described by Davis and others in 2004. In Old Cairo, the archaeological monitoring program of the groundwater-lowering project was able to record buried archaeological remains and a changing landscape from the Late Period to modern times.[21] However, there is a danger here of being satisfied with an accurate record while an original monument and its archaeological context are destroyed through lack of will or finances to salvage it. Contractors at heritage sites in Egypt have, in general, shown themselves reluctant to include a sufficient level of archaeological involvement during project implementation and to include archaeologists in the project design stage, when mitigation strategies can be incorporated with maximum efficiency and minimum financial cost. Early consultation between engineers and archaeologists can produce a development proposal in which potentially harmful engineering is designed to avoid archaeologically sensitive parts of the project area, thus conserving buried remains in situ.

Authenticity

Authenticity involves preserving as much of the original as possible, as well as avoiding intrusive and unsympathetic modern features such as arenas for sound and light or stage performances, electricity posts such as those running through the middle of the main temple at Tanis, and even even high-rise buildings overlooking an ancient site. It also includes protective measures that preserve authenticity and avoid invasive action: for example, walkways over original temple pavements to protect the stones, rather than replacing the worn-out slabs with mismatched modern stones.

It can also be interpreted as the demarcation of what is original and what has been added, but authenticity is a much more complex question. Sometimes the solution can be straightforward, as at the Shunet el-Zebib, where new bricks used to rebuild were stamped on the concealed upper surface with the project name and date. At other times, the solution needs to be imaginative. For example, the funerary temple of Merneptah at Thebes contained many blocks from the nearby temple of Amenhotep III, reused so that their original decoration was turned into the walls. The whole temple has been developed as an open-air museum with a special display inside the rebuilt second pylon where the 19th Dynasty decoration scheme is intact on the outside, and the visitor can enter the pylon to see the other faces of the blocks with the beautiful and instructive Amenhotep III relief.

Minimum Intervention and Reversibility of Treatment

Minimum intervention is usually a reliable way of maintaining authenticity and often brings its own benefits of sustainability. A successful pilot project carried out by ARCE along these lines was to protect the tombs of Ramesses I and Sety I (KV 16 and 17) in the Valley of the Kings from rare but disastrous flash flood water. Archaeological evidence

FIGURE 6.6. Valley of the Kings. Floodwater control project in the valley beside the tombs of Ramesses I and Sety I, showing the entrances protected by baffle walls and approached by steps. Photo: Chip Vincent, June 2005.

shows that the tomb entrances were positioned well above the contemporary valley floor, possibly to avoid flooding, and the material now filling the valley is redeposited ancient debris and excavators' dumps. The risk from flooding has been greatly increased by modern archaeological dumping, which has filled up the originally deep ravines. By excavating the modern fill to a level just above the ancient surface, the tomb entrances have been restored to a relatively high and safe level and the ancient deposits in the area have been preserved in situ. Walls and steps were built in front of tomb entrances from limestone set in a lime and clay mortar, materials which are functional and aesthetically compatible with the surroundings (Fig. 6.6).

Palimpsest Approach versus Single Phase

The Venice Charter states: 'A monument is inseparable from the history from which it bears witness and from the setting in which it occurs.' The era of Mariette and the *sebbakhin* saw the removal of the palimpsest landscape of accumulated evidence for occupation, adaptation, and abandonment that today would be understood as giving meaning to sites. However, the question of how to preserve what remains of different and often incompatible periods is often troubling.

The ARCE project to clean the Roman wall paintings in the Luxor temple is an example of the dilemmas sometimes presented by palimpsest remains. The paintings are located in the room beyond the hypostyle hall, converted into the *sacellum* of the Roman legionary fortress and consecrated for the imperial cult. Wilkinson made freehand watercolours of the whole room sometime before 1853, but much of what he saw is now lost. The surviving frescos are now endangered by atmospheric pollution, humidity, and ultraviolet radiation and are being cleaned and documented before they are too far gone to justify the expense and effort involved.

The frescos, of the highest artistic quality, were painted on a plaster layer applied over the 18th Dynasty reliefs that have not been seen since the end of the third century AD. The question of what to do after conservation is tricky; should the frescos be preserved *in situ* or removed to a safe location, such as the Luxor Museum? Removal of the frescos would deprive the temple of important evidence for its later use belonging with other architectural alterations of the same phase. If left in situ they would need protection, probably in the form of a structure that would add a modern intrusive feature. Continued exposure to humidity and air pollution from tour boats moored nearby will contribute to their further deterioration. If they were removed, the New Kingdom reliefs would be revealed and made available for study and display, but moving the frescos could damage them. Familiarity and nostalgia for a monument may sway judgments, but personal taste should not influence vital conservation measures.

Rebuilding Only When Necessary for Stability, Safety, and Survival (Loss Compensation)

At certain sites, rebuilding missing parts is the only way to stabilize a ruined structure. This might involve reconstruction, patching, or replacement of building materials or retouching paintings *in trateggio*. The huge 2nd Dynasty mud-brick funerary monuments at Abydos and Hieraconpolis are exceptionally well preserved, with some wall sections still standing close to their original height, but elsewhere endangered by various structural problems and close to collapse. There is an argument here for leaving such structures alone and allowing them to fall gracefully into further ruin.

As these monuments are the oldest free-standing structures in Egypt, a building study was implemented at the Shunet el-Zebib at Abydos to document the standing remains, evaluate present conditions, and propose remedial measures. It revealed that the Shunah faces four main causes of structural weakness: walls undercut in the late Roman period when Christian hermits carved cells into the thickness of the brickwork, deep tunnels made by dogs and foxes, heavy wasps' nests which pull off brickwork, and sections of brickwork shearing off along vertical seams in the walls. In addition, termites have consumed the organic temper in the original bricks and weakened their carrying capacity.

FIGURE 6.7. Abydos: Shunet el-Zebib. New brickwork being added to protect damaged ancient masonry and support an overhanging wall section. Photo: Chip Vincent, June 2004.

The most fragile sections were protected with scaffolding and sandbags. Selected areas such as the hermits' cells were excavated and recorded. Sample mud-bricks were analysed to determine the 'recipes' used by the ancient builders so that they could be replicated to ensure compatibility with the surviving ancient brickwork. New bricks were made and were used to construct buttresses containing reinforcing layers to support endangered sections, to fill in the hermits' cells (now fully documented) and animal burrows, and to underpin eroded walls (Fig. 6.7). Replacement brickwork is reinforced with steel rods, nylon rods, and a tough plastic grid to bridge structural cracks.

An important question raised during this project was how much alteration of the original is justified for stability. For example, the jambs and lintel of the west entrance were rebuilt to act as buttresses for the walls on either side, although not enough survives of the original on which to base the reconstruction. But without the jambs, the walls would eventually collapse and the rebuilding was justified because it anticipated future problems, as well as addressing present needs.

Use of Traditional and Compatible Materials Wherever Possible

The use of inappropriate materials in conservation is widespread and usually results from the wish to find a quick solution for a long-term problem. An old method of strengthening structures or connecting stone elements for anastylosis (reconstructing fallen architectural elements, especially columns) was to insert iron bars. In many cases these have now corroded, swelling to as much as four times their original diameter and splitting stonework apart. Portland cement is especially harmful due to its high salt content and hardened strength, which often exceeds that of the original structure to which it is applied. For example, the long history of restoration at the Giza Sphinx and the detrimental effects of unsuitable materials applied by unqualified teams are usefully summarised by Esmael in 1992 and Hawass in 1998. Furthermore, new stonework frequently alters the form of the original, compromising its authenticity and historic value, as well as masking important architectural and archaeological evidence.

Preservation through Reburial

Already, in 1931, the Athens Charter recommended reburial for sites not scheduled for immediate restoration when remains are threatened beyond their capacity and with deterioration beyond the scope of available financial and practical means. As a conservation approach, reburial is gaining in popularity, as described in a series of papers edited by Stanley-Price and Burch in 2004. Unfortunately, it is still rarely applied in Egypt. Reburial puts a strong emphasis on the need for proper recording and demands that scholars adopt a more rigorous approach to archaeological recovery, recording, stabilisation, and interpretation than has been the case at many sites in Egypt. Ultimately, however, the choice is between the preservation of the monument or surrendering it to all the forces of destruction mentioned above, especially in areas closed to visitors and lacking site management. Archaeologists have often left incomplete excavations open with remains exposed and vulnerable under hostile conditions that eventually consume their discoveries. Mud-brick structures are particularly vulnerable, but stone buildings also suffer. A much-damaged site which would still benefit from reburial is the abandoned, half-excavated Hathor Temple at Memphis, discovered by chance in 1971 and described by el-Sayed Mahmud, and then partly excavated so that the tops of the walls and Hathor-head column capitals were exposed. The rest of the temple and its surroundings were never excavated and remain in this condition until today, with salt efflorescence and vegetation gradually destroying the uncovered remains (Fig. 6.8).

The temple-palace at Medinet Habu is an early example of reburial for preservation. This building was ransacked by the *sebbakhin* and then dug out by Burton, who left unsupported stone doorjambs and wall lining slabs exposed. After excavation and recording, the decision was made to preserve the foundations by reburying them in sand and building a replica in brick on top to preserve it in facsimile and present the palace to scholars and visitors. The doorjambs and wall lining slabs were incorporated into the replica.

A similar procedure was used recently at Giza to preserve an Old Kingdom mud-brick house in the settlement south of the Sphinx, described by Lehner et al. in 2006. The site

FIGURE 6.8. Mit Rahinah-Memphis. The 19th Dynasty temple of Hathor. Photo: Michael Jones, June 2006.

is threatened by high groundwater and erosion from rain. It was reburied in sand after excavation and full documentation so that an exact replica could be built at a higher level over the original. The method was adopted in this case as the alternative to capping the mud-brick walls as has been done effectively at other sites, for example, in the funerary temple of Sety I at Qurna and in the temple beside the North Pyramid at Dahshur. Capping the walls is an effective means of protecting them from the weather, but it requires regular maintenance and does not solve present or future groundwater problems.

MultiDisciplinary Approach

The use of the term *cultural heritage management* automatically implies a holistic approach to monument conservation and maintenance. Very often, a project will deal with only one aspect of a monument – for example, the painted decoration – and ignore other needs. Sometimes this is due to financial limitations, and sometimes to lack of commitment. One example of a holistic approach to conservation is the Chicago House project at the Small Temple of Amun in the Medinet Habu enclosure. The archaeological investigation and architectural survey were completed before World War II. Recent work has focused on cleaning and conservation of the painted reliefs inside the 18th Dynasty part of the temple. The encrusted dirt and soot were removed mechanically, and the walls were cleaned using chemical solvents, resulting in the discovery of more original details, such as hieratic and demotic texts, thus greatly enhancing the epigraphic record. The temple roof, which leaked during water from rainfall, was repaired with new sandstone blocks quarried at Gebel Silsila, the source of the original blocks. The examination and recording of numerous sculpture fragments led to the reconstruction of the cult statue of Tuthmosis III and Amun, which was replaced in its original position in the sanctuary. Thus this project has combined archaeology, architectural survey, epigraphic recording, stone conservation, and wall painting conservation in order to treat the whole building in context – a holistic approach in which all aspects of the work complement and inform each other. The final outcome will be comprehensive publication and a comprehensible display and presentation to visitors.

Such long-term projects are able to deal with the multiple problems of conserving and preserving ancient buildings on a scale commensurate with the magnitude of the task. The sustained work of the Egyptian–French Centre in Karnak, continuing the operations of Lacau and Chevrier in the early twentieth century, combines recording, excavating, cleaning, and conservation of the Karnak temples to provide public access to tourists and scholars both at the site itself and through regular publications.

Maintenance

The ultimate aim of cultural heritage management is long-term maintenance in order to preserve the monuments for future generations. A major obstacle to achieving this, identified by Naguib Amin, is the out-of-date attitude to archaeological sites. '. . . most – not all – active national and international [archaeological] missions are racing after discoveries and research results, without involvement in actions aiming at long term site preservation.' He argues for a radical shift in policy, focusing on the present and future state of the remains, rather than trying only to reconstruct the past.

Monitoring current conditions and recording data for future planning are essential. There is still no standard regular monitoring system applied to all sites, although some of them are better cared for than others. This means that there are few data on which to base long-term protection. For example, decorated buildings should be regularly photographed *in toto* and in detail so that conditions can be checked. A standard monitoring procedure is urgently needed throughout the country on all sites on a regular basis, and evaluation criteria for monitoring need to be established and clear guidelines formulated on what is being monitored and to what end. Mitigation of damage, or the causes of damage, should also be dealt with promptly. At the moment, a widespread response is to either ignore the damage or close the site; even the latter procedure can have adverse effects through neglect, as can be seen at the Apis House in Memphis, mentioned above.

A controversial subject is that of the dismantled boat discovered at the foot of the Great Pyramid in 1954. Its painstaking restoration by Hagg Ahmed Yussef over the following 13 years was a triumph of deduction and patience and is described in the study by Lipke. However, the final reconstruction was installed over the pit in which it had been found, in a specially constructed museum with large south-facing windows but no temperature or humidity control. Inevitably, many of the timbers were damaged. Air conditioning has now been installed and blinds fitted on the windows. Although the building itself is a blot on the ancient landscape, the location preserves authenticity. A second pit nearby was found to contain a similar dismantled boat, but an investigation sponsored by the National Geographic in 1988 showed that removal of overlying sand and rubble had allowed air and moisture to enter the pit, jeopardising the timbers, and conserving them may no longer be feasible.[22]

The tomb of Sety I in the Valley of the Kings (KV 17) is another case in point. This richly decorated but damaged tomb has been closed since 1981 because of structural instability. In 1997–9, ARCE conducted a conditions survey, examining the geology and structure, the condition of the painted decoration and reliefs, internal humidity and temperature, and requirements for a conservation project.[23] The tomb is narrow and very deep and is unsuitable for large tourist group visits. So far, the motivation and the finances to conserve it have been lacking, but a regular monitoring programme is required to help minimise further deterioration.

The whole of the Valley of the Kings is one of the most endangered sites, as it is one of most visited, with up to 7,000 people per day. The Ministry of Tourism aims to increase this number to 12,000 daily by 2014. It is obvious that protection measures are necessary and some mitigation is already in place, improving the desperate overcrowding. The entry ticket to the Valley allows access to only three tombs, but unfortunately most tourists want to visit the same easily accessible tombs near the centre of the Valley. Consequently the tombs of Ramesses IX (KV 6), Ramesses VI (KV 9), and Ramesses III (KV 11) are overvisited and frequently crowded beyond their carrying capacity. A visit to the tomb of Tutankhamun, which has suffered noticeable degradation, has for a long time needed a separate and more expensive ticket, and the number of visitors is limited. Guides are no longer allowed to talk inside tombs, thus reducing the length of group visits.

Some measures are actually exacerbating the situation; for example, the heavy floor-to-ceiling glass panels protecting the mural decoration are difficult to clean and trap heat, humidity, and dust. The diesel trains that bring tourists into the Valley produce noise and fumes as well as leaking oil. They detract from the dignity of the Valley and are unsuitable for a heritage site.

A recent site management plan prepared by Weeks and Hetherington for the World Monuments Fund outlines a comprehensive program of improvements and monitoring. This includes the most essential factor – restricting the number of visitors at any one time. They also advocate the regular monitoring of temperature and humidity so that the 'carrying capacity' – the maximum number of visitors before deterioration begins – can be estimated.

Additional mitigations are suggested, such as low-heat lighting, air-flow systems to reduce heat and humidity, and replacing the present glass protective panels with much smaller Plexiglas barriers. At the moment, improvements to the infrastructure and the measures taken to protect the tombs lag so far behind the ever-increasing tourist numbers and international cultural heritage management practices that it is difficult to see how the tombs will survive. The ultimate conservation solution may be replicas, not only for the Valley of the Kings, but also for selected tombs in the Valley of the Queens and private tombs. So far, this has been dismissed for financial reasons, but replicas at Lascaux and Altimira have proven the success of this approach when the original is definitively closed and the replica is accurate and sited in a comparable environment with easy visitor access. Laser scanning is now available to make precise replicas without damage to the original.

Where tourism overloads, especially at the 'must-see' sites of the Giza Pyramids and the Valley of the Kings, the effect is as shocking for the visitor as for the ancient monuments whose survival it threatens in such a rapacious world. Tung's 2001 account of Cairo's cultural heritage is a vivid and realistic assessment. Access, both intellectual and physical, to sites is two-edged – it can harm or preserve. A well-managed site depends in the first place on the protection afforded its monuments and environment, and only when that is achieved, on providing access and accurate information to all interested parties. This is achieved by a detailed assessment of the conservation needs, the maximum visitor numbers, visitor access, and infrastructure. A comprehensive plan for the management of the archaeological heritage is essential to ensure that the responsible authorities can maintain control of the inevitable conservation needs.

A controversial project taking place at the time of writing illustrates this. As part of a government initiative to develop southern Egypt, Luxor, as the wealthiest city in the area, is scheduled for large-scale development, focused mainly on the tourist potential. Work began in 2006 and President Mubarak officially launched the project in January 2007, with wide press coverage. Central to its design, laid out by Abraham and Bakr in the concept paper, is the restoration of the complete length (2.4 kilometers) of the avenue of sphinxes as a major tourist attraction. The complexities of accommodating tourism and economic development in historic towns were discussed by Orbashli in 2000.

Only the portions of the avenue near the temples were excavated before, while the rest remained buried under alluvium, later mediaeval occupation, and the modern town. When clearing began in 2006, many of the sphinxes were missing and most of the pedestals badly preserved. Unfortunately, there was no archaeological impact study before work began, nor any geophysical reconnaissance to inform on the state of survival of the sphinxes. The task of stabilising and conserving the remains after they have been uncovered will be lengthy and expensive and if they are to be preserved in the future, a perpetual conservation monitoring and maintenance program will be necessary.

The concept paper states that 'the Avenue of Sphinxes will accommodate thousands of tourists, both day and night, in an atmosphere that transports the stroller back across the centuries'. To do so the Avenue of Sphinxes will have to be partially or fully restored, as indeed the concept paper recognises. Such an outcome not only brings into question the safety of the archaeological remains and the means to safeguard them, but also presents the worrying possibility that the aim is to restore the sphinxes fully to create a barren simulacrum à la Hollywood, concealing and risking the original heritage. It is ironic that Egypt, whose ancient culture provided such inspiration for some of the great movie epics, now finds the fantasy more compelling than the real thing.

Egyptian hospitality towards foreign scholars is legendary and has fostered a long tradition of archaeological and Egyptological collaboration. Thus the authorities allow foreign-funded and -managed projects to work on individual sites and SCA projects, but these have little or no impact on Egyptian governmental decisions affecting the long-term survival and integrity of heritage sites, rendering many of them little more than cosmetic and temporary solutions to large-scale problems. Cultural heritage can only be managed successfully on a national scale by government agencies empowered to protect it, since they are capable of financing the work sufficiently and they maintain a constant presence while foreign donors and projects come and go. Yet developments in Luxor illustrate the problems in Egypt when decision-making is the prerogative of higher authorities and those responsible have to respond to crises. As Sedky again points out, 'values and interests such as the historical integrity and the authenticity of historic areas and monuments are likely to be compromised.' The dilemma is best expressed in the form of questions that take us back to the first in this series of practical approaches to cultural heritage management: what is the perceived value and significance of the Pharaonic culture and who are the principal stakeholders? At the beginning of the twenty-first century the monuments and sites that have survived from ancient Egypt are receiving another new identity, demonstrating how culture is a continuous process. Heritage management is an important part of the process and it is now imperative for archaeologists, conservationists, and heritage managers to be more proactive in making sure that what we have inherited is protected and preserved.

NOTES

1. Pritchard 1950: 251–2.
2. Cleere 2000: 1–19.
3. Abdul-Qader 1960: 228–79; pls. XL and XLI.
4. Gamblin 2006: 19–25.
5. Säve-Söderbergh 1987; VATTENBYGGNADSBYRÅN (VBB) 1976.
6. Hawass 2003.
7. Von Beckerath 1966: 43–55.
8. Anthes 1956: 4–65, pls. 1–5, 13, 14, 20–23; Jeffreys et al. 1984: 25–32; pl. VII.
9. Hawass 2000: 3–5.
10. Hawass 2000: 6.
11. See www.quarryscapes.no (accessed 29 December 2006).
12. Seel August 2006: 76–83; see www.centamin.com (accessed 29 December 2006).
13. Norwich 1991: 45–52.

14. See www.icomos.org (accessed 25 August 2006).
15. See The Getty Conservation Institute publications Agnew and Bridgland 2006; Teutonico and Palumbo 2002; Avrami et al. 2000.
16. Sedky 2005: 113–30.
17. Rashed 1994: 5.
18. See aljazeera.net, *Statue fatwa riles artists*, Monday 3 April 2006. (Accessed 25 August 2006).
19. El-Iraqi 2006: 109.
20. El Amir 1948: 51–6; pls. XV–XVII; Jones 1990: 141–7, pls. VI and VII.
21. Sheehan forthcoming.
22. El-Baz 1988: 512–33.
23. Jones 2003: 252–61.

PART III

ART AND ARTIFACT

Objects as Subject

CHAPTER 7

ART OF ANCIENT EGYPT

Rita E. Freed

A culture of mystery and beauty, ancient Egypt has been a source of fascination worldwide and for millennia. Its writings – whose meaning was lost for nearly 1,500 years – were thought to contain sacred knowledge. Its awesome deities challenged and were ultimately subsumed by Christian theology and iconography. But more than those aspects, it was the monumentality of Egyptian temples and the beauty of Egyptian sculpture that attracted pilgrims to the Nile banks since the time of the ancient Egyptians themselves.

Today we admire Egyptian art and make efforts to understand it. It seems clear that Egyptian art, like many other aspects of Egyptian society, represents a balance of opposites. For example, it is frequently monumental yet capable of displaying exquisite detail; often it is intended to be timeless, yet like a photograph it can capture a moment in time; it can be coldly formal or intimate and playful. What is certain is that it delights and fascinates the modern eye just as it earned the admiration and awe of foreign cultures of its own time.

Egyptian artists are well known for their ability to work in stone. Limestone, sandstone, and granite were readily available in different parts of the Nile Valley. Basalt, greywacke, diorite, and quartzite quarries were scarcer and more remote, yet those stones were particularly prized for their color or ability to accept a high polish. Recent research has identified many of these quarries and has shed light on the makeup of the mining expeditions that worked them.[1] Abandoned works make it clear that sculptures were roughed out at the quarry site, so that the least possible weight was transported to the final workshop.

Tools were simple. Balls of dolerite and other hard stones were used as pounders to rough out the desired shape. Copper or, from the New Kingdom on, bronze chisels were used to further refine the work, and an abrasive of powdered stone produced the final polish. Soft stones such as limestone and sandstone were brightly painted, while only select details were painted on harder stones.

Some of the finest and most sensitively carved examples of Egyptian relief and sculpture were executed in wood, although only a small fraction of what was made has survived. Hard woods had to be imported – cedar from the Levant and ebony from further south in Africa – and because it was scarce, the Egyptians developed complex techniques of joinery, inlay, and veneering. Much more work needs to be done to identify the nature and precise origin of the woods used.

A few preserved examples demonstrate that at least as early as the late Old Kingdom, large-scale and expressive works were made of copper hammered over a wood core. The recent cleaning of two 6th Dynasty examples shows just how skilled the Egyptians were at modeling realistic likenesses in this material.[2] From the Middle Kingdom onward, hollow casting of copper made the creation of exquisitely detailed works possible. Knowledge of bronze working came in the New Kingdom, but it was in the subsequent Third Intermediate Period that many of Egypt's finest creations in that medium were produced. Large in scale and inlaid with gold and silver, these represent highpoints in both technology and artistry.

Regardless of the material, Egyptian artists generally worked according to a fixed set of rules known as the canon of proportion. By placing a grid of equal squares over the human figure, artists were able to reproduce it in the same way, regardless of size or medium. As has recently been demonstrated, both the number of squares in the grid and the relative proportion of body parts changed periodically, although often only subtly, throughout the 2.5 millennia of its use. The use of the canon and grid made it possible for Egyptian artists to continue to reproduce the same styles and forms. This contributes greatly to making Egyptian art so distinctive and recognizable.

Although our modern eye appreciates Egyptian works as art, the artists who created them did so for the message they conveyed or the purpose they served. Often they were not meant to be seen, because they were hidden away in tombs where they could serve as a substitute for the body should anything happen to it. In part for this reason, they were not generally intended to be a true portrait of an individual, but rather an idealized image of beauty of the time. It was through its inscription that a statue or relief was linked to a specific person. Through what our modern view would consider magic, statues and reliefs were brought to life so that they could function in the afterlife in the same way as what they depicted functioned in this life.

Current research is shedding light on the origins of Nile Valley Egyptian civilization, pushing back its date. In the desert fringes around the Second Cataract and further south, pottery from about 7000 BC already displays sophisticated overall decoration that bears testimony to an innate desire to make utilitarian objects beautiful. It also showcases their makers' ability and innate desire to create beauty through minimal means and understatement. From about the same period in the Delta come representations of human heads and entire figures from both funerary and domestic contexts. Although their significance is unclear, they share the same minimalist esthetic with the objects from the South. Recent work in the archaeology of the Eastern and Western Desert wadis is demonstrating the vast extent of early trade routes and cultural contacts.

By about 4000 BC permanent settlements proliferated along the Nile Valley in Upper Egypt and shared a similar culture often referred to as the Nagada Culture, named after the site of Nagada just north of Thebes, where it was first identified. Vast cemeteries yielded a variety of ceramics and personal effects. Pottery from the earliest phase was the result of a multistep and labor-intensive process that included hand coiling, pebble burnishing, slipping with red ochre, and painting white line decoration. Scenes included landscapes combining aerial and profile views, animal trapping, and the earliest representation of one human smiting another, iconography that would continue throughout Egyptian history. Seldom were two vessels alike. Graves also included utilitarian objects such as combs made of ivory or greywacke palettes for grinding eye paint. The softness of both those materials made them easy to carve, and artists augmented their outlines to suggest the shapes of the mammals, birds, fish, and reptiles abundant along the Nile and its banks. The imagination and creativity of these early artists was seldom surpassed.

As time passed, communities increased in size and complexity. Greater demand for material goods resulted in more being made, but their mass production led to simplification and stylization. Although still handmade, pottery characteristic of the later Nagada Culture is decorated in red paint on an unslipped, buff ground. Men in boats and overall motifs of spirals, wavy lines, or abstract dots are common themes found in many areas.

Major centers of population developed and their leaders extended their power beyond local borders. Primary among these was Hierakonpolis in Upper Egypt just south of Thebes, a site whose continuing excavations are constantly revising our understanding of the nature and scope of Predynastic and Early Dynastic culture. It is clear that the types of objects produced previously for utilitarian purposes acquired significance as a vehicle for propaganda. One example from Hierakonpolis, now in the Egyptian Museum, Cairo, is the Narmer palette.[3] It copies the material and shape of earlier palettes for grinding eye paint, although it is substantially larger. Its main side and reverse are covered with relief carving. Artists divided the surface into registers and carved scenes depicting Narmer, the first king of a unified Egypt, overcoming enemies in a variety of ways, both in a human and in a divine sphere.

It is noteworthy that so many of the hallmarks of Egyptian style and iconography are already present on this object made around 3000 BC. Size is equated with hierarchy, and the king, as the most important figure, is also the largest. Behind him on the main side of the palette on the largest register stands his sandal bearer, but he is approximately one-fourth the king's size. Narmer wields a mace overhead in one hand and in the other clasps the hair of a supplicant enemy. In this manner the instant prior to action is shown, although the next gruesome moment is clear. Similarly, on the obverse, bound and decapitated enemies are neatly laid out with their heads between their legs, a vivid reminder of the outcome of battle. Egyptian art, for the next 3,000 years, was seldom a violent art, although the implication and results of violence were present.

Narmer is depicted from a combination of profile and frontal viewpoints. By doing this, the artists made every individual element of his figure recognizable, even though it did not represent the way it would have been viewable from any given point. Facial features are rendered in true profile except for the eye, which for the sake of clarity and simplicity is shown frontally. From the shoulders to the hips, the torso is frontal, but the legs are in profile and the far leg is extended forward. In this manner, not only are the salient aspects of each part of the body shown, but also they occupy the maximum amount of space, thereby providing a sense of power and balance. This manner of depicting the body also became the Egyptian norm.

Attitudes and attributes depicted on the Narmer palette were understood and repeated by artists working three millennia later. For example, on the main side of the palette, Narmer wears a tall crown that was identified with his homeland of Upper Egypt. On the reverse, in smaller scale, he wears a flat-topped crown with a diagonal projection at the rear. This headgear is associated with Lower Egypt (the Delta), the territory he subjugated, thereby unifying Egypt for the first time.

What the king did on a human scale, the gods repeated in the divine sphere. The falcon god Horus was associated with kingship. Above and to the right of the king wearing the Lower Egyptian crown, Horus snags a human-headed clump of papyrus plants. Papyrus, growing in the marshy Delta, was identified with that area. Although not present on the Narmer palette, lotus flowers, found abundantly in the Nile, symbolized Upper Egypt. On the main side of the palette in the lowest register, a powerful bull breaks through a city wall, forcing a melee of its citizens into a free fall. The bull was also synonymous with kingship, and it is the power of the bull that the king calls upon when he wears the bull's tail at the back of his kilt.

Although much of the style and iconography of the palette continues in use, other aspects appear again only rarely. The large central register of the palette's obverse is occupied by two large, mythical animals interpreted as a cross between a leopard and a serpent ("serpopards"). Their origin may lie in ancient Elam (Persia) or Mesopotamia, and they bear testimony to rich interconnections at the beginning of the third millennium BC. On the palette, two men use brute force to pull the beasts' long, entwined necks apart. The area their necks encircle, which is further set off by a raised frame border, recalls the original function of the palette as an aid in grinding eye paint.

Therefore, while the Narmer palette hearkens back to the past, it also sets a path toward the future. Here at the beginning of the emergence of Egypt as a unified country, it conveys a multitude of messages about the power of kingship, religion, and social order. A remarkable and innovative art object, it explores balance, symmetry, and clarity. Sophisticated and intricate interior detailing is offset by broad unadorned planes. Contemporary attempts at three-dimensional sculpture lag far behind the Narmer palette in their ability to realistically portray their subject.

In the two dynasties following Narmer, Egypt's Early Dynastic Period, artists excelled in the carving of fancifully shaped stone vessels and other minor arts. However, their attempts to create three-dimensional naturalistic human sculpture still show a period of experimentation. The squatting statue of Hetepdief[4] is charming but awkward. The names of the last three kings of Dynasty 2 carved into the shoulder suggest that it was made at the end of that dynasty or the beginning of the next. Proportionally the head is too large for the body, and it projects too far forward. Head and torso merge together without a neck, but the transition between them is cleverly masked by a heavy round wig extending to the shoulder blades. In comparison to the head, the torso is far more schematically rendered, and the limbs are barely differentiated from the torso mass. This, as well as the lack of neck, suggests that the artists were unable to liberate narrow forms from the rock matrix with the tools at hand, namely copper chisels, stone pounders, and abrasives. What they achieved was far more geometric than naturalistic. This geometry and the original shape of the stone may be seen from viewing the statue either frontally or from the side.

By the Dynasty 4 artists not only had mastered the challenge of carving naturalistic human forms in hard stone, but also achieved a formula for doing so that was admired and copied by succeeding dynasties. The Egyptian ideal for the standing figure, both male and female, is elegantly expressed in a dyad featuring Menkaure and his wife (Fig. 7.1). Menkaure was the builder of the third pyramid at Giza, and the dyad comes from the Valley Temple of that pyramid. Giza was one of several royal necropolises, all of which were located in the vicinity of the capital, Memphis.

In keeping with the idea that the right side is dominant, Menkaure stands to the right of his queen. His left foot is forward, although his weight rests squarely on his right leg. In this manner he occupies space and presents a powerful impression, although he is immobile. He has broad shoulders, a narrow waist, and pronounced muscles in his arms and legs. In contrast, his queen's body is decidedly feminine, with narrow shoulders, a tiny waist, small hips, and an abdomen so slender that the outline of her pubic triangle is visible even though she is clothed. (The hem of her sheath dress may be seen just above her ankles.)

King and Queen share similar facial features, although the shape of her face is rounder. Both gaze forward impassively, looking neither at the observer nor at each other. They are not young or old, but ageless and immortal. He stands with his arms at his sides. Her right arm extends behind his back, allowing the hand to wrap around his right arm. Her left arm extends in front of her torso and her fingers touch his left arm. Despite this, there is no tenderness or emotion in their position. Rather, the queen's gesture is one of association and of recognition of his higher status. The two represent an ageless, timeless ideal. Egyptian artists followed this model for both royal and nonroyal sculptures for the next two millennia.

Menkaure and his Queen probably never resembled their statue. As mentioned above, although Egyptian art was not created as portraiture, a few exceptions, such as Ankhaf in the Old Kingdom (Fig. 7.2), demonstrate that when the artists wished to render true portraits, they had the skills to do so. The vast majority of sculptures in the Old Kingdom were created for tombs and sealed away in an inaccessible room (*serdab*). Perhaps for that reason they represent the owner as he wished to be remembered, that is, with a perfect body in the ideal of youth, rather than how he actually looked. Ankhaf, on the other hand, was set up in an outdoor chapel, a place where outsiders could view him and leave offerings of food and drink for him to consume in the afterlife. Perhaps for that reason, an attempt was

FIGURE 7.1. King Menkaure (Mycerinus) and queen (MFA #11.1738). Photo: Courtesy of and ©
Museum of Fine Arts, Boston.

made to personalize him. In other instances, personalization was achieved by means of an
inscription. To change the identity of a statue one only had to change the inscription, a
practice that was carried out with some frequency in later dynasties.

Although the perfect formula for the human body had been achieved by Dynasty 4, the
first half of the Old Kingdom was still a time of innovation. New poses, sizes, materials,
statue types, and groupings were tried, and the results showcased the prosperity and creative
spirit of the time. Although not a lot is known about the organization of artists, it is clear
from their tombs that they enjoyed privileged status. Exceedingly rarely, however, can an
artist be associated with a given work. Unlike the Greek artists, Egyptian artists did not sign

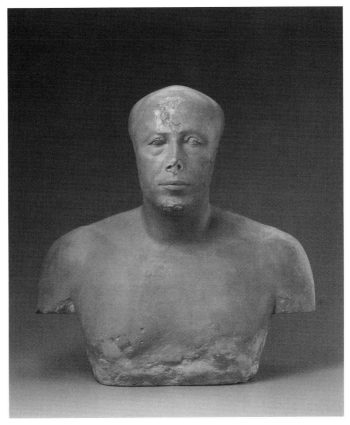

FIGURE 7.2. Bust of Prince Ankhhaf (MFA #27.442). Photo: Courtesy of and © Museum of Fine Arts, Boston.

their creations. Representations of sculptors at work indicate that a single piece was often a team effort, with different artists working on different aspects at the same time. It is likely that a master supervised and corrected the overall work and executed fine and important details such as the face. More junior artists and apprentices would have been responsible for the basic roughing out of the piece, simpler aspects of the torso, and, in the case of reliefs, minor figures and background details.

As the Old Kingdom flourished, its administration grew more complex. Anybody with a bureaucratic title was entitled to burial in a royal necropolis, and the demand for tombs and their contents increased accordingly. Carefully sculpted, innovative works of the Fourth and early Fifth Dynasties gave way to bland pieces executed in a limited variety of poses, often small in scale and crude in execution.

A series of events brought down the central authority at the end of the 6th Dynasty. With no king, there were no royal building projects and there was no royal support for artists.

The country fragmented, and control reverted to a series of city-states known as nomes. Each had its own leader or nomarch who was buried locally in a tomb created by a native artist. As time went by, and with limited, if any, access to earlier works, artists veered farther and farther from the earlier ideals, and many areas developed their own, easily identifiable styles, which make up in charm what they lack in sophistication.

After more than a hundred years the Theban nome gained supremacy, and a ruler named Mentuhotep (II) gradually reunited the country, thereby establishing what is known as the Middle Kingdom. Three-dimensional works by local Theban artists early in Mentuhotep II's reign display a blocky, almost brutal style. In relief, long thin limbs, small heads, high waists, and elongated lower bodies appear awkward in comparison with Old Kingdom works. Facial features in both sculpture and relief also tend to be thick and elongated. As the country came together, the earlier artistic production of the Memphite area became accessible, and artists copied it directly, one even admitting so in a biographical inscription on his funerary stela. Even within Mentuhotep's funerary monument at Deir el Bahari, the change to earlier, canonical proportions and a more polished style is apparent in the relief-carved walls.

By the early 12th Dynasty, artists had mastered the style of the Old Kingdom, and superficially, at least, their works resembled those earlier. A comparison between the seated diorite statue of Khafre[5], the predecessor of Menkaure, from his funerary complex at Giza and the ten seated statues of King Sesostris I,[6] the second king of Dynasty 12, from his funerary temple at Lisht to the south of Giza makes this evident. Their torsos are similarly proportioned, their dress is the same, and their faces are ageless and impassive. There is no doubt that the latter copies the earlier. What is lacking in the copy, however, is the artistry of a sculpture creating an original work. The copy, that is, Sesostris I, has fussier torso modeling and a slight smile that makes him appear almost effeminate.

More so than earlier, kings of the Middle Kingdom made their power known through monuments they built countrywide, rather than concentrating primarily on their funerary temples. Long and prosperous reigns provided the necessary resources. Temples showing the king adoring local and national deities sent the message that he provided for the well-being of the populace and deserved their homage and their awe. Sculpture now served propaganda purposes as well as funerary needs. But the traditional expressionless and ageless faces did little to reinforce this need. Perhaps at least in part for that reason, the physiognomy of the king underwent a gradual change. The face of Sesostris II, the fourth monarch of the 12th Dynasty, exhibits slight folds of flesh running diagonally between his nose and mouth and additional folds at the corners of his mouth. His image is not one of youthful power but one of wisdom and maturity. These same hallmarks may also be seen in his queen – the first time a high-status female is shown with signs of age (Fig. 7.3). By the reign of his son and successor, Sesostris III, slight folds became deep furrows. Eyes projecting from sunken sockets were further highlighted by pouches underneath. This was the image the populace saw as they passed by temples like Mentuhotep II's at Thebes. It was one that must have inspired fear and awe and sent the message that the king was all-powerful.

FIGURE 7.3. Head of a female sphinx (MFA #2002.609). Photo: Courtesy of and © Museum of Fine Arts, Boston.

The fierce expression of Sesostris III becomes somewhat muted during the reign of his son and successor, Amenemhat III. The emphasis shifts from the eyes, which are generally less pronounced, to the mouth and chin, which project outward as if in a sullen pout. As before, private individuals are represented according to the royal style, or at least as close as they can be. A great industry arose for the production of small-scale private art, not only for tombs, but also for cenotaphs at Abydos, homeland and mythological burial place of Osiris, god of resurrection. Because of a change in religious thought that gave the general populace access to that holy site, those who could afford it to left a statue or stela there. By doing so they could take part in Osiris' yearly resurrection drama and achieve the same result themselves. These efforts for the common man imitate contemporary style but vary greatly in quality.

By Dynasty 13, officials high in the bureaucracy became the real governing power over a long line of kings with short and largely ineffectual reigns. The weakened central power succumbed to the Hyksos invasion in the Delta and the Kerma invasion in the south, and as recent discoveries have shown, the invaders even came close to taking Thebes. Little native Egyptian art was produced during this Second Intermediate Period.

Rulers in Thebes in Dynasty 17 gradually expelled the foreigners from Egypt and re-established the monarchy, inaugurating a period known as the New Kingdom. Not surprisingly, in its blocky, noncanonical shapes and overlarge but poorly integrated facial features, art of late Dynasty 17 and early Dynasty 18 greatly resembles Theban art of the early Middle Kingdom and was probably influenced by it. Later rulers pushed beyond Egypt's borders to establish an empire that stretched from the Orontes River in Syria to Gebel Barkal at the Nile's Fourth Cataract in the South. New Kingdom art, particularly painting, benefited from these international contacts, which brought not only new inspiration but also new raw materials.

Because Thebes was both the homeland of the ruling family and centrally located in the empire, the city and its environs acquired a new importance in both the religious and political spheres. Beginning with Thutmosis I, the second king of Dynasty 18, the Middle Kingdom shrine on the East Bank dedicated to the local god Amen was greatly expanded. Its walls were decorated with reliefs displaying the exploits of the reigning king on the battlefield, his gratitude to Amen, and the gifts of long life and power he received in return for it. Beginning with Thutmosis I's father Amenhotep I, kings located their mortuary monuments across the river. Funerary temples were constructed at the desert edge, but to thwart robbers, tombs were hidden in the crevices of high cliffs accessed by a narrow wadi (dry river bed) now known as the Valley of the Kings. Their titled officials were buried in the hills nearby. The demand for artists to decorate these monuments increased commensurately with the growing wealth of the monarchy.

Sculpture, reliefs, and paintings of the early New Kingdom again returned to the past for inspiration, and artists replicated classical and canonical early Dynasty 12 models, particularly those of Sesostris I, whose numerous monuments might still have been visible countrywide. In some instances artists succeeded so well that it can be difficult to distinguish reliefs of Sesostris I, for example, from those of Amenhotep I. By the time of the joint rule of Hatsehpsut and her stepson Thutmosis III, the demand for statuary and relief increased geometrically.

Hatsheptsut built monuments depicting herself, her stepson, and her gods not only at Karnak and across the river at Deir el Bahari, where she located her funerary temple, but also at more remote places like Aswan, where the pair erected a temple to the local goddesses Satet and Anuket. Possible because of her influence, works acquired a decided feminine quality. Blocky torso proportions of the very early New Kingdom slimmed down and became more refined. Smaller eyes were extended outward by cosmetic lines and surmounted by high and sharply arched brows, whose outer edges paralleled the cosmetic lines. Hatshepsut's dainty lips curled upward in a sweet, feminine smile.[7] Although her proportions and facial features grew somewhat more masculine toward the end of her rule, her works are often indistinguishable from those made during the solo thirty-three-year-long rule of Thutmosis III.

The tour de force of Hatshepsut's reign is her funerary temple, mentioned above. Three porticoed terraces sculpted into a bay of cliffs at Deir el Bahari across the river from Karnak display an elegance and sophistication that far surpass Mentuhotep II's funerary temple beside it, and after which it is loosely modeled. The walls of the terraces provide ample space for Hatshepsut to tell the story of her divine birth and her earthly exploits, all carefully rendered in low raised relief. The latter include the transport of obelisks from Aswan to Karnak and the receipt of exotica from Punt, including the Queen of Punt herself, grossly obese and apparently suffering from elephantiasis. The pillars of the terraces, the ramps connecting them, and the causeway that once led to her Valley Temple were adorned with more than 200 statues, nearly all of which were reduced to fragments by Thutmosis III during his sole rule.

Some of the finest works of the first half of the 18th Dynasty are not its royal edifices, but private tombs at Thebes, created for the burgeoning administrative class. The stiff formalism of the Middle Kingdom was gradually replaced by more crowded compositions, freer line, spontaneity, rich colors, and exquisite detailing, and some of this change may have been due to foreign influences, particularly from the Aegean. Hunt scenes depict animals in full flying gallop over naturalistic terrain or in the agony preceding death. Female musicians worked themselves into a frenzy entertaining their patrons at funerary banquets.[8] Foreigners arrived by foot or ship with their exotic goods. Tomb equipment included foreign imports as well as Egyptian imitations in local materials. Scholars dispute whether Minoan style wall paintings recently found in a palace at Avaris of the time of Thutmosis III are the work of Minoan painters or Egyptians copying Minoan style.

A village of artisans who built and decorated the royal tombs grew up at Deir el Medina, not far from the Valley of the Kings. They were also available for private hire. Thanks to this village and the records its inhabitants left behind, a great deal is known about their organization and methodology. They worked in teams, or gangs, and the privilege of working as an artisan was passed from father to son. Each gang had its distinctive style, and scholars have been able to identify their work in multiple tombs.

The 18th Dynasty was a high point in the production of minor arts, thanks to the availability of precious metals and stones and the ability of artists to transform them into objects that both delighted the eye and served a function. For example, seductive servant girls dressed only in cowrie-shell girdles were transformed into mirror handles, promising rejuvenation and rebirth to the mirror's owner. The slightly flattened disk that reflected its owner's image was symbolic of the sun, reborn with the dawn of every new day.

Egypt's prosperity reached its height under Amenhotep III. He built more and larger monuments than anybody before him, including at least two 17.3-meter-high statues of himself made of single blocks of quartzite, a stone prized for its brown/red color, which the Egyptians identified with the sun. Its name in Egyptian is *"bia,"* meaning "marvel." These statues, today known as the Colossi of Memnon, marked a pylon in his enormous funerary temple and nearby palace. Ongoing excavations there are bringing to light many more statues that are colossal in scale or imaginative in their subject matter.

During Amenhotep III's long (37 years) and peaceful reign there was a gradual change in religious ideology, particularly with regard to the prominence of the sun god. Art, especially the depiction of the human body, was one of the byproducts of this change. In comparison to earlier in the dynasty, on both royal and private sculpture, eyes became narrower, and cheekbones more prominent. Overall, there was a tendency toward fussiness, apparent particularly in overlarge and very detailed wigs. As time passed these aspects became even more exaggerated. For example, eyes were reduced to mere flattened ovals elongated by thick, flat upper lids extending outward toward the temples and similarly shaped brows running parallel to them. Sometimes the eyes were further emphasized by an incised line between the upper eyelid and brow. This almost manneristic appearance is enhanced by a thin ridge outlining the lips and filtrum. Further, the upper lip not only dips in the center, but also extends slightly over the lower, thereby giving the king a slight overbite.

Fashion also changes during the reign of Amenhotep III. On both men and women, the tightly wrapped or clinging garments traditional in earlier reigns were abandoned in favor of longer and more voluminous tunics and dresses, whose careful pleating follows the body contours and contributes to their opulent effect.

Amenhotep III made his interest in the solar cult clear through the attributes he wore on his monuments, including uraeii (royal cobras) with sun disks that adorned royal wigs and garments or necklaces made of golden disks, the so-called "Gold of Honor." On one statue found in his solar court addition to the Luxor Temple, Amenhotep III wears a collar, a pectoral, armlets and bracelets, and an apron of uraeii with sun disks atop their heads. The surface area of all his ornaments was left rough so that gold, also a solar symbol, would adhere. In the last years of his rule, Amenhotep III's focus on the sun god and its rejuvenative aspects manifested itself in his new body form. His head took on the shape of a solar sphere, and his torso acquired a child-like pudginess – the first time a royal body was depicted as anything less than trim (Fig. 7.4).

Finally, and presumably at the very end of his rule, the king's statues lost all of their manneristic stylization and he was depicted in long robes covering a decidedly protruding abdomen and almost feminine breasts. His face again assumed an oval shape, his eyes became naturalistic protruding orbs, and his lips formed a fleshy pout. This last style, seen on a pair of statues from his funerary temple, may have been made at the time of a co-regency with his son, Amenhotep IV, in whose sole reign even more dramatic changes took place. Whether or not there was a co-regency and how it may have influenced art remains a controversial topic.

Artistically, as well as from a religious and political standpoint, the reign of Amenhotep IV is one of the most intriguing and problematic in the history of pharaonic Egypt. This king too elevated the sun god to special prominence and ultimately proclaimed it, in the form of Aten – the radiance of the sun – as Egypt's only god. Aten was depicted as an abstract disk with radiating lines ending in human hands that presented hieroglyphs for life and power to the king and his wife, Nefertiti. This represented a sharp break with past

FIGURE 7.4. Kneeling Amenhotep III as the god Neferhotep (MFA # 1970.636). Photo: Courtesy of and © Museum of Fine Arts, Boston.

tradition, where divinities were represented in human form, animal form, or a combination, but certainly not in a nonfigural manner.

Amenhotep IV continued his father's legacy of vast building projects. During the first five years of his reign, he erected at least four large temples and a palace in and around Karnak, particularly on its east side, to catch the first rays of the rising sun. In many ways the past repertoire of temple scenes was unsuitable for Aten, and the king's artists found inspiration in the private sphere. Simple and small-scale scenes of life in the service of Aten, such as food preparation, temple building, and depictions of nature, appeared on temples for the first time. Traditional large-scale reliefs of the gods were replaced with large-scale scenes of the king and his wife – and their growing family of daughters – offering to Aten, whose rays embraced them.

Colossal statues of the king erected in the courtyard of one of his Karnak temples show him with a grossly elongated face and slit eyes whose upper lids project out like a shelf. High cheekbones emphasized his sunken cheeks. A long, thin nose whose nostrils form a "V" echoed the shape of the mouth, whose corners were connected to the edge of the nostrils by a diagonal incised line. A drooping lower lip leads the eye to a sharply attenuated chin.[9]

The king's body was depicted in an equally strange manner. His head seems precariously balanced on a long sinewy neck that bends forward. An emaciated lower torso with the suggestion of breasts broadens into enormous, feminine hips. Arms were decidedly spindly. On most of the statues or statue fragments the king wears a tightly wrapped pleated kilt. However, on at least one, no clothes are represented, leading many to believe it is a representation of Nefertiti. At least two dozen of such statues stood as piers around an open courtyard, where the sharply raking sunlight further emphasized their strange modeling and imbued them with an even more surreal quality. Reliefs from the temple walls show not only the royal family, but also those who served the king depicted with the same non-canonical proportions. This commonality of representation is one argument against the theory proposed by some that the king's depiction is a true portrait of a monarch with a disease whose effects would have included his oddly distorted body. Had this been the case, however, one would expect the symptoms to have worsened with time. On the contrary, the opposite occurred, and later representations of the royal family and their court display softer modeling and body proportions that are closer to those of their traditional Egyptian predecessors.

By five years into his reign, and despite his massive building program at Karnak, Amenhotep IV abandoned Thebes for an area significantly downriver, uninhabited prior to his time. With boundary stones he marked out an area about 15 kilometers long on both sides of the river and dedicated the area to Aten. There he established a new capital city, naming it "Akhetaten" ("Horizon of Aten"), and moved there with his family and court. Today it is known as Amarna or Tell el Amarna, after the tribes living nearby. At about the same time he changed his name from Amenhotep IV ("Amen is Satisfied") to Akhenaten ("Life Spirit of Aten") and abandoned all connections to Amen and his priesthood.

The king made the new capital a glorious affair with temples, palaces, administrative buildings, and private houses arranged along a road on the east bank of the river. Mud-brick palaces were plastered and painted with some of the liveliest scenes Egyptian artists ever produced, a *trompe l'oeil* of the natural world around them.[10] Made first of mud-brick, temples were soon rebuilt in limestone carved in sunk relief and brightly painted or inlaid with faience. Although these were dismantled and the stone reused as ballast in later constructions, from the pieces recovered it seems clear that their decoration reflected life at Amarna. They display an intimacy and poignancy that represents a new vocabulary for Egyptian artists. Meaning was conveyed through a simple hand gesture, the tilt of a head, or even empty space.[11]

Temple walls featured the king, queen, and royal daughters, who eventually numbered six, galloping every morning in chariots from their palace in the far north to the temples in the center of Akhetaten, offering to Aten, and then returning along the same road at nightfall. Accompanying them were rows of bowing officials, attendants, and the army, heralded by trumpeters. En route, typical activities along the river and riverbank were depicted. Art became the vehicle for this ceremonial display of royal power and vitality, and the life-sustaining warmth of the sun dictated that these aspects be shown true to life, at least within certain constraints. Although many details were naturalistically rendered, the equation between size and hierarchy was maintained so that all life at Akhetaten was dwarfed by the royal family. Interestingly, the same themes with the same constraints were featured in the forty-four tombs of high officials carved into the eastern cliffs.

The colossal statuary of Akenaten and Nefertiti that lined courtyards and processional ways and fronted pylons of Aketaten's temples and ceremonial palaces was an important aspect of their architecture. Until recently this was known mainly from depictions in temples and tombs. Recent assembly of the thousands of fragments to which these statues were reduced has demonstrated the accuracy of the representations. Yearly more are coming to light.

Akhenaten's theology and political philosophy seems to have evolved through his seventeen years of rule and, with it, his style of depicting the human figure. The sharp eccentricities of the early regnal years gradually softened into more realistic representations. As the royal family aged, artists experimented with ways of depicting it. One statue of Nefertiti shows her with a lined face and sagging breasts.[12] A remarkable group of nonroyal heads and faces found in the same Amarna sculptor's workshop as the famous Nefertiti bust feature lined foreheads, crows' feet, and sagging jowls.[13]

Shortly after the death of Akhenaten, his religious experiment ended, and ultimately a young Tutankhaten was pushed to abandon Amarna to return to Thebes and the worship of Amen. In addition to changing his name to Tutankhamen, he restored the glories of Karnak, erecting numerous statues to the gods and himself in the process. Although the experiment with Aten was over, the elements of naturalism Aten's worship had fostered in art remained. On faces, three-dimensional eyes, high cheekbones, sensuous lips, and a slightly pendant chin differered little from what Akhenaten's artists created at the end of his reign. Male bodies with slight breasts, rounded hips, and low-slung belts underlining protruding stomachs also resembled late Amarna works. In all likelihood, the artists who worked at Amarna made these too. These artists went to the Memphite region as well, where sculptures and reliefs at Saqqara show their unmistakable hand.

In the Valley of the Kings, the tombs of Tutankhamen, Aye, and, to somewhat lesser extents, Horemheb and Ramesses I, bear the Amarna stamp, particularly in their figural representations. In the nonroyal sphere, and particularly at Saqqara, tombs not only exhibit late Amarna body forms, but also continue their depictions of age, emotion, spontaneity, and naturalism.

As time passed and as Akhenaten's artists died, naturalistic representations and scenes of daily life were replaced by more formal, repetitive poses and themes heavily grounded in the religious sphere. The transition between the two approaches is nowhere more vivid than in the temple that Seti I, the second king of Dynasty 19, erected in honor of Osiris and five other gods – and himself as well – at Abydos. Exquisitely and imaginatively patterned wigs, garments, and jewelry are juxtaposed with slightly modeled but otherwise unadorned surfaces. The subjects are carved so that they are higher than their backgrounds (raised relief), a more complex and time-consuming technique than simply incising into a surface (sunk relief). An occasional tender gesture or imaginative interpretation breaks the temple's solemnity.[14] These subtleties represent the heritage of Amarna. Yet the themes are the age-old ones of offering sustenance to families of gods in return for intangibles such as long life and a prosperous rule.

Seti I's illustrious and long-lived successor, Ramesses II (Ramesses the Great), is better known for the number and scale of his building projects than for the quality of their execution. One way for his artists to accomplish the king's objectives of promoting his power and leadership was to work in sunk, rather than raised, relief. Another technique was to usurp the monuments of his predecessors by removing their names and adding his. He particularly chose to emulate Amenhotep III, the king who until then was Egypt's largest builder both in number of monuments and their size. Because many of the latter's monuments showed him with a plump body and fussy detailing – both aspects that ran counter to the traditional canon of proportion – Ramesses II's artists slimmed down Amenhotep III's torso and shaved away the raised lines on his face. Updating the look, they also added pierced ears, lines on the neck, and occasional jewelry. This substantial makeover has resulted in a hybrid that until recently caused great confusion among Egyptologists.

But Ramesses II's artists did more than recarve earlier monuments. Those statues his artists created tended to be large in scale and summary in execution (Fig. 7.5). Unabashedly he used art as propaganda to promote his omnipotence and omnipresence. This is nowhere more vivid than in the many rock-cut temples he erected in Nubia along the river, of which Abu Simbel is justifiably the most famous. Nubians traveling downstream could not help but be awed by the four 20-meter-high seated statues of the king staring down at them. This edifice, like many others Ramesses II built far from the constraints of traditional religious decorum, is as much a monument to himself as it is to the gods. Here Ramesses presented himself as a god among gods in both relief on the temple walls and sculpture in the innermost shrine, where Ramesses the King is shown worshipping Ramesses the God. Although he was not the first to do so, he did it more often and more blatantly than any predecessor.

The topic repeated with most frequency on Ramesses the Great's temples is the story of a battle he fought in his fifth regnal year in Syria at Kadesh against the Hittites, a rising power originating in an area that is now Turkey. By ruse, the Hittites surprised the Egyptians

FIGURE 7.5. Head and shoulders from a colossus of Ramesses II (MFA# 89.558). Photo: Courtesy of and © Museum of Fine Arts, Boston.

and cut Ramesses off from most of his army. The fact that the king escaped with his life was enough to warrant his retelling the story on temple walls in increasing narrative detail throughout his rule. What is never depicted is the outcome of the battle, namely the fact that the Hittites retained Kadesh.

Despite the many dozens of children prominently displayed on his monuments, after Ramesses the Great was succeeded by his thirteenth son Merneptah, his bloodline disappears. Yet another nine kings take the name Ramesses in his honor. Most prominent among them art-historically and historically was Ramesses III, first king of the 20th Dynasty. He was forced to fend off potential invaders on the Mediterranean coast, and gruesome scenes of carnage resulting in his victories over the so-called Sea Peoples are writ large on his funerary temple at Medinet Habu in Western Thebes, much as the Battle of Kadesh is on

FIGURE 7.6. Amulet of Harsaphes (MFA #06.2408). Photo: Courtesy of and © Museum of Fine Arts, Boston.

the temples of his namesake. Architecturally Medinet Habu's high walls and fortified gate reflect the danger outside.

In the private sphere, tomb decoration and statue styles show an increased religiosity following the Amarna interlude. Scenes of mummification, judgment, and paradise replace scenes of daily life. Personal devotion to the gods is shown in three dimensions as well. Priests present images of the gods they serve. Thoth, god of writing, sits atop the shoulders of a cross-legged scribe as he practices his art. Seldom are these sculptures carved with the delicacy or artistry of earlier private works. In that way they are comparable to contemporary royal material. However, at times they display a refreshing creativity of pose

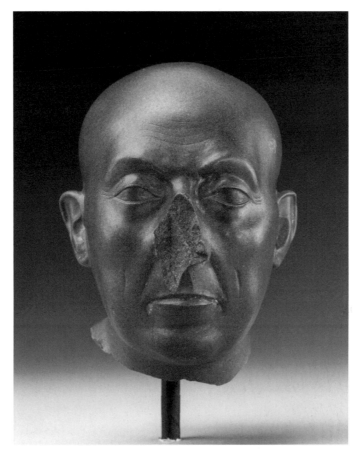

FIGURE 7.7. Head of a priest (The Boston Green Head) (MFA #04.1749). Photo: Courtesy of and © Museum of Fine Arts, Boston.

in their effort to broadcast their closeness to their god.[15] To date, with the absence of an inscription, it can be very difficult to arrange them chronologically within the Ramesside Period.

Struggles between the priesthood and the military led to Egypt's fragmentation in the Third Intermediate Period. Of all the intermediate periods, it produced the most stone sculpture, although it often is merely a repetitive echo of Dynasty 28. The cube statue, ideally suited to display piety in temples, was the most common form. In metals, however, the creativity of the Third Intermediate Period is unsurpassed. Large-scale hollow-cast bronzes, richly inlaid with gold and silver,[16] most often depict priestesses. Royal burials interred within the temple enclosure wall at Tanis included copious amounts of precious metal, not only in the form of jewelry but also vessels, masks, and entire coffins. These and other finds of gold and silver (Fig. 7.6) have led scholars to believe that the pious priests who removed the New Kingdom royal mummies from their individual tombs and reburied them in large caches may have recycled some of what earlier robbers left behind.

The 25th Dynasty saw rulers from Nubia on the throne of Egypt, and they took great pride in restoring and augmenting Egypt's monuments, particularly in Thebes, whose reverence for Amun they shared. They depicted themselves superficially in pharaonic poses and attributes, but tailored them to their own outlook and beliefs. Strong round faces with prominent cheekbones, broad noses, and fleshy lips distinguish them from their Egyptian counterparts. Close-fitting caps, two uraeii, and tall plumes often, although not always, replace the more traditional pharaonic crowns. Ram heads resting at the base of the neck and at each shoulder broadcast their reverence for Amun, whom they worshipped as a ram.

The change in physiognomy from the characterless sweetness of the Third Intermediate Period to the powerful depictions of Nubian rulers impacted the private realm tremendously. A number of striking depictions of powerful Theban nobility can only be described as portraiture, not only as far as the face in concerned, but the body as well.[17]

This trend continued into the next dynasty, the 26th, after the Nubians were forced out of Egypt by the Assyrians, who sacked Thebes but retreated afterwards, leaving officials of likely Libyan, or at least Western Delta, ancestry to govern as vassals. Taking over, they made every effort to establish their legitimacy as native rulers, in part by imitating the style of the New Kingdom. Yet the previous style persisted in private sculpture, and 25th Dynasty realism existed side by side with idealized, smiling faces that hearkened back to the time of Egypt's glory.

These two styles continued to exist in tandem until Egypt's conquest by Alexander the Great in 331 B.C. Perhaps thanks to the internationalism of the times coupled with some 3,000 years of experience in working with stone, pharaonic Egypt's waning days produced some of its finest and most expressive works (Fig. 7.7).

NOTES

1. See especially R. and D. Klemm 1993.
2. For Cairo JE 33035 post-cleaning and JE 33034 prior to cleaning see *The Treasures of Ancient Egypt from the Egyptian Museum in Cairo* 2001: 84–5.
3. Cairo JE 32169, illustrated in Saleh and Sourouzian 1987: no. 8.
4. Saleh and Sourouzian 1987: no. 22.
5. Saleh and Sourouzian 1987: no. 31
6. Saleh and Sourouzian 1987: no. 87 and *Treasures of Ancient Egypt* 2001: 111.
7. Roehrig 2005: frontispiece.
8. Quirke and Spencer 1992: 140–41.
9. Freed, Markowitz, and D'Auria 1999: 20–21.
10. Freed et al. 1999: 122, fig. 83.
11. Freed et al. 1999: 119.
12. Freed et al. 1999: 127.

13. Freed et al. 1999: 427, no. 139.
14. Claverly 1958: pls. 20, 23.
15. *Treasures of Ancient Egypt* 2001: 205.
16. Andreu, Rutschowscaya, and Ziegler 1997: 177.
17. Wenig 1978: 172.

CHAPTER 8

ANCIENT EGYPT IN MUSEUMS TODAY

Arielle P. Kozloff

THE ANCIENT TEMPLE AS ANCESTOR OF THE MODERN MUSEUM

The first museums of Egyptian art were the ancient temples and tombs themselves. Walls were decorated with scenes carved or painted by thousands of artists over many centuries. Corridors and chambers were filled with statues of gods and goddesses, kings and queens, and courtiers and officials of many dynasties. Interaction between works of art and the public came on festival days when the temples and cemeteries became the centers of celebration, their pictured walls reminding viewers of historic glories or eternal truths, and statues bidding passers-by to speak to the gods through them as intercessors. Even the most sacred cult statues were brought out from the temples' darkest recesses for processions through towns.

When temples became too crowded with statuary, priests cleaned house. They did not destroy the objects' magical powers by beheading them or erasing their inscriptions. They buried them whole, as if storing them away. Pharaohs, too, renovated temples, tearing down old walls and using them as rubble fill within the hollows of their new structures. These *cachettes* and filled pylons became the first storage areas, and they served their purpose well, preserving tens of thousands of works of stone, bronze, and other materials in pristine condition for the millennia.

At the Eighth International Congress of Egyptologists in Cairo in 2000, Regine Schultz covered many of the same issues discussed here in her paper, "Museology, Egyptology, and Marketing Interests: A Contradiction?" with responses by Anna Maria Donadoni Roveri, Ali Radwan and Maarten Raven, published in Zahi Hawass, ed., *Egyptology at the Dawn of the Twenty-First Century* (Cairo, 2002), pp. 95–106.

Except for the geographic spread and the evolution in the surrounding civilizations, museums of the twenty-first century are similar in many ways to the temples and tombs of antiquity. They house the same sorts of objects and are presided over by a priesthood of specialists – curators and conservators – trained in their arcane meaning and methods of care. These individuals collect, study, display, and elucidate items in the spaces assigned to them until overcrowding requires them to store the excess away or even deaccession the surplus.

Today, Egyptian collections are major attractions in museums.[1] What visitors hope for when they view these relics of the past are experiences that will "change them . . . alter their experience to the world . . . make it come alive anew for them, so that they can walk away at a different angle to the world."[2] It may not be quite the religious experience of millennia past, but for many there is indeed an element of the spiritual, the transcendental.

TODAY'S MUSEUM – WHERE ART THOU, MUSE?

The Latin word "museum" comes from the Greek *Mouseion*, shrine of the Muses. Not one of the nine traditional Greek Muses is a patron of the visual arts, though many of the major collections of Egyptian antiquities are housed in art museums. Yet, the architecture of many early museums in Europe, the United States, and even Cairo reflects the ancient form. Walking up grand staircases to columned entrances of these beaux-arts buildings and antique palaces sets the visitor's mood toward reverence and thoughtful contemplation of the treasures inside. In a sense, for the first 150 serious and stately years of modern museum history, the architecture was the Muse.

Ironically, toward the end of the twentieth century all of the Muses from Clio (History), to Terpsichore (Dance), to Calliope (Poetry), to Euterpe (Music), and even to Thalia (Comedy) have taken up residence in the great halls as museums have aimed their offerings to attract larger audiences. Long gone is the purist approach to the museum as a place for the quiet appreciation of works of art. In the early twenty-first century, they are "more like multifaceted amusement centers."[3]

The seismic force setting off this sea-change was none other than our own King Tut. While his first traveling exhibition in 1962 was a fairly modest affair, the second U.S. tour, organized by the Metropolitan Museum's director Thomas Hoving in the 1970s, became "the most spectacular museum success in American museum history."[4] Millions of people who otherwise never visited museums saw Tut. In a nation where 50 percent of the adult population did not know the abbreviations BC and AD,[5] suddenly there were popular King Tut songs, dances, political cartoons, and even reincarnations of ancient Egyptian royalty among Hollywood stars. Since Tut, museums have displayed temporary exhibitions of Egyptian antiquities on a frequent basis to keep the visitor pump primed. In 2005, King Tut returned once again to America.[6] In terms of commercialism, the Tut exhibition of the early twenty-first century is far beyond what even Hoving might have dreamed. If architecture was the

Egyptian antiquities curator's Muse for the first 150 years, King Tut has been the Muse – despite some protestations to the contrary – since 1978.

EGYPT'S OWN MUSEUMS

All of the recorded treasures from Tutankhamen's tomb belong to Egypt, and most reside in the cavernous Cairo Museum on el-Tahrir square. Each rendition of King Tut was organized with the intent of raising money to build a new museum in Cairo to replace the present one, which opened in 1902. This protracted project, called the Grand Egyptian Museum, is blossoming toward construction near the Great Pyramid, hopefully by 2010,[7] but several smaller museums have already been completed or are nearly opened at this writing. Thus, the general landscape of homeland Egyptian museums has changed dramatically over the past two decades, especially during the tenure of Zahi Hawass as Secretary General of the Supreme Council of Egyptian Antiquities.[8]

Meanwhile, the present, French-designed neoclassical building, now under the direction of Wafaa El-Saddik, houses more than 120,000 objects, from Narmer's palette to the treasures of Tutankhamen, Thuya and Yuya, and the Ramesside kings, to the two-story-tall colossal pair statue of Amenhotep III and Tiy – the largest Egyptian statue housed indoors anywhere in the world – to the mummies of the New Kingdom pharaohs.[9] Several small renovation projects have been undertaken when possible to update some of the galleries. A separate modern museum houses artifacts from the Coptic Period (Figs. 8.1 and 8.2).

The Luxor Museum opened in 1975 to show artifacts connected to the Theban area.[10] Some of its treasures include a large painted tomb wall from the Valley of the Nobles showing Amenhotep III enthroned and many talatat blocks from Amenhotep IV's temple at Karnak put together like pieces from a jigsaw to form the original image. Two of its sculptural masterpieces are the sublime graywacke portrait of Thutmose III and the monumental alabaster group of the crocodile god Sobek enthroned with his arm draped avuncularly around the shoulder of a more diminutive Amenhotep III. In 1989, a *cachette* of statues of Amenhotep III was found at Luxor temple. This find required a new wing added onto the 1975 building in 1992.[11]

Near the Luxor Museum is the Mummification Museum, the first of its kind in the world, which opened in 1997. Covering more than 2,000 square meters, it has nineteen display cases displaying mummies of both humans and animals, embalming fluids and tools, and funerary objects such as canopic jars, ushabtis, and amulets.

On the west bank of Thebes is a gemlike museum on site at Merenptah's mortuary temple. While the largest part of the museum is outdoors, a building of pylon width houses sculptural fragments and reliefs found there, many from the reign of Amenhotep III. "The outer and inner appearance of the museum has been restricted to the utmost simplicity of form," thus not interfering with the landscape and architectural remains surrounding it.[12]

FIGURE 8.1. Exterior, Coptic Museum, Cairo. Photo: Courtesy of Dr. Zahi Hawass.

Funded by UNESCO, the Nubia Museum opened in Aswan in 1997 and won the Aga Khan Award for Architecture in 1999–2001. Covering 7,000 square meters (a total of 50,000 for the extended grounds and garden), it houses 3,000 antiquities representing all periods from Prehistoric through Islamic. An outdoor exhibition space holds ninety monumental sculptures and architectural elements.

The Imhotep Museum is slated to open soon at Saqqara, and several other site museums are in the planning stages: the Ikhnaton Museum in Minya, a site museum at Amarna, and another at Sohag. The National Museum of Egyptian Civilization is already under construction in Fustat. This museum "provides an opportunity to exhibit numerous almost unknown collections, including, for the first time, the treasures from Helwan," which have been stored for more than fifty years in the basement of the Cairo museum.[13]

The Supreme Council of Antiquities has been generous in lending individual objects and entire exhibitions abroad in order to raise money for these ambitious projects, but they note that this amount of travel is hard on the artifacts and they hope that they will not need to continue sending their treasures abroad once their projects have been completed.[14]

In Egypt, virtually all of the curatorial staff has been trained in some aspect of archaeology or Egyptology. Even so, according to Zahi Hawass, "the biggest challenges facing museums in Egypt are the lack of trained curators, and the lack of modern collections management

FIGURE 8.2. Display case, Coptic Museum, Cairo. Courtesy of Dr. Zahi Hawass.

systems. We are addressing both of these issues through ongoing projects. ARCE [the American Research Center in Egypt] is sponsoring a museum training project at the Egyptian Museum, Cairo, which will develop a new collections management system for this museum, set up a registrar's office, and train a group of young registrars. A team is currently building a new database for the museum that will form an essential part of the new system. This initiative will also cover the Luxor Museum, the Nubia Museum, and the new Imhotep museum."[15] (See Fig. 8.3.)

In addition, the British Museum, at the behest of Keeper W. Vivian Davies, has for several years sponsored an in-house training program for native Egyptian and Sudanese curators, currently under the supervision of Neal Spencer and Marcel Marée. In this program, individuals already working in the field are brought to London to study contemporary conservation, installation, registration, and handling techniques under the guidance of British specialists.

FOREIGN MUSEUMS AND ANCIENT EGYPT'S PLACE WITHIN THEIR WALLS

Outside of Egypt, mostly in Europe and North America, several types of museums house Egyptian antiquities today. They range from vast, richly appointed royal palaces such as the Louvre to tiny, overstuffed garrets such as the Petrie collection of University College,

FIGURE 8.3. Imhotep Museum. Photo: Courtesy of Dr. Zahi Hawass.

London. Some, such as Turin's venerable Museo egizio, are devoted entirely to Egyptian antiquities. Others, such as Leiden's Rijksmuseum van Oudheden,[16] are general antiquities and anthropological collections with an art bias. Still others are encyclopedic fine art museums that either started with Egyptian collections at their core or embraced Egyptology early on.

The largest collection outside of Egypt, comprising 90,000 objects from dynastic Egypt and exponentially higher numbers from the Sudan, is housed at the British Museum.[17] The keystone of this collection is the trilingually inscribed block from Rosetta, captured by the British from the French army at Alexandria in 1801. The Younger Memnon, a colossal portrait of Ramesses the Great, was taken from the Ramesseum by the former circus strongman-turned-"archaeologist" Giovanni Belzoni under commission to Henry Salt, British Consul General in Egypt, during the early nineteenth century. Later came over-life-size portraits of Amenhotep III from Karnak and a pair of colossal red granite lion figures from Soleb, in Nubia. From other collectors came exquisite fragments of wall painting, glass vessels, and so on. Interest in Nubia has become particularly strong in recent years, and the department has renamed itself, recognizing Egypt and the Sudan equally.

The Museum of Fine Arts, Boston, counts its collection of over 60,000 objects as one of the largest and most comprehensive in the world. "By the time the Egyptian department formally came into being in 1902, [its] Egyptian collection was already the largest in the United States."[18]

Excavations by the joint Harvard MFA expedition directed by George Andrew Reisner gave Boston its most famous masterpieces, in particular a colossal alabaster statue of Mycerinus, group statuary of the same king, and the lifelike portrait bust of Ankh-kaf.[19]

The Louvre's Egyptian collection (Fig. 8.4) – some 35,000 objects strong – is based on the ancient royal collections, augmented by thousands of objects brought back to France by private collectors in the mid-nineteenth century.[20] The brilliant artistic quality of many of the smaller objects is a tribute to the aesthetic taste of these collectors. Jean-François Champollion, the decipherer of hieroglyphs, was its first curator, and ironically, the collection would have been much larger if France had acquired the huge collection of objects amassed by the French consul in Egypt, Drovetti. When it was refused, Champollion arranged for it to be bought by the King of Sardinia and set up in Turin – in the first museum of Egyptology ever established.[21] Somewhat later, Auguste Mariette excavated at Saqqara, discovering the Serapeum, and brought back to Paris one of the Louvre's most famous statues, the Red Scribe. Mariette was also the founding father of the Egyptian Antiquities Service, as well as the Cairo Museum.

Berlin's Egyptian collection was reunited in 2005 after more than half a century of diaspora during and after the Second World War.[22] It is now entirely housed, along with arguably the most famous Egyptian sculpture in the world, the bust of Nefertiti, in the Neues Museum on Museum Island. This and many other masterworks of Amarna sculpture were excavated by Ludwig Borchardt in 1912.

The Metropolitan Museum's collection is about the same size as the Louvre's. Excavations in the Theban area by Albert Lythgoe, Herbert Winlock, and Ambrose Lansing added immeasurably to the museum's holdings, especially the grand, colossal statues of Hatshepsut from Deir el Bahri, the treasure of gold jewelry belonging to three princesses of Thutmose III, and the painted wood funerary models from the Middle Kingdom tomb of the Chancellor Meket-Re.[23] Two architectural favorites are the Old Kingdom mastaba of Per-neb, an early purchase, and the Temple of Dendur, a gift to the citizens of the United States for their contributions toward saving the temples of Abu Simbel. Many fine additions were made over the years by purchase, including a number of beautiful late Dynasty 18 objects acquired from the collection of the Earl of Carnarvon.

Other American collections in Brooklyn, Cleveland, Toledo, Kansas City, and San Francisco, for example, were built almost entirely from purchases on the open antiquities market in Europe and New York. John D. Cooney, curator at Brooklyn from the 1930s until the early 1960s, made the most of funds left by Charles Edwin Wilbour and bought one masterpiece after another, building what is, arguably, piece for piece the finest ancient Egyptian art collection in the world.[24] Cooney was one of the first curators to show Egyptian objects as works of art rather than as primitive archaeological ancestors of "real" art – Greek and Roman sculpture and vases.[25]

The elegant Miho Museum, built on a mountaintop in Shigaraki Prefecture, Japan, by I. M. Pei under commission from the Shumei family, houses masterpieces of Egyptian, ancient Near Eastern, Chinese, and Japanese works of art.[26] Its collection was gathered entirely by

FIGURE 8.4. Egyptian sculpture, exhibit hall, The Louvre. Photo: Courtesy of The Egyptian Department of The Louvre.

purchase and features two important Egyptian sculptures: a life-size painted wood striding sculpture of an official named Nakht and an over-life-size granodiorite Ptolemaic queen recut in antiquity from a Dynasty 18 statue of Queen Tiy. The original must have been similar to a statue found in 2006 at the Temple of Mut, Karnak.[27]

COLLECTING IN THE TWENTY-FIRST CENTURY – WHO OWNS EGYPT'S PAST?

To say that attitudes toward collecting archaeological artifacts have changed at the end of the twentieth century would be an understatement. Long gone are the days when the Egyptian government allowed excavators to keep a portion of the objects they discovered. And long gone is the open antiquities market in Egypt. According to Egyptian Law No.117 of 1983, all antiquities found in Egypt are the property of the state and may not be removed from Egypt without official permission, normally granted only for special exhibitions or for conservation work done abroad. A new law under consideration makes the possession of antiquities within Egypt illegal, requiring "all owners of Egyptian antiquities [to] hand over all objects to the SCA, which in turn will install them in their archaeological store-houses."[28]

There is a certain amount of irony in an archaeologically rich country claiming sole ownership of its treasures at the same time that it raises money from the collector nations for renovation, restoration, and construction of museums and archaeological sites on the grounds that we all share the same heritage. There is also a certain amount of consternation among both public and private collectors who would rather see interesting and beautiful objects exhibited, published, and displayed than reburied in archaeological storerooms.

Of course, Egypt is not alone among archaeologically rich countries in enacting such laws. Italy, Greece, Turkey, China, Mexico, and others have done the same. The collector nations, as well, have legislated to support these bans, and internationally, they have come together under UNESCO to search for common ground. A few art-rich countries, such as England and Japan, have proactive trading laws that require objects of the highest national cultural importance to remain at home while allowing the thousands of less important works of art to be sold abroad.

Since 2000, a number of objects smuggled from Egypt have been found abroad and returned. These have included some important statuary, as well as Greco-Roman mummy masks and papyrus fragments. In 2002, Frederick Schultz, a New York antiquities dealer, was found guilty in a U.S. federal district court for conspiring to smuggle and possess looted Egyptian artifacts. The conviction was based not on U.S. law, but on the 1983 Egyptian law claiming ownership of all antiquities.[29] Thus, many collectors now trace back the history of prospective purchases to 1982 or earlier before buying.

In some cases, the objects returned have a long history outside of Egypt. In 1999, the Michael C. Carlos Museum acquired a collection of Egyptian mummies from the Niagara Falls Museum in New York State, where they had been since the early twentieth century. One of these was identified as the mummy of Ramesses I, the grandfather of Ramesses the Great, returned to Egypt in 2003, and placed on view in the Luxor Museum.

Currently, Egypt demands the repatriation of a late Dynasty 18 mummy mask acquired by the St. Louis Art Museum in 1998 from a well-known gallery. The heavily painted and glass-inlaid mask of Ka-nefer-nefer was excavated at Saqqara in the early 1950s. By one account it was given to the excavator to sell, and by another, it went to the Cairo Museum, from which it disappeared.[30]

Despite the challenges, both museums and private individuals continue to collect Egyptian antiquities. Both, on occasion, also deaccession. Museums normally do this at public auction as a matter of transparency with the hope of turning storage fillers into cash for more exhibition-worthy objects.

KEEPERS AND CURATORS – MAKING THEIR MARKS WITH SPECIAL EXHIBITIONS AND REINSTALLATIONS

At about the same time as the second Tut exhibition, a new generation of curators was gradually taking over from the previous one. The new generation was competitive and

FIGURE 8.5. Hatshepsut Exhibit. Photo: Courtesy of R. Dreyfus.

energetic. While they continued to acquire, to excavate, and to publish in much the same way as had their predecessors, the new area in which they excelled – perhaps inspired by the success of Tut – was special exhibitions, the largest ones including loans from many different countries. The richness, variety, and sheer number of superb exhibitions created in the past 30 years make it impossible to list all of them here, but a few of them can be listed according to the types of shows they represent.

Perhaps the most obvious type of exhibition is one identified with a particular pharaoh,[31] such as Brooklyn's "Cleopatra's Egypt," Cleveland and the Louvre's "Egypt's Dazzling Sun," Hildesheim's "Ägyptens Aufstieg zur Weltmacht," and San Francisco and the Metropolitan Museum's "Hatshepsut" (Fig. 8.5). Some exhibitions covered longer periods,[32] such as the joint New York/Paris/Toronto venture, "Egyptian Art from the Age of the Pyramids," and Boston's "Egypt's Golden Age" and "Pharaohs of the Sun." Other exhibitions centered on topics[33] such as gender issues, materials, mummies, and mummy portraits. Cincinnati's "Mistress," Rhode Island School of Design's "Gifts of the Nile," and Boston's "Mummies and Magic" are just a few of these. Nubian antiquities rated several studies, including Munich's and London's.[34] At the other end of the spectrum were the encyclopedic shows[35] such as Vienna's "Gott, Mensch, Pharao," Cleveland and the Louvre's "Pharaohs," the University of Pennsylvania Museum's "Searching for Ancient Egypt," and the Palazzo Grassi's "The Pharaohs." Small, in-house "focus shows"[36] are the luxury of museums large enough to have several exhibition spaces. The Metropolitan has produced "Animals in Ancient Egypt," "The Art of Medicine," and "The Royal Women of Amarna." The Louvre has mounted "Les artistes de Pharaon." These temporary exhibitions left lasting legacies in the form of catalogs – large and small – that greatly enriched the Egyptological literature.

At the Metropolitan Museum, except for housing King Tut, Christine Lilyquist stayed out of the special exhibition mill, concentrating instead on her collection's reinstallation. This project with the architects Kevin Roche and John Dinkeloo was "perhaps the most ambitious installation of ancient Egyptian objects in the world.[37] The museum and architects decided to place every single object on display in more or less chronological order. Accomplished in three phases over a period of 12 years, the result was a counterclockwise hippodromic design with the large sculpture and many of the masterpieces in the center and on the edges of the oval track, each given its spatial due. Smaller side galleries cached here and there hold shelf upon shelf of tightly packed smaller treasures or plainer objects, along with some popular favorites, such as the Middle Kingdom faience hippo, "William," to encourage and reward the visitor's extra effort.

The Met lavished great expense on climate control, both active and passive.[38] These efforts were directed not only at the large gallery spaces, but within individual cases (micro-climates), taking into account the different needs of human and animal remains, ancient linen, wood, bronze, and so on. In the words of the pharaohs, "never had the like occurred before this time." It takes an "angel" to stand behind such an effort financially, and the Met had that in their great patron, Lila Acheson Wallace, "who bore the costs not only of design and construction but of personnel and of allocations in the museum, so that the project could be completed as rapidly as it was."[39]

In Paris, I. M. Pei's 1997 redesign of the entrance, admissions, and commercial areas of the Grand Louvre forced a reinstallation of the Egyptian collection and provided a bit more space, since one of the entrances from outside was blocked off, unfortunately allowing no quick access to ancient Egypt. Here again curators desired to place as many objects as possible on view. Only a certain amount of change in the format of the galleries could be achieved, since the ground floor necessarily held the heaviest statues, coffins, and temple elements. However, some of the galleries on that level were rearranged into themes central to Egyptian civilization, such as agriculture and the importance of the Nile River, while the galleries in the floor above were arranged to present chronologically the objects that would fit well into the antique palace chambers.

Victoria Newhouse made a study of the difference between the Parisian and the New York approach to special exhibition design with particular regard to the exhibit, "Egyptian Art in the Age of the Pyramids."[40] At the Grand Palais Ziegler used the bright, rich hues and elements of ancient decorative design to "color-code" various parts of the exhibition, and in particular to separate royal from nonroyal sculpture. At the Met, Dorothea Arnold preferred muted sand tones and separated her two types by placement. New Yorkers would probably have been horrified by the Parisian design, and Parisians would probably have been bored with the New York design, but each worked well within its own walls and for its own public.

The British Museum's Egyptian galleries actually lost square footage due to Norman Foster 's redesign of the former Library into a public services center, including ticketing, shops, and cafes, with a tiny special exhibition gallery perched above the old reading room, now encased in stone like a time capsule. Most of the 90,000 objects, the largest collection of Egyptian artifacts outside Egypt, are in storage. The department, however, led by keeper W. Vivian Davies, has an active and generous lending program, and nearly a thousand of its objects are on loan to special exhibitions in institutions throughout the world at any given time.[41]

Like the Louvre's, the British Museum's Egyptian collection is on two floors, with the heaviest and largest sculpture on the ground floor and the smaller, lighter objects upstairs. A relatively new feature of the installation is a gallery devoted entirely to Nubia. The Museum of Fine Arts, Boston, is another of the few museums that have devoted entire galleries to ancient Nubia. This room, comprising mostly small material, is on the ground floor, as well as another room devoted mostly to funerary material, while contrary to the British Museum and the Louvre, the large, heavy pieces, such as the colossal seated Mycerinus, the Middle Kingdom granodiorite Sennuwy, and Ptolemy VIII's gateway, are on the floor above.

Many of the older collections have been renovated in recent years, including those in Turin, housed in Guarino Guarini's Palazzo dell'Accademia delle Scienze; at the Oriental Institute, Chicago, which opened in May 1999; at the Ashmolean Museum, September 2003; and at the Fitzwilliam Museum, May 2006.[42]

With Cleveland's major renovation by Rafael Vignoly due to open in 2008, the Egyptian galleries will hopefully be reinstalled in space fifty percent larger than before in order to place virtually all of the museum's artifacts on display. A small collection of only about 500 objects, Cleveland's is better suited to a thematic display, and current plans call for three themes: royal and divine, private, and funerary. These are essentially the same ideas used by Champollion when arranging the Louvre's Egyptian holdings in the early nineteenth century, and it works well for small collections chosen more for aesthetic impact than to fill historical or archaeological gaps.

Most of these installations, as wonderful as they are, suffer from the same problem: inadequate or incorrect lighting. Some museums show their stone sculpture in galleries with large windows, aiming for the sunlight to work its magic as it did in the homeland, where the sun was literally and figuratively divine. The problems are (1) that sunlight cannot be controlled and (2) that neither the intensity nor the color of the sunlight in New York, Paris, and London, for example, is anything like that in Egypt. As John Walsh, director emeritus of the J. Paul Getty Museum, has written, "of the hundreds of millions of dollars expended by museums for new construction and upkeep each year, very little gets spent to improve the lighting – being certain that the light is sympathetic and as correct for the objects as it can possibly be . . . There is a whole literature on museum lighting, mostly unread by curators and architects."[43]

CACHETTES AND PYLONS

The storage areas of the Museum of Fine Arts, Boston, were at one time legendary for, as the myth goes, a cat who made her home there quite happily until she gave birth to several kittens and was adopted by a staff member. Then the trouble started, first with a spurt in the rodent population, and then, once they were eradicated, with an efflorescence of the insects that the mice used to eat. Nowadays, Egyptian art storage at the MFA is a model of organization and nearly surgical cleanliness. It is almost as spacious as the galleries above, with every item carefully photographed and documented under the aegis of a staff member whose full-time job is to administer this area. In almost all up-to-date museum storage rooms, as in Boston, "space-saver" shelves and cabinets, which can be rolled slowly along tracks, allowing one open aisle at a time among several units, have greatly increased capacity.

Egyptian collection storage rooms increasingly came under scrutiny and demand for updating in the last decades of the twentieth century with increased sophistication in the area of object conservation. A hundred years earlier, the field was more one of restoration – putting together fragments to create a more complete object, with little attention to creating friendly environments for the various materials in order to care for them better long-term. Now, as was the case at the Met's reinstallation, conservators have become as important to the process of planning installations and storage areas as are the curators.

Conservation has also become a more visible part of curatorial work and publications. Lawrence Berman's catalog of the Egyptian collection of the Cleveland Museum of Art includes a condition report on each object by conservator Patricia Griffin. Many of the more technically interesting pieces are accompanied by long materials-and-construction analyses by the same author. Florence Dunn Friedman's catalogue for the exhibition *Gifts of the Nile: Ancient Egyptian Faience* includes an entire chapter by Paul T. Nicholson on materials and technology.

MUSEUM AS EDUCATOR

The two banes of every museum goer's visit, and therefore every curator's career, are labels and seats. There are too many or too few of the former, and definitely not enough of the latter. The print on the labels is too small or the labels are too large, or they say too much, or they do not say the right things. They are placed too high in the case for the handicapped and children or too low for tall people with back problems. And then, as Regine Schultz, curator of Egyptian art at the Walters Art Gallery, asked, "How do you prepare labels for a local, urban public that is 50 percent illiterate?"[44] At the other end of the spectrum, the Metropolitan's installation of Hatshepsut used the phrase "Hathoric wig" on a label, as though a large number of their audience would know the meaning of that phrase or would have the wits to look it up.

FIGURE 8.6. Museum staff in conference, British Museum. Courtesy of S. Woodhouse.

School children often study ancient Egypt in their primary school years. A number of museums have created special programs for them, including Cleveland's Egyptomania package, which includes workbooks and "teacher resource" guides. Several museums have on-site study centers devoted to school children.

Symposia and special research opportunities are provided by some museums for staff and visiting colleagues. The British Museum (Fig. 8.6) is especially strong in this area, producing an important symposium every July in conjunction with the annual Sackler lecture. The papers are then published in a monograph. Some of the subjects covered in recent years[45] have been Nubia, temples, and the Theban necropolis. In addition, the Department maintains on its own premises a large library run by Egyptologist Susanne Woodhouse, an invaluable resource for both staff and colleagues. In the Western Hemisphere, the greatest library resource is the Wilbour Library of Egyptology at the Brooklyn Museum.[46] Once housed within the Egyptian department on the museum's third floor, the library has now been moved to the museum's central library, with plans to refurbish the original space and discussions under way for a new space. However, reorganization within the museum has now virtually destroyed the curatorial departments, dividing the curatorial staff between two "teams," one for collections and one for exhibitions,[47] thus casting a shadow on the Wilbour Library's future.

One of the few museums actively engaged in producing catalogs of discrete portions of its large collection is the Louvre. Recent additions to its publications list include volumes on ushabtis, ancient shoes, Old Kingdom sculpture, Middle Kingdom sculpture, and Greco-Roman terra cottas.[48]

THE WORLD WIDE WEB – EGYPTOLOGY'S ELECTRONIC FALSE DOOR

The World Wide Web is today's version of the ancient false door – the magic portal into another world – except with a reverse directional flow. Sitting at home, school, wherever, in front of an impenetrable piece of hardware, the living pass – as if by magic – across oceans, through walls and locked doors, into Egyptological collections throughout the world. Virtually anything one writes about the Web and how museums use it today will be out of date tomorrow. Even so, looking at a selection of Web sites opens a window into the personalities and priorities of each museum.

The Cairo Museum starts its Web site (www.egyptianmuseum.gov.eg) with a brief introduction of the museum's history. Each month a new Piece of the Month is featured, June 2006 being a triad of Menkaure. Search options allow the virtual visitor to view 250 objects arranged in the following categories: jewelry, funerary objects, Tutankhamen, and statuary. Each object is clearly identified by title, date, material, and so forth, with a brief paragraph giving insight and information for the general visitor. Another option is a virtual tour of the museum's galleries, room by room, with a tiny map showing the location in red; however, it is hard to use because the pictures are so small.

A Web site that excels in such a feature is the British Museum's (www.thebritishmuseum. ac.uk), designed by Nigel Strudwick. A map of each gallery has thumbnail images of the more important or intriguing works of art. Clicking on a thumbnail brings up a larger, beautifully photographed image and a great deal of relevant information. One more click makes the picture nearly full screen size.

The Louvre's Web site (www.louvre.fr) has 191 of the Louvre's more important Egyptian objects available for remote viewing. Those who wish more in-depth study are invited to contact the research department.

On the Museum of Fine Arts, Boston, Web site (www.mfa.org), the Egyptian, Nubian, and Greek and Roman departments are found within *The Art of the Ancient World*. Twenty-five well-chosen Egyptian objects form the highlights tour. Particularly satisfying is the advanced search, which allows the virtual visitor to enter a keyword, such as "Menkaure," and arrive at page after page of statues of all sizes and related funerary implements, all from Reisner's excavations at Giza.

The Metropolitan Museum's pithy and informative introduction to the Egyptian department and its history (www.metmuseum.org) reads like a vintage *Encyclopaedia Britannica* entry on the history of collecting Egyptian art in America. Their search process is more cumbersome than Boston's and sometimes yields surprising results. For example, a keyword search for Amenhotep III turned up fifty-two European paintings in addition to the desired objects, because the Roman numeral "III" occurred somewhere in their labels.

Electronic resources such as these did not become widely available until the eve of the twenty-first century. Now up-to-date museums throughout the world devote enormous financial and human resources to creating, revamping, enlarging, and designing collection Web sites. Their sophistication, ease of use, attractiveness, and breadth of information have grown exponentially in the few years since their inception and will undoubtedly continue to grow in the years to come.

And so, the question: Why bother going to museums if we can see everything we want on line?[49] The practiced museumgoer already knows the answer: Photos lie – or at least, they misrepresent, not intentionally, but inevitably. First is the question of scale. Monumental objects and small ones are all formatted to fit the size of the medium. We are used to this in television and are not likely to confuse the size of an aspirin bottle with the size of a Toyota because we are very familiar with these objects; however, the scale and impact of the unfamiliar ones are extremely difficult to judge even for professionals and even with the dimensions listed nearby. Second, photos and electronic images depend on lighting that casts some aspects into shadow, and rarely do they allow or invite truly close observation.

These and other failings of the small screen are apparent with experience. No online "hit" can compare with viewing in person the Metropolitan Museum's voluptuous yellow jasper lips of Queen Tiy or standing at the foot of the supercolossal limestone pair statue of Amenhotep III and Queen Tiy in the central hall of Cairo's Egyptian Museum. No photo can catch the shimmer, joy, and sense of piscatory movement in the British Museum's core-formed glass fish. But one has to have seen the original to understand the difference, with what John Walsh calls "a lingering examination of the original" that totally absorbs the viewer and transforms him or her emotionally and spiritually.[50]

The in-person experience has also changed a great deal with technological advances. In 1958, the National Gallery in Washington introduced radio receivers to pick up educational transmissions about its masterpieces.[51] In 1963, the Metropolitan Museum introduced an updated version, and gradually many if not most museums hired companies to help them write tapes to be played in gadgets slung over the shoulder. The latest innovation along this line is the iPod, the tiny mobile device onto which seemingly infinite recordings can be downloaded from a computer and then played back at will. Such is the actor Sam

Waterston's reading of a script prepared for him to accompany the Hatshepsut exhibition at the Metropolitan Museum.

THE FUTURE OF EGYPTOLOGY IN MUSEUMS

Most European museums are supported by governments. In the United States, most are private, with some supported partially or wholly by local, state, or federal government. Publicly supported institutions increasingly look to the private sector for support and vice versa. This has created new dimensions in the way museums are built and organized.

The current generation of museum trustees in the United States includes numbers of graduates of business schools and tends to search for "profit centers" within museums as ways of providing income. The Dendur wing serves that purpose for the Metropolitan, as it is often rented out as a reception or party space. Its glass shell architecture and space have served to inspire other such spaces, such as that planned in Cleveland, even though Cleveland's museum is not at the center of a thriving metropolis.

Thanks to King Tut, the relative success or failure of exhibitions and, in fact, of museums themselves is rated by the box office. Curators have also started to measure success by attendance, "even though they have had to witness their own status fall as a byproduct of this same process. . . . They have now become merely one division in a far-flung operation comprising education and public relations, special events and security, preparations and gift shops – terrifically expensive business in which the centrality of their own role could not help being eroded."[52]

It is true that contemporary audiences are attracted by novelty, excitement, and glitter, but many of those who come to art museums also come for a quality experience. For all of Tut's glamor, the exquisiteness of each object is also irrefutable. James Cuno has written about people going to museums in the days following September 11, "just to be there, quietly, safe in the company of things that are beautiful and impossibly fragile, yet that have lasted for centuries through war and tumult to lay claim still on our imaginations."[53] And Neil MacGregor has written of London's National Gallery staying open during the Blitz, showing one Old Master at a time, and that visitors feel it is "a place where ordinary people and rich patrons alike can touch base and feel they are part of a lively learning community, a place where they can know that they are not alone."[54]

In these gleaming glass and granite galleries where even the most fragile objects have an eternal presence, the effort that goes into acquiring, protecting, installing, elucidating, reexamining, and conserving is almost invisible to the public. This is what curators do. It takes years of study and hard work to achieve what appears effortless. Deep down the public understands this, because what they expect most from the great museums is authenticity and authoritativeness. Thus, the degree to which specialized curatorial work is either supported or eroded is the degree to which museums will continue to provide knowledge, entertainment, aesthetic quality, and stimulus for the imagination and spirit in the future.

NOTES

1. Newhouse 2005.
2. Cuno 2004: 73.
3. Lewis 2006: 36.
4. Lewis 2006: 36. On Hoving's organization of the exhibition, see: Hoving 1993: 401–14.
5. This figure comes from studies done by U.S. museum education departments for the American Association of Museums.
6. Wiese and Brodbeck 2004.
7. El-Saddik 2005: 31–5; Mansour 2005: 36–41.
8. Hawass 2005: 7–22.
9. Saleh and Sourouzian 1987;. Bongioanni and Croce 2001.
10. Romano 1979.
11. El-Saghir 1992.
12. Jaritz 2001: 20–3.
13. Radwan 2005: 87–90.
14. Zahi Hawass, personal communication, June 8, 2006.
15. Zahi Hawass, personal communication, June 9, 2006.
16. Schneider 1996.
17. James and Davies 1983; Andrews 1984; Edwards 1969.
18. Berman 2003: 11.
19. Dunham 1958.
20. Ziegler 1990.
21. Donadoni et al. 1988.
22. Staatliche Museen Preussicher Kulturbesitz 1982; Fay 1985; Priese 1991.
23. Hayes 1990.
24. Cooney 1956; Bothmer and Keith 1970; Fazzini 1975; Fazzini et al. 1989; Ferber et al. 1987.
25. See Jenkins 1992: 102 for early attitudes toward Egyptian artifacts.
26. Kozloff 1997: 10–40.
27. Ikram et al. 2006: 55.
28. El-Aref 2005.
29. Pearlstein 2005: 21–4.
30. Slayman 2006: 20.
31. For these exhibitions see the following: Brooklyn: Fazzini and Bianchi 1988. Cleveland and the Louvre: Kozloff and Bryan 1992. Hildesheim: Eggebrecht 1987. San Francisco and the Metropolitan Museum: Roehrig *et al.* 2005.
32. For exhibitions for longer periods see the following: New York/Paris/Toronto: Arnold et al. 1999. Boston: Brovarski et al. 1982; and Freed et al. 1999.
33. For exhibitions focusing on specific topics see the following: Cincinnati: Capel and Markoe 1996. Rhode Island: Friedman 1998. Boston: D'Auria et al. 1988.
34. Wildung 1996; Welsby and Anderson 2004.
35. For the "encyclopedic" exhibitions see the following: Vienna: Seipel 1992. Cleveland and the Louvre: Berman and Letellier 1996. University of Pennsylvania: Silverman 1997. The Palazzo Grassi: Ziegler 2002.
36. For the "focus shows" mentioned see the following: The Metropolitan Museum of Art: Allen 2005 and Arnold 1996. The Louvre: Andreu 2002.
37. Lilyquist 1984: 85–91.

38. Barrette 1985: 81–4.
39. Lilyquist 1984: 91.
40. Newhouse 2005: 108–41
41. For example, Russmann 2001; Taylor and Strudwick 2005.
42. On the renovation of these older collections see the following: Turin: Newhouse 2005: 137; for Chicago: Teeter 2000: 41–3; for the Ashmolean Museum: Whitehouse 2004: 12–13.
43. Walsh 2004: 91.
44. Personal communication, April 27, 2006.
45. Nubia: Friedman 2002. Temples: Quirke 1997. The Theban Necropolis: Strudwick and Taylor 2003.
46. Houlihan 2003.
47. Kennedy 2006.
48. Bovot 2003; Montembault 2000; Ziegler 1997; Delange 1987; Dunand 1990.
49. For related thoughts, see Stille 2002: 3–39, 332–9.
50. Walsh 2004: 79 ff.
51. Kennedy 2006.
52. Lewis 2006: 36.
53. Cuno 2004: 49.
54. MacGregor 2004: 42–5.

CHAPTER 9

ARTIFACT CONSERVATION AND EGYPTOLOGY

Susanne Gänsicke

The ancient Egyptians were masters in the field of preservation, specifically of perishable, organic substances and most notably of human and animal remains. In their desire to secure the elements of mortal life for an eternal one, the Egyptians provided a lasting repository of their existence. Thus have survived, in addition to a rich architectural heritage, sculpture and written records, remarkable items of daily use, decorated furniture, jewelry, and funerary materials, sometimes in visually almost unchanged condition, which continue to delight and astound us today.

The fascination with Egypt dates back to ancient times. The concentrated and systematic effort with which Western archaeology in the nineteenth century began to explore, collect, and study ancient civilizations, however, provided an unparalleled flow of objects into rapidly forming collections. The work of these archaeologists was accompanied by activities of treasure hunters and for hundreds of years travelers returned from Egypt with antiquities, while other objects found their way through the labyrinthine world of the art market. As a result, Egyptian objects can be found almost worldwide in diverse institutions such as large encyclopedic museums, small specialized museums, universities, and private and other collections. Museums outside of Egypt by and large focus on managing their existing collections, which are augmented by occasional acquisitions, but do not receive objects from active excavations. Museums in Egypt, in contrast to collections elsewhere, continue to be enriched by additions from ongoing archaeological activities.

In the following chapter, the general principles of conservation practice and their development over time, as well as how they relate to the needs of Egyptology, will be introduced. Emphasis will be given to institutional collections as opposed to conservation during excavation, which, although closely related to conservation in a museum laboratory, is a separate discipline within the field. The multifaceted role that conservators and other conservation professionals play in meeting increasing demands on collections will be discussed and the changing standards of the profession, often led by technological developments, will be illustrated. Appendices provide material-specific information, a glossary of common conservation terminology, and other resources for further exploration of conservation issues and issues related to the study and preservation of Egyptian collections.

DEVELOPMENT OF THE CONSERVATION PROFESSION

In Egypt, sealed tomb chambers have provided an almost ideal setting due to the absence of natural light and relatively stable climatic conditions. Tombs did not prevent, however, the introduction of insects, mold activity, groundwater, or chemicals interacting with and altering the entombed objects. Other Egyptian objects originate from more diverse environments. Architectural elements from temples and palaces were exposed to weathering conditions. Some objects are excavated in the agricultural areas, where the soil provides a moist and often saline matrix. More recently, significant objects have also been retrieved from salt water of the ocean bed, for example, in the ancient port of Alexandria. The rate at which materials degrade is furthermore influenced by original use, manufacturing flaws, or inherent defects.

Early archaeologists were acutely aware that by unearthing and exposing ancient artifacts they also greatly endangered them. Driven by their concerns about damage and loss, some nineteenth-century archaeologists, such as William Flinders Petrie, experimented in developing methods of preservation for artifacts, and it is known that favorite recipes were exchanged among colleagues.[1] The true pioneers of conservation, however, were chemists. The first chemical laboratory devoted to the preservation and study of ancient materials was founded by Friedrich Rathgen in Berlin in 1888 and his handbook on conservation of antiquities, translated into English in 1905, influenced and guided many in their work.[2] In Egypt, the British chemist Alfred Lucas began working for the Antiquities Service in 1923. He is most notable, next to his involvement in the treatment of objects from the tomb of Tutankhamun, for his extensive analytical work on Egyptian materials, which to date remains a vital resource.[3] In the following decades many leading museums set up laboratories and workshops whose operations were based on varying scientific standards.

The conservation profession as it exists today stems from further developments in the second half of the twentieth century, when the first academic training programs were instituted, and national and international professional organizations were founded. Prior to then, most training was apprenticeship based and much of the profession was crafts oriented. Conservators at present are professional hybrids who combine expertise in different disciplines, including art history, chemistry, materials science, and studio art, with exquisite hand skills. Conservation comprises five fundamental functions: examination, documentation, stabilization, restoration, and prevention. In their actions, conservators are bound by a professional code of ethics.[4] Conservation and preservation professionals can perhaps be best compared to the medical profession, which has evolved in comparable ways. Most scientific techniques employed in the examination of objects are borrowed from medicine: x-radiography, CT scanning, and other sophisticated quantitative and qualitative techniques used by analytical chemistry. A heavy focus lies on prevention; treatments are carried out with less intervention using increasingly sophisticated methods; and much of the care is given by practitioners. Similarly, in museums, conservators are supported by collections care specialists, conservation engineers, mount makers, preparators, art handlers, art packers, and installers.

Five universities in North America offer conservation training at the graduate level; one of these programs offers a specialization in archaeological conservation. During their studies, conservators tend to specialize in different categories of materials such as paintings, books, paper and photography, textiles, or objects. The last discipline, focused on three-dimensional objects of all materials and historic backgrounds, exists mainly in the English-speaking world, and predominantly in North America, where the encyclopedic nature of most museums generated a need for this broad specialization. In contrast, conservators in Europe tend to concentrate on a particular type of material, such as stone, metals, or polychromed wood, or on a classification such as archaeological conservation, and training programs exist at a much greater variety of levels in private studios and at colleges and universities.

To date, no program in the West offers exclusive training in the conservation of Egyptian objects, and specialization usually occurs within a framework of employment, most often by conservators of objects or archaeological materials. International symposia have focused on the conservation and technical study of Egyptian materials, and a substantial body of conservation literature deals with their specific problems.[5] Recently, in the tradition of Lucas's work, an updated review of the analysis of materials and techniques has been published.[6]

CURRENT CONSERVATION PRACTICES

On the whole, conservation of Egyptian materials does not differ from conservation of any other types of objects: the same principles are valid. Naturally, a number of particulars are unique to Egypt. Certain materials were predominantly used, manufactured, or invented in Egypt, such as Egyptian faience, certain pigments, and the use of specific organic varnishes and surface coatings, as well as the entire group of substances related to mummification. Intrinsic characteristics of natural Egyptian materials, such as sedimentary limestone, can lead to very specific problems. Soil chemistry, arid desert conditions, and other factors of the Egyptian environment produce deterioration patterns that differ from those observed on archaeological objects from, for example, northern Europe.

It is common practice in archaeology to block-lift delicate objects or complexes that may be surrounded by soil and to excavate and treat them under controlled laboratory conditions. As mentioned above, such work will rarely be required on Egyptian objects in Western collections today. Some Egyptian collections outside of Egypt, however, contain material excavated many decades ago, which has never been treated and which sometimes resides, still heavily encrusted with soil, in original excavation crates.

Conservation treatments are approached mindful of the materials from which objects are made, of their original appearance, and of all aspects – ancient and modern – that may have led to alteration. The environmental conditions to which objects have been exposed have a profound impact on their condition, as their chemical stability and structural integrity are affected by various internal and external factors, leading to more or less apparent alterations. Some of those changes take place over long periods of time, while others can occur quickly and may be noticed even over very short periods. Most chemical and structural changes are permanent and cannot be reversed, but some ongoing destructive processes can be controlled or halted, preventing or minimizing future damage. Fundamental to modern conservation is the principle of reversibility, which demands that materials and methods should be selected on the basis that they will remain removable without altering or damaging the original materials, and for their stability and aging properties.

Conservation practice makes a distinction between conservation of archaeological materials and conservation of decorative or fine art.[7] Particularly, the first contact with and examination of freshly excavated objects can be compared with aspects of forensic science, as every minute detail can provide information about the ancient context. Original surface treatments such as paint or patination may be barely discernible, and organic residue in containers may not be visible but reside in microscopic traces. Thus, even light cleaning can only proceed after thorough examination.

In archaeological collections, the fragmentary and incomplete condition of objects is often fully acceptable. At the same time, while still of archaeological origin, many Egyptian objects are considered to be fine art and are thus supplied with a high degree of integration of losses and cosmetic treatment. Conservators aid in the reconstruction and, thus, interpretation of objects, and through skilled work damaged pieces of artwork can be resurrected. Opinions about how much restoration is appropriate or how much restoration should be integrated with the original material can radically change over time. Likewise, the understanding of how much age an object is allowed to show varies. Depending on the institutional identity and philosophy, different standards apply and the conservator's obligation to preserve all ancient physical evidence can conflict with curators' vision of restoration and presentation.

Equally, thoughts about what aspects of an object were deemed worth preserving have changed. In past centuries, mummies were sometimes destroyed in the search for embedded precious metal items! Most curators place greater value on excavated objects, which can be fully understood in a well-provenanced context, than on pieces without secure provenance. Fiscal and spatial restrictions of institutions can also influence the selection of conservation priorities. Chosen objects, selected either for their significance in themselves or for their role within a specific collection, may receive involved and lengthy treatments, while others, often large groups of repetitive materials, may be better served by proper documentation and storage without treatment.

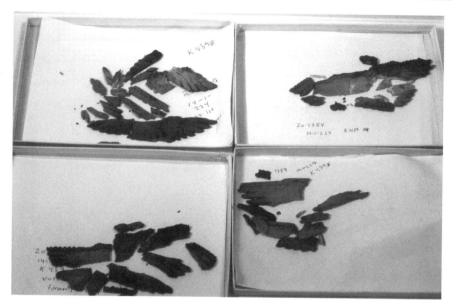

FIGURE 9.1. Fragments of vulture-shaped ivory inlays before treatment. Kerma, Sudan, Tumulus IV, tomb K 439. Late Classic Kerma, 1630–1600 BC. Photo: Courtesy of S. Gänsicke.

Excavated objects were frequently treated in the field, but specifics of field treatments were often only scantily recorded. Even less is known about the recent history of undocumented objects. Some old restorations were done by highly skilled sculptors; their preservation in conjunction with ancient fragments can be of considerable importance. Many interventions were carried out with the best intentions using the prevalent methods of the time, but it has become apparent that often the materials used did not age as well as the ancient substances they were meant to preserve. Thus, today's treatments address not only damage that occurred over millennia, but also damage related to recent treatments.[8]

In the late nineteenth century, the use of natural materials such as wax, glue, and shellac to strengthen objects and to mend breaks was widespread. Melted wax, for example, was applied to objects during excavation when they were too fragile to be lifted. While in the short term successful, the wax treatments often darkened and severely disfigured the objects over time (Fig. 9.1). Prolonged soaking in organic solvents to remove such wax allowed the reconstruction of ancient ivory inlays at the MFA (Fig. 9.2). Glue and shellac, on the other hand, become brittle or contract over time and, thus, easily cause damage of softer ancient surfaces to which they were applied (Fig. 9.3). In the early twentieth century, synthetic resins began to be used as they became available, but some discolored and others become intractable, making it difficult to undo joins and repairs. As mentioned, surface cleaning is irrevocable and the term *overcleaned* is commonly used in reference to some older treatments. Metals excavated in Egypt, in particular bronze and silver, tend to

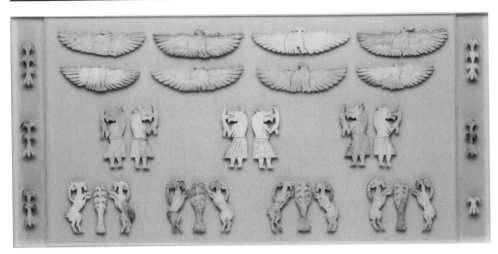

FIGURE 9.2. Twenty-four reconstructed ivories mounted in a suggested original arrangement that would have decorated the footboard of a burial bed. Kerma, Sudan, Tumulus IV, tomb K 439. Late Classic Kerma, 1630–1600 BC. Photograph © Museum of Fine Arts, Boston.

be heavily corroded due to acidic or alkaline soil conditions. The corrosion can be thick and disfiguring to such a degree that the shape of an object is hard to discern. In the worst cases, corrosion leads to complete disintegration and loss. In the past, aggressive chemical and electrochemical cleaning methods were used both to halt corrosion and to expose a surface with the metallic luster that we are accustomed to on modern metals. In the process, the metallographic structure of the ancient metal may be forever altered and information about the manufacturing process lost. Surface details embedded within the corrosion products are discarded. Often the chemicals used were not completely neutralized, resulting in secondary corrosion, which can also be caused by inappropriate adhesives (Fig. 9.4).

Salts that have impregnated a material during burial react to fluctuations in relative humidity with changes in their state of crystallization. The pressure related to the formation of salt crystals within or underneath the surface can lead to severe damage (Fig. 9.5). Decades ago, stone with such salt-related problems was soaked in water, with hopes of washing out saline contaminants. Since then, it has been proven that such baths can be extremely harmful, endangering the composition of certain types of stone. Often original polychromy was washed away.

Today, unstable objects, such as corroding metals or objects impregnated with salts, often are successfully stabilized using less aggressive methods, including local consolidation and tightly sealed environments with stable relative humidity.

Retreatment and reinterpretation based on new scholarship allows sometimes surprising results. Ten years ago, sandstone blocks of a relief at the Museum of Fine Arts, Boston (MFA), were recognized as elements of a monumental gateway.[9] Extensive treatment and

FIGURE 9.3. Previously used adhesive darkened and contracted over time and damaged the original underlying surface of this ceramic bowl. Predynastic Period. 3950–3100 BC. Emily Esters Sears Fund. MFA 03.1581. Photo: Courtesy of S. Gänsicke.

ingenious engineering solutions resulted in a full-sized reconstruction, which traveled to three exhibition venues within the United States and is now on permanent display in Boston (Figs. 9.6 and 9.7).

Technological development has continued to change and advance the conservation profession. Increasingly refined and sophisticated analytical techniques allow a much greater degree of material identification, aided by growing databases of ancient materials and techniques. Thus, treatment of as yet untreated excavated material is approached more cautiously. Less invasive and highly controlled techniques have become prevalent, for example, the use of lasers in cleaning of mostly inorganic surfaces. Products are often borrowed from many other industries and are rarely developed specifically for conservation purposes. Recently, the use of cyclododecane, a volatile waxlike material, which can be melted and used to stabilize surfaces similarly to old-fashioned wax, has been used during excavations. It has a unique characteristic: over time, by sublimation it converges from a solid to a gaseous phase, thus leaving the ancient surface without any residue, eliminating unwieldy retreatments.

FIGURE 9.4. Bronze vessel showing turquoise-colored corrosion caused by an inappropriate adhesive. Tomb W 354/4 Meroe, Sudan. Meroitic Period. MFA 24.964. Photograph © Museum of Fine Arts, Boston.

The digital revolution has had a large impact on all aspects of documentation. Digital imaging allows immediate results, annotation, linkage to databases, and electronic dissemination and sharing of information. Special software allows virtual manipulation of objects, and imaging techniques have allowed visualization of underlying materials, designs, or shapes recorded in ultraviolet, in infrared light, or with the use of CT scanners. Databases have greatly facilitated data management of conservation records.

FIGURE 9.5. Detail of a limestone stele with severe surface disintegration due to the action of soluble salts. 5011, Sheikh Farag, Egypt. First Intermediate Period. 2100–2061 BC. MFA 25.659. Photograph © Museum of Fine Arts, Boston.

THE ROLE OF SCIENCE IN CONSERVATION

A number of large museums maintain departments for scientific analysis, often integrated with or connected to the conservation laboratories. Institutions without in-house facilities or lacking certain analytical techniques draw on the services of other museums or scientific laboratories. In general, analytical techniques can be divided into those that are nonde-structive (examination in ultraviolet or infrared light, X-Radiography, energy-dispersive

FIGURE 9.6. Installation of sandstone blocks from a gateway as a flat relief in the Late Period galleries of the Museum of Fine Arts, Boston, in 1931. Koptos, Egypt. Greco-Roman Period. Reign of Ptolemy VIII, 170–116 BC. MFA 24.1632, 24.1633. Photograph © Museum of Fine Arts, Boston.

X-ray fluorescence, Raman spectroscopy) and those that require samples, which may be tiny (scanning electron microscopy, Fourier transform infrared spectroscopy, gas chromatography/mass spectrometry, high-performance liquid chromatography, X-ray diffraction). Examination by CT scanning has been employed to investigate mummies and three-dimensional objects; it is commonly performed through collaboration with hospitals or industrial services.[10]

Scientific analysis of artwork is used to investigate a variety of subjects. Identification of materials and techniques employed in the manufacture of objects and of sources of raw materials is of considerable interest to archaeologists, Egyptologists, and conservators. The complexity of such examinations ranges from basic identification of a particular type of material, such as a pigment or metal alloy, to comprehensive research projects, such as investigation and reconstruction of an ancient production process or development of a chronology of manufacturing techniques. Research projects that center on questions of origin of materials such as metal ores, stones, or organic substances often require highly sophisticated analytical techniques and large, comparative databases.

Most museums require their conservators and scientists to examine potential acquisitions of antiquities, after issues of legal provenance have been cleared, to identify prior repairs

FIGURE 9.7. The reconstructed gateway from an enclosure of a temple at Koptos. Koptos, Egypt. Greco-Roman Period. Reign of Ptolemy VIII, 170–116 BC. MFA 24.1632, 24.1633. Photograph © Museum of Fine Arts, Boston.

and to assess the stability of an object and the integrity of its materials. In other cases, objects that have entered collections in the past may require careful reevaluation. A limited group of techniques, such as thermoluminescence and radiocarbon dating, are able to provide direct dating of ancient substances. Frequently, however, a combination of techniques helps to authenticate an object. x-radiography and elemental analysis, for example of a bronze figure, are useful in revealing repairs and alteration, manufacturing techniques, and alloy composition, necessary for comparison of similar excavated and datable examples. Most metals will form corrosion products over time that are highly distinct and can be

173

distinguished from modern patination. On the other hand, it is much more difficult to date a carved stone: deterioration patterns are less conclusive and petrographic identification may indicate a stone's source but not when it was carved. Increasingly, growing knowledge about ancient materials and work processes is helpful, but many questions remain very difficult to answer.

Analysis of materials and deterioration products is crucial to support the formulation of appropriate treatments. For example, different types of corrosion require specific chemical treatments, while the identification of soluble salts aids in the development of proper approaches for their stabilization.

Testing and evaluation of new conservation materials and techniques are predominantly conducted in university programs and at conservation institutes, but in many cases, studies have been undertaken in museum laboratories.

Increasing emphasis in the field of conservation is being placed on the prevention of damage to objects. A wide range of environmental factors can significantly influence an object's longevity. Conservation science aids in monitoring and evaluating exhibition materials used in case construction and for storage purposes, which will be discussed in greater detail below.

MUSEUM ACTIVITIES AND INTERACTION WITH CONSERVATION

Presentation, interpretation, and use of collections have changed according to trends. Often exhibition design has a direct impact on the safety and preservation of objects. Many institutions, for example, favored the vertical display of mummy cases, despite conservators' arguments that weak structural joins of wooden sarcophagi and human remains contained within them suffer from an upright position. Similarly, architectural elements such as reliefs, architraves, offering chapels, and gateways and much stone sculpture are better experienced by the visitor when viewed without the barrier of vitrines, yet any exposed surface suffers the risk of vandalism or simply soiling due to pollution or direct handling. Softer stones and polychrome surfaces can only endure limited cleaning and can show wear caused by repeated dusting. Some museums, such as the Metropolitan Museum in New York, have exhibited their Egyptian collections in their entirety with the use of condensed displays in study collections. Other institutions only display a fraction of their holdings, with the majority in storage. Such different approaches present different sets of problems and challenges for the preservation of these collections.

As mentioned, the environment, which includes biological activities, has a vital impact on materials. Exposure to high light levels promotes degradation of organic substances and certain pigments. Higher temperatures accelerate chemical processes such as corrosion, tarnish, and degradation. Fluctuating levels of relative humidity can lead to disastrous results in composite materials, which react with dimensional changes at different rates – flaking surfaces and paint layers may result. Certain general rules apply: metals are best kept dry to prevent corrosion or formation of tarnish, while organic materials are better kept at higher levels of humidity to prevent cracking and desiccation. Supervision of environmental conditions and their monitoring by mechanical or digital means, as well as monitoring of insect activity, fall into the sphere of conservation.[11]

Many collections are housed in older or historic buildings without climate control. The retrofitting of such buildings is often of prohibitive cost or for other reasons impossible. In these situations, exhibition cases and storage furniture can be fitted with chemicals to buffer humidity levels and create microclimates. The key to a successful microclimate lies in a well-sealed system with a minimal amount of leakage. Exhibition cases are most successful if they have a compartment that can be accessed from the outside, often under the exhibition deck, without removal of glass panels or the object itself, in order to exchange buffering or desiccating agents.

While exhibition cases and storage cabinets provide safety from physical damage and theft, they can have dangerous side effects.[12] In the past, cases and cabinets were often constructed from wood or wood products, and collections housed in them have shown new types of corrosion and efflorescence. This type of damage is directly related to gaseous pollution by acidic products released by construction materials. Wood is known to emit acetic acid, while formic acid derives from formaldehyde, often used in adhesives found in some types of particle board and plywood. A former favorite for case interiors, felt, consists of wool, which emits sulfur that can lead to tarnishing of metals and can attract insects. Ancient metal surfaces – or historic and modern ones, for that matter – cannot be cleaned repeatedly without loss of surface details. Thus, more recently, all materials that come into contact with artwork, in exhibition cases, storage cabinets, and shipping crates, are scrutinized and tests of proposed case material are conducted in conservation laboratories on a routine basis. The use of inert materials such as glass, Plexiglas, and metal for construction ultimately provides the best results. The interior atmospheres of cases can be further purified by the addition of materials to absorb gaseous pollutants using active or passive methods. Oxygen-free cases fed with inert gases provide the ultimate protection and have been employed to house unique cultural icons: the American Declaration of Independence and the royal mummies at the Cairo Museum.[13]

Installation, movement, and handling of objects require the advice of conservators who are familiar with the objects they have treated. As museums in many parts of the world are addressing the risk or reality of earthquakes, conservators and collections care specialists have paid increasing attention to properly securing objects. Small artifacts with stable surfaces are often secured with a small amount of wax. More delicate objects require the manufacture of custom-made armatures, which may consist of metal or custom-formed supports of synthetic resins. Jewelry, cartonnage, or bead nets are often secured on handmade forms that lend support to areas of fragility. Larger objects such as heavy sculptures and architectural fragments are sometimes mounted on metal frames, the design of which frequently is the outcome of interdisciplinary consultation with architects and structural engineers. Applied armatures allow heavy machinery such as forklifts and gantries to grasp

175

the mounts rather than the fragile edges of the actual objects; in earthquake zones metal armatures are used to secure the mounted objects.

One of the major challenges and contradictions in preserving art in a museum is the mandate to make art accessible, although limited exposure would be most beneficial to its preservation. This might demand a permanent museum display, but more often it also requires objects to be shipped great distances and suffer the rigor of travel, as the many popular Egyptian shows currently circling the globe can attest. To address these needs, a growing number of American museums have added specialized exhibitions conservators to their staffs, who develop strategies to minimize impact of travel and display to prevent wear or actual damage. Communications between museums a long time prior to the actual opening date of an exhibition focus on all particular needs of specific loan objects to secure that they will be met. The planning processes can be difficult. If a multivenue exhibition, for example, is scheduled to travel to international institutions, language barriers and varying standards for display and conservation can be problematic. Conservators and other museum specialists typically travel with the objects from their collections to monitor unpacking, installation, and the condition of objects. Detailed written reports and photographs document changes during exhibition and provide details on all existing damages, areas of fragility, or concern.

Beyond consultation on safekeeping of objects on exhibition and while on loan, conservators in many institutions are deeply involved in formulating plans for disaster preparedness.

CONCLUSIONS

Conservators are advocates for the preservation of the collections with which they have been entrusted. They carry out their work in collaboration with other museum staff, striving to maintain the highest standards of the profession, while developing innovative solutions to meet the needs of their collections along with comprehensive risk management. A look backward to the beginnings of conservation demonstrate that every generation of caretakers covers only a very short period of time in the long life of an object. As philosophies have changed within a short time frame, we recognize that any intervention has thus to be carried out in a fashion that must not hinder future treatment and research and that prevents side effects. A growing understanding of interactions and changes in materials has led to a more conservative stance.

NOTES

1. Petrie 1904.
2. Rathgen 1905.
3. Lucas 1932; Gilberg 1998.

4. American Institute for Conservation, *Code of Ethics and Standards of Practice*. 1717 K Street, NW, Suite 200, Washington, DC 20036.
5. Watkins and Brown 1988; Brown, Macalister, and Wright 1995; Schorsch forthcoming.
6. Nicholson and Shaw 2000.
7. Cronyn 1990; Pye 2001.
8. Gänsicke et al. 2003.
9. Larkin 1995.
10. Wildung 1992 [1993].
11. Thompson 1994.
12. Hatchfield 2002; Tétreault 2003.
13. Maekawa 1998.
14. Muros and Hirx 2004.
15. Tite 1987; Vergès 1992; Ellis and Newman 2005.
16. Bradley and Hanna 1986; Bradley and Middleton 1988; Garland and Rogers 1995; Nunberg, Heywood, and Wheeler 1996; Gibson *et al.* 1997; Thickett, Lee, and Bradley 2000; Rodriguez-Navarro et al. 1998.
17. Gale and Stos-Gale 1981; Newman 1990; Frantz and Schorsch 1990; Becker, Pilosi, and Schorsch 1994; Drayman-Weisser 1994; Beale 1996; La Niece et al. 2002.
18. Jaeschke and Jaeschke 1990; Chiotasso and Sarnelli 1996; Newman 1998; Scott et al. 2004; Farrell, Snow, and Vinogradskaya 2006.
19. Hatchfield 1986; Hatchfield and Koestler 1987; Blanchette et al. 1994.

APPENDIX 1
Most Common Ancient Egyptian Materials: Their Uses and Prevalent Damages as a Result of Burial or Exposure

Material	Specific materials and their use	Leading factors that cause changes in condition	Common treatments
Ceramic/faience[14] (Selected references to conservation and analysis of the different materials can be found in endnotes)	*Ceramic (mostly earthenware):* – undecorated: vessels, figures, coffins, molds – decorated (burnished, fired paint, inlays, applied paint, varnish): vessels, figures, coffins *Egyptian faience:* – beads, amulets, tiles, vessels, small sculptures	*Chemical:* – water, acidic or alkaline soil conditions: leach out components of body and weaken ceramic – stains (organic or inorganic): disfigure surface – salts: impregnate the body, can lead from surface loss to complete disintegration – accretions: deposits on surface, disfiguring, can lead to loss of surface *Physical:* – impact: cracking, breakage – abrasion: loss of surface detail/decoration – thermal shock: cracking, breakage – plant roots: deposits on surface, cracks, breaks – interaction with original content: can lead to swelling and results in cracking of ceramic	*Surface:* – removal of soil/dirt/accretions/ stains using mechanical or chemical methods – consolidation of surface, glaze or surface decoration *Structural:* – desalination, commonly in baths – consolidation of ceramic body – reattaching broken parts/reassembly of broken object – compensation of losses
Glass[15]	*Glass:* – vessels, amulets, beads, inlays *Glass frit:* – amulets, paint, glaze	*Chemical:* – water, acidic or alkaline soil conditions: leaching of glass components leading to corrosion – stains (organic or inorganic): disfigure surface – improper composition of glass: can lead to disintegration – accretions: deposits on surface, disfiguring, can lead to loss of surface	*Surface:* – removal of soil/dirt/accretions/ stains using mechanical or chemical methods – consolidation of corroded surface *Structural:* – reattaching broken parts/reassembly of broken object – compensation of losses

Stone[16]

Igneous rock (plutonic):
- granite, granodiorite, quartzdiorite: sculpture, coffins, architectural elements

Igneous rock (magmatic):
- basalt, porphyry

Metamorphic rock:
- marble, gneiss, serpentine: figures and sculpture, small utilitarian items

Sedimentary rock:
- schist/graywacke, sandstone, quartzite, limestone, calcite, anhydrite: architecture, sculpture, coffins, vessels

Other:
- minerals, semiprecious stones: jewelry, inlays, pigments

Physical:
- impact: cracking, breakage
- abrasion: loss of surface detail/decoration
- thermal shock: cracking, breakage
- plant roots: deposits on surface, cracks, breaks
- interaction with original content: can lead to swelling, cracking

Chemical:
- water, acidic or alkaline soil: leaching, etching, dissolution, can lead to expansion of clay layers in sedimentary stone and result in cracking
- biological agents: stains, etching
- exposure to metals or organic compounds: staining
- corrosion of embedded metallic particles or veins: leads to cracking of igneous rock
- salts: impregnate the stone, can lead from surface loss to complete disintegration
- accretions: deposits on surface, disfiguring, can lead to loss of surface and applied decoration

Physical:
- weathering agents and mechanisms: water, freeze–thaw cycles, thermal expansion, abrasion by wind-blown particles
- corrosion of metal dowels or clamps: can lead to cracking

Human intervention:
- vandalism, iconoclasm, reuse
- environmental pollution: deposit of crusts, leaching

Surface:
- removal of soil/dirt/accretions/ stains using mechanical or chemical methods
- consolidation of surface or surface decoration

Structural:
- removal of salts using poultices
- passive control of salts at controlled relative humidity
- consolidation of friable or unstable stone
- reassembly of broken parts, sometime using internal dowels
- filling of losses for support
- external armatures for support and transport

(continued)

APPENDIX 1 (continued)

Material	Specific materials and their use	Leading factors that cause changes in condition	Common treatments
		Seismic activity: – dislocation, breakage	
Metals[17]	*Gold and gold leaf:* – jewelry, surface decoration, vessels, funerary items *Silver:* – jewelry, vessels, surface decorations *Electrum:* – jewelry, vessels, surface decorations *Copper and copper alloys:* – sculptures and figures, vessels, utilitarian items, blades, architectural elements *Iron:* – blades, utilitarian items *Lead:* – figures, amulets	*Chemical:* – water, acidic or alkaline soil: corrosion, accretions – salts: active corrosion/chemical instability – alteration of surface: loss of patina, polish, plating – disfiguring corrosion – tarnish *Physical:* – impact: deformation, cracking, breakage – abrasion: loss of surface detail/decoration – plant roots: deposits on surface, cracks, breaks – accretions: deposits on surface, disfiguring, can lead to loss of surface – failure of joins due to corrosion	*Surface:* – removal of soil/dirt/accretions/stains using mechanical or chemical methods – removal of disfiguring corrosion – consolidation of surface decoration such inlays, patination, or gilding – preservation of organic materials replicated by corrosion products (pseudomorphs) *Structural:* – treatment of active corrosion using corrosion inhibitors or other chemical methods – reassembly – application of support materials
Miscellaneous organics[18]	*Plant fibers:* – basketry/ropes/papyrus/mats *Flax (linen):* – textiles, sails, cartonnage *Feathers:* – fans *Fur/hair:* – wigs, clothing, furniture	*Biodeterioration:* – fungal (rot)/bacterial/insects: surface damage, structural damage, disintegration *Chemical:* – water, acidic or alkaline soil: decomposition *Physical:* – impact: breakage	*Surface:* – removal of soil/dirt/accretions/stains using mechanical or chemical methods – consolidation of brittle/unstable substances *Surface:* – reattaching broken elements

	Skin/leather: – clothes, furniture, weapons *Bone/ivory:* – sculpture, furniture *Food:* – funerary items *Resin/bitumen/wax:* – varnish, painting, mummification, ointment, incense *Human and animal remains:* – mummification	– light and high temperature: advances deterioration – changing relative humidity: cracks, splits, flaking of surface decorations/gilding	– consolidation of weak body of material – application of outer, supporting materials, such as tissue paper – filling of losses *Treatment of active infestation:* – chemical, thermal, or anoxic methods
Wood[19]	*Acacia:* – boats, masts, coffins *Sycamore fig:* – roof timbers, wagons, coffins *Tamarisk:* – construction, coffins, fuel *Date palm:* – roofing *Cypress:* – construction, statuary, furniture, monumental doors *Cedar from Lebanon:* – boats, monumental doors, sculpture, coffins *Ebony:* – furniture, inlays, sculpture *Painted/decorated/gilded surfaces:* – possible on all wooden surfaces	*Biodeterioration:* – fungal (rot)/bacterial/ insects: surface damage, structural damage, disintegration *Chemical:* – water, acidic or alkaline soil: decomposition – nonbiological deterioration (alkaline conditions) *Physical:* – impact: breaks, cracks, damage to surface decoration – light and high temperature: advances deterioration – changing relative humidity: cracks, splits, flaking of surface decorations/gilding – failure of joins	*Surface:* – removal of soil/dirt/accretions/ stains using mechanical or chemical methods – consolidation of brittle unstable substances *Structural:* – reattaching broken elements – consolidation of deteriorated wood – application of outer supporting materials, such as tissue paper – filling of losses *Treatment of active infestation:* – chemical, thermal, or anoxic methods

APPENDIX 2
Glossary of Conservation Terms

Abrasion: Partial or complete loss of original surface due to mechanical action.

Anoxic: Treatment of active infestation through asphyxiation in an oxygen-free microenvironment.

Accretion: Deposit of a foreign substance on the surface of an object, often accumulated over long periods of time during burial or by repetitive exposure to drips.

Art Sorb®: A product used to create or buffer specific levels of relative humidity in display cases, storage units, or packing crates.

Biodeterioration: Damage caused by living organisms such as insects, fungi, plants, and vertebrates, which may lead to physical losses of substances or to chemical deterioration as the result of secretion of chemicals.

Bronze disease: A process of cyclic corrosion of copper and copper alloys caused by the presence of chlorides, introduced during use or burial. Copper chlorides disintegrate at elevated levels of relative humidity and form small amounts of acid, which continuously further dissolves metallic copper. Bronze disease can be controlled with low relative humidity and the use of corrosion inhibitors.

Chip: An area of surface loss, usually small, most often caused by mechanical impact.

Conservator: A professional responsible for the various aspects of preservation and safekeeping of artwork, including examination, documentation, treatments, and preventive conservation.

Collections care specialist: A professional focused on aspects of preventive care, such as environmental control, handling, mount making, installation, packing, storage housing and maintenance, and integrated pest management.

Consolidation: Stabilization of a structurally weakened material by introducing a substance that will strengthen it. Most often a synthetic resin will be applied in dilute solution, which after setting will bridge gaps and fissures.

Corrosion: Degradation of a substance due to the presence of moisture and salts. Mostly refers to corrosion of metals, but also to deterioration of glass.

Corrosion inhibitor: A chemical compound or scavenger used to protect metals from, or reduce the rate of, tarnishing and corrosion.

Crazing: Surface damage visible as a network of fine cracks due to deterioration on glass and glazes, paint layers, and varnishes on a micro scale.

Data logger: A small instrument used to record temperature and relative humidity in galleries, exhibition cases, and shipping crates. Data can be downloaded to a computer. Various types of data loggers exist, including wireless devices.

Desiccated: An artificially dried environment, usually created by using silica gel. Also used to describe a deterioration state of organic objects, which have lost flexibility and have become embrittled.

Desalination: Treatment procedures aimed at removing or reducing soluble salts from the bodies of objects using a variety of baths or poultices.

Deterioration: Disintegration of a substance due to action of chemical or physical factors.

Discoloration: Color change of a surface due to staining after contact with foreign organic or inorganic substances or due to alteration such as fading or darkening after exposure to light.

Efflorescence: The formation of salt crystals on a surface. The source of salts may be intrinsic or can be related to original use, the burial environment, or modern treatment or pollutants.

Electrolytic reduction: A method favored in the late nineteenth and the earlier part of the twentieth century for remove corrosion layers from metal objects using a chemical solution (electrolyte) and electric current.

Erosion: Weathering caused by chemical or physical factors, such as water, wind-blown particles, freeze–thaw cycles, and chemical reactions.

Exfoliation: The irreversible loss of scales, flakes, or layers from a surface. Exfoliation may occur on exterior stones due to weathering, deterioration from salts, or freeze–thaw action.

Flaking: Type of deterioration causing small surface areas to detach from a substrate due to action of soluble salts, changes in dimensions due to humidity changes, or degradation of organic binders and varnishes.

Gesso: A white ground layer applied to stone, wood, cartonnage, and sometime metals, prior to application of paint, varnish, or gilding. Egyptian gesso commonly consists of finely ground calcium carbonate and organic binders; on stone surfaces Egyptian gesso can be of a pink color.

Hygrothermograph: This device records temperature and relative humidity on a chart, commonly over a period of one week. It is being replaced by digital data loggers.

Insect damage: Various forms of damage and loss inflicted by insects on organic materials, which can result in surface loss, tunneling, and complete disintegration.

Iridescence: Discoloration and color variations of deteriorated glazes and glass surfaces caused by the corrosion of glassy materials, which results in different diffraction of light.

Mineralization: Extreme state of corrosion of metal objects in which the metallic core has reverted into nonmetallic minerals.

Mold: Mold damage, related to a variety of fungi, can occur during burial in humid environments. It can lead to deterioration of organic materials and often to staining on inorganic substances. Mold control in a museum environment relies mostly on low levels of relative humidity.

Patina: A surface condition developed over long periods of time due to handling or exposure, which generally is viewed as desirable as a sign of age and authenticity.

Pitting: Deterioration pattern on metal, stone, or ceramic surfaces, caused most often by the presence of soluble salts resulting in small craterlike losses or corrosion pits.

Pollutant: In a museum environment, natural and human-made products such as materials used for cases and storage furniture, including wood products, paints, adhesive, fabrics, and gaskets, have the potential to emit harmful acidic gases that can lead to corrosion, tarnishing, and deterioration of artwork.

Poultice: A soft, permeable substance, dampened with an aqueous or solvent-based solution, which is applied to surfaces to solubilize and remove stains, accretions, or salts.

Powdering: An unstable surface condition caused by the actions of soluble salts, insect activity, or deterioration of binding material in paint layers.

Preventive conservation: Measures taken to prevent further or future damage to objects by providing pollutant-free storage and display conditions and appropriate light, humidity, and temperature levels.

Restoration: Treatment of artwork to re-create its original appearance, shape, and function as the primary aim with lesser or no emphasis on full preservation. Also used to describe filling of losses.

Reversibility: A guiding principle of conservation requiring that conservation treatments and interventions should be and remain removable in the future.

Salt decay: Damage caused to objects due to the presence of soluble salts. Salts react to changes of relative humidity, and different salts or mixtures of salts crystallize at different levels. The process of crystallization causes internal pressures that lead to surface damage such as powdering, flaking, and disintegration.

Silica gel: A synthetically made form of pure silica used to control humidity levels in exhibition cases, storage units, and shipping containers.

Soluble salts: Water-soluble chemicals, which can occur naturally in soil and water, and are introduced into the bodies of objects during burial. Salts can also be present as natural components in sedimentary stones or can interact with objects due to human-made pollution. Most common in archaeological contexts are chlorides, nitrates, and sulfates.

Spalling: A deterioration pattern of stone or ceramics in which the surface breaks up in layers, often as a result of salt action, freeze–thaw cycles, or swelling of clay layers.

Staining: Discoloration as a result of contact with or penetration by a foreign substance of organic or inorganic nature.

Subflorescence: Formation of salt crystals below the surface of a material, such as ceramic or stone, that can lead to surface damage and loss.

Tarnishing: Chemical alteration of metal surfaces, most commonly due to exposure to sulfur, resulting in darkening.

Wear: Loss of surface finish or substance due to use or handling.

APPENDIX 3
Professional Resources

The two national conservation associations of the United States and the United Kingdom offer a wide range of resources and advice to their members, as well as to the public.

American Institute for Conservation (AIC)
1156 15th Street, NW, Suite 320
Washington, DC 2005–1714, USA
Phone (202) 452 9545, Fax (202) 452 9328
http://aic.stanford.edu/

International Institute for Conservation (IIC)
6 Buckingham Street, London WC2N 6BA, UK
Phone +44 (0)20 7839 5975, Fax +44 (0)20 7976 1564
http://www.iiconservation.org/

Web-based resources:

Two major databases contain resources and abstracts related to conservation, preservation, research, and analysis of cultural heritage:

BCIN (Bibliographic Database of the Conservation Information Network) is hosted by the Canadian Heritage Information Network (CHIN),
http://www.bcin.ca/

AATA Online (Art and Archaeology Technical Abstracts) is produced by the Getty Conservation Institute (GCI) in association with IIC and with the International Centre for the Study of the Preservation and Restoration of Cultural Property (ICCROM),
http://aata.getty.edu/nps/

Conservation and Art Material Encyclopedia Online (CAMEO), developed by Conservation and Collections Management at the MFA and hosted by the MFA Web site, is a database of more than 10,000 entries on materials used in conservation, art, architecture, and archaeology,
http://www.mfa.org/_cameo/frontend/home.asp

PART IV

TEXTS

Words of Gods and Men

CHAPTER 10

THE EGYPTIAN LANGUAGE

James P. Allen

Ancient Egyptian is the world's oldest and longest continually attested language. It existed as a living language from its first appearance in writing, about 3200 BC, until sometime in the eleventh century AD, the probable date of its last known original compositions.[1] After the Islamic conquest of Egypt in AD 642, it was gradually replaced by Arabic, the language of Egypt today, although its latest stage survives in the scriptures and rituals of the Egyptian Coptic Church.

Egyptian belongs to the family of North African and Near Eastern languages known as Afro-Asiatic or Hamito-Semitic.[2] On the African, or Hamitic, side, it is related to Berber and the group of Cushitic and Chadic languages such as Beja and Hausa, and on the Asiatic side to Akkadian, Hebrew, Arabic, and other Semitic tongues. Within this spectrum, Egyptian is both central and unique: it has features found in North African and Semitic languages but is closely allied to neither group.

As all languages do, Egyptian evolved and changed over its nearly four thousand–year lifespan. Modern scholarship divides this history into five major stages, known as Old Egyptian, Middle Egyptian, Late Egyptian, Demotic, and Coptic. Coincident with these are the four primary scripts with which the language was written: hieroglyphic, hieratic, demotic, and Coptic. Because Egyptian is attested only in written form, our understanding of its phonology, grammar, and lexicon is in part theoretical.[3] Following the decipherment of hieroglyphs in 1822, the study of ancient Egyptian has been a process of continuing refinement in our knowledge of the language.

WRITING

With the exception of Coptic, the basis of all Egyptian writing is the hieroglyphic system. In its original and most representative form, this system consists of images drawn from the environment and imagination of the ancient Egyptians, which were used to convey the sounds and words of the language. The images, known as hieroglyphs, are of two basic types, usually called ideograms and phonograms. Ideograms represent individual words or concepts of the Egyptian language as pictures: for instance, a pair of open lips, used to write the word meaning "mouth." Phonograms are also pictures, but they are used to express sounds rather than words or ideas: the sign for the word "mouth" was also used to write the consonant *r* (see Fig. 10.1). Phonograms stand for one, two, or three consonants; hieroglyphic writing did not represent individual vowels, although several of its signs could be used to indicate that a word began or ended in a vowel. Select groups of phonograms were also employed in a system known as "group writing" to reflect the vocalization of foreign names and words, based on the syllabic value of these groups in Egyptian words.[4]

In the hieroglyphic system, some words are written regularly as ideograms and others only with phonograms. Most words combine the two kinds of signs, with phonograms expressing the consonantal structure of the word and a final ideogram representing the semantic class to which the word belongs; in this latter use, ideograms are traditionally known as determinatives.[5] The word *sn*, meaning "brother," for example, usually consists of two signs with the value *sn* followed by the determinative of a seated man, denoting the class of "human male"; the writing of the word *snt*, "sister," adds the phonogram *t* and uses the determinative of a seated woman.

This system is at once both flexible and opaque. The use of determinatives makes it possible to express in writing nuances of meaning that do not exist for single words in the spoken language: for instance, the sign of a seated god following the phonograms for *sn* indicates that the word refers to a divine rather than human "brother." The omission of vowels, however, sometimes conceals grammatical information that can be retrieved only from the context, if at all. This is particularly troublesome in verb-forms, where differences in meaning could be conveyed by changes in vocalic structure (as in English *sang* versus *sing*) that are not reflected in writing.

The use of hieroglyphs to represent sounds rather than the objects that the signs themselves depict is undoubtedly derived from an original system that was purely pictographic. This development is based on the rebus principle, by which images can be used to write unrelated words with similar sounds: for example, the pictures of an eye, a bee, and a leaf to write the English phrase "I believe." Unlike Mesopotamian cuneiform, whose development from pictograms to a complete writing system can be traced over several millennia, Egyptian hieroglyphic writing displays the use of phonograms in its earliest examples, about 3200 BC.

Hieroglyphs are the standard script of ancient Egyptian on monuments. Their prevalence in temple inscriptions is reflected in their name, derived from the Greek for "sacred carvings";

SIGN	CONVENTIONAL TRANSCRIPTION	VALUE
(vulture)	ꜣ	originally a liquid (*r* or *l*), later a glottal stop
(reed-leaf)	*j* or *i*	indicates a syllable beginning or ending in a vowel
(two reed-leaves)	*y*	*y*
(human arm)	ꜥ	Semitic *ꜥayin* (guttural *a*)
(quail chick)	*w*	*w*; also indicates a syllable ending in a vowel
(human leg)	*b*	*b* (soft, as in Spanish *cabo*)
(a mat)	*p*	*p*
(horned viper)	*f*	*f*
(owl)	*m*	*m*
(water)	*n*	*n*; occasionally *l* (dialectical?)
(human lips)	*r*	*r*; occasionally *l* (dialectical?)
(house plan)	*h*	*h*
(rope)	*ḥ*	Semitic *ḥa* (a harsh *h*)
(uncertain)	*ḫ*	*kh* (as in German *ach*)
(udder)	*ẖ*	*khʸ* (palatalized *kh*)
(doorbolt)	*z* or *s*	originally *th* (as in **th**ink), later *s*
(bolt of cloth)	*s* or *ś*	*s*
(body of water)	*š*	*sh* (as in **sh**ip)
(hill)	*q* or *ḳ*	Semitic *qaf/qoph* (guttural *k*)
(basket)	*k*	*k*
(jar stand)	*g*	*g*
(loaf of bread)	*t*	*t* or *tʰ* (as in *top*)
(hobble)	*ṯ*	*tʸ* (as in British *tune*)
(human hand)	*d*	"emphatic" *t*, or *t* (as in American *butter*)
(cobra)	*ḏ*	"emphatic" *tʸ*, or *tʸ* (as in British *fortune*)

FIGURE 10.1. The Egyptian hieroglyphic "alphabet" (signs for single consonantal phonemes). Image by J. Allen.

the Egyptians themselves called them "god's words." They were also used to write some religious texts, such as the Book of the Dead, with a simpler form of the signs, known as cursive hieroglyphs. The language of hieroglyphic inscriptions is usually either Old or Middle Egyptian. Hieroglyphs continued in use after the development of Late Egyptian and

FIGURE 10.2. Hieratic inscription with hieroglyphic transliteration below. Image by J. Allen.

Demotic, but the basic grammar of the inscriptions remained that of Middle Egyptian. The last dated hieroglyphic inscription was carved in AD 394.

For writing on papyri or ostraca a more cursive form of the hieroglyphic script was used, known as hieratic. Both Old and Middle Egyptian documents were written in hieratic, and Late Egyptian is primarily attested in this script. Some hieratic signs bear little resemblance to their hieroglyphic counterparts (see Fig. 10.2), and the script also employed numerous ligatures. Demotic developed around 650 BC from an even more cursive form of hieratic; the stage of the language known by the same name is written only in this script (Fig. 10.3). In the last centuries of Egyptian civilization, demotic was employed in most secular documents while hieratic was retained for religious papyri; the last known demotic text was written in AD 452.

During the Ptolemaic and Roman periods, most literate Egyptians could read and write Greek as well as demotic; the Rosetta Stone, which became the key to the decipherment of hieroglyphs, contains a decree of 196 BC inscribed in hieroglyphic, Demotic, and Greek. In some demotic magical texts, Greek characters were also used as glosses of Egyptian words, to ensure their proper vocalization; a few such Egyptian texts were written entirely in these characters, with a number of additional signs derived from demotic. This script, known as Coptic, was eventually adopted for the translation of Christian scriptures into Egyptian; it became the sole form of Egyptian writing after knowledge of the earlier scripts was lost (Fig. 10.4).

Demotic and Coptic are the only stages of the language in which there is a one-to-one correspondence between the language and its script. Old and Middle Egyptian were written in both hieroglyphic and hieratic, and Late Egyptian primarily in hieratic. Except in the latest Coptic manuscripts, none of the scripts employed either punctuation or word separation.

PHONOLOGY

Coptic is the only stage of ancient Egyptian in which the full phonological inventory of the language is shown in writing. It is also the only stage to reflect regional differences in pronunciation and grammar consistently. More than a dozen dialects of Coptic are

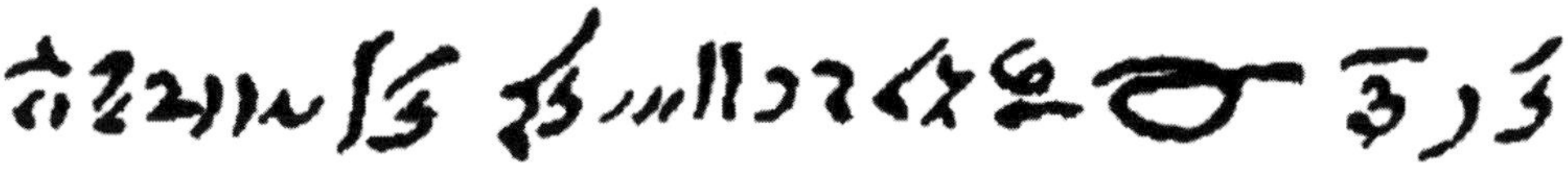

$$\underline{d}d.f \; n.w \; m\text{-}jr \; \underline{h}sf \; t\mathfrak{z} \; ntj \; jw.j \; \underline{d}d.s \; \underline{d}d.w \; p\mathfrak{z}y.n \; nb \; {}^c\mathfrak{z}$$

FIGURE 10.3. Demotic inscription with transliteration below. Image by J. Allen.

attested; the major ones are Sahidic and Akhmimic (spoken in southern Egypt), Fayumic, and Bohairic (from the Delta). The Coptic alphabet consists of the twenty-four letters of the Greek alphabet, an additional six for sounds that existed in Egyptian but not in Greek, and a monogram for *ti*.[6] These represent twenty-one to twenty-four phonemes in the major dialects: seven vocalic (*a, ĕ, ē, ī, ŏ, ō, ū*) and eighteen consonantal (*b, p/p^b, f, m, n, r, l, h, ḫ, s, š, k, k^b, k^y/t^{hy}, t, t^b, t^y*, and a glottal stop).[7] Bohairic is distinguished by its use of the four aspirated consonants, which do not exist in the other dialects.

The phonological inventory in earlier stages of the language can be reconstructed in part from that of Coptic.[8] In common with most Afro-Asiatic languages, Egyptian had three basic vowels (*a, i,* and *u*). These became the seven of Coptic through two historical processes: a distinction between short and long vowels in stressed syllables, with concomitant reduction to an indeterminate vowel in unstressed syllables; and a vowel shift, which took place between 1300 and 700 BC.[9] These changes can be traced in part through cuneiform transcriptions of Egyptian words: for example, Coptic *šmūn/ḫmūn* (Egyptian *ḫmnw*) "eight" < **ḫ^y emúne* (Neo-Assyrian *ḫe-mu-ni*) < **ḫamána* (Middle Babylonian *ḫa-ma-ana*).

The consonantal phonemes of Coptic are descended from twenty-five discernible in earlier Egyptian, usually transcribed as ꜣ, *j* or *ỉ, y, ꜥ, w, b, p, f, m, n, r, h, ḥ, ḫ, ẖ, z* or *s, s* or *ś, š, q* or *ḳ, k, g, t, ṯ, d,* and *ḏ*. Of these, ꜣ represented a liquid of some sort in Old and Middle Egyptian, perhaps an alveolar flap (the *r* in Spanish *pero* "but") if *r* was an alveolar trill (the *r* in Spanish *perro* "dog"); by Late Egyptian it had become a glottal stop or *y* in most words. In most dialects the liquid *l* seems to have been an allophone of ꜣ, *n,* and *r* (or vice versa) until Demotic. The consonant *j*, pronounced as a glottal stop in some words and as *y* in others, primarily indicated the presence of a vowel at the beginning or end of words or the hiatus between two vowels; phonemic *y* was most often written with a pair of the usual sign for *j*. The consonant ꜥ seems to have originally represented alveolar *d*, at least in some dialects, but had become a uvular glide (Semitic *ꜥayin*) by Late Egyptian, and probably before then. The consonants *ẖ* and *š* represented a single phoneme in Old Egyptian, perhaps *ḫ^y* (a palatalized velar fricative), but were distinguished thereafter, with *š* having the value of a palatalized alveolar fricative (Semitic *shin*); in Middle Egyptian, *ẖ* usually represented *ḫ^y*, but by Late Egyptian it had coalesced with its unpalatalized counterpart *ḫ* and a new grapheme was invented to represent *ḫ^y* (the digraph *ḫj*, demotic *ẖ*). The consonant *z* was phonemic only in Old Egyptian, where it may have represented an unvoiced dental fricative (the *th* in English *think*); by Middle Egyptian it was merely an allograph for *s*. The phonemes *t* and *t̲* were alveolar stops, the latter palatalized (*t^y*). Palatalization also distinguished *d* and *d̲*, but the phonological value of these two consonants in contrast to *t* and *t̲* is less certain: the distinction between the two pairs has been interpreted as one of voice (unvoiced *t/t^y* versus voiced *d/d^y*), aspiration (aspirated *t^h/t^hy* versus unaspirated *t/t^y*), or "emphasis" (unemphatic *t/t^y* versus emphatic *t̲/t̲^y*).[10]

The evolution of the Egyptian consonantal phonemes into those of Coptic is a complex history of loss, assimilation, dissimilation, and reacquisition and is complicated further by the fact that dialectical differences are generally imperceptible before Coptic. Nonetheless, two primary trends can be detected: alveolarization, through which pharyngeal, uvular, and velar consonants moved forward to become alveolars (for example, Old Egyptian *kw* "you" > Old/Middle Egyptian *t̲w* > Middle/Late Egyptian *tw*), and a gradual reduction of the consonantal phonemic inventory, from the twenty-four consonants of Old and Middle Egyptian to the eighteen of Coptic.

THE LEXICON

The vocabulary of ancient Egyptian is fairly sparse, comprising some ten thousand lexical entries other than proper names. A large number of these have Semitic cognates: for example, the preposition *n* "to, for" (Akkadian *ana*), the noun *jzr* "tamarisk" (Hebrew *ʾēšel*), and the verb *ḥsb* "count" (Arabic *ḥasaba*). Others, however, are African, such as the adjective *nfr* "good" (Beja *nafir*) and the numeral *fdw* "four" (Hausa *fudu*). Interestingly, some hieroglyphs reflect a Semitic substrate that has disappeared in historical Egyptian: the image of a hand has the value *d* (as in Hebrew and Arabic *yad* "hand"), while the word for "hand" is *d̲rt* (from the verb *nd̲r* "grasp"); the hieroglyph of a cow's ear can have the value *jdn* (compare Akkadian *uznu* "ear"), although the word for "ear" is *msd̲r* (derived from the verb *sd̲r* "sleep, lie").

Egyptian words belong to one of seven lexical categories: nouns, pronouns, prepositions, adjectives, adverbs, verbs, and particles. Most adjectives are participial forms of verbs rather than a distinct category: for example, *nfr* "(what is) good," from the verb *nfr* "become good." All native nouns and verbs have roots of two to six consonants; this distinguishes Egyptian from Semitic languages, where the norm is three. Basic verb roots consist of two to four consonants, which can be extended by means of prefixation and reduplication: for example, *t̲ḥn* "shine," *st̲ḥn* "cause to shine," *t̲ḥnḥn* "glitter." Prefixation is productive only in the earliest attested stages of the language and there only for the causative *s*; other prefixes, such as the reflexive *n* (e.g., *nḫrḫr* "be downcast," from *ḫr* "fall"), had been lexicalized by the time of Old Egyptian. Reduplication is historically nonproductive as well; full reduplication is essentially limited to biliteral roots (such as *snsn* "fraternize" from *sn* "kiss"), although a few

Letter and Name	Value	Letter and Name	Value
ⲁ ⲁⲗⲫⲁ	a (as in *father*)	ⲧ ⲧⲁⲩ	t
ⲃ ⲃⲏⲧⲁ	b (soft, as in Spanish *cabo*)	† (none)	= ⲧⲓ
ⲅ ⲅⲁⲙⲙⲁ	k (mostly in Greek loanwords)	ⲩ ϩⲉ	w after vowels except ⲟⲩ = ū (as in *soup*); i in Greek loanwords
ⲇ ⲇⲁⲗⲇⲁ	t (as in American *butter*; mostly in Greek loanwords)	ⲫ ⲫⲓ	= ⲡϩ in most dialects; Bohairic p^h (as in *pot*)
ⲉ ⲉⲓ	e (as in *set*)	ⲭ ⲭⲓ	= ⲕϩ in most dialects; Bohairic k^h (as in *kiss*)
ⲍ ⲍⲏⲧⲁ	s (mostly in Greek loanwords)	ⲯ ⲫⲓ	= ⲡⲥ
ⲏ ϩⲏⲧⲁ	ē (as in *reign*)	ⲱ ⲱ	ō (as in *hope*)
ⲑ ⲑⲏⲧⲁ	= ⲧϩ in most dialects; Bohairic t^h (as in *top*)	ϣ ϣⲁⲓ	sh (as in *ship*)
ⲓ ⲓⲱⲧⲁ	ī (as in *pizza*), usually written ⲉⲓ	ϥ ϥⲁⲓ	f
ï ⲓⲱⲧⲁ	y	ϧ ϧⲁⲓ and	kh (as in German *ach*), in Bohairic (ϧ) and Akhmimic (ⳉ)
ⲕ ⲕⲁⲡⲡⲁ	k	ϩ ϩⲟⲣⲓ	h
ⲗ ⲗⲁⲩⲇⲁ	l	ϫ ϫⲁⲛϫⲓⲁ	t^y or d^y in most dialects; Bohairic t^y (as in British *fortune*)
ⲙ ⲙⲏ	m	ϭ ϭⲓⲙⲁ	k^y in most dialects; Bohairic t^{hy} (as in British *tune*)
ⲛ ⲛⲉ	n	susperscript (e.g., ⲙ̄ⲛ)	indistinct e (as in *condiment*)
ⲝ ⲝⲓ	= ⲕⲥ		
ⲟ ⲟⲩ	o (as in *hop*)		
ⲡ ⲡⲓ	p		
ⲣ ⲣⲱ	r; l in Fayumic		
ⲥ ⲥⲏⲙⲙⲁ	s		

FIGURE 10.4. The Coptic alphabet. Image by J. Allen.

examples from triliteral roots are attested in Old Egyptian (e.g., *nḏdnḏd* "perdure," regularly *nḏdḏd*). Nouns and pronouns have either masculine or feminine gender. Masculine gender is morphologically unmarked; feminine nouns are distinguished by a final *t* (*snt* "sister" versus *sn* "brother").

Lexical history is the least studied aspect of ancient Egyptian, but changes in the meanings of words and in vocabulary can be traced throughout time, as in all languages. Examples are the noun *ẖt* "body," ancestor of Coptic *he/ẖe* "manner," and the noun *pr* "house," largely replaced by *ꜥwj* in the Late Period (Coptic *ēi*). The most consistent change affected the formation of the causative roots of verbs. Prefixation of *s* had become lexicalized by Middle Egyptian, by which time causatives were usually formed grammatically by means of the verb *rḏj* "give" governing a specific form of the dependent verb: thus, *smsj* "cause to give birth" (from *msj* "give birth") was regularly replaced by a form of *rḏj* plus *msj.s* "that she give birth." This construction was later grammaticalized and became a new causative root in Coptic (*tmesio* "cause to give birth").

Grammar: History

Old Egyptian is the name given to the earliest recorded form of the language, which lasted from the first extensive text, the tomb inscription of Metjen (Dynasty 4, ca. 2560 BC), into the First Intermediate Period. It is attested primarily in tomb biographies and the funerary literature known as the Pyramid Texts. These two corpora exhibit slight distinctions in grammar, which were probably chronological in origin: the Pyramid Texts generally preserve the language spoken before the middle of Dynasty 5, while most tomb biographies represent the form current after that point. Dialectically, Old Egyptian probably reflects the speech of the Memphite area, where it is primarily attested.

Middle Egyptian is closely related to the later phase of Old Egyptian but may reflect the dialect of Thebes rather than that of the north.[11] Its classical form is represented by the literature of the Middle Kingdom, but it was retained as the basic language of monumental inscriptions and religious texts for the remainder of ancient Egyptian civilization. Elements of Late Egyptian appear in Middle Egyptian texts of the late Second Intermediate Period (Papyrus Westcar, ca. 1600 BC), occasionally in monumental inscriptions of Dynasty 18, and more frequently in texts of the Amarna and Ramesside periods and later. This blend of older and more current forms of the language is sometimes called Traditional or Late Middle Egyptian.

Late Egyptian itself is primarily attested by texts of the Ramesside Period, but it had probably replaced Middle Egyptian as the spoken language before Dynasty 18. It shares certain morphological features with Old Egyptian and probably also originated in the north.[12] The purest form of Late Egyptian is represented by hieratic letters and administrative documents of Dynasties 19–20; literary texts and monumental inscriptions tend to retain Middle Egyptian features that had disappeared from the colloquial language.

Demotic, which first appeared in the Saite Period (ca. 650 BC), is essentially a later form of Late Egyptian, written in a distinct script, and Coptic bears the same relationship to Demotic. Demotic was the primary language and script of Egypt until the end of its ancient civilization; it was used not only in colloquial documents such as letters and accounts but also for literary and religious texts and even for some monumental inscriptions carved in stone, such as the Rosetta Stone. Coptic was primarily the language and script of Christian Egypt; until the demise of Demotic, most of its texts were scriptural or religious in nature.

The history of the Egyptian language as a whole can be divided into two phases: early, comprising Old and Middle Egyptian; and late, including Late Egyptian through Coptic. The early phase is primarily synthetic in morphology, signaling differences in meaning through changes in the form of words (as in English *sing* versus *sang* and *song* versus *songs*); the late phase is largely analytic, with different meanings conveyed by word phrases (as in English *sing* versus *will sing*). This distinction affects both nouns and verbs. In addition, Egyptian sentence structure exhibits a historical movement away from an original verb-subject-object (VSO) word order and toward one in which the subject precedes the verb

(SVO). These developments can be traced throughout the history of the language, with the greatest change occurring between Middle and Late Egyptian.

GRAMMAR: NOUNS

In use, nouns are either singular or nonsingular. The latter is the marked form. Plurals are distinguished morphologically by the phoneme *w* appended to the end of masculine nouns and inserted before the final *t* of feminines: *snw* "brothers," *snwt* "sisters." The language also possessed a dual, marked by a final *wj* (masculine) or *j* (feminine): *snwj* "(two) brothers," *sntj* "(two) sisters." The dual was productive only in Old Egyptian; thereafter, it was generally applied only to nouns that were regularly paired (e.g., *jrtj* "eyes").

Case was not a feature of nouns in historical Egyptian, but the language may originally have used the common Afro-Asiatic system of three cases: nominative, marked by final *u*; genitive, with final *i*; and accusative, with final *a*. Traces of these are perhaps to be recognized in some Coptic descendants: for example, nominative *u* (> *ē*) in *snēu* "brothers" < **sanúwu* versus *son* "brother" < **san* < ***sanu*, and genitive *i* (> *a*) in *hraf* "his face" < **haríf* versus *ho* "face" < **har* < ***haru*.[13]

The ending *t* of singular and plural feminine nouns is sometimes omitted in writing, reflecting its loss in pronunciation. This process, which began already in the Old Kingdom, is comparable to that which produced the *tā' marbūtah* of Arabic (e.g., *hikāyah* "history" < **hikāyat*). It also affected the feminine form of adjectives and attributive verb forms, such as participles, and eventually extended to the final *t* of masculine nouns as well (e.g., *ht* "wood" > Coptic *še/he*). The ending was retained before a pronominal suffix, as in Arabic, but generally not in constructs, unlike Arabic: *r ḏbst.f* "with respect to him" > Coptic *etbē'tef* (cf. Arabic *hikāyatuh* "his history") but *r ḏbst psy* "with respect to this" > Coptic *etbe-pai* (cf. Arabic *hikāyat-misri* "Egypt's history").

In Old and Middle Egyptian, common nouns can be defined or undefined (*sn* "the brother" or "a brother"); this feature is unmarked morphologically and determined only by context. By Late Egyptian the language had developed definite and indefinite articles: the former from a demonstrative pronoun (masculine *ps*, feminine *ts*, plural *ns* "the"); the latter from the numeral "one" (masculine *wˁ*, feminine *wˁt*), with the noun *hnw* "some" as plural. Since these regularly indicate gender and number, morphological marking of the same features on the noun itself is sometimes ignored in writing, although it was retained phonologically in many cases: for example, *ts sn* "the sister" (Coptic *tsōne*), *ns sn* "the brothers, the sisters" (Coptic *nesnēu*). This produces an analytic compound, in which the article conveys grammatical information (definition, gender, and number) and the noun carries the lexical component. Because most nouns retained their synthetic phonology, the compound was often only partly analytic, but fully analytic constructions are attested for some nouns in Coptic (e.g., *tše're* "the daughter," *enše're* "the daughters").

Grammar: Pronouns

Egyptian has three basic categories of pronouns: personal, demonstrative, and interrogative. In Old and Middle Egyptian, personal pronouns have four different forms, depending on their use in sentences: independent, used primarily as subjects in nonverbal sentences; dependent, used as the subject of an adjectival predicate or the object of a verb; suffix, appended to verbs as subjects, to prepositions as objects, and to nouns as possessives; and stative, used as obligatory suffixes with the verb form of the same name. A fifth form, used as subject in certain verbal constructions, is primarily a feature of later Egyptian, although it appears in some Middle Egyptian texts. For the most part, these pronouns have Afro-Asiatic cognates: for example, *jnk* "I" (independent form: **anák* > Coptic *anok*), Akkadian *anāku*, Berber *nk*, Arabic *anā*. They generally retained the same morphology from Old Egyptian to Coptic; major changes affected the second- and third-person singular independent pronouns between Old and Middle Egyptian (2ms *ṯwt*, 2fs *ṯmt*, 3ms *swt*, 3fs *stt* > 2ms *ntk*, 2fs *ntṯ*, 3ms *ntf*, 3fs *nts*) and the third-person plural suffix pronoun between Middle and Late Egyptian (*sn* > *w*). All personal pronouns originally possessed a dual form, which was lost after Old Egyptian.

Demonstrative pronouns also distinguish singular and plural, and originally dual. They were used both dependently and as adjectives. In the latter use they usually follow the noun, but the pronouns *pꜣ/tꜣ/nꜣ* (m/f/pl) "this, these" always precede it. This set, primarily a dialectical or colloquial feature in Old and Middle Egyptian, developed into the definite article of Late Egyptian, Demotic, and Coptic. It also formed the base of a set of analytic possessives in those later phases of the language, generally replacing the older suffix pronouns: for example, Old/Middle Egyptian *jtj.k* "your father" > Late Egyptian *pꜣy.k jtj* > Coptic *pek-eiōt*.[14]

Grammar: Verbs

The verbal system is the aspect of ancient Egyptian that underwent the most change throughout the history of the language. In all phases, however, verb forms can be divided into five basic categories: predicative, stative, imperative, attributive, and nominal. Verb forms also express essentially the same range of semantic features in all phases: these include transitivity (transitive versus intransitive, a lexical feature); state; tense, aspect, and mood; voice (active versus passive); and syntactic function. The varieties of these features, however, and the means by which they are expressed in the verb, differ from one stage of Egyptian to the next, and substantially so between its early and late phases.

In the early phase, comprising Old and Middle Egyptian, verb forms are primarily synthetic: almost exclusively so in the earliest stage of Old Egyptian, less so in Middle Egyptian. Predicative forms, usually grouped under the heading of the "suffix conjugation," belong to one of six subcategories, called the *sḏm.f*, *sḏm.n.f*, *sḏmt.f*, *sḏm.jn.f*, *sḏm.ḫr.f*, and *sḏm.kꜣ.f*.[15] The *sḏm.f* itself represents six forms, known as perfective (or indicative), imperfective (or circumstantial), subjunctive (or prospective), prospective (or "*sḏmw.f*"), passive, and prospective passive (or *sḏmm.f*). All but the passive forms and *sḏmt.f* are active in voice and can be made passive by means of the suffix *tw* (*tj* in Old Egyptian), appended to the end of the form (but before a suffix pronoun: e.g., *sḏm.n.tw.f*); the *sḏmt.f* is essentially neutral with respect to voice.

The stative, also known as the old perfective, is a single form distinguished by a set of obligatory pronominal suffixes. It corresponds to the stative of Akkadian and the perfect of other Semitic languages, such as Arabic, with much the same suffixes. In function it expresses state, usually with the implication of a previous action: for example, *šm.tj* "(you are/have) gone," *smn.w* "(they are/have been) established." The imperative is a single form as well, though its morphology varies depending on whether it is addressed to one or more than one referent; Coptic descendants of the imperative indicate that its vocalization also differed depending on the referent's gender.

The category of attributive forms includes five participles and three relative forms, all equivalent to relative clauses in other languages (and historically in Egyptian itself). Participles correspond to a relative clause in which the subject is identical to the term modified; the relative forms are used when these two elements are not identical: for example, *zꜣ sḏm* "a son who hears/who is heard," *zꜣ sḏm.k* "a son whom you hear." Four of the five participles are distinguished by aspect (perfective versus imperfective) and voice (active versus passive); the fifth, neutral with respect to voice, is marked for tense (future). The three relative forms include the perfective and imperfective *sḏm.f* and the *sḏm.n.f*. The lexical componenent of attributive forms is marked with endings that reflect the gender and number of the referent (e.g., *zꜣt sḏmt.k* "a daughter whom you hear").

Nominal forms of the verb are those that express the action of the verb itself without other connotations. These include a large variety of verbal nouns, one specific set of which, distinguished by its syntax, is known as the infinitive. The other nominal forms of early Egyptian are the negatival complement, used to express the verb in certain negative constructions, and the complementary infinitive, used as the object of another form of the same verb. These last two forms were replaced by the infinitive in later stages of Egyptian, a process that began already in Middle Egyptian. All the nominal forms are neutral with respect to voice.

The eleven predicative forms all express action and various aspects, moods, and voices. The *sḏm.n.f* and its normal passive counterpart, the passive *sḏm.f*, are essentially perfect, denoting completed or prior action; the *sḏmt.f* has the same basic value and generally serves as the counterpart of these two forms in specific constructions. The *sḏm.jn.f*, *sḏm.ḫr.f*, and *sḏm.kꜣ.f* each denote consecutive action, generally in the past, present, and future, respectively; the *sḏm.ḫr.f* also carries the connotation of necessity ("he has to hear"). The six forms of the *sḏm.f* were distinguished by morphology and vocalization. The distinctions are not visible for all lexical verbs but have been deduced paradigmatically: for the verb *stp* "choose," for example, passive *stpw* and prospective passive *stpp* are distinguished from unmarked *stp*; for *msj* "give birth," prospective *msjw* from unmarked *msj*; for *tmm* "close," imperfective and prospective *tmm* from unmarked *tm;* and for the irregular verb *rdj* "give," imperfective and subjunctive *dj* from prospective *rdjw* and unmarked *rdj*. The perfective *sdm.f* basically denotes simple action, commonly in past contexts ("he heard"); the imperfective, incomplete action; and the prospective forms, action that lies in the future with respect to the moment of speaking or another verb or clause. Together with the passive *sdm.f*, these are indicative in mood and as such contrast with the subjunctive, which denotes the action of the verb as contingent, possible, or desirable.

The primary verbal system of early Egyptian as a whole distinguishes four basic semantic features: state, mood, voice, and aspect. The first distinction exists between the stative, which denotes state, and all other forms, which express action; the stative is neutral with respect to mood, voice, and aspect. The subjunctive and imperative are marked for mood; all other forms are indicative in sense. Passive voice is marked in the passive and prospective passive *sdm.f* and the perfective and imperfective passive participles; all other forms are either active or neutral in voice. Aspectual distinctions exist in the predicative and attributive forms, which are marked for completed, incomplete, prospective, or consecutive action: these include the *sdm.n.f*, passive *sdm.f*, *sdmt.f*, and relative *sdm.n.f* (completed action); the imperfective *sdm.f*, participles, and relative forms (incomplete action); the prospective *sdm.f* and participle (prospective action); and the *sdm.jn.f*, *sdm.hr.f*, and *sdm.ks.f* (consecutive action; at least the last also with an aspectual connotation). All other forms are aspectually unmarked. Tense is not a primary distinction in any of the verb forms, although it is often a connotation, particularly of the prospective forms.

Besides the aspectual features of primary forms, early Egyptian also expresses the notion of ongoing action, similar to the English imperfect, by means of the SUBJECT-*sdm.f* construction, in which the subject of an imperfective *sdm.f* is co-referential with a preceding subject in the same clause: for example, *s(j) jw.s* "she is coming" (Pyr. 282b). This can be specified temporally by means of a form of the verb *wnn* "be": *wn.s jw.s* "she was coming, she used to come" (with the perfective *sdm.f* of *wnn*), *wnn.s jw.s* "she will be coming" (with the prospective *sdm.f* of *wnn*). In the second phase of Old Egyptian and later, the SUBJECT-*sdm.f* construction gave way to one in which the imperfective *sdm.f* was replaced by the preposition *hr* "upon" and the infinitive: for example, *sr(jw) hr hzt.tn* "the official is blessing you," literally, "the official (is) upon your blessing."[16] A similar construction, with the preposition *(j)r* "to," expresses the future, perhaps originally with a sense of inevitability: *sr(jw) r ms mnht* "the official (is) to see the clothing."[17] Both constructions are traditionally called "pseudoverbal," because the verb is expressed by the infinitive rather than by a predicative form. They are the ancestors of the Coptic "First Present" and "Third Future" tenses, respectively, and are often designated with those names.

In Middle Egyptian, the predicative prospective forms have largely disappeared except for *wnn* and in a few grammaticalized constructions, replaced by the subjunctive and the "Third Future." Old Egyptian distinguishes between preterite and perfect expressions of the past tense, the former largely expressed by the perfective *sdm.f* ("he heard") and the latter by the *sḏm.n.f* of transitive verbs ("he has heard") and the stative of intransitives (*šm.w* "they have gone"). This distinction has disappeared in Middle Egyptian, where the *sḏm.n.f* and stative in affirmative statements, and the perfective *sḏm.f* in the negative construction *nj sḏm.f*, have both preterite and perfect meanings. Old Egyptian is also distinguished, particularly in its older phase, by the use of verb forms marked by the prefix *j* (e.g., subjunctive *j.ḏḏ.f* "he should speak"). This feature, probably dialectical in origin, is also largely absent from Middle Egyptian.[18]

The verbal system of Late Egyptian differs significantly in its morphology from that of the earlier language. Only four of the older predicative forms have survived: the perfective, subjunctive, and passive *sḏm.f*, and the *sḏm.n.f*, with the use of the last two forms largely restricted to administrative and literary texts. The stative exhibits a gradual loss of its pronominal suffixes throughout the lifespan of Late Egyptian, eventually distinguishing only between the first-person singular and all other persons and numbers. The older imperative survives for a few verbs but the language has also begun to create a new imperative, formed from the infinitive with the prefix *j*. The eight attributives of Old and Middle Egyptian have been reduced to two, an active participle and a relative form, both essentially neutral with respect to aspect and tense; a passive participle, uniformly past in meaning, is also found in administrative texts.[19] Of the nominal forms, only the infinitive is preserved, filling the function of both the older infinitive and negatival complement; the construction using the complementary infinitive has not survived, and the other verbal nouns have become lexicalized.

This substantial reduction in the inventory of synthetic verb forms is offset by an increase in analytic constructions, which both replace and enhance the older forms. The perfective *sḏm.f* has both preterite and perfect meanings, like the Old Egyptian *sḏm.f* and *sḏm.n.f*, respectively. Late Egyptian uses the First Present in place of the imperfective *sḏm.f*. The subjunctive *sḏm.f* retains its earlier uses and modal values, including the expression of the intentional future (English *I will hear*); the Third Future is used for indicative future statements (English *I shall hear*).

Demotic uses essentially the same predicative system, with some differences and additions. The jussive sense of the subjunctive *sḏm.f* is now expressed analytically, with the verb form governed by the imperative *mj* "give, cause" (*mj sḏm.f*, later *mj jr.f sḏm* "let him hear"). Aorist meaning is no longer carried merely by the First Present but also by a new analytic construction *ḫr sḏm.f*, later *ḫr jr.f sḏm*, "he hears." The perfective *sḏm.f* has mostly a preterite sense, with a new analytic construction used for the perfect: *wꜣḥ.f sḏm* "he has heard." These new constructions reflect not only the gradual replacement of the older synthetic forms by analytic counterparts but also the general movement of the language toward a word order in which the subject precedes the verb: for example, Late Egyptian *sḏm.f* "let him hear" > early Demotic *mj sḏm.f* "cause that he hear" > later Demotic *mj jr.f sḏm* "cause that he do hearing." In Coptic these two trends have resulted in a system that is completely analytic. The perfective *sḏm.f* has become analytic *af-sōtem* < *jr.f sḏm*, literally "he did hearing." Early Coptic retains the Demotic distinction between preterite and perfect, but this eventually disappears as the perfect *haf-sōtem*, descendant of Demotic *wꜣḥ.f sḏm*, loses its initial consonant and merges with the preterite; the distinction is retained, however, in negations (preterite *empef-sōtem* versus perfect *empatef-sōtem*). The subjunctive *sḏm.f* has disappeared: the Third Future is now used for jussive statements (*efe-sōtem* "he should hear, let him hear"), while the older jussive has an optative meaning (*maref-sōtem* "may he hear" < *mj jr.f sḏm*). To express the indicative future Coptic has created a new form, known as the First Future, descendant of a construction that first appears in Late Egyptian: *tina-sōtem* "I will hear" < *twj m n'j r sḏm* "I (am) going to hear."

From Late Egyptian through Coptic, the predicative system as a whole exhibits a basic distinction between forms that are marked for tense, mood, or aspect and those that are not. The latter is based on the First Present, with the infinitive as predicate in statements of action and the stative as predicate expressing state (and the past tense of intransitive verbs): *st (ḥr) sḏm* "she hears, she is hearing" > Coptic *s-sōtem*,[20] *st 'ḥ'* "she is standing/has stood up" > Coptic *s-ohe*. The former include the synthetic perfective and subjunctive *sḏm.f* in Late Egyptian and Demotic but have become completely analytic in Coptic, with the infinitive as predicate and an additional morpheme to mark tense, mood, or aspect: for example, optative *sḏm.f* "may he hear" > *mj sḏm.f* > *mj jr.f sḏm* > *maref-sōtem*. Reflecting the Coptic forms, the unmarked forms are known as the bipartite system (subject plus infinitive/stative) and the marked forms as the tripartite system (subject plus marker of tense/mood/aspect plus infinitive).

GRAMMAR: CLAUSES AND SENTENCES

In common with most Afro-Asiatic languages, Egyptian can form a statement without a predicative verb form. In such statements, commonly called "nonverbal sentences," the predicate is either nominal (noun, pronoun, attributive or nominal verb form), adjectival (adjective or participle), or adverbial (adverb or prepositional phrase). The nominal and adverbial constructions exist in all phases of the language; Demotic and Coptic have lost the adjectival predicate, replacing it with a special form of the adjective-verb. The First Present and Third Future are originally adverbial-predicate constructions, and adverbial predicates are part of the bipartite system in Late Egyptian through Coptic.

In Old and Middle Egyptian, relationships between clauses can be signaled by context alone. The subjunctive *sḏm.f*, for example, serves as initial predicate not only in main clauses but also in dependent clauses of purpose and content: *jr.n.f ṯꜣw n jb, 'nḫ fnḏw.sn* "He has made air for the heart, that their noses might live," *ḏd.n.f ḥꜣ.f ḥn'.j* "He said he would fight with me."[21] The language also employs distinct morphemes of subordination, particularly for constructions that cannot be subordinated by context or morphological change: for instance, *ntj ḥr sḏm* "who is hearing," with the relative pronoun *ntj* as subject of the First Present, as opposed to *sḏm* "who hears," with the participial form of the verb. Use of these subordinating elements, often called "converters," is more frequent from Late Egyptian onward, as the language loses its synthetic forms.

Old and Middle Egyptian employ the *sḏm.f* and *sḏm.n.f* relative forms not only as attributives but also as initial predicates in noun clauses, such as those that serve as the object of a verb or preposition. These two functions, comparable to the use of *that* clauses in English, are distinguished not only by context but also by the presence or absence of a correlative ending. In attributive use, the relative forms carry an ending that signals agreement in gender and number with their antecedents; in noun clauses, the forms have no such ending: for example, *zꜣt mrrt.k* "the daughter that you love," with the feminine singular imperfective relative *mrrt.k* (from the verb *mrj* "like, desire"), versus *rḫ.tj mrr.j ṯw* "you know that I love you," with the unmarked imperfective relative *mrr.j*. The unmarked relative forms are also used as grammatical predicates in main clauses to signal that the logical predicate is some other element of the sentence (usually an adverb, prepositional phrase, or dependent clause): *mrr.k wš.tw ꞌryt.k ḥr jb* "Why do you want your household to be destroyed?"[22] This last use of the relative forms is commonly called "emphatic" in studies of Egyptian grammar. Later stages of the language no longer use the relative forms as predicates in noun clauses as objects of verbs or prepositions, but they do retain the emphatic construction, albeit with different verb forms: for example, Late Egyptian *j.jr.k jy ḥr jb* "Why have you come?," with the relative form *j.jr.k jy* (compare the attributive *pꜣy.j jw j.jr.j sḫpr.f* "my dog that I raised," with the relative form *j.jr.j sḫpr.f*), Coptic *entak-bōk etōn* "To where have you gone?," with the relative form *entak-bōk* (compare *entopos entak-bōk eroou* "the places to which you have gone," with the same relative form).[23]

The function of the emphatic constructions was a relatively late discovery in the study of the Egyptian language. The Coptic relatives in this use were initially thought to be secondary forms of the various predicative tenses (and for that reason are usually called Second Tenses: e.g., Second Present, Second Perfect). It was not until 1944, with the publication of Polotsky's *Études de syntaxe copte*, that their true value was recognized. Even then, Egyptology was slow to accept Polotsky's analysis. Well into the 1960s, the understanding of the Egyptian verbal system was predominantly that of Gardiner's Middle Egyptian grammar (Gardiner 1964), which recognized forms such as *mrr.k* as an imperfective variety of the predicative *sḏm.f*. Since then, however, Polotsky's approach has become the standard theory of Egyptian grammar, for all phases of the language.

While the semantic value of the emphatic forms (or Second Tenses) is now universally recognized, their syntax is still a matter of debate. Polotsky analyzed the emphatic sentence as one in which the emphatic form served as nominal subject to a nonverbal predicate: thus, *entak-bōk etōn* was understood as a sentence in which the adverbial phrase *etōn* "to where" was the syntactic predicate and the verb form *entak-bōk* "you have gone" as its nominalized subject:

literally, "that you have gone (is) to where." More recently, and based in part on modern linguistic theory, such sentences have been analyzed as containing a verbal predicate but with the specialized form of that predicate indicating or reflecting the fact that the logical predicate lies elsewhere in the sentence.[24] In the example under discussion, therefore, *entak-bōk* "you have gone" is understood as a phrase containing the grammatical predicate and its subject, while *etōn* "to where" is an adverbial adjunct. As in most such questions, however, the verb-phrase reflects background information and the interrogative phrase contains the focus of new interest. This is the reverse of normal sentences, in which the verbal predicate itself carries the new information.

The study of Egyptian grammar is currently divided between proponents of these two analytical approaches. A similar division is reflected in the analysis of verb forms or constructions that have adverbial function. The school inspired by Polotsky characterizes these as morphologically adverbial, while more recent analysis, which distinguishes between form and function, sees them as predicative forms in adverbial use: the difference is reflected, *inter alia*, in the name of the *sḏm.f* known as the circumstantial or imperfective form.

Today, nearly two hundred years after the hieroglyphic script was deciphered, ancient Egyptian can be read and understood nearly as well as any other language. There are still gaps in our understanding of some words and grammatical constructions, but these are few and impact mostly finer nuances rather than overall meaning. Major progress still remains to be made, however, in the study of individual words in order to refine their precise meaning. The future of Egyptian language studies now seems to belong to lexicography.

NOTES

1. For the earliest attestations see Dreyer 2000; for the latest, Kahle 1954: 193.
2. See Loprieno 1995: 1–5.
3. The pronunciation of Coptic in the rituals of the Egyptian Coptic Church is heavily influenced by the phonology of Arabic and does not always correspond to that which modern scholarship has reconstructed for the ancient language.
4. See Hoch 1994: 487–512.
5. For these semantic classes, and the use of determinatives, see Goldwasser 1995 and 2002.
6. Many Coptic manuscripts also employ a superliteral stroke representing an epenthetic vowel (or "schwa"): e.g., ϩⲙ̄ϩⲁⲗ (*h'mhál*) "servant." Because this varies in writing with ⲉ (*ĕ*) – e.g., ϩⲉⲙϩⲁⲗ (*hemhál*) – it can be considered an allograph of that vowel; the orthography is comparable to the use of *e* and the apostrophe in English: e.g., *heaven* and poetic *heav'n*. The vowel ⲓ (*ī*) is sometimes marked by a diaresis to indicate its full phonetic value in diphthongs: e.g., ⲉⲓ (*ey*) versus ⲉⲓ (*ei = ī*).
7. The letters ⲅ, ⲇ, and ⲍ, used primarily in writing words of Greek origin, are essentially allographs of ⲕ, ⲧ, and ⲥ; ⲝ, ⲫ, and ⲧ are monograms for ⲕⲥ, ⲡⲥ, and ⲧⲓ. The characters ⲯ, ⲭ, and ⲑ are monograms for ⲡϩ (*ph*), ⲕϩ (*kh*), and ⲧϩ (*th*) in all dialects except Bohairic, where they are the aspirated counterparts of ⲡ, ⲕ, and ⲧ, respectively; the letter ϭ is the aspirated form of ⲭ (*tʸ*) in Bohairic and the palatalized consonant *kʸ* in all other dialects. The distribution of Bohairic

π/ϣ (p/pᵇ) and Fayumic ρ/λ (r/l) is not phonemic. The velar fricative ḫ (ⳉ/ϧ) does not exist in Sahidic and Fayumic. The glottal stop is reflected by doubled vowels in most dialects but either has disappeared or is not represented in Bohairic.

8. For Egyptian phonology, see Loprieno 1995: 28–50 and Peust 1999.

9. See Edgerton 1947. The distinction between short and long vowels was conditioned by syllable structure, with short vowels in closed syllables (ending in a consonant) and long vowels in open syllables: e.g., *san "brother" > *săn > Coptic **cон** (sŏn) versus *sanat (*sá-nat) "sister" > *sānat > Coptic **cⲱⲛⲉ** (sōne).

10. For an overview of these theories, see Peust 1999: 80–83.

11. See Allen 2004: 9–10.

12. The classic study is Edgerton 1951.

13. Loprieno 1995: 55–6.

14. In transcription, suffix and stative pronouns are usually written as part of the word to which they are appended, separated by a dot or by two short strokes (jtj=k, pꜣy=k jtj).

15. The verb sḏm "hear," with the 3ms pronominal suffix f "he," is traditionally used as a paradigmatic form in studies of Egyptian grammar. In transcription, dots normally separate the suffixes jn, ḫr, and kꜣ from the verb to which they are appended.

16. Cited in Edel 1964: § 928. See Vernus 1990: 163–93.

17. Cited in Vernus 1990: 13.

18. See Allen 2004: 6–7.

19. See Černý and Groll 1984: 463–95. Both the active participle and the relative have regular and periphrastic forms: j.sḏm and j.jr sḏm, j.sḏm.f and j.jr.f sḏm. The former are usually past and the latter present, but the extent to which this constitutes a real morphological dichotomy is unclear. All four can be regarded as essentially unmarked for tense and aspect.

20. The preposition ḥr is often omitted in this construction in Late Egyptian, and was probably left unexpressed, or expressed only as a vowel, in pronunciation.

21. Cited in Allen 2000: 251 and 253.

22. Gardiner and Sethe 1928: pl. 6, 4–5. Literally, "You want that your house be destroyed on account of what?" where the prepositional phrase ḥr jḫ "on account of what" is the logical predicate.

23. Gardiner 1932: 67, 9–10, and 6, 14–15; Steindorff 1951: 208 and 229. The examples in this sentence have the literal meanings "you have come on account of what?" "my dog that I raised him," "you have gone to where?" and "the places that you have gone to them"; the two attributive clauses each have an obligatory pronoun coreferential with the antecedent.

24. See the discussion in Allen 2000: 404–8.

CHAPTER 11

ANCIENT EGYPTIAN LITERATURE

John L. Foster and Ann L. Foster

Are there any here today like Hordjedef?
    Is there another like Imhotep?
There has not come in our time one like Neferty
    or Khety, the best of them all.
I give you the names of Ptahemdjehuty
    or Khakheperreseneb.
Is there another like Ptahhotep
    or the equal of Kaires?

Those sages who saw into the future –
    what came from their mouths came to be;
It is found as wisdom and truth
    inscribed on their papyrus rolls.
The children of others are given to them
    to be co-heirs with their own;
And the sacred knowledge they saved for the world
    can be followed and known in their writings.
They themselves are dead and gone,
    but their names are immortal in books.

This passage from Papyrus Chester Beatty IV, written around 1200 BC, names several of the famous writers in the Egyptian literary tradition as seen in the eyes of a scribe of the 20th Dynasty. Thus we have contemporary evidence as to who the famous writers were; and, in fact, five of those named above have pieces still surviving today, some in fragments, and some apparently complete. The passage also shows evidence of a rich literary tradition belonging to one of the world's oldest civilizations. Over the span of the past four or five millennia the losses from that literature must surely have been considerable; today ancient Egyptian literature is a literature in ruins. Nevertheless, what we have is substantial and well worth the effort to study and enjoy it.

The list of authors quoted above mentions only the wise men of the culture – those looked to for guidance and moral direction. But these sages had a second function, alluded to in the passage, which was closely allied to the wisdom they were famous for: educating the young. Khety, one of the wise men mentioned above, writes in his "Instruction" to his little son, Pepi:

> It is good to study many things
>> that you may learn the wisdom of great men.
> Thus you can help to educate the children of the people
>> while you walk according to the wise man's footsteps.
> The scribe is seen as listening and obeying,
>> and the listening develops into satisfaction.
> Hold fast the words which hearken to these things
>> as your own footsteps hurry,
> And while you are on your journey
>> you need never hide your heart.
> Step out on the path of learning –
>> the friends of Man are your company.

This Company in Khety's passage was composed of wise men and teachers, yet it also included scribes with priestly, artistic, accounting, and secretarial duties. Most important for our purposes, these writers of hieroglyphs and hieratic were also the composers of literature: of hymns and prayers, of love songs, of stories and tales, of various didactic and educational pieces, and of royal encomia. Examples of all of these survive.

The term *literature* is spoken of in two ways, as referring to (1) anything written down; or (2) writing of excellence, writing with an imaginative and creative dimension (that is, *belles lettres*), writing including the poetry, fiction, criticism, and essays of a people. We will be referring to the second usage of the word in this chapter. We will also really only be considering literature from the pharaonic period and written in the stages of the language known as Old Egyptian, Middle Egyptian, and Late Egyptian.

The surviving literature of ancient Egypt commences during the Old Kingdom with pieces concerning the resurrection of the dead king and his return to his proper home among the gods. These are found in the Pyramid Texts; examples date to the end of the 5th Dynasty (from the tomb of King Unis) and then to subsequent kings of the 6th Dynasty. Many of the Pyramid Texts are cast as lyrics, pieces with songlike qualities; they commemorate events as the king takes his rightful position in heaven among his peers, or as he flashes gloriously across the sky like a bolt of lightning, or like a star fading in the dawn as he goes to rest in the arms of his father, Atum. Collectively such pieces give an imaginative picture of the deceased kings' lives beyond the grave, and in doing so they offer us the earliest surviving body of Egyptian literature:

> A pale sky darkens,
>> stars hide away,
> Nations of heavenly bowmen are shaken,
>> bones of the earth-gods tremble –
> All cease motion, are still,
>> for they have looked upon Unis, the King,
> Whose Soul rises in glory, transfigured, a god,
>> alive among his fathers of old time,
>>> nourished by ancient mothers.

These lyrics are clearly full of rich imagery, and the authors exercise the use of metaphor and simile with great skill, a skill that remains a part of the Egyptian literary tradition throughout its long life.

There is another kind of lyric literature surviving from this period (6th Dynasty) but to a much lesser degree, songs. The most complete occur within tomb biographies. In the tomb of Weni at Abydos, for instance, there is a song of victory commemorating an army for its success under the command of Weni in a series of couplets, one line of which is repeated in the manner of a refrain:

> This army returned in triumph
>> after destroying the land of the Bedouin;
> This army returned in triumph
>> after leveling the land of the sandfarers;
> This army returned in triumph
>> after tearing down its sanctuaries;
> This army returned in triumph
>> after cutting down its fig trees and vines;
> This army returned in triumph
>> after setting fire to all its dwellings;
> This army returned in triumph
>> after killing the troops in it by the tens of thousands;
> This army returned in triumph
>> after taking a great multitude of the troops therein as captives –
> And I was praised by his Majesty for it above anything.

Other songs are only partially preserved, with merely a line or two recorded as a caption in a tomb scene.

Of the preserved writings from this period, the tomb biography is relatively common. Yet its literary merit is minimal, however rich in the facts of social history. Only the portion known as the "Catalogue of Virtues" demonstrates literary characteristics, though they become formulaic and repetitive with multiple use over time. From the tomb of Pepi-ankh:

> I was honored by the king;
>> I was honored by the Great God;
>>> I was honored by the people.
> I was one beloved of my father;
>> I was one praised by my mother;
>>> I was one beloved of his brothers and sisters.

There may have been earlier selections, but these we can actually point to. They demonstrate that the literature was in being by around 2300 BC and that it was of the kind we would call lyric.

Another kind of writing with examples appearing in the Old Kingdom (unless surviving examples are pseudonymous and attributed to these earlier authors) is the didactic or moral genre. Of the examples, the most obvious and common are the instructions. One of the earliest of these is the "Maxims of Ptahhotep" (one of the authors lauded in the earlier passage from P. Chester Beatty IV), consisting of some forty-five bits of advice for his son given in his old age by the vizier to King Izezi of the 5th Dynasty. This wisdom literature had solidified into a specific form, in which a famous father garners the experiences of a lifetime and passes them on to a son. King Izezi is delighted to have Ptahhotep make the request to codify his experience; for, as the king says, "No one is born wise!"

Maxim 16

> If you would be a leader,
>> spread wide good governance by means of your edicts.
> Do deeds of distinction
>> so that the days which come after remember them.
> Carping does not occur in the midst of praise;
>> it is when hatred develops that the crocodile slips in.

With the Middle Kingdom comes what has traditionally been known in Egyptology as the period of classic ancient Egyptian literature, even called by some the apex of the ancient Egyptian tradition. This may be an oversimplification, but we surely see a burgeoning of examples and types dating to the Middle Kingdom, and many are very finely written. For example, didactic literature flourishes, including the instruction. But for the most part the wisdom literature as a whole displays a wider range. "The Teaching for Merikare" not only exhibits the wisdom characteristic of the genre but also contains a great deal of historical material for Merikare to digest. "The Teaching of King Amenemhat for His Son, Senusret" is really an apologia for the father's life as he returns after death to speak with his son on

FIGURE 11.1. Photograph of a portion of Papyrus British Museum 10274 recto (also known as Papyrus Butler), which records a passage from "The Eloquent Peasant." The hieratic is written in black ink and in columns. The columns are read from right to left and from top to bottom within each one. Photo: Courtesy of the British Museum. Copyright the Trustees of the British Museum.

affairs of the kingdom. "The Man Who Was Tired of Life" is a dialogue between a despairing man and his soul (*ba*) over the philosophical problem of suicide:

> Who is there to talk to today?
>> Gentleness is dead;
>>> brute strength bears down on everyone.

"The Admonitions of an Egyptian Sage" is really an outcry over the degeneration of Egyptian culture as it is invaded and overrun by foreigners from Lower Egypt. "The Prophecy of Neferty" (again a work attributed to one of the five authors in the opening stanzas of this chapter) takes the form of a prophecy that notes the decay of Egyptian civilization as it awaits regeneration under King Amenemhat:

> Rê withdraws himself from mankind
>> so that he shines down but fitfully –
> One never knows when midday happens,
>> one cannot distinguish shadows,
> There is no splendor to see by
>> – eyes cannot stream with tears.

And finally, "The Tale of the Eloquent Peasant" (Fig. 11.1) is a blend of the didactic and narrative genres. It is a story as far as the overall structure is concerned: a peasant sets off to trade his goods but is waylaid by an official who tries to rob him, with the result that the peasant is provoked into a series of speeches in defense of *maat* or justice. The point is that while all these pieces belong to the didactic genre, their subject matter is quite varied.

Lyric pieces also occur and we begin to see hymns to the gods and kings as well as more spells and prayers in the Coffin Texts. Here is an encomium to Senusret III:

His Protecting Power

He came to us to seize the Southland,
    and the Double Crown was firm on his head.
He came, he united the Two Lands,
    he mingled the Sedge and the Bee.
He came, he ruled the Egyptians,
    he placed the desert under his control.
He came, he protected the Two Lands,
    he pacified the Two Banks.
He came, he nourished the Egyptians,
    he dispelled their troubles.
He came, he saved the nobles,
    he let the throats of the commoners breathe.
He came, he trampled the foreigners,
    he struck down the tribes who did not fear him.
He came, he descended to his frontiers,
    he rescued those who had been injured.
He came, his arms received the veneration
    for what his power had brought to us.
He came, he helped us raise our children,
    we have buried our elders with his blessing.

And it is in the Middle Kingdom that the tale or story appears. This is the final genre of Egyptian literature: narrative. Some of the most appealing pieces of ancient Egyptian literature are of this kind, perhaps because they are cast in a form so familiar to our own types of literature.

"The Tale of Sinuhe" dates to this period and is considered by many to be a masterwork in the canon of ancient Egyptian literature. Sinuhe is a high-ranking member of the court of King Senusret at the beginning of the 12th Dynasty, attached to the harim of Queen Neferu. He overhears word of a plot to overthrow the king and runs off to Syria–Palestine (Retenu) to save his life. He is successful in his attempt and ends up at the court of King Amunenshi, who welcomes him. Sinuhe allies himself with Amunenshi, defeats the local champion in single combat, and is made general of the army. He has a stellar military career with Amunenshi, but misses his homeland:

Splendid my tent here, and wide my domain –
    but I still have dreams of the palace.

So he writes to Senusret, asking forgiveness, and the king immediately grants it. Sinuhe travels back to Egypt, has a welcoming audience with the king, and is reinstated in his former place at court. When he dies, he is given a pyramid in the royal burial ground. The tale is modeled on a tomb biography, a narration which gives an account of the subject's life and deeds:

> It was his Majesty who did all this for me;
> > no simple man has ever had so much.
> And I enjoyed the sunshine of his royal favor
> > until my day of mooring dawned.

Sinuhe is a loyal servant – except for the one failure, when he runs away from his duty thinking his king is about to be overthrown; and he spends most of his life coming to terms with that failure. King Senusret, on the other hand, is depicted with a truly royal capacity for understanding and forgiveness in his treatment of Sinuhe. And though the tale of Sinuhe's adventures is exciting enough, it is really his concurrent growth in character as he comes to terms with his failing and finally reconciles with his king and himself that makes this such a fine piece of literature.

One point ought to be mentioned here, since it concerns the narrative genre in general, and sometimes the didactic as well. This is the phenomenon of "embedding." Embedding occurs when one genre is interrupted for a time by another – for instance, a lyric passage inserted in the midst of a narrative. This occurs in "Sinuhe" where the protagonist's hymn of praise to King Senusret interrupts the narrative, or his prayer of thanks for his victory over the hero of Retenu, or the princesses' song of intercession with the king for Sinuhe. All three of these instances show the lyric mode interrupting the narrative. The same phenomenon occurs in the "Eloquent Peasant" to such an extent that it is difficult to tell whether the piece is a narrative with lyric interruptions or the reverse.

"The Tale of the Shipwrecked Sailor" is another of the Middle Kingdom stories that we have in virtually complete form, although it seems to belong to a cycle of tales, the remainder of which are missing from the papyrus. The sailor is attempting to comfort his captain for an unsuccessful expedition by telling him of a similar voyage he had made:

> But let me tell you just a little story, a bit like this,
> > which happened once upon a time to me.
> I was traveling to the region of the royal mines
> > and had descended to the Great Green Sea
> In a grand two-hundred-foot-long vessel
> > (its width was seventy feet from rail to rail),
> The crew within it, one hundred twenty
> > of the finest men in Egypt.
> Let them see sky, let them see land,
> > braver were their hearts than lions;
> They could foretell a storm before its coming,
> > foul weather before ever it occurred.

What he fails to convey is that he himself fared very well as a result of this disastrous expedition, returning to Egypt with treasures for the king – something that the sailor's captain could not offer. The general situation, so misapplied by the sailor, and his comments, which are so often wide of the mark, serve to add an aura of delightful humor to the tale. The above passage continues:

> A storm came up – with us on the open sea –
>   and no chance for us to reach harbor;
> The wind grew sharp and made a constant moaning,
>   and there were hungry fourteen-foot-high waves!
> A piece of wood of some sort hit me,
>   and then the ship was dead.
> Of all those fine men, not a one survived.

The sailor himself is a comic character – assertive, blustery, overconfident, forgetful of past favors, and unaware of the ironies of his speech and situation. And the giant talking serpent that the sailor meets on the magical island is a perfect foil for him.

The New Kingdom provides us with more numerous examples of literary pieces than the earlier Old and Middle Kingdoms, as well as an even greater variety of the types within each genre. All three genres are well represented. In the lyric genre, hymns, prayers, and spells continue to be composed, while new kinds of songs are developed: the love song and the so-called Harper's Song. Here is an example of a spell from the Ramesside period:

> Spell for Causing the Beloved to Follow After
>
> Hear me, O Rê, Falcon of Twin Horizons,
>   father of gods!
> Hear me, you seven Hathors
>   who weave fate with a scarlet thread!
> O Hear, all you gods of heaven and earth! –
>
>   Grant –
> That this girl, true child of her mother,
>   pursue me with undying passion,
> Follow close on my heels
>   like a cow seeking pasture,
>   like a nursemaid minding her charge,
>   like a guardian after his herd!
>
> For if you will not cause her to love me,
>   I must surely abandon the day,
>   consumed to dust in the fire of my burning.

213

The bulk of the lyric genre consists of hymns and prayers. We can use the wonderful "Hymn to the Aten," possibly by King Akhenaten himself, as an example. The king prays to his "father," Aten, describing the wonders of creation and giving thanks for them: the Nile, the nurturing rain, the chick in the egg, cities, towns, fields:

> How various is the world you have created,
> each thing mysterious, sacred to sight,
> O sole God
> beside whom is no other!

Akhenaten closes his hymn by asking that Aten "lift up the creatures of earth for your Son." The overall tone of the poem borders on the ecstatic.

The love songs offer a type of lyric poem totally different from the religious poem. First of all, the love songs are secular, offering characters and situations that express the varieties of human love. And their tone and mood run the gamut from the shy and retiring to deep and even erotic longing. One young woman lies abed at night alone and longs for her lover:

> I love you through the daytimes,
> in the dark,
> Through all the long divisions of the night, . . .

Another invites her lover to go swimming with her, promising to wear a swimsuit that goes sheer in the water; or a third is overcome by confusion when she meets her secret love on horseback coming along the road. There is even a poem to Queen Nefertari, requiring decorum on the part of the author since it is written to a queen and inscribed on a wall of Luxor Temple (Fig. 11.2), that exhibits tenderness in its loving description:

> This was a princess.
>
> Of the line royal, lady most praiseworthy
> and a woman of charm, sweet for love,
> Yet Mistress ruling two countries,
> the Twin Lands of Sedge and Papyri.
>
> See her, her hands here shaking the sistra
> to bring pleasure to God, her father Amun.
> How lovely she moves,
> her hair bound with fillets,
> Songstress with perfect features,
> a beauty in double-plumed headdress,
> And first among harim women
> to Horus, Lord of the Palace.
>
> Pleasure there is in her lips' motions,
> all that she says, it is done for her gladly,

FIGURE 11.2. Queen Nefertari and the poem, "For a Portrait of the Queen," from Luxor Temple, Court of the Statues, West Wall, North of Door. This love song is written in columns, one in front of the figure of the queen and five behind her. The columns are read from left to right and from top to bottom within each one. Photo by the authors.

> Her heart is all kindness, her words
> > gentle to those upon earth.
> One lives just to hear her voice.

Another kind of poem from the lyric genre is the Harper's Song. There are only a few of these, and they form a strange interlude in the literature; for they seem to question the sacred Egyptian principle of eternal life, urging the hearer to *carpe diem*, "seize the day":

> Grieve not your heart, whatever comes;
> > let sweet music play before you;
> Recall not the evil, loathsome to God,
> > but have joy, joy, joy, and pleasure!

The harper's song from Inherkhawy's tomb says just this:

> All who come into being as flesh,
> > pass on. . . .

> Let your heart be drunk on the gift of Day
> > until that day comes when you anchor.

The lyric genre includes the widest range of subjects from ancient Egypt, and among them appear the poems often called the "schoolboy" poems, written by schoolboys, or by instructors aiming to improve student work. Of these, beside chastisements and other calls to duty, there is the occasional piece reflecting the life of the student. For instance, "Longing for Memphis" shows the schoolboy tired of his studies and longing to be out of the schoolroom and off to the big city. He prays to Ptah, Lord of Memphis, to help him concentrate on his schoolwork:

> O Lord of the City friendly to young scribes,
> > be at peace with me!
> > > Grant me to rise above this day's infirmities!

The didactic genre continues in the New Kingdom with earlier works copied ("The Instruction of Khety") as well as new compositions such as "The Instruction of Amenemope," which closely follow the structure of "The Maxims of Ptahhotep" from the Old Kingdom:

> Give ear to hear my words,
> > and give your mind to searching into them.
> Great benefit is yours if you will place them in your heart,
> > while failure follows the neglect of them.

One unique text in the didactic genre, found on a single ostracon from Deir el-Medineh, is "Menna's Lament." It is Menna's letter to his wayward son, Pay-iry, admonishing him to change the course of his life. It aches with the love and frustration of a father who believes he has done everything he should for his son, yet the son has gone wild:

> As for the son who should obey his father,
> > that text holds good for all eternity, they say.
> But then you did not pause for any admonition
> > with which I warned and warned you long ago.

Variations do occur among the examples of instructions, and it is unclear whether these differences reflect an evolutionary pattern or are due to the chances of preservation.

Regarding New Kingdom narratives, several survive, including the longer and complete "Tale of the Two Brothers" and "The Contendings of Horus and Seth." These narratives shows stylistic characteristics different from those of the earlier carefully crafted narrations of the Middle Kingdom that use the full gamut of literary devices. These have a looser style, with frequent repetitions and an emphasis on the chain of events rather than the development of characters within the work or the use of literary devices that lend richness to the meaning and imagery.

The first New Kingdom tale is of marital infidelity causing a rift between brothers who had been like father and son. A long and painful misunderstanding ensues – the elder brother killing his unfaithful wife and the younger (who had been falsely accused by the wife) emasculating himself and going into exile. Over a period of years, the rift between the brothers is slowly healed and the two trade positions of influence and power. In the end, Bata, the younger, becomes king and Anubis, the elder, is appointed crown prince by his younger brother, as the two become reconciled.

"The Contendings of Horus and Seth" is the narrative – rather poorly presented – of the battle for supremacy between the uncle and the nephew in the Osirian family. The Ennead generally back the cause of Horus, while Rê champions Seth. They bicker back and forth until Horus is finally awarded the Kingdom of Egypt and Seth given a position as aide to Rê.

Narratives using more literary devices and language also occur in the New Kingdom. One that is particularly interesting in this respect is an embedded narrative section in "The Battle of Kadesh." It describes the events of the battle of Ramesses II and his Egyptian forces against the Hittites. But with its focus on Ramesses and his thoughts and actions during his solitary stand in the battle as well as the tone of the poem itself, Ramesses becomes a heroic character and the passage becomes "proto-epic":

> So, I prayed at the far end of the world,
>   and my voice echoed through Thebes;
> And I found that Amun would come
>   once I cried out to him.
> He put his hand in mine
>   and I was happy.
> And he called as if behind me,
>   "Go forward! I am with you!
>   I am your Father, my hand is in yours!
> I am stronger than hundreds of thousands of men!
>   I am the Lord of Battle, Lover of Victory!"

Though outside of the scope of this study, the Late Period also produced works from these genres: hymns and prayers continued to be written, Onkhsheshonkhy is a fine example of an instruction, and the stories of Prince Khaemwas continued the tradition of the narrative.

These then – the lyric, the didactic, and the narrative – are the basic forms in which the literature was cast, each form having stylistic characteristics and each having a variety of subdivisions.

Ancient Egyptian literature, it seems, was essentially a verse literature, although this point is not accepted by all scholars. For ancient Egyptian verse literature, even basic points of prosody remain under scholarly discussion, particularly because the orthography of the pre-Coptic language did not reflect vowels, and the pronunciation of words can only be surmised. This makes a metrical assessment of ancient Egyptian verse problematic, and to some scholars, impossible. Nonetheless, Gerhard Fecht developed a metrical method for analyzing ancient Egyptian verse based on later Coptic metrics. He contended that the line is composed of a set number of *kola* (groups of syllables), with each *kolon* possessing one stress and based on grammatical groupings of words.

Another approach to ancient Egyptian prosody began with the line itself and used nonmetrical criteria for analysis. In this view, the individual verse line of all ancient Egyptian literary genres consists of a single grammatical clause; and two such clauses constitute the Egyptian couplet, the structural unit that builds up the literary passage. Other unit arrangements occur – the two-element verse line, the singlet, the triplet, the quatrain – but these additional arrangements do not occur often enough to break the couplet rhythm. The evidence for this comes from the red dots above the lines inked onto some texts appearing on either papyri or ostraca. These, called "verse points," mark clauses, and thus verse lines of text. If one rearranges continuous lines of original text based on the verse points (as in a poem in English), one discovers that lines of verse are formed and, moreover, that each such line constitutes a clause. Further, grammatically these clauses seem to join together, forming sentences composed of couplets; and this phenomenon has been termed the "thought couplet." That all three kinds of Egyptian literature are structured similarly – in couplets – is also evidence for suggesting that all the literature (*belles lettres*) is in verse. In the lyric and didactic kinds, this couplet structuring is strictly adhered to; while in some narrative examples it seems to be more relaxed.

Other than this matter of the verse flow being built up from clauses in couplets, Egyptian verse utilizes the same devices as other literatures – metaphor, alliteration, repetition, vivid imagery, personification, characterization, symbol – and all the myriad ways of enhancing meaning. For example, vivid imagery has already been noted in the Pyramid Texts. Metaphors and similes are frequently used to enrich meaning and images. A metaphor from a hymn to Thoth,

> Let us offer praise to Thoth,
>   the plumbline which is true in the center of the balance,

shows that the god's honesty is not just unswerving, but is not able to be skewed, just as a plumbline is held straight by gravity. Another example of a metaphor is from a poem called "The Memphis Ferry":

> O Memphis, my city, beauty forever! –
>   you are a bowl of love's own berries.

A simile occurs later in the same poem:

> Oh, I'm bound downstream on the Memphis ferry,
>   like a runaway, snapping all ties, . . .

where the young man is likening himself to a boat that has snapped its mooring rope, having been caught in the strong current and pulled away. This is especially effective in that it is echoed in the image of the ferry he has just stepped into to go to Memphis.

Characterization is another device used and is wholly at work in both "The Tale of Sinuhe" and "The Shipwrecked Sailor." In the first, Sinuhe's character develops, providing one of the primary actions of the story. In the second, the sailor's character remains the same – in spite of the tremendous events that might make another man reform – and provides the basis of much of the story's humor.

Yet another literary device is personification, and this is evident in a portion of the second stanza of "The Great Hymn to Osiris" from the New Kingdom stele of Amenmose:

> It was for him chaos poured forth its waters,
>> and the north wind drove upstream;
> Sky would make breeze for his nostrils
>> that thereby his heart might find peace;
> For his sake green things grew, and the
>> good earth would bring forth its riches.
> Sky and its stars obeyed him,
>> for him the great gates of heaven stood open;
> Praise of him thundered down southern skies,
>> he was adored under northern heavens;
> The circling, unfaltering stars
>> wheeled near his watchful eye,
> And the weary ones, who sink below seeing –
>> with them was his very dwelling.

Here various natural phenomena, particularly celestial ones, are personified in their acts on behalf of Osiris and their desire to perform them.

Repetition is used and includes the sound repetition of alliteration as well as the grammatical, syntactic, and thematic repetitions that make up *parallelism*. The "Victory Song of Weni" shows repetition, not just in the use of the same words in the first line of each couplet, but also in the destructive activity the army exerts upon its enemy in each of the second lines of each couplet. The exact nature of the destructive acts varies, but they all have the same effect on the army's opponent – complete ruin. The fourth song in praise of Senusret III, "His Protecting Power," also shows intentional repetition. Here it is working with more complexity than in Weni's song. As in Weni's song, the same phrase, "He came," opens each couplet. With the exception of the opening couplet and the concluding two couplets, additional repetitions can be seen. The second half of the first line and the second line of each subsequent couplet tell how the king actively does something to benefit Egypt. Then within each couplet the parallelism occurs in the object of the verbs and varies from couplet to couplet. In the second and seventh couplets, the objects are the same; they just go by different names: "Two Lands" is paired with "Sedge and Bee" and "foreigners" with "tribes that did not fear him." But an interesting tension is introduced with the objects in

FIGURE 11.3. Ostracon OIM 17002–17003: the beginning of "The Instruction of Hordjedef." Photograph of ostracon with hieratic text preserved on the surface. The hieratic writing is in black ink and is read from right to left. Verse points are in red ink and raised to the upper part of each register. Note the lighter color and cleaner surface of more recent breaks: the upper left surface, the central fissure, and the upper right. Photo: Courtesy of the Oriental Institute of the University of Chicago.

other couplets that are juxtaposed. In the third couplet it is "Egypt" and "the desert"; in the fourth it is "the Two Lands" of the north and south juxtaposed with "the Two Banks" of the Nile-oriented east and west; in the fifth it is "nourishing" as opposed to "dispelling their troubles"; and in the sixth it is "the nobles" and "the commoners" of Egypt. It concludes with a similar juxtaposition, the children and the elders of Egypt, which shows that all of Egypt benefits from the interest and blessings of the king.

One caution: the term *poetry*, so widely used today, is actually inappropriate to apply wholesale to the literature of ancient Egypt. For Egyptian literature, the proper distinction is between *verse* and *prose*. For example, pieces from the lyric genre are written in verse, while the greatest of them, particularly some of the love songs and hymns, rise to *poetry*.

Many of the pieces survive only in fragments. But there is a partial remedy for this. There are often multiple partial copies of a given text that, when arranged into a "parallel text" edition, can improve the original. The process begins with a photograph of the original text – in our example, an ostracon (Fig. 11.3). The script is then differentiated from its background and

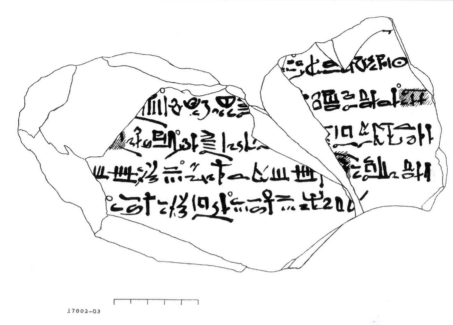

17002–03

FIGURE 11.4. Ostracon OIM 17002–17003: the beginning of "The Instruction of Hordjedef." Hieratic phase of transcription. The details of the photographic image of the stone have been removed, leaving the hieratic writing in its position relative to the outline and the main surfaces of the stone. The red ink of the verse points is denoted as outlines around the small circles of each point. (Standard procedure for hieratic drawn in red ink is to outline it as well.) Hatching indicates areas of uncertain, often worn, writing. Image copyright of the authors.

reproduced (Fig. 11.4). If hieratic, it is then transcribed into hieroglyphs (Fig. 11.5) and, when they are present, divided into verse lines by the verse points (Fig. 11.6). Once this has been completed for each separate source for a text, the parallel text edition is formed.

First, the most complete copy of the text is arranged in a single horizontal line of signs. Then copies of the passage from other sources, generally ostraca or papyri, are written horizontally beneath the matching signs of the first copy (Fig. 11.7). That is, the various copies are drawn "in parallel" to the first copy. Since most texts with multiple copies show minute variations, one can see the varying signs drawn by the ancient copyists, compare them with the other renderings on other copies of the passage, and make a judgment as to which copy used the best interpretation of the original text. Often, this re-examination of multiple texts improves a reading. In addition, longer gaps in a text can be filled from secondary texts. Comparing the examples and making these choices, the most complete version of the text is assembled, forming what is known as an "eclectic text" (Fig. 11.8).

For instance, take the opening of "The Instruction of Hordjedef," a work of another of the five authors from the opening of this chapter. An ostracon from the Oriental Institute Museum of the University of Chicago, number 17002–17003, preserves a fair amount of the

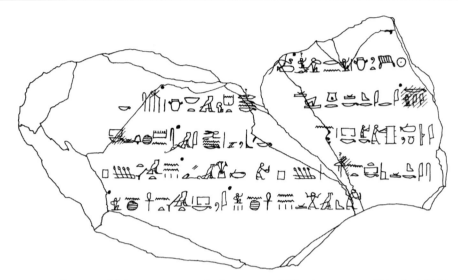

FIGURE 11.5. Ostracon OIM 17002–17003: the beginning of "The Instruction of Hordjedef." Hieroglyphic phase of transcription. The hieroglyphic equivalents of the hieratic signs are substituted on the same outline of the stone. Verse points are now solid small circles. (Standard procedure for indicating red ink in a hieroglyphic rendering of a text is to underline signs. Verse points may be outlined or solid.) Signs only partially preserved in the original are now restored in the broken areas if possible. Hatching remains in areas of uncertain or abraded writing. Image copyright of the authors.

first part of the piece. Figures 11.3, 11.4, and 11.5 illustrate Ostracon OIM 17002–17003 in the first steps of the documentation process described above. Figure 11.6 then divides the text of O. OIM 17002–17003 into its verse lines – or, more correctly, the fragments thereof.

Looking at the ostracon, we can see that the "tail" of a sign appears at the break line of the stone at the top right. This shows that a line of hieratic originally occurred there. Below this, the name *Aut-ib-re* begins this copy of the text and then the stone is again broken. The text resumes with the next line (again, beginning at the right) with a slightly obliterated series of signs, then a quite legible series of more signs, then a break through the original stone (note the recent mend), then another series of quite legible signs, and then another break. Verse points occur near each end of this line of text. The signs between these verse points are reproduced in Fig. 11.7 in parallel text format with the same lines from other ostraca that also preserve this passage to some degree or another. One can immediately see how one copy augments another.

For example, the line divisions of single ostraca are subsumed into the line divisions of the original, complete piece. The lower case Roman numerals in Fig. 11.6 are expanded (i becomes final text lines 1, 2, 3, and the first half of 4) or contracted (xiii becomes the end of line 14 and the beginning of line 15, with the break in the stone noted at the end of xiii and beginning of xiv being present at the time of composition and thus not a break in the text at all) to fall into their places in the shape of the original text.

FIGURE 11.6. Ostracon OIM 17002–17003: the beginning of "The Instruction of Hordjedef." Division into verse lines. The hieroglyphic text of ostracon is now rendered in preserved, probable verse lines (lower case Roman numerals) on the basis of the verse points present in the original text. Broken edges of the stone that intersect the text are noted. Image copyright of the authors.

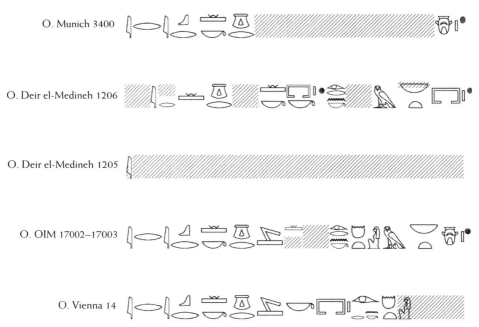

FIGURE 11.7. Parallel text reconstruction for signs appearing between verse points in the third line of Ostracon OIM 17002–17003: the beginning of "The Instruction of Hordjedef." Of these ostraca that preserve this part of the instruction, O. Munich 3400 appears first because it is generally the most complete. In this section, however, O. OIM 17002–17003 is most complete and can be used to restore the others. Conversely, the middle of the line from O. OIM 17002–17003 is damaged and missing and is thus itself restored using O. DeM 1206 (with verse point!) and supplemented by O. Vienna 14. Note that the text is now read from left to right. These two lines are ultimately verse lines 7 and 8 from the complete text. This reconstruction is adapted from Wolfgang Helck, *Die Lehre des Djedefhor und Die Lehre eines Vaters an seinen Sohn*, Kleine Ägyptische Texte 8, Wiesbaden: Otto Harrassowitz, 1984. Image by the authors.

The parallel text edition makes possible the recovery of a more accurate text – free of the various schoolboy errors prevalent in many of the ostraca texts, since these were often practice pieces for scribes in training. For example, line xii of O. OIM 17002–17003 ends incorrectly – the scribe has placed the verse point too soon in the line, perhaps mistaking the forearm with palm down (here used as part of the spelling of the word) for another use the sign is put to, the means to designate the end of a stanza (and, implicitly, the end of a line). It should be placed in the middle of line xiii. The correct (and corrected) version appears in the eclectic text of Fig. 11.8. And from this eclectic text comes our translation:

1   Beginning of the Teaching
2   made by the Overseer and Prince,
3   King's Son, Hordjedef,

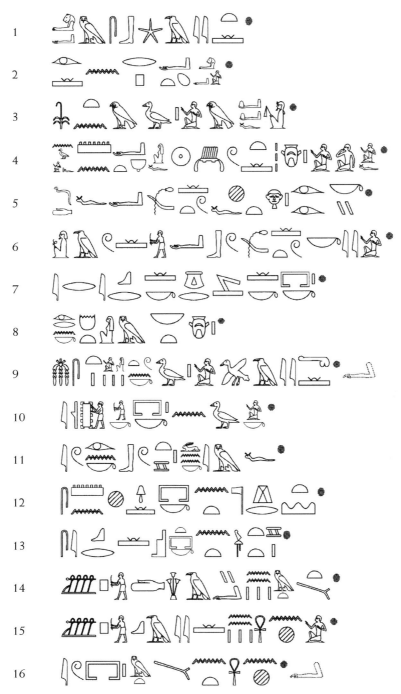

FIGURE 11.8. Eclectic text for the beginning of "The Instruction of Hordjedef." This comprises the first sixteen lines of the text and is the length of the text originally written on O. OIM 17002–17003. Verse points appear at the ends of the lines as large dots. Stanza ends are denoted by the hieroglyph of an arm with palm facing down appearing after the verse points in lines 9 and 16. Gray tone here indicates red ink on the original text. Another standard practice is to underline signs originally in red ink. Note that, though not utilized in any of the ostraca forming this eclectic text, red ink was also often used for the first hieroglyphs of a new stanza. This red portion is known as a "rubric." Image by the authors.

4   for his Son, whom he reared, Autibre.
5   He says: Correct yourself in your own eyes;
6   take care that another does not reprove you.
7   If you are wise, found your household;
8   take to yourself a woman as loving lady
9   that a male child be born to you.

10   Build your estate for your son,
11   that a place where you are be created for you.
12   Embellish your dwelling in the Land under God,
13   make splendid your dwelling in the West.
14   Accept that death is bitter for us;
15   accept that life is exalted for us;
16   the house of Death is for the Ever-Living.

The source of many of these ostraca is the scribal school of western Thebes, now the site of Deir el-Medineh, where a huge trash pit was uncovered some years ago with thousands of fragments containing texts, literary and nonliterary, written by the students as they copied their lessons. Once the lessons were completed, the ostraca were discarded. As another example of the parallel text process, we can take the didactic text known as "The Instruction of Khety" for his son Pepi, usually known as "The Satire on the Trades." Until recently this text survived in two papyri – quite unreliable – and dozens of ostraca. Yet it was one of the most copied of the Deir el-Medineh texts. The French scholar Georges Posener spent much time studying and cataloguing these ostraca, adding over a hundred pieces (mostly partial duplicates) to the store of copies. Though scribal errors are rampant in these ostraca, the body of comparative sources is large, which leads to a vast improvement in the passage once the parallel text analysis reconstructs an eclectic text. It is only after this compilation of a more accurate original that the modern scholar first makes the literal translation into English (in our case) and then, should purposes dictate, the literary translation.

It has been less than two hundred years since the key to translating the ancient Egyptian language was discovered – a fraction of the time the language itself was in use, from about 3000 BC (and probably earlier), until on into the early Christian era. During the time since Champollion, not only the very sounds and values of the ancient Egyptian signs had to be discovered, but also the nature of the sentence, the meanings of words, as well as the specific ages of documents and their contributions to forming a reliable history of the country. And none of these ongoing endeavors even touch on the nature and content of ancient Egyptian literature. Literary investigations had to wait on results of grammatical studies, the compiling of dictionaries, and the earliest tentative translations.

The problem of word meanings was particularly difficult in the nineteenth and earlier twentieth centuries, as the root meanings of words were pursued. From the earliest days of the translation of the literature, there have been two methods. First is the *literal* trans-lation, wherein the core, literal meanings of the words are employed – the denotations of the words and the original flow of the sentences are used in the translation. The second method is the *literary* translation, in which a wider leeway is chosen, one in which the spirit of the original rather than the letter is sought. The former method has the drawback of masking or marring any of the literary values or beauty of pieces originally meant to convey material intended to be imaginative or beautiful. The problem with the literary translation is the possibility of departing too far from the literal meaning of the words used in the original Egyptian. The problem of use of the literal or literary translation is still with us.

Today the student of ancient Egyptian literature is able to stand on the shoulders of at least three generations of scholars specific to this field. Yet full training must be accomplished in components. There is no single program in just ancient Egyptian literature. Instead, the student must learn the ancient Egyptian language in its various stages as a discipline in itself. Separately, the student must also learn literary theory. Only after both have been mastered can a true understanding and appreciation of the literature of ancient Egypt *as literature* be accomplished. Many universities teaching the ancient Egyptian language also have pro-grams in comparative literature, and a sympathetic faculty might be persuaded to develop a combined course of study in a degree program. Most scholars working in the discipline today have completed a degree in Egyptology and have acquired a knowledge of literary theory during an earlier degree, in guided reading, or through independent study. Most of these scholars, too, are employed as Egyptologists, though those additionally trained in comparative literature or related fields may have jobs in such academic departments in a college or university.

As for the state of the field itself, much remains to be done. The understanding of the language, as discussed above, remains basic in many respects important to a literary under-standing of a work, so that nuances of meaning, constructions, and cultural values are still to be elucidated. In addition, it is still possible to search texts for heretofore unknown items of literary quality. And the history of ancient Egyptian literature has yet to be fully fleshed out, including exploration to discern if there are other literary genres, such as the tomb biography, to add to the canon we have now. Then, though true literary critiques of texts have been done, the potential for additional work is still great. For example, as discussed earlier, the question of prosody in ancient Egyptian literature is still being addressed from very different perspectives. Among others, one aspect of prosody still worth pursuing is the careful determination of the dividing line between verse and prose. Another field of study continues to be investigating the place, if any, of oral tradition in the general literary tradition of ancient Egypt, since so many of the current texts seem to bear evidence of oral handling. Yet another major area of potential study is the relation of styles in ancient Egyptian liter-ature to those of neighboring cultures. Biblical parallels have most often been considered, but could be explored further; and the literature of sub-Saharan African traditions, of the

Greco-Roman tradition, and even the later Arabic literature of Egypt must contain potentially fruitful comparative materials for various aspects of literary studies.

But no matter what the vagaries of preservation, the challenges of recovery, and the differences in translation and interpretation, ancient Egyptian literature is without doubt another of the rich legacies from the land of the Nile.

APPENDIX
Some Sources for the Study of Ancient Egyptian Literature

Full citations for the works listed here are given in the bibliography for this chapter.

A. Primary sources are numerous and may be found in the references and notes of the works cited in the bibliography. However, as an illustration of the Deir el-Medineh ostraca discussed in some detail in this chapter, the following publications may be noted: Černý and Gardiner 1957; Guess 1990; Lopez 1978–84; Posener 1938–80.

B. Secondary sources include the following:

Parallel text editions: Among others, Helck published literary texts in this format in the series *Kleine Ägyptische Texte*, which is the basis for the example in Fig. 11.7 (Helck 1984).

Commentaries: Commentaries are generally found in monographs and articles within scholarly journals and cover all of the various topics touched on within this chapter. This ranges from studies of orthography and spelling through consideration of the intentions of the author as well as the use of literary devices. Bibliographies within the other sources cited here provide more specific references.

C. General assessments of ancient Egyptian literature as literature as well as surveys of the field can be divided into encyclopedic and single author works. For encyclopedic works see Assmann and Blumenthal 1999; Assmann, Feucht, and Grieshammer, 1977; Loprieno 1996; Moers 1999; Spuler 1970. See also various topical discussions listed alphabetically in Helck, Westendorf, and Otto 1975–1992; Redford 2001. For single-author works, see Assmann 1992; Brunner 1986; Brunner-Traut 1978; Burkard 1993; Burkard and Thissen 2003; Parkinson 2002; Posener 1951; Posener 1956; Posener 1971; Redford 1995.

D. Specific topical assessments of ancient Egyptian literature by genre:

Hymns: Plas 1986; love songs: Fox 1985; Mathieu 1996; Schott 1950; Vernus 1992; prosody: Burkard 1983; Fecht 1965; Foster 1988; Lichtheim 1971–2; Mathieu 1988, 1990, 1994, and 1997; Schenkel 1978; stories and tales: Hollis 1995; wisdom texts: Hermann 1959; Hornung and Keel 1979; Leclant 1963; Williams 1992.

E. Translations: Most have an introductory essay with short, introductory prefaces to each piece and associated bibliographies.

Assmann 1999; Barucq and Daumas 1979; Bresciani 1969; Brunner 1988; Brunner-Traut 1963; Brunner-Traut 1985; Erman 1966; Foster 1992; Foster 1995; Foster 2001; Lefebvre 1949; Lichtheim 1973–80; Parkinson 1997; Rocatti 1994; Simpson, Ritner, Tobin, and Wente 2003.

F. Some tools of the translator include, but are not limited to:

Grammars: Allen 2000; Gardiner 1973; dictionaries: Erman and Grapow 1971; Faulkner 1981; Hannig 1995; index of hieratic forms: Möller 1965; hieroglyphic computer font: Berg and Aubourg 2000; literary theory: Preminger and Brogan 1993.

Chapter 12

Egyptian Religious Texts

Ronald J. Leprohon

Textual material of a religious nature is ubiquitous in ancient Egypt, perhaps due to accident of preservation; much of this documentation comes from tombs and temples, built of durable materials. Domestic architecture, whether royal or private, was made of more perishable materials. Notwithstanding Kemp's cautious warnings to the contrary, spiritual matters appear to have been of paramount importance in ancient Egypt. From birth and its attendant dangers, to unexplained illnesses and unforeseen misfortunes, to death – that greatest of unknowns – the ancient Egyptians seemed to have felt the need to communicate with the unseen forces (which we call divinities) whom they believed responsible, whether positively or negatively, for such events. They composed a myriad of texts to placate or honor their gods, an act they felt gave them a degree of control over their own lives.

Since storytelling is innate in human beings, it is likely that composing and recounting tales about the gods was the first step in this process.[1] This small sampling of religious texts will begin with myths and, remembering the importance of the power of spoken word in ancient Egypt,[2] will go on to official temple ritual, where some of those sacred tales were retold in formal contexts. Next, texts detailing personal piety will demonstrate – for example, with personal names – that knowledge of the sacred stories can be assumed for the entire population. The last section will examine the mortuary literature, composed to give the Egyptians psychic comfort about death and its aftermath. Many of these categories are perforce somewhat arbitrary, since various elements could be woven into a single text. For example, a narrative tale could use religious symbolism that would have been well known to the original audience; a protective spell could contain allusions to well-known mythological episodes, the happy outcome of which would be magically transferred to the earthly recipient; or a hymn to the god Osiris could contain a lamentation meant to be sung by his sisters Isis and Nephthys (e.g., Pap. Berlin 3008).[3]

Sacred History – Myths
Cosmogonies

Creation stories, which are common to all societies throughout world history, answer such existential questions as "Who are we?" and "Who made us, where, and when?" and explain the world and its phenomena. The Egyptian material is not always immediately accessible to the modern reader, because of how the ancient Egyptians saw natural occurrences. As H. A. Frankfort suggested,[4] what the modern mind sees as an "It" was perceived as a "You" by the ancients. One example of this approach is the ancient explanation of the Nile flood. The Egyptians did not know about the "Why," the early summer rains in northern Ethiopia, which caused the Blue Nile to overflow its banks and start running north, causing the Nile to rise in Aswan in mid-July. They therefore asked "Who?" in this instance, the god Hapy, an anthropomorphic deity who was said to reside in the caverns of the first Cataract area and be responsible for the inundation.

Another obstacle is that the full mythical narratives often have to be pieced together from diverse sources. The ancient Egyptians – for reasons that can be endlessly debated – never felt the need to write down treatises of their complete theology. Two famous examples of this lack are the myth of Osiris and the creation account from Heliopolis; the former, apart from Plutarch's later account, must be pieced together from a number of allusions found in the Pyramid Texts and from scattered references in hymns to the god, while the latter must be gathered hither and yon in the Pyramid Texts. This absence of a full narrative led Assmann to suggest that myth did not exist in Egypt before the period of the New Kingdom.[5] Others have taken a more moderate approach, proposing that, although full mythical narratives are not found in corpora such as the Pyramid Texts, perhaps the myths were relegated to the sphere of oral tradition.[6] In 2002 Goebs also cogently argued that the context in which the myths are found must be taken into consideration. The position taken in this chapter – admittedly not completely unassailable – will be that myths did indeed exist as far back as the Old Kingdom, when the Pyramid Texts were carved on the inner walls of royal pyramids, and that traces of them can in fact be found in the corpus. As the present writer sees it, since the Pyramid Texts were written to help the deceased king with his rebirth, it should not be surprising to find stories of the birth of the world within their many-layered utterances.

In ancient Egypt, the creation accounts were very much a reflection of the world as the Egyptians saw it. Every spring, the Nile flood would subside and what first emerged from the water were triangular-shaped islands of rich black earth. These little mounds represented the promise of new life, which led to the notion that all creation must have begun exactly the same way.

Heliopolis: The first creation story is from Heliopolis, Egyptian Iunu, or "Pillar-Town." Out of dark and inert water called the Nun, a small hill appeared, on which the god Atum-Khepri manifested himself. The text is full of puns, which underscores the power of the spoken word: "Hail to you Atum and hail to you Khepri, the one who came into being (*kheper*) by himself, as you become high (*qai*) in this your name of Hill (*qa*), and as you come into being (*kheper*) in this your name of Khepri" (PT, § 1587). Atum then begins masturbating to fashion the god Shu and the goddess Tefnut, who represent the polarity of air and moisture, respectively, one a preserving and the other a decomposing agent. Another version has Atum creating the two deities through the use of puns: "What you [Atum] sneezed (*ishesh*) was Shu and what you spat out (*tef*) was Tefnut" (PT, § 1652). This first pair of deities then produce the earth-god Geb and the sky-goddess Nut, who, in turn, beget two further divine pairs, Osiris and Isis and Seth and Nephthys. This last generation represents the link between the earthly and the divine world and the beginnings of the political realm on earth. Known by the Greek word Ennead in modern scholarship, this divine family was called *pesdjet*, "(Group of) Nine," by the Egyptians, a feminine word that presumably alluded to the group's cosmic procreative powers.

Hermopolis: From the Middle Kingdom, with additional texts from later periods, the next creation story comes from the city of Hermopolis, the Greek designation for Egyptian Khemnu, "Eight-Town." Clearly a local memory of the area's own creation myth, the tale contains four pair of male and female divinities, the former represented as frogs and the latter as snakes. Called "the Eight Infinite Ones" by the Egyptians (CT Spell 76), they are usually referred to by another Greek term, the Ogdoad, in Egyptological literature. Compared to the Heliopolitan tradition, the Hermopolitan is a more abstract doctrine. These eight deities are Nun and Nunet, symbolizing the primeval waters of the earlier Heliopolitan tradition; Heh and Hehet, representing the concept of the flood; Keku and Kekut, embodying the darkness; and Tenem and Tenemet, signifying straying or lack of direction. With the ascendancy of Amun during the New Kingdom, theologians replaced the last couple with Amun and Amunet, representing the invisible but active breath of life. These deities appear simultaneously and set the inert primeval mass in motion; this movement churns up the mud of the primeval waters, which condenses into a hill that emerges from the floodwaters. From this hill, called the Island of the Flame, the sun appears out of a water lily in some accounts, or out of a primordial egg in others.

Presumably aware of the Heliopolitan account and borrowing from it, the Hermopolitan theologians wrote that the god Atum emerged "from the *heh*-flood, from the *nun*-ocean, from the *keku*-darkness, and from the *tenem*-lack of direction" (CT Spell 76), that is, from the Ogdoad. They also referred to their Ogdoad as "the fathers and mothers who came into being at the very beginning, who gave birth to the sun and created Atum." [7] Thus did they reassure their faithful that their own cosmogony was simply part – but a major part – of the other great creation story emanating from Heliopolis.

Memphis: The third major creation account centers on the god Ptah of Memphis; hence its customary name, The Memphite Theology. Its source is the so-called Shabako Stone, a 25th Dynasty copy of an earlier worm-eaten papyrus. Long thought to date to the Old Kingdom, the Memphite Theology has now been convincingly dated by Schlögl to the Ramesside Period. The main means of creation is through the god's mind (*ib*, often rendered as "heart") and tongue, that is, will and the power of the spoken word. The god needed only to think of something and then pronounce its name to make it occur, reminding us of the well-known New Testament passage "In the beginning was the Word and the Word was with God" (John 1:1).

A number of points connect the Memphite Theology to the previous creation accounts. The introductory passage by King Shabako mentions that he ordered the text copied on behalf of "his father Ptah-Tatenen," a syncretistic god associating Ptah with the Memphite deity whose name means "the land that has arisen," a reference to the primeval hill that emerged out of the waters of the Nun at the time of creation in the earlier Heliopolitan myth. The creation account then introduces "The gods who came into being by means of Ptah," followed by a list of eight deities, including Ptah-Nun and Ptah-Nunet. The number eight may be a coincidence but, given the Hermopolitan Ogdoad, is certainly noteworthy; perhaps the Memphite theologians were actively seeking to connect their doctrine to the earlier one. Next, "Through the mind and through the tongue did it come into being (kheper) as the image of Atum" (Shabako Stone, col. 53), linking Ptah with his Heliopolitan counterpart. Another passage ties Ptah's own Ennead with "that phallus and those hands of Atum" (Shabako Stone, col. 55), seemingly a direct correlation with the Heliopolitan Atum's creative act.

This notion of a creative mind that names things was not new to Egypt, as the deities Sia and Hu – personifications of divine perception and utterance, respectively – are known as far back as the Old Kingdom (PT, §§ 267b–d, 300c, etc.). The belief that something had to be named before it could exist is also found on Pap. Berlin 3055, a 22nd Dynasty papyrus that describes the primeval condition as a time when "the name of any thing had not yet been conceived."[8] Far from being contradictory, these three creation accounts are actually complementary. Egyptian theologians were obviously aware of various accounts and, instead of competing with them, chose to integrate earlier stories into their own, in a clear demonstration of a sense of spiritual compromise.[9] Where earlier scholars chose to see competition between the various cities and their priesthoods, perhaps one should see accommodation and creative thinking. Current research includes detailed study of the cosmogonic stories as found in the Coffin Texts, or from particular sites such as the Khonsu Temple at Karnak; examinations of particular genres of text, such as Late Period hymns, in which the creation motifs reflect earlier New Kingdom traditions at the same time as they show great innovation; and studies on such specific topics as the use of the number seven in myth, or the influence of ancient Egypt on Old Testament theologians.[10]

Tales of the Divine

Osirian Cycle: The importance of the Osirian cycle is second to none, since it informs so many aspects of ancient Egyptian culture, from the obvious funerary texts to protective ("magical") spells and amulets to personal names that demonstrate how well all strata of Egyptian society knew the tale. The full saga is only recorded by the first century AD Greek writer Plutarch; as with the cosmogonies, the Egyptians never wrote the complete story down. Some pharaonic material, however, contains parts of the story, allowing comparison of this earlier material to Plutarch's narrative.

In the first of the three portions of the story, the god Geb gives the office of kingship to Osiris. Osiris is said to be a good and beneficent ruler. His jealous brother Seth murders Osiris by throwing a chest containing his body into the river. His sister – and wife – Isis discovers him in Byblos, and she takes the chest back to Egypt, thus revivifying the king. Seth again kills Osiris, but this time cuts the body into fourteen pieces, which he scatters over Egypt. Isis looks for Osiris anew and eventually finds all the pieces, save for the phallus, so that an artificial phallus has to be supplied to Osiris. Isis brings him back to life again long enough to conceive a child. Osiris then descends to the underworld to rule the dead. The second part of the cycle has Isis hiding in the marshes of the Delta, where she gives birth to Horus, whom she protects from scorpion and snakes. The third part tells of a now-grown Horus avenging his father, through a number of battles with Seth, in one of which Horus loses his eye. When the god Thoth heals the eye, it is said to be "hale" (*udjat*), an icon that became ubiquitous in ancient Egypt. Horus eventually claims the throne through a divine legal judgment. This portion is told in a protracted, and sometimes comical, series of events in which Isis often intervenes on her son's behalf.[11] One of the sequences, a homosexual attack by Seth on Horus, has generated much discussion, notably by Parkinson, who, in 1995, investigated the difference in approach to the subject in literary and nonliterary texts; Walls, who more recently has looked at the episode from a Freudian point of view; and Amenta, who connects the *topos* to magical texts and suggests that the condemnation of homosexual activities was simply prompted by its inability to further mankind's procreation.

The first and most obvious theme of the full story is that the death of Osiris and his subsequent rebirth assured ordinary Egyptians of the possibility of their own resurrection. Second, the loving ministrations of Isis gave all women a role model as wife, mother, and protectress. The last role made her important as a healer and explains the many references to that particular portion of the cycle in so-called magical spells.[12] As Quirke rightly pointed out,[13] the many roles Isis plays throughout the legend make her the unifying element, the one common actor in the whole cycle. A third major theme is the importance of tribunals, since a divine court of law eventually gave Horus his father's inheritance. This decision must surely have encouraged the population to use the local courts to settle their disputes instead of taking matters into their own hands. This theme is underscored by the behavior of Horus and Seth in the third part of the cycle, where the former continually presents his case to the divine court in a calm and rational way, while Seth keeps losing his temper and challenging Horus to fight. The final outcome in court must have left no doubt to anyone listening to the tale as to which behavior was the better one to emulate.

Destruction of Humanity: The myth traditionally known as the Destruction of Mankind[14] contained in the first part of the so-called Book of the Divine Cow, tells of the aging god Re who discovers that mankind – his creation – has been plotting against him. He convenes a divine council to seek their advice; there, he is told to send his eye, in the form of Hathor, to destroy humanity. Hathor then turns into the bloodthirsty Sekhmet ("the Powerful One") and begins to enjoy her destructive work so much that Re repents and decides he must save his creation from total annihilation. To achieve this, 7,000 jugs of beer mixed with red ocher are spread over the fields; seeing what she thinks is blood, she begins to drink the beer and, drunk, "failed to recognize mankind," thus saving humanity.

Apart from some explanations on the formation and the structure of the world found in the second part of the tale, the main theme of the Destruction story is that mankind brought on its own misfortunes by "[devising] plans to be enemies of Re." This is echoed in *The Instructions to King Merykare*, a Middle Kingdom text that tells how the creator god "slew his foes and reduced their children because they had planned rebellion." This theme of an angry creator god deciding to punish his rebellious creation is well known to many other ancient cultures, as Schmidt has shown.

OFFICIAL CULT
Ritual Texts

Stories about deities made them more accessible and made it easier for the ancient Egyptians to cope with the unknown world, but they also dealt with the gods directly, through actions and words. Texts containing ritual activities must have existed in great quantities in ancient Egypt, if the list of documents contained in a library such as the temple of Edfu's "House of Books" is to be believed[15]; given the fragile nature of papyrus, however, only a small sampling of these survive today. Records of foundation ceremonies, with texts and images, are found on temple walls. Elaborate lists of festivals and illustrations of a few of these, accompanied by captions that complement the reliefs,[16] were also carved on temple walls. Additional texts can be found on stelae, such as King Piye's great victory stela, part of which describes him performing ritual ceremonies at the temple of Re in Heliopolis. Texts describing ritual acts are also found on papyrus.

The major purpose of the temple ritual was the preservation of the cosmos from chaos through interaction between the king – officially always the actor, although in practical terms his role had to be delegated to priests – and the gods. The king offered sustenance to the gods, who, in turn, promised the king peace and prosperity. A few extant texts with detailed instructions for the officiants help us flesh out this ritual. The introductory section of the previously mentioned Pap. Berlin 3055 reads: "The beginning of the recitations (lit., 'spells') of the sacred rites that are carried out in the temple of Amun-Re, king of the gods, in the course of every day, by the great *wab*-priest who is in his day." What follows is a list of acts called "striking the fire," "taking the censer," "placing the incense upon the flame," and so on, after which come the actual words to be spoken during the cultic acts. The ritual could also contain allusions to mythological episodes such as the triumph of Horus over Seth, symbolizing the victory of order over chaos.[17]

Further ceremonies dealt with the institution of kingship. One of the most discussed texts is the late Middle Kingdom Ramesseum Dramatic Papyrus. The text consists of a ritual drama complete with dialogue for actors and stage directions, written in clearly delineated vertical columns, which are, in turn, separated by horizontal lines to distinguish the various parts. The papyrus was long considered to be part of a Sed Festival celebration; Quack has recently proposed that it deals with the old king's death and the new monarch's accession. A similar text is found on the left side of the previously mentioned Shabako Stone. Its design and content recall those of the Ramesseum Dramatic Papyrus, and its purpose is to affirm the right of Horus – that is, the reigning king – to rule over Egypt.

Another intriguing text that re-creates the Osirian Cycle is the late second century BC text known as the Triumph of Horus, from the temple of Edfu. As devised by Fairman – a conception that has not met with complete approval[18] – it consists of a prologue; act 1, with five scenes; act 2, with two scenes; act 3, with three scenes; and an epilogue. Each scene is laid out similarly: an introductory line of text lies above the full scene; below this, columns of text on the left constitute the script, to the right of which are representations, complete with captions. The full drama essentially consists of the same actions done repeatedly, representing the triumph of Horus (once again symbolizing the reigning king) over his enemies, notably the god Seth. Gillam has staged the actual play and fully examined the question of performance and drama in ancient Egypt.

Recent work on temples[19] include a full study by Wilkinson; Beinlich and others' investigations on various topics from the daily ritual performed there to the iconography of the deities; Ullmann's study of the royal mortuary temples and the term "House of Millions of Years"; Mohamed's volume on festivals and their logistical impact on the economies of the communities involved; and Goyon's publication of the "Ritual for Appeasing Sekhmet," wherein the king was introduced as the offspring of the "Eye of Re" and thus put under its protection. Late Period temples have also been investigated, notably Leitz's volume on Greco-Roman period temple inscriptions, as well as his bibliography of such texts.

Hymns

While some texts were performed in the formalized context of temples, others offer a more personal relationship with the deity. Hymns were recited or chanted, perhaps even sung, as the representation in the early Middle Kingdom Theban tomb of Senet – complete with two harpists shown under the text (Fig. 12.1) – would seem to indicate. Written in verse form, using mostly couplets but sometimes also triplets and even quatrains, the hymns are exquisitely composed, and they reveal the believers' deeply held convictions regarding the deities. Space does not allow a catalogue of these prayers,[20] but they were composed in honor of Amun-Re, Hathor, Isis, Maat, Osiris, Ptah, Re, Sekhmet, Sobek, Thoth, the Nile, and even the king, to name a few of the recipients. Most are written on papyrus, but a few,

FIGURE 12.1. Harp players and hymns to Hathor, Early Middle Kingdom Tomb of Senet. Redrawn from N. de Garis Davies and A. H. Gardiner, *The Tomb of Antefoker, Vizier of Sesostris I, and his Wife Senet (No. 60)*, Theban Tomb Series 2. London: Egypt Exploration Society, 1920, pl. 29. Drawing by Barbara Ibronyi.

such as the stela Louvre C286, which bears many of the episodes known from Plutarch's narrative of the Osiris story, are carved on stone.

The hymn to the syncretistic sun god Amun-Re in Pap. Leiden I 350 is an exceptional example of the craft of the ancient author, who skillfully wove themes from one stanza to another. The first four stanzas are lost, but Stanza 5 deals with Amun's daily rebirth from the underworld to usher in a new day, followed by Stanza 6, which describes Amun's reign over the whole world. Stanza 7 then relates Amun's gifts as healer, after which his ability to sustain life is described in the eighth stanza, a theme reiterated in the ninth stanza, where Amun-Re is acclaimed as creator god, followed by the provenance of this creation – Thebes – in the tenth. Because he has earlier been described as rising, the next stanza (numbered 20; from here on, the figures are in multiples of tens) illustrates the sun god's journey across the cosmos, with the sun's enemies being destroyed in stanza 30 and a reiteration of the god's self-creation in stanza 40. Stanza 50 details the might of the god, comparing him to a falcon, a lion, and a bull, all symbols connected to royalty, fitting images for the so-called King of the Gods. This is continued in stanza 60 with Amun's dominion over the entire world, followed in stanza 70 by the god's beneficences, again echoing royal imagery, here as the shepherd of his people. Next come a number of sections where Amun-Re is described as a primeval god, using the stanza numbers as puns; thus stanzas 80 and 90 mention the god's Ogdoad and Ennead, respectively. Two more stanzas (100 and 200) recount his early manifestations, while stanza 300 sums them up with a mention of Amun, Re, and Ptah, three creator gods. Stanzas 400 to 600 then chronicle the god's powers, with the latter echoing the Memphite Theology in its mention of the divinities Sia and Hu. The penultimate section relates Amun-Re's dominion over the cosmos, with the poem culminating in stanza 800 with passages about mooring in the west, that is, references to death.

The puns just mentioned are, in fact, very much part of the poet's craft, as he plays throughout with the number of the given stanza and the themes explored therein. Thus, stanza 5 uses the words *diu* "five," *duat* "underworld," and *dua* "to praise." Stanza 6 plays on the word for "six," *sisoo*, and the "regions," *suau*, the god controls. Other puns include those between *medj*, "ten," and *mety*, the "pattern" for which every other city Thebes is said to be; *maba*, "thirty," and the *maba*-harpoon that destroys the sun's enemies; *hemu*, "forty," and *hemu*, "to fashion," which the god is said to do for himself.

Phrases and themes can also be borrowed from one hymn to another. Compare, for example, an 18th Dynasty hymn to Amun found in Pap. Bulaq 17 and published by Luiselli, where the demiurge is said to have "created the Tree of Life" (stanza 1), to Pap. Leiden I 350, where Amun-Re's seed is proclaimed as "the Tree of Life" (stanza 600). A few comparisons can also be made between Pap. Bulaq 17 and Akhenaten's Great Hymn to the Aten. In stanza 5 of the former, the creator god is said to have "distinguished [mankind's] nature and made their lives, and also separated skin (color) one from the other" which can be paralleled by Akhenaten's declaration that "their skins are different because you [the Aten] have distinguished the foreigners" (col. 8). The end of the same stanza in the Amun hymn states that "the cattle grow languid when you [Amun] shine," which can be likened to Akhenaten's assertion that "all herds are at peace in their pastures" once the sun disk has risen (col. 5). An iconographic correspondence can also be made between Amun and Aten. In stanza 6 of Pap. Bulaq 17, Amun is called the "Truly Unique One, with many hands," surely a precursor to the subsequent illustrations of the Aten, whose multiple sun rays end in hands bestowing life.[21]

Parallels have also been drawn between Akhenaten's Great Hymn and the Biblical Psalm 104, which celebrates Yahweh's creation. Column 5 of the Aten hymn declares that "Birds have flown from their nests, their wings in praise of your life force," which finds a parallel in Psalm 104:11–12: "Beside them the birds of heaven nest, they sing among the branches." Similarly, compare the Aten hymn's "You have made an inundation (lit. "a Nile") in the sky that it may descend upon them [foreign lands] and make waves upon the mountains like the sea" (cols. 9–10) to Psalm 104:13: "From your palace on high you water the mountains; by your labor the earth abounds." And finally, the Hymn to the Aten's "How manifold is that which you do, although it is hidden from sight! O sole god, there is no other beside you; you created the earth according to your wish" (cols. 7–8) can be likened to Psalm 104:24's "How manifold are your works, O Lord! In wisdom you have made them all; the earth is full of your creations." Given the centuries between the composition of the Aten Hymn – a text that was presumably proscribed soon after Akhenaten's reign – and of Psalm 104, one should certainly not infer that the Psalmist borrowed directly from the Egyptian text, but the numerous parallels are certainly intriguing.[22]

Much work has been done on the study of hymns recently, notably the meticulous examinations of the metrical format of the songs by Patanè and Mathieu. Other welcome projects are fresh publications of long known but often inaccessible texts, such as the previously mentioned Pap. Bulaq 17, as well as Pap. Berlin 3049, a 22nd Dynasty document studied by Gülden. Hornung's masterful study of Akhenaten's religion,[23] among other topics, finally laid to rest the claim that it was monotheistic; and the texts from that period have also been masterfully translated by Murnane.

PERSONAL WORSHIP

The texts used in official temple contexts were unavailable to much of the population, who had limited access to the temples.[24] Religious material from the nonelite is, nevertheless, represented in written sources,[25] from graffiti in shrines and temples, to prayers written on stelae or papyrus; even everyday letters reveal a certain degree of religiosity, as Baines's 2001 study of the divinities invoked in the introductory formulas has shown. It must be stressed that this material was not from the poor, but from the vast majority of the population, from all socioeconomic strata. This so-called popular religion is not a separate strand of ancient Egyptian religion, but simply a different manifestation of the same beliefs.

Everyday Protection

Birth, always considered a dangerous occasion, was accompanied by magical spells to protect the mother and hasten the process. One example underscores what has already been said about the ancient Egyptians' knowledge of their myths: "O Re and Aten . . . Isis is suffering from her behind, as a pregnant woman. Her months have been completed according to the (proper) number, in pregnancy with her son Horus, the avenger of his father . . . It is not I who have said it . . . it is Isis who has said it . . . Take care of the child-bearing of N born of N in the same manner."[26] The pregnant woman is compared to Isis, and the gods are encouraged to help her just as they had helped Isis in mythical times. Although anepigraphic and thus beyond the scope of this chapter, a polychrome illustrated birth brick recently discovered at Abydos must be mentioned. It shows a seated mother and her newborn flanked by images of the goddess Hathor, associating the mother with the goddess.[27] Such objects, which were often inscribed with Spell 151 of the Book of the Dead, must have been common, but few have survived. Other texts with magical significance are the so-called stelae of Horus on the Crocodiles, also known as *cippi* of Horus. These round-topped stelae depict a young Horus trampling crocodiles beneath his feet and holding snakes, scorpions, and gazelles in his hands; the incantations written on the monuments were designed to avert or heal wounds suffered from these animals, as Ritner has shown.

Throughout their lives, constant brushes with unknown forces compelled the ancient Egyptians to compose ever more protective spells. One is the so-called Spell for the Protection of a Child, which addresses a number of spirits, exhorting them to "flow out . . . failing in that for which you came," and ends with the emphatic statement "Against you have I made a protection!" Graffiti left at shrines implore the deity to "Do good, do good," to "Grant him [the writer] a good endowment," or "Let favor be his <with> gods and men."[28] Such texts assume that the deities invoked will hear the petitions and, indeed, there is a category of monuments referred to as ear-stelae – recently studied by Morgan – the central focus of which is ears carved on their surfaces to enable the deities to hear the supplicants' pleas. This belief is further supported by appeals to gods who are said to "hear" (*sedjem*) pleas and petitions.[29] In another genre of text the author plays an intermediary role, promising to pass petitions on to the divinity in return for offerings. One example is a statue left at Deir el Bahari, part of which reads: "The Royal craftsman Tjawy says: I am a sistrum player for Hathor, who hears the petitions of any young girl who weeps, and who has put her trust (in) Hathor. . . . Give (me) sustenance in your presence, and then I shall speak to Hathor, who hears pleas. . . ."[30] Another instance of appeals to gods was oracular questions put to the statues of the divinities as they passed by the population during festival processions. There, the supplicant was said to "go," "stand," or "say" before the god, as well as "call to" the deity, who, in turn, expressed approval of the request by "moving forward," "walking forward," or "addressing" the petitioner; disapproval was expressed by the god "walking backward" or being "angry." It is to be noted that the texts never mention the god actually saying anything; only the priests carrying the god are responsible for the god's response.[31]

Penitential Texts

Stelae that confess specific sins and plead for the god's mercy appear in the Ramesside period. Although these have often been said to have been the result of the aftermath of the Amarna heresy and the subsequent fury of the gods, it may simply be that these were the products of a loosening of the restrictions found in previous periods, as Podemann Sørensen has suggested. In one example, a man named Neferabu confesses to having "sworn falsely by Ptah, lord of Maat" and was subsequently afflicted by blindness. He ends his prayer with a declaration that Ptah "taught me (a lesson)"[32]

Personal Names

Although little is known about the process of naming a child, onomastics are an overlooked source for elucidating personal religious beliefs. For example, and notwithstanding the iconographic evidence that does not show people directly praying to gods before the New Kingdom, Archaic Period theophoric names demonstrate how personal contact with divinities did occur before the New Kingdom. A few examples suffice: Iy-en-(i)-Min ("Min comes to me") and Ma-en-(i)-Neith ("I have seen Neith") hint at individuals to whom a god has made an appearance; Inet-Neith ("The one [fem.] whom Neith has brought forth") and Iri-en-Anubis ("The one [masc.] whom Anubis has created") suggest parents praying for an offspring who, in gratitude, name the child after the divinity after the birth; and, finally, Mer-netjer ("The one whom the god loves") and Inedj-en-Khnum ("The one whom Khnum has protected") allude to personal protection accorded by a deity to an individual.[33]

Similarly, another group of theophoric names help corroborate that all ancient Egyptians knew their myths. For example, the name Pa-en-iat ("The one who belongs to the primordial mound") associates the recipient of the name with the sacred mound from which the demiurge appeared, as does Ni-su-pauti-tawy ("He belongs to the primordial god of the two lands"), as *pauti* is a generic term for the creator god. The Osirian cycle is also well represented in theophoric names. Since Akh-bit (also known as Chemnis) is the Delta site where Isis gave birth to Horus, the names Aset-em-akh-bit ("Isis is in Akh-bit") and Pa-en-ta-net-akh-bit, ("The one [masc.] who belongs to the-one [fem.]-of-Akh-bit") refer to the second part of the Osirian cycle, when Isis hid in the Delta marshes. Isis' role as protectress is further represented by the name Nakht-Aset-er-ou ("Isis is strong against them"), the generic pronoun "them" referring to the malevolent forces against which Isis battled. Horus is also well represented. The name Hor-sa-Aset ("Horus is the son of Isis") describes the relationship between Horus and Isis; similar names are the touching Hor-em-qeni-Aset ("Horus is in the embrace of Isis") and Hor-em-akh-bit ("Horus is in Akh-bit"), recalling the name seen earlier. Horus' association with his father is also attested, as we find names such as Hor-nedj-it-ef ("Horus is his father's protector") and Hor-her-set-it-ef ("Horus is on his father's throne"), the latter leaving no doubt of the outcome of the struggle between Horus and Seth.

FUNERARY TEXTS

The funerary ritual's purpose was to ensure the deceased, whether royal or private, a successful transition to a happy afterlife. Not surprisingly, the textual material contains a great many references to the myth of Osiris, as the latter's resurrection and rebirth reassured the ancient Egyptians that they could achieve the same. The texts are probably the best known of all ancient Egyptian religious material and feature prominently in most books on ancient Egypt.[34]

Pyramid Texts

Found in the Saqqara pyramids of the last king of Dynasty 5 and all the kings and a few queens of Dynasty 6, as well as one Dynasty 8 ruler, the Pyramid Texts are the oldest collection of religious material from ancient Egypt. They consist of over 700 spells without, however, any single pyramid containing the entire collection. The most important recent work on this corpus is by J. P. Allen, whose fresh translation of 2005 will remain the standard English rendering henceforth. His decision to publish the texts from each pyramid separately highlights the extent of the changes from one pyramid to another and allows an integrated study of each pyramid's selection of spells. Allen has also masterfully reconstructed the order in which the texts are to be read (1994). Whereas an earlier generation of scholars such as Schott wished to read the texts in the direction a visitor to the pyramid would, that is, from outside in, Allen has convincingly argued that the spells are meant to be seen from the king's point of view, that is, from the inside out. He has also established that the burial chamber represented the Duat-underworld, while the antechamber symbolized the Akhet-horizon. Although it is anepigraphic and therefore beyond the scope of this chapter, recent research has also shown that the serdab, at the eastern end of the antechamber, represents the Mansion of Osiris, a stopping place on the deceased's way to the sky.[35] The full catalog of spells in a given pyramid thus narrate the king's journey out of the burial chamber into the antechamber, and from there to the sky via the exit corridor found in the north end of the antechamber.

The Pyramid Texts contain a variety of genres of spells. Protective spells are found on the west wall of the burial chamber over the king's sarcophagus, at the eastern end of the antechamber, and at the beginning of the northbound corridor leading out of the pyramid; their placement suggests that they safeguarded the outer portions of the king's chambers. The resurrection ritual is found on the south wall of the burial chamber and in the passageway between the burial chamber and the antechamber, while the offering ritual, including the Opening of the Mouth ceremony, is found on the north wall of the burial chamber, to the left of the king. And in the antechamber and the corridor are ascension and transformation spells, so-called personal spells meant to be used by the deceased himself.

As part of the resurrection ritual in the burial chamber, the king is first assured: "Not dead have you departed, but alive have you departed" (PT § 134a). Once the king has been told to "Raise yourself" (PT § 657e), he is free to move toward the sky. In the passageway leading to the antechamber, the king is prompted to "Go stand at the Akhet's door" (PT § 255). This is underscored by PT § 257, a spell at the western end of the antechamber, which tells the king that he has "emerged from the Duat," and PT § 496, a text on the northwest corner of the antechamber, which mentions opening "the door of the Akhet." Once the king has turned left into the exit corridor, the door of the sky is ordered to "open a path" for the king (PT § 502).

Recent books on the Pyramid Texts are the previously mentioned translation by Allen and the studies edited by Bickel and Mathieu on the relationship between the Pyramid Texts and the Coffin Texts. Work on individual aspects of these texts includes investigations of the divine genealogies in the corpus and the list of enemies the king was likely to encounter in the other world.[36] Studies on individual spells have also been published, such as those on the famous Cannibal Hymn. Eyre concentrated on the performative aspect of the hymn, with its word plays and metaphoric use of language, while Goebs viewed the text as a description of the sunrise, where the night stars are said to be swallowed by the rising sun god as they disappear one by one from the sky. Another important recent study is the investigation of the Dynasty 6 Saqqara tomb of the noble Ankhmahor by Vischak, which compares the sequence of images in the tomb to the layout of texts inside the pyramid chambers.

Coffin Texts

Because so little royal funerary material has survived from the Middle Kingdom, private burials must provide a glimpse of the funerary beliefs of that period. The most important corpus is known as the Coffin Texts because it was mostly written in cursive hieroglyphs on the panels of coffins; the ancient Egyptians referred to this collection as "The Book of Making a Man's Voice Be True in the Realm of the Dead" (CT Spell 1). Although they were long thought to have originated in the First Intermediate Period, recent discoveries have shown that the genesis of the Coffin Texts is significantly earlier. A coffin from Dakhleh Oasis dating to the late Old Kingdom contains partial imprints of what appear to be a number of Coffin Texts spells; additionally, part of the Book of Two Ways, which comprises CT spells 1029–1186, has been found within an Old Kingdom Pyramid Texts corpus. Conversely, two sheets of papyri glued together found in the funerary temple of King Pepy I, which contain parts of PT spell 217 on one side and spell 690 on the other, date to Dynasty 12.[37] Therefore, the chronological divide between the Pyramid Texts and the Coffin Texts is significantly blurred, and the two corpora should probably not be considered distinct.[38] The Coffin Texts continued to be used well into the Late Period, as Gestermann has established.

Each coffin was meant to be a miniature version of the pyramid chambers, with some of the Coffin Texts spells placed deliberately in specific areas of the coffin as Barguet has shown. Thus, CT spell 229, which exhorts a deity to "place my head on my neck for me," is usually placed at the head (northern) portion of the inner panels, while CT spell 236, placed by the deceased's feet, enjoins another deity to "give me my legs, that I may walk on them." Enough exceptions to such patterns exist, however, to defy consistency.

The Coffin Texts spells number 1,186 but, as with the Pyramid Texts, no one coffin includes more than 200 spells.[39] There are a number of themes in the Coffin Texts, some of which are known from the Pyramid Texts, such as the resurrection and offering rituals and protective spells. Other types of spells provision the deceased, provide safe passage through obstacles, and transform. Accompanying the spells are some illustrations, such as the friezes of objects found near the deceased inside the coffin, the Fields of Hetep of spells 464–8, and the previously mentioned Book of Two Ways.

Recent studies of themes in the Coffin Texts include investigations into the hazards the deceased could meet in the underworld, such as having to walk upside down or eating feces, and the spells composed to help the dead avoid such unpleasantness; the possibilities of the deceased's cyclical rebirth and renewal through the symbolic representations of astronomical references; and the various kinds of mortuary liturgy included therein.[40] Specific portions of the corpus have also been considered. The ritual landscape encountered in the Book of Two Ways has been examined by Robinson, and a number of spells from the same body of texts have elucidated the different concepts of the afterlife as conceived by the author(s) of the collection.[41] Integral studies of individual coffins have permitted valuable observations on the functions of the coffins as funerary objects. Willems's highly detailed study of the placement of the spells and the illustrations on a single coffin has clarified the relationship between the various parts of the coffin. Meyer-Dietrich's equally detailed study looks at the texts and illustrations as actual performance aids in the funerary ritual. Shalomi-Hen's paleographical studies of the texts, specifically the determinatives on divine names, provide insights into the ancient Egyptian's perception of the divine. A number of useful dictionaries and concordances of the Coffin Texts have also been recently published.[42]

Book of the Dead

The so-called Book of the Dead is a collection of texts the Egyptians called "The Book of Going Forth by Day." Usually regarded as a New Kingdom composition, Geisen's careful investigation of a now-lost queen's coffin has allowed her to redate it to Dynasty 13, with the important conclusion that the Book of the Dead spells found on it are now the earliest such spells found. Like the relationship between the Pyramid Texts and the Coffin Texts, the Book of the Dead shows affinities with its predecessors. For example, BD spell 6, the so-called Shabti Spell, which released the deceased from corvée labor in the underworld, goes back to CT spell 472; BD spell 30, the "Spell for not allowing the deceased's heart to create opposition against him," hearkens back to CT spells 20 and 113; and BD spell 17, which presents a summary of the full Book of the Dead, recalls CT spell 335, "(Spell for) Going out into the day from the realm of the dead"; and BD spell 110, which describes the Field of Offerings, goes back to CT spells 464–8.

Nearly all the Book of the Dead spells are personal spells, in that they were meant to be used by the deceased. Examples are BD spell 25, which helped the deceased remember their names; BD spells 31 and 32, used as protection against crocodiles; and the all-important BD spell 44, which prevented the deceased from "dying again." Also significant were the transformation spells (BD spells 76–88), which allowed the deceased to metamorphose into various shapes that allowed more freedom;[43] and BD spells 144–7, which helped the dead through various underworld doorways and gateways. As with the Coffin Texts, certain spells contain glosses in parts of the texts. One example is BD spell 17, where the editors query the meaning of certain passages, indicating – as Lapp has shown – that even the ancient theologians had difficulties understanding some of the passages they were copying. Although mostly written in cursive hieroglyphs on papyri, certain spells became so closely identified with their purpose that they came to be inscribed on specific objects. Examples of these are the previously mentioned BD spell 6, which was carved on shabti figurines and placed in the tomb, and BD spell 30, which was carved on the underside of scarabs and placed close to the heart on the mummy itself.

One major innovation in the Book of the Dead is the series of vignettes that illustrate the texts. A full study of the iconography of the Book of the Dead, a difficult and gargantuan task, remains to be done. Another innovation is Book of the Dead spell 125, the so-called Declaration of Innocence. Often referred to as the Negative Confession, it is in fact nothing of the sort, as the deceased denies having done a number of misdeeds that range from social to cultic transgressions.

Much of the most important recent scholarship on the Book of the Dead has appeared in two major series, the *Handschriften des Altägyptischen Totenbuches* (HAT) and the *Studien zum Altägyptischen Totenbuch* (SAT), which deal with specific papyri and topics, respectively. So far, Book of the Dead papyri dating to Dynasty 18, the Ramesside, the Third Intermediate, and the Late and Ptolemaic Periods have been published in the HAT collection; new papyri are also part of the SAT series.[44] The SAT series has offered a general bibliography of the Book of the Dead; a list of occurrences of spells in Third Intermediate Period papyri; an index of a Late Period papyri; studies on specific spells; and ritual books.[45] General studies on the corpus, as well as the history of its transmission, such as that of Rößler-Köhler, are also available. Another significant advance is that of Stephen Quirke, who, in his Web site for University College, London, has not only translated much of the Book of the Dead but also added a most welcome transliteration of the original Egyptian.

Other Funerary Texts

The New Kingdom royal books of the Underworld, known collectively as the Book of Amduat, from the Egyptian *imy-duat*, "what is in the underworld," include the Books of Gates, of Caves, and of Caverns, to name a few. The theme of all these compositions is the sun god's nautical journey through the underworld during the twelve hours of the night, with the king as part of the divine crew, the culmination of which was the sun's successful rebirth at dawn. Mostly inscribed on the walls of the New Kingdom royal tombs, they are accompanied by vivid illustrations that depict the topography of the underworld, complete with gates and their fierce guardians, as well as its inhabitants. These have been described in great detail by Hornung,[46] and more recently studied by Wiebach-Koepke, Darnell, and Hegenbarth-Reichardt. The Book of Amduat in the tomb of Thutmosis III has recently been published by Barré, complete with CD-ROM disk.

Among nonroyal funerary texts, the most ubiquitous is the Offering Formula, which begins with the phrase "An offering that the king gives, and that god N has given." It has been repeatedly discussed in the literature, with the most recent being Franke's study, which convincingly argued that the king and the god were always meant to be parallel givers of the offerings, and thus that no historical change occurred between the Old Kingdom and the First Intermediate Period. Another significant nonroyal text is the Appeal to the Living. Found on tomb facades, commemorative stelae, and statues, as well as in quarries and mines, it urges passers-by – who are still on earth and living – to recite prayers in honor of the text's author. The latter, who often styled himself as a well-equipped *akh*-spirit, promised in turn to watch over the offerers from his vantage point in the other world. A recent study of this genre by Shubert has analyzed the texts from the Old to the late New Kingdom.

CONCLUSION

From Erman's description of the ancient Egyptians' beliefs as "unparalleled confusion" and Gardiner's characterization of these as "unmitigated rubbish," the world of scholarship has produced individuals such as Siegfried Morenz, who very much wrote "from the heart" as a believer, and Jan Assmann, whose elaborate theories mix a standard Egyptological approach with more current theories on theology, culminating with J. L. Foster's eloquent plea to respect the religion of Egypt and take it seriously.[47] The varied religious texts that have survived from ancient Egypt continue to reveal more about the civilization that produced them.

NOTES

1. See Baines 1991: 94; Loprieno 1996: 49.
2. Sauneron 1969: 125–9; Ritner 2001: 321–2.
3. See, respectively, on religious symbolism, Baines 1996; protective spells, Pinch 1994: 18–32; Guilhou 1995; Pap. Berlin 3008, Lichtheim 1980: 116–21.
4. Frankfort 1971: 12.
5. Assmann 1977, 1982.
6. For example, Baines 1991: 102–3; Baines 1996; and Zeidler 1993. See also Morenz 1996.
7. Sethe 1929: 52.
8. Barucq and Daumas 1980: 293.
9. Hornung 1982: 237–43.
10. See, respectively, Coffin Texts: Bickel 1994; Khonsu Temple: Mendel 2003; Hymns: Knigge 2006; Seven: Rochholz 2002; Old Testament: Currid 1997.
11. Simpson 2003: 91–103.
12. Borghouts 1978: 30, 31, 40, 43, etc.
13. Quirke 1992: 67.
14. Simpson 2003: 289–98.
15. Sauneron 1969: 138.
16. Spalinger 2001.

17. A few sections of this text can be found in Barucq and Daumas 1980: 287–97; and Ritner 1997. For the allusions to mythological episodes see Ritner 1997: 55.
18. Fairman 1973; but see O'Rourke 2001.
19. Wilkinson 2000; Beinlich 2002; Ullmann 2002; Mohamed 2004; Goyon 2006; Leitz 2004 and 2005.
20. For fresh and accessible translations, see Foster, 1995a.
21. Barucq and Daumas 1980:197, n. [ac].
22. See Foster, 1995b: 1759.
23. Hornung, 1999a.
24. For discussions on the areas where the population was allowed access, see Bell 1997:164–70; Teeter 1997: 4–5; Wilkinson 2000: 71, 99. Bell's and Teeter's conclusions have been challenged by Baines 2001: 31.
25. For graffiti, see, e.g., Jacquet-Gordon 2003; for nontextual evidence of religious participation, see, e.g., Pinch 1993.
26. Borghouts 1978: 40.
27. Wegner 2002; Wegner 2006: 35. For a recent study of such objects, see Roth and Roehrig 2002.
28. The examples given here are taken from Borghouts 1978: 41–2; and Sadek 1987: 53–6.
29. Guglielmi and Dittmar 1992.
30. Cf. Pinch 1993: 333–4, with a slightly different reading.
31. For a recent and accessible study of oracles, see Kruchten 2001.
32. See Simpson 2003: 287–8.
33. For these and other examples, see Hornung 1982: 44–6.
34. For a recent study in English, see Grajetski 2003.
35. Mathieu, 1997b.
36. Divine genealogies: Köthen-Welpot 2003; lists of enemies: Meurer 2003.
37. For the Dakhleh coffin: Valloggia 1986: 74–8; Book of Two Ways: Pierre-Croisiau 2004: 268; Pepy I funerary temple papyri: Berger-el Naggar 2004.
38. Mathieu 2004; see also Allen 2006.
39. For the full number: Willems 1996: 138, 411; for the lesser number: Allen 1988: 40.
40. For the hazards of the Underworld see Topmann 2002; for the astronomical references, Wallin 2002; for the mortuary liturgy, Assmann 2002.
41. Backes, 2005a.
42. See Molen 2000, 2005; along with an electronic version: Plas and Borghouts 1998.
43. For recent studies of these spells, see Servajean 2004; Lüscher 2006.
44. For these papyri see, respectively, Dynasty 18: Munro, 1995a, 1995b; Ramesside: Munro 1997; Third Intermediate Period: Munro 1996, 2001; Late Period: Verhoeven 2001; Ptolemaic Period: Lüscher 2000; Falk 2006; Munro 2006; new papyri in the SAT series: Stadler 2003.
45. For the SAT series bibliography see Gülden and Munro 1998; Third Intermediate Period: Munro, 2001b; Late Period: Backes, 2005b; specific spells: Lüscher 1998; ritual books: Munro 2004 and Beinlich 2000.
46. Hornung, 1999b.
47. Erman 1971: 261; Gardiner 1957: 55; Morenz 1973: xvi; Assmann 2001; Foster, 1995a: 8.

AFTERWORD

THE PAST IN THE FUTURE

Egyptology Tomorrow

Richard H. Wilkinson

Egyptologists, like all students of ancient cultures, focus on the past and do not presume to predict the future; nevertheless, a number of ongoing developments in the discipline have been mentioned in this book. The constraints of space mean that it is only possible to give a very few further examples here, but some emerging patterns are clear.

The use of new scientific and technological tools – in some cases within a very short time after their development – clearly is increasing in areas of Egyptology as widely separated as biomedical study, mapping, dating, recording, and conservation. For example, the recent development of a new type of pottery dating through lipid analysis that dates ceramic objects by means of the residual traces of fats placed in the vessel – or even oils from the skin of those who anciently held them – is of great interest to Egyptologists conducting excavations and may, when perfected, help to revolutionize our ability to understand otherwise difficult archaeological contexts. Similarly, the programs of conservation recently completed in the tombs of Nefertari and other royal monuments employed new and sometimes little-known methods of preservation that should greatly increase the chances of survival of these heritage monuments. Such interactions can only serve to further the integration of Egyptology with the wider field of ancient studies and, in turn, to encourage and enable similar developments in the future.

Cooperation between Egyptologists and other specialists both within the field and from related disciplines will certainly increase if present trends continue, and there is no reason to doubt that this will be the case. This fact may be seen in the changes in university and college courses and programs in Egyptology that have occurred in recent years. Once Egyptology was an area in which a fairly narrow and predictable curriculum of study was followed; now students preparing for a career in some aspect of Egyptological study often have the opportunity to study a far wider range of approaches and materials both within and without their chosen field. In many cases this has led to the taking of second bachelor's or master's degrees before the doctorate on the part of students wishing to develop wider perspectives and training, as well as academic programs accepting courses from – or interaction with – other areas of study.

Newer avenues of research within Egyptology – some only now beginning to be explored – will doubtless open up further understandings in the field. The presence of symbolism in ancient Egyptian culture, for example, has long been understood, but has received comparatively little in-depth study. A number of recent formal studies have focused on various aspects of the symbolic "landscapes" created by the ancient Egyptians in their art and literature, however. Such studies appear to indicate a growing interest in and understanding of this aspect of Egyptian thought.

In a similar manner, the application of principles of psychology and sociology to Egyptology is in its infancy but may provide new approaches to and understandings of ancient behavior at both the individual and collective levels. Gender issues have received increasing attention over recent decades in terms of women's roles and responsibilities, and this trend has recently been furthered by a call for the parallel study of the unique aspects of the roles of men in Egyptian society, indicating in a small but telling way an ongoing broadening and deepening of perspective.

There has also been a literal broadening of study that is ongoing. For well over a century Egyptologists concentrated mainly on the Nile valley as the central area of monumental remains, but more recently the field has embraced much more of the total geographic sphere of ancient Egypt through studies of the desert, delta and coastal areas.

Rather than focusing on the quest for "hidden tombs and treasures" – as was undeniably the case in Egyptology's infancy – more informed Egyptological fieldwork now primarily seeks information rather than things. This attitude does not negate or render useless new discoveries of major sites, features, or artifacts, but puts those discoveries in a context that has often been lacking and that has still to become ubiquitous. There has also been a distinct emphasis in recent years on dealing with monuments and sites that are in danger of deterioration rather than just searching for those previously undiscovered. Egyptological museum work has seen many parallel developments, and new studies of objects and collections – often done in conjunction with their conservation – are providing rich results. While basic enough, these newer approaches to what is already known go hand in hand with changed attitudes toward new discoveries, and they provide the foundation for much work that will be done in the future.

The individual chapters of this book have repeatedly touched upon areas where change is present or imminent in Egyptology, and this situation certainly indicates that the discipline is not only alive, but also continuing to grow. Only time will reveal the specific major developments that will occur in the field, of course, but today's Egyptology gives promise of a continued increase in our understanding of all aspects of this ancient culture. This will certainly remain the ultimate goal of Egyptology tomorrow.

BIBLIOGRAPHY

Chapter 1: Archaeology and Egyptology

Aston, B. G. *Ancient Egyptian Stone Vessels: Materials and Forms*, Studien zur Archaeologie und Geschichte Altaegyptens, 5. Heidelberg, 1994.

Bard, K. A. *From Farmers to Pharaohs: Mortuary Evidence for the Rise of Complex Society in Egypt*, Monographs in Mediterranean Archaeology, 2. Sheffield, 1994.

Bietak, M. *Avaris: The Capital of the Hyksos: Recent Excavations at Tell el-Dab'a*. London, 1996.

Curl, J. S. *The Egyptian Revival: An Introductory Study of a Recurring Theme in the History of Taste*. London, 1982.

Dawson, W. R., and E. P. Uphill. *Who Was Who in Egyptology*, 2nd ed. London, 1972.

De Vartavan, C. *Hidden Fields of Tutankhamun: From Identification to Interpretation of Newly Discovered Plant Materials from the Pharaoh's Grave*, Triade Exploration's Opus Magnum Series, 2. 2nd ed. London, 2002.

Description de l'Égypte, ou recueil des observations et des recherches qui ont été faites en Égypte pendant l'expédition de l'armée française. Antiquités. 9 vols. Paris, 1809–22.

Drower, M. S. *Flinders Petrie: A Life in Archaeology*. London, 1985.

El-Daly, O. *Egyptology: The Missing Millennium: Ancient Egypt in Medieval Arabic Writings*. London, 2005.

Fisher, M. M. *The Sons of Ramesses II*, Agypten und altes Testament, 53. 2 vols. Wiesbaden, 2001.

Gomaa, F. *Khaemwese, Sohn Ramses II und Hoherpriester von Memphis*, Ägyptologische Abhandlungen, 27. Wiesbaden, 1973.

Greener, L. *The Discovery of Egypt*. New York, 1967.

Habachi, L. *The Obelisks of Egypt*. New York, 1977.

Iversen, E. *Obelisks in Exile*. 2 vols. Copenhagen, 1968–72.

———. *The Myth of Egypt and Its Hieroglyphs in European Tradition*. Princeton, NJ, 1993.

Jacquet-Gordon, H. "A Tentative Typology of Egyptian Bread Moulds." *Studien zur altaegyptischen Keramik* (1981): 11–24.

James, T. G. H., ed. *Excavating in Egypt: The Egypt Exploration Society, 1882–1982*. London, 1982.

Meskell, L. *Archaeologies of Social Life: Age, Sex, Class, et Cetera, in Ancient Egypt.* Oxford, 1999.

Orton, C., P. Tyers, and A. Vince. *Pottery in Archaeology*, Cambridge Manuals in Archaeology. Cambridge, 1993.

Reid, D. M. *Whose Pharaohs? Archaeology, Museums and Egyptian National Identity from Napoleon to World War I.* Berkeley, CA and Los Angeles, 2003.

Wenke, R. J. "Anthropology, Egyptology and the Concept of Cultural Change." In *Anthropology and Egyptology: A Developing Dialogue*, ed. Judith Lustig, 212–33. Sheffield, 1997.

Wortham, J. D. *British Egyptology: 1549–1906.* Newton Abbott, 1971.

Chapter 2: History and Egyptology

Algaze, G. *The Uruk World System: The Dynamics of Expansion of Early Mesopotamian Civilization.* Chicago and London, 2005.

Assmann, J. *The Mind of Ancient Egypt: History and Meaning in the Time of the Pharaohs.* New York, 1996.

Bauman, R. *Verbal Art as Performance.* Prospect Heights, IL, 1977.

Birch, S. *History of Egypt.* London, 1879.

Bleiberg, E. J. "Historical Texts as Political Propaganda during the New Kingdom." *Bulletin of the Egyptological Seminar* 7 (1985–6): 5–14.

Bower, G., J. Black, and T. Turner. "Scripts in Memory for Tests." *Cognitive Psychology* 11 (1979): 177–220.

Breisach, E. *Historiography, Ancient, Mediaeval and Modern.* Chicago, 1994.

Brugsch, H. *Histoire de l'Egypte.* Leipzig, 1859.

———. *Geschichte Aegyptens.* Leipzig, 1877.

Brunner-Traut, E. "Wechselbeziehungen zwischen schriftliche und muendlicher Uberlieferung im alten Aegypten." *Fabula* 20 (1979): 34ff.

Burke, K. *A Rhetoric of Motive.* Berkeley, CA, 1971.

Burke, P., ed. *New Perspectives on Historical Writing.* University Park, PA, 1992.

Castillos, J. J. *The Predynastic Period in Egypt.* Montevideo, 2002.

Chomsky, N. *Language and Politics.* Montreal, 1999.

———. *Propaganda and the Public Mind.* Cambridge, 2001.

Cohen, A. *The Politics of Elite Cultures: Explorations in the Dramaturgy of Power in a Modern African Society.* Berkeley, CA, 1981.

Derchain, P. "Eloquence et politique. L'opinion d'Akhtoy." *Revue d'Égyptologie* 40 (1989): 37–47.

Doherty, L. E. "The Internal and Implied Audience in *Odyssey* 11." *Arethusa* 24 (1991): 145–76.

Doxey, D. *Egyptian Non-royal Epithets in the Middle Kingdom.* Leiden, 1998.

Eagleton, T. *Marxism and Literary Criticism.* London, 1989.

———. *The Ideology of the Aesthetic.* Oxford, 1990.

———. *Literary Theory: An Introduction.* Oxford, 1996.

———. *The Idea of Culture.* Oxford, 2000.

———. *After Theory.* New York, 2003.

Edel, E. *Die aegyptisch-hethitische Korrespondenz aus Boghazköy.* Oplade, 1994.

Evans, J. A. S. *Herodotus, Explorer of the Past.* Princeton, NJ, 1991.

Felling, C. "Epilogue." In *The Limits of Historiography: Genre and Narrative in Ancient Historical Texts*, ed. C. S. Kraus, 325–60. Leiden, 1999.

Finnegan, R. H. *Oral Poetry: Its Nature, Significance and Social Context.* Cambridge, 1977.

Foley, J. M. "Indigenous Poems, Colonialist Texts." In *Orality, Literacy and Colonialism in Antiquity*, ed. J. A. Draper, 9–35. Atlanta, 2004.

Foucault, M. *The Archaeology of Knowledge and the Discourse on Language*. New York, 1972.

————. *Language, Counter-memory, Practice*. Ithaca, NY, 1980.

Foxhall, L. "The Running Sands of Time: Archaeology and the Short-Term." *World Archaeology* 3 (2000): 484–98.

Friedrich, R. "Homeric Enjambement and Orality." *Hermes* 128 (2000): 1–19.

Gaballa, G. A. *Narrative in Egyptian Art*. Mainz, 1977.

Gadamer, H.-G. *Philosophical Hermeneutics*. Berkeley, CA, 1977.

Grimal, N. *Les termes de la propaganda royale egyptienne de la XIXe dynastie a la conquete d'Alexandre*. Paris, 1986.

Grimal, N., and B. Menu. *Le Commerce en Egypte ancienne*. Cairo, 1998.

Gundlach, R., and W. Seipel, eds. *Das frühe aegyptische Koenigtum*. Wiesbaden, 1999.

Hadot, P. *Qu'est-ce que la philosophie antique?* Paris, 1995.

Hauser, A. *The Social History of Art*, Vol. IV. New York, 1985.

Hearon, H. E. "The Implications of 'Orality' for Studies of the Biblical Text." *Oral Tradition* 19 (2004): 96–107.

Hegazy, S. *The Reign of Nectanebo I*. Ph.D. thesis. University of Budapest, 1989.

Helck, W. *Historisch-biographische Texte der 2. Zwischenzeit und neue Texte der 18. Dynastie*. Wiesbaden, 1975.

————. *Die Lehre des Djedefhor und die Lehre eines Vaters an seinen Sohn*. Wiesbaden, 1984.

Hendrickx, S., Friedman, R. F., Cialowicz, K. M., Chlodnicki, M., eds. *Egypt at Its Origins: Studies in Memory of Barbara Adams*. Leiden, 2004.

Hoffmeier, J. K. "The Problem of 'History' in Egyptian Royal Inscriptions." In *VICongresso internazionale di egittologia*, Atti I, 291–99. Turin, 1992.

Hofmann, B. *Die Koenigsnovelle: "Strukturanalyse am Einzelwerk."* Wiesbaden, 2004.

Janssen, J. J. *Commodity Prices from the Ramessid Period*. Leiden, 1975.

Kaiser, W. "Zu den Quellen der aegyptischen Geschichte Herodots." *Zeitschrift für ägyptische Sprache und Altertumskunde* 94 (1967): 93–116.

Lloyd, A. B. *Herodotus Book II: A Commentary*, 3 vols. Leiden, 1975–88.

————. "Herodotus' Account of Pharaonic History." *Historia* 37 (1988): 22–53.

Louden, B. "Eumaios and Alkinoos: The Audience and the Odyssey." *Phoenix* 51 (1997): 95–114.

Lustig, J., ed. *Anthropology and Egyptology*. Sheffield, 1997.

Malek, J. "La division de l'histoire de l'Egypte et l'Egyptologie moderne." *Bulletin de la Société Française d'Égyptologie* 138 (1997): 6–17.

Mark, S. *From Egypt to Mesopotamia: A Study of Predynastic Trade Routes*. London, 1997.

Menu, B. *Recherches sur l'histoire juridique, economique, et sociale de l'ancienne Egypte*, Vol. II. Cairo, 1998.

Minchin, E. *Homer and the Resources of Memory*. Oxford, 2001.

Momigliano, A. *The Classical Foundations of Modern Historiography*. Berkeley, CA, 1990.

Moorey, P. R. S. *From Gulf to Delta and Beyond*. Beersheva, 1995.

Otto, E., ed. *Fragen an die altaegyptische Literatur*. Wiesbaden, 1977.

Porter, B. W. "Authority, Polity and Tenuous Elites in Iron Age Edom." *Oxford Journal of Archaeology* 23 (2004): 373–96.

Posener, G. *L'Enseignement loyaliste. Sagesse egyptienne du Moyen Empire*. Geneva, 1976.

Purkiss, D. "What We Leave Out." *Times Literary Supplement*, Oct. 13, 2006.

Rabinowitz, P. J. "Truth in Fiction: A Re-examination of Audience." *Critical Inquiry* 4.1 (1977): 121–41.

Redford, D. B. "The Historiography of Ancient Egypt." In *Egyptology and the Social Sciences*, ed. K. Weeks, 3–20. Cairo, 1979.

_____. *Pharaonic King-Lists, Annals and Daybooks*. Mississauga, Ontario, 1986.

_____. "Scribe and Speaker. The Interface between the Written and the Oral in Ancient Egypt." In *Writings and Speech in Israelite and Ancient Near Eastern Prophecy*, ed. E. Ben Zvi and M. H. Floyd, 145–218. Atlanta, 2000.

_____. "The Writing of the History of Ancient Egypt." In *Egyptology at the Dawn of the Twenty-first Century*, Vol. II, ed. Z. Hawass, 1–12. Cairo, 2003.

Reichl, K. *The Oral Epic Performance and Music*. Berkeley, CA, 2000.

Rice, M. *Egypt's Making: The Origins of Ancient Egypt 5000–2000 BC*. London, 1991.

Richardson, S. "Truth in the Tales of the Odyssey." *Mnemosyne* 49 (1996): 393–402.

Rothman, M. S., ed. *Uruk Mesopotamia and Its Neighbors*. Santa Fe, NM, 2001.

Rubin, D. *Memory in Oral Tradition: The Cognitive Psychology of Epics, Ballads and Counting-Out*. Oxford, 1995.

Rydberg-Cox, J. A. "Oral and Written Sources in Athenian Forensic Rhetoric." *Mnemosyne* 56 (2003): 652–65.

Said, E. *Culture and Imperialism*. New York, 1993.

Shank, R., and R. Abelson. *Scripts, Plans, Goals and Understanding: An Inquiry into Human Knowledge Structures*. Hillsdale, NJ, 1977.

Shubert, S. B. *Those Who (Still) Live on Earth: A Study of the Egyptian Appeal to the Living Texts*. Ph.D. thesis. University of Toronto, 2006.

Sim, S. *Derrida and the End of History*. New York, 1999.

Simpson, W. K. "Belles Lettres and Propaganda." In *Ancient Egyptian Literature. History and Forms*, ed. A. Loprieno, 435–46. Leiden, 1996.

Spencer, J., ed. *Aspects of Early Egypt*. London, 1996.

Spiegel, J. "Die Phasen der aegyptischen Geistesgeschichte." *Saeculum* 1 (1950): 1–48.

Stone, L. "The Revival of Narrative." In *The Past and Present Revisited*, ed. L. Stone, 74–96. London, 1987.

Tannen, D. "What's in a Frame? Surface Evidence for Underlying Expectations." In *New Directions in Discourse Processing*, ed. R. O. Freedle, 137–81. Norwood, NJ, 1979.

Tefnin, R. "Image, ecriture, recit. A propos des representations de la bataille de Qadesh." *Göttingen Miscellen* 47 (1981): 55–76.

Thomas, K. "New Ways Revisited: How History's Borders Have Expanded in the Last Forty Years." *Times Literary Supplement*, Oct. 13, 2006.

Tillyard, S. "All Our Pasts: The Rise of Popular History." *Times Literary Supplement*, Oct. 13, 2006.

Trigger, B. G. *Early Civilizations: Ancient Egypt in Context*. Cairo, 1993.

Van den Brink, E. C. M. and T. E. Levy, eds. *Egypt and the Levant: Interrelations from the 4th through the Early 3rd Millennium B. C.E.* London, 2002.

Vanseveren, S. "La Formule homerique. Problemes et definition." *Les Etudes Classiques* 66 (1998): 225–36.

Vansina, J. *Oral Tradition as History*. Madison, WI, 1985.

Warburton, D. *State and Economy in Ancient Egypt: Fiscal Vocabulary of the New Kingdom*. Fribourg-Goettingen, 1997.

Wiedemann, A. *Aegyptische Geschichte*. Gottha, 1884.

Wilkinson, T. A. H. *Early Dynastic Egypt*. London and New York, 2001.

Willett, J., ed. *Brecht on Theatre: The Development of an Aesthetic*. London, 1964.

Williams, R. J. "Literature as a Medium of Political Propaganda in Ancient Egypt." In *The Seed of Wisdom*, ed. W. S. McCullough, 14–30. Toronto, 1964.

Yamagata, N. "Plato, Memory and Performance." *Oral Tradition* 20 (2005): 111–29.

Zevit, Z. "Cognitive Theory and Memorability in Biblical Poetry." *Ma'ariv* 8 (1992): 199–212.

Chapter 3: Medical Science and Egyptology

Aufderheide, A. C. *The Scientific Study of Mummies.* Cambridge, 2003.

Balabanova, S., F. Parsche, and W. Pirsig. "First Identification of Drugs in Egyptian Mummies." *Naturwissenschaften* 79 (1992): 358.

Balout, L., and C. Roubet. *La Momie de Ramses II.* Paris, 1985.

Benson, G., S. R. Hemingway, and F. N. Leach. "The Analysis of Wrappings of Mummy 1770." In *The Manchester Museum Mummy Project*, ed. A. R. David, 119–32. Manchester, 1979.

Birkett, D. A., C. L. Gummer, and R. P. R. Dawber. "Preservation of the Sub-Cellular Ultrastructure of Ancient Hair." In *Science in Egyptology: Proceedings of the 'Science in Egyptology' Symposia*, ed. A. R. David, 367–70. Manchester, 1986.

Bucaille, M. "Interet actuel de l'etude radiologique des momies pharaonique." *Annals of Radiology* 19 (1979): 475–80.

Buckley, S. A., and R. P. Evershed. "Organic Chemistry of Embalming Agents in Pharaonic and Graeco-Roman Mummies." *Nature* 413 (2001): 837–41.

Campbell, J. "Pharmacy in Ancient Egypt." In *Egyptian Mummies and Modern Science*, ed. A. R. David. Cambridge, forthcoming.

Cerutti, N., A. Marin, D. Savoia, and E. R. Massa. "Perspectives on malaria in Egyptian mummies from the Gebelen site." In *Mummies in a New Millenium. Proceedings of the 4th World Congress on Mummy Studies, Nuuk, Greenland, September 4th–10th, 2001*, eds. N. Lynnerup, C. Andreasen, and J. Berglund, 101–104. Copenhagen, 2003.

Cockburn, A., R. A. Barraco, T. A. Reyman, and W. Peck. "Autopsy of an Egyptian Mummy." *Science* 187 (1975): 1155–60.

Cockburn, A., and E. Cockburn, eds. *Mummies, Disease and Ancient Cultures.* Cambridge, 1980.

Cockburn, A., E. Cockburn, and T. A. Reyman, eds. *Mummies, Disease and Ancient Cultures.* Cambridge, 1998; 2nd ed.

Connolly, R. C., and R. G. Harrison. "Kinship of Smenkhkare and Tutankhamen, Confirmed by Serologic Micromethod." *Nature* 224 (1969): 325.

Contis, G., and A. R. David. "The Epidemiology of *Bilharzia* in Ancient Egypt: 5000 Years of Schistosomiasis." *Parasitology Today* 12, No. 7 (July, 1996): 253–5.

Counsell, D. C. "Pharmacological Applications in Egyptology." In *Egyptian Mummies and Modern Science*, ed. A. R. David. Cambridge, forthcoming.

Curry, A. "The Insects Associated with the Manchester Mummies." In *The Manchester Museum Mummy Project*, ed. A. R. David, 113–17. Manchester, 1979.

Curry, A., C. Anfield, and E. Tapp. "Electron Microscopy of the Manchester Mummies." In *The Manchester Museum Mummy Project*, ed. A. R. David, 103–11. Manchester, 1979.

David, A. E., and A. R. David. "Preservation of Human Mummified Specimens." In *The Care and Conservation of Palaeontological Material*, ed. C. Collins, 73–88. Oxford, 1995.

David, A. R., ed. *The Manchester Museum Mummy Project.* Manchester, 1979.

———, ed. *Science in Egyptology: Proceedings of the 'Science in Egyptology' Symposia.* Manchester, 1986.

———, ed. *Egyptian Mummies and Modern Science.* Cambridge, forthcoming.

David, A. R., and R. Archbold. *Conversations with Mummies.* London, 2000.

David, A. R., and V. C. Garner. "Asru, an Ancient Egyptian Temple Chantress: Modern Spectrometric Studies as Part of the Manchester Egyptian Mummy Research Project." In *Molecular and Structural Archaeology: Cosmetic and Therapeutic Chemicals*, eds. G. Tsoucaris and J. Lipkowski, 153–62. Dordrecht, 2003.

David, A. R., and E. Tapp, eds. *Evidence Embalmed.* Manchester, 1984.

David, A. R., and E. Tapp. *The Mummy's Tale*. London, 1992.

Deelder, A. M., N. De Jonge, O. C. Boerman, Y. E. Fillie, and J. P. Rotmans. "Sensitive Determination of Circulating Anodic Antigen in *Schistosoma mansoni* Infected Individuals by an Enzyme-Linked Immunosorbent Assay Using Monoclonal Antibodies." *American Journal of Tropical Medicine and Hygiene* 40 (1989): 268–72.

Deelder, A. M., R. L. Miller, N. De Jonge, and F. W. Krijger. "Detection of Schistosome Antigens in Mummies." *Lancet* 335 (1990): 724.

Dawson, D. P., S. Giles, and M. W. Ponsford, eds. *Horemkenesi, May He Live Forever! The Bristol Mummy Project*. Bristol, 2002.

Dawson, W. R., and P. H. K. Gray. *Catalogue of Egyptian Antiquities in the British Museum, Vol. 1: Mummies and Human Remains*. London, 1968.

Flaherty, T., and T. Haigh. "Blood Grouping." In *The Mummy's Tale*, eds. A. R. David and E. Tapp, 154–61. London, 1992.

Goudsmit, J., and D. Brandon-Jones. "Evidence from the Baboon Catacomb in North Saqqara for a West Mediterranean Monkey Trade Route to Ptolemaic Alexandria." *Journal of Egyptian Archaeology* 86 (2000): 111–19.

Harer, W. B. "Pharmacological and Biological Properties of the Egyptian Lotus." *Journal of the American Research Center in Egypt* 22 (1985): 49–54.

Harris, J. E., P. V. Ponitz, and M. S. Loufty. "Orthodontics' Contribution to Save the Monuments of Nubia: A 1970 Field Report." *American Journal of Orthodontics* 58 (6) (1970): 578–96.

Harris, J. E., and K. E. Weeks. *X-Raying the Pharaohs*. New York, 1973.

Harris, J. E., and E. S. Wente, eds. *An Atlas of the Royal Mummies*. Chicago and London, 1980.

Harwood-Nash, D. C. E. "Computed Tomography of Ancient Egyptian Mummies." *Journal of Computer Assisted Tomography* 3, No. 6 (1979): 768–73.

Hawass, Z. "Press Release. Tutankhamun CT Scan"; available at http://guardians.net/hawass/press_release_tutankhamun_ct_scan_results.htm, accessed 8 March 2005.

Horne, P. D., and P. K. Lewin. "Electron Microscopy of Mummified Tissue." *Canadian Medical Association Journal* 117, No. 5 (1977): Report, Section 7.

Ikram, S., and A. Dodson. *The Mummy in Ancient Egypt*. London, 1998.

Isherwood, I., H. Jarvis, and R. A. Fawcitt. "Radiology of the Manchester Mummies." In *The Manchester Museum Mummy Project*, ed. A. R. David, 25–64. Manchester, 1979.

Lambert-Zazulak, P. I. "The International Ancient Egyptian Mummy Tissue Bank at the Manchester Museum." *Antiquity* 74 (2000): 44–8.

Leek, F. F. "Teeth and Bread in Ancient Egypt." *Journal of Egyptian Archaeology* 58 (1972): 126–32.

———. "The Dental History of the Manchester Mummies." In *The Manchester Museum Mummy Project*, ed. A. R. David, 65–78. Manchester, 1979.

Lewin, P. K., "Palaeo-Electron Microscopy of Mummified Tissue." In *Nature* 213 (1967): 416–17.

Lucas, A., and J. R. Harris, *Ancient Egyptian Materials and Industries*, 4th ed. London, 1962.

Merrillees, R. S. "Opium Trade in the Bronze Age Levant." *Antiquity* 36 (1962): 287–92.

———. "Opium Again in Antiquity." *Levant* 11 (1979): 167–71.

Miller, J. "Palaeodontology." In *Egyptian Mummies and Modern Science*, ed. A. R. David. Cambridge, forthcoming.

Miller, J., and C. Asher-McDade. "The Dental Examination of Natsef-Amun." In *The Mummy's Tale*, eds. A. R. David and E. Tapp, 112–20. London, 1992.

Miller, R. L., G. J. Armelagos, S. Ikram, N. De Jonge, F. W. Krijger, and A. M. Deelder. "Palaeoepidemiology of Schistosoma Infection in Mummies." *British Medical Journal* 304 (1992): 555–556.

Miller, R. L., N. De Jonge, F. W. Krijger, and A. M. Deelder. "Predynastic Schistosomiasis." In *Biological Anthropology and the Study of Ancient Egypt*, ed. W. V. Davies and R. Walker, 54–60. London, 1993.

Miller, R. L., S. Ikram, G. J. Armelagos, R. Walker, W. B. Harer, and C. J. Shiff. "Diagnosis of *Plasmodium falciparum* Infections in Mummies Using the Rapid *Para* Sight-F Test." *Transactions of the Royal Society of Tropical Medicine and Hygiene* 88 (1994): 31–32.

Moodie, R. L. *Roentgenologic Studies of Egyptian and Peruvian Mummies*, Anthropological Series 3. Chicago, 1931.

Murray, M. A. *The Tomb of Two Brothers*. Manchester, 1910.

Neave, R. A. H. "The Reconstruction of the Heads and Faces of Three Ancient Egyptian Mummies." In *The Manchester Museum Mummy Project*, ed. A. R. David, 149–57. Manchester, 1979.

———. "The Facial Reconstruction of Natsef-Amun." In *The Mummy's Tale*, ed. A. R. David, 162–7. London, 1992.

Nicholson, P. T., and I. Shaw, eds. *Ancient Egyptian Materials and Technology*. Cambridge, 2000.

Nunn, J. F. *Ancient Egyptian Medicine*. London, 1996.

Paabo, S. "Preservation of DNA in Ancient Egyptian Mummies." *Journal of Archaeological Science* 12 (1985): 411–17.

Pain, S. "Parasites in Paradise." *New Scientist* No. 2320 (8 December 2001): 34–7.

Parsche, F., and G. Ziegelmayer. "Munich Mummy Project – A Preliminary Report." In *Science in Egyptology: Proceedings of the 'Science in Egyptology' Symposia*, ed. A. R. David, 81–6. Manchester, 1986.

Raven, M. J., and W. K. Taconis. *Egyptian Mummies: Radiological Atlas of the Collections in the National Museum of Antiquities at Leiden*. Turnhout, 2005.

Ruffer, M. A. "Remarks on the Histology and Pathological Anatomy of Egyptian Mummies." *Cairo Scientific Journal* 10 (1910): 3–7.

Rutherford, P. "Immunocytochemistry and the Diagnosis of Schistosomiasis: Ancient and Modern." *Parasitology Today* 15 (1999): 390–91.

Sandison, A. T. "Reconstruction of Dried-Up Tissue Specimens for Histological Examination." *Journal of Clinical Pathology* 19 (1955): 522–523.

Smith, G. E. *The Royal Mummies*. Cairo, 1912.

Smith, G. E., and W. Dawson. *Egyptian Mummies*. London, 1924. Reprint, London, 1991.

Smith, G. E., and F. Wood-Jones. *Report of the Human Remains*. In *The Archaeological Survey of Nubia. Report for 1907–1908*, ed. G. A. Reisner, Vol. II, 7–367. Cairo, 1910.

Strouhal, E. "Embalming Excerebration in the Middle Kingdom." In *Science in Egyptology: Proceedings of the 'Science in Egyptology' Symposia*, ed. A. R. David, 141–54. Manchester, 1986.

Tapp, E. "Disease in the Manchester Mummies." In *The Manchester Museum Mummy Project*, ed. A. R. David, 95–102. Manchester, 1979.

Tapp, E., P. Stanworth, and K. Wildsmith. "The Endoscope in Mummy Research." In *Evidence Embalmed*, eds. A. R. David and E. Tapp, 65–77. Manchester, 1984.

Tapp, E., and K. Wildsmith. "The Autopsy and Endoscopy of the Leeds Mummy." In *The Mummy's Tale*, eds. A. R. David and E. Tapp, 132–53. London, 1992.

Taylor, J. H. *Mummy, the Inside Story*. London, 2004.

Wilkinson, C., B. Brier, R. Neave, and D. Smith. "The Facial Reconstruction of Egyptian Mummies and Comparison with the Fayuum Portraits." In *Mummies in a New Millenium: Proceedings of the 4th World Congress on Mummy Studies, Nuuk, Greenland, September 4th–10th, 2001*, eds. N. Lynnerup, C. Andreasen, and J. Berglund, 141–6. Copenhagen, 2003.

Wilkinson, C. "The Scientific Facial Reconstruction of Ancient Egyptians." In *Egyptian Mummies and Modern Science*, ed. A. R. David. Cambridge, forthcoming.

Chapter 4: Site Survey in Egyptology

Adams, R. *Heartland of Cities: Surveys of Ancient Settlement and Land Use on the Central Floodplain of the Euphrates.* Chicago, 1981.

Alcock, S., and J. Cherry. *Side by Side Survey: Comparative Regional Studies in Mediterranean Survey.* Oxford, 2003.

Amin, N. *The Historical Sites of Egypt, Vol. I: Ash-Sharqiyyah Governorate.* Cairo, 2005.

Barta, M., and V. Bruna. "Satellite Imaging in the Pyramid Fields." *Egyptian Archaeology* 26 (2005): 3–7.

Becker, H., and J. Fassbinder. "In Search of Piramesses – The Lost Capital of Ramesses II in the Nile Delta (Egypt) by Caesium Magnetometry." In *Archaeological Prospection*, ed. J. Fassbinder and W. Irlinger, 146–50. Munich, 1999.

Bietak, M. *Tell el-Dab'a II, Der Fundort im Rahmen einer archäologisch-geographischen Untersuchung über das ägyptische Östdelta.* Vienna, 1975.

———. "The Present State of Egyptian Archaeology." *Journal of Egyptian Archaeology* 65 (1979): 156–160.

Bubenzer, O., and A. Bolten. "In Egypt, Sudan and Namibia, GIS Helps Compare Human Strategies of Coping with Arid Habitats." *Archnews* 25 (2003): 2.

Butzer, K. *Early Hydraulic Civilization in Egypt: A Study in Cultural Ecology.* Chicago, 1976.

Chlodnicki, M., R. Fattovich, and S. Salvatori. "The Italian Archaeological Mission of the C.S.R.L.-Venice to the Eastern Nile Delta: A Preliminary Report of the 1987–1988 Field Season." *Cahier de Recherches de l'Institut de Papyrologie et d'Égyptologie de Lille* 14 (1992): 45–62.

Daressy, G. "A Travers les Koms du Delta." *Annales du Service des Antiquités de l'Égypte* 12 (1912): 169–213.

Darnell, J. *Theban Desert Road Survey in the Egyptian Western Desert*, Vol. 1: *Gebel Tjauti Rock Inscriptions 1–45 and Wadi el-Hôl Rock Inscriptions 1–45.* Oriental Institute Publications 119. Chicago, 2004.

Engelbach, R. "The Aeroplane and Egyptian Archaeology." *Antiquity* 10 (1929): 470–3.

Graham, A., and J. Bunbury. "The Ancient Landscapes and Waterscapes of Karnak." *Egyptian Archaeology* 27 (2005): 17–19.

Hoffmeier, J., and S. Moshier. "New Paleo-environmental Evidence from the North Sinai to Complement Manfred Bietak's Map of the Eastern Delta and Some Historical Implications." In *Timelines: Studies in Honour of Manfred Bietak, Vol. II: Orientalia Lovaniensia Analecta, 149*, eds. E. Czerny, I. Hein, H. Hunger, D. Melman, and A. Schwab, 167–76. Leuven, 2006.

Jeffreys, D. "Introducing 200 Years of Ancient Egypt: Modern History, Ancient Archaeology." In *Views of Ancient Egypt since Napoleon Bonaparte: Imperialism, Colonialism and Modern Appropriation*, ed. D. Jeffreys, 1–3. London, 2003.

———. "Memphis 2004." *Journal of Egyptian Archaeology* 91 (2005): 8–12.

Jomard, M. "Description des Antiquites d'Athribis, de Thmuis, et de Plusieurs nomes du Delta Oriental." *Memoire du Description de l'Égypte* 9. Paris, 1820.

Kemp, B., and S. Garfi. *A Survey of the Ancient City of El-'Amarna.* London, 1993.

Knisely-Marpole, R. "Kite Aerial Photography in Egypt's Western Desert." *Aerial Archaeology Research Group Newsletter* 23 (2001): 33–7.

Lawrence, W., M. Imhoff, N. Kerles, and D. Stutzer. "Quantifying Urban Land Use and Impact in Egypt Using Diurnal Imagery of the Earth's Surface." *International Journal for Remote Sensing* 23 (2002): 3921–3937.

Morrow, M., and M. Morrow. *Desert RATS: Rock Art Topographical Survey in the Eastern Desert.* London, 2002.

Mumford, G. "Reconstruction of the Temple at Tell Tebilla (East Delta)." In *Egypt, Israel and the Ancient Mediterranean World: Studies in Honour of Donald B. Redford*, ed. G. Knoppers and Å. Hirsch, 267–86. Leiden, 2004.

Mumford, G., L. Pavlish, and C. D'Andrea. "Geotechnical Survey at Tell Tabilla, Northeastern Nile Delta, Egypt." In *Egyptology at the Dawn of the Twenty-first Century: Proceedings of the Eighth International Congress of Egyptologists. Cairo, 2000. Vol. 1: Archaeology*, eds. Z. Hawass and L. Pinch-Brock, 361–8. Cairo, 2003.

Owen, G. "Looking Down at Amarna." *Aerial Archaeology Research Group Newsletter* 6 (1993): 33–37.

Parcak, S. "Satellites and Survey in Middle Egypt." *Egyptian Archaeology* 29 (2005): 28–32.

————. "Satellite Remote Sensing Methods for Monitoring Tell Sites in the Middle East." *Journal of Field Archaeology* (forthcoming).

Pavlish, L. "Archaeometry at Mendes: 1990–2002." In *Egypt, Israel, and the Ancient Mediterranean World: Studies in Honor of Donald B. Redford*, ed. G. Knoppers and A. Hirsch, 61–112. Leiden, 2004.

Poidebard, A. *La trace de Rome dans le désert de Syrie*. Paris, 1934.

Porter, B., and R. Moss. *Topographical Bibliography*, 2nd ed. Oxford, 1960–99.

Ur, Jason. "Corona Satellite Photography Ancient Road Networks: A Northern Mesopotamian Case Study." *Antiquity* 77 (2003): 102–115.

Van den Brink, E. "A Geo-archaeological Survey in the East Delta, Egypt: The First Two Seasons, a Preliminary Report," *Mitteilungen des Deutschen Archäologischen Instituts Abteilung Kairo* 43 (1987): 4–31.

Vercoutter, J. *Mirgissa I*. Paris, 1976.

Wendorf, F., A. Close, and R. Schild "A Survey of the Egyptian Radar Channels: An Example of Applied Field Archaeology." *Journal of Field Archaeology* 14 (1987): 43–63.

Wilkinson, T. "Archaeological Survey of the Tell Beydar Region, Syria 1997." In *Tell Beydar Environmental and Technical Studies*, eds. K. Van Lerberghe and G. Voet, 1–37. Begijnhof, 2002.

Wilson, P. "Sais (Sa el-Hagar) Fieldwork, 2004–05." *Journal of Egyptian Archaeology* 91 (2005): 1–8.

Yoshimura, S., J. Kondo, S. Hasegawa, T. Sakata, M. Etaya, T. Nakagawa, and S. Nishimoto. "A Preliminary Report of the General Survey at Dahshur North, Egypt, Annual Report of the Collegium Mediterranistarum." *Mediterraneus* 20 (1997): 3–24.

Chapter 5: Epigraphy and Recording

Arnold, D. "The Destruction of the Statues of Hatshepsut from Deir el-Bahri." In *Hatshepsut: From Queen to Pharaoh*, ed. C. Roehrig, with R. Dreyfus and C. A. Keller, 270–76. New York, New Haven, CT, and London, 2005.

Baines, J. "Communication and Display: The Integration of Early Egyptian Art and Writing." *Antiquity* 63 (1989): 471–82.

————. "The Earliest Egyptian Writing: Development, Content, Purpose." In *The First Writing: Script Invention as History and Process*, ed. S. D. Houston, 150–89. Cambridge, 2004.

Bell, L. D. "The Epigraphic Survey: The Philosophy of Egyptian Epigraphy after Sixty Years' Practical Experience." In *Problems and Priorities in Egyptian Archaeology*, ed. J. Assmann, G. Burkard, and V. Davies, 43–67. London and New York, 1987.

————. "New Kingdom Epigraphy." In *Ancient Egypt: Essays*, ed. N. Thomas, 105. New York, 1996.

Bickel, S. *Untersuchungen im Totentempel des Merenptah in Theben III: Tore und andere wiederverwendete Bauteile Aomenophis' III*. Beiträge zur ägyptischen Bauforschung und Altertumskunde 16. Stuttgart, 1997.

Bryan, B. "Painting Techniques and Artisan Organization in the Tomb of Suemniwet, Theban Tomb 92." In *Colour and Painting in Ancient Egypt*, ed. W. V. Davies, 63–72. London, 2001.

Calverley, A., and A. H. Gardiner. *The Temple of King Sethos I at Abydos*, 4 vols. Chicago and London, 1933–58.

Caminos, R. "The Recording of Inscriptions and Scenes in Tombs and Temples." In *Ancient Egyptian Epigraphy and Palaeography*, ed. H. G. Fischer, 3–25. New York, 1976.

–––––––. "Epigraphy in the Field," In *Problems and Priorities in Egyptian Archaeology*, ed. by J. Assmann, G. Burkard, and V. Davies, 57–67. London and New York, 1987.

Černý , J., ed. *Graffiti de la montagne thébaine*, 4 vols. Cairo, 1969–74.

Champollion, J.-F. *Précis du système hiéroglyphique des anciens égyptiens*, 2 vols. Paris, 1827–8.

–––––––. *Monuments de l'Égypte et de la Nubie*, 4 vols. Paris, 1835–45.

–––––––. *Notices descriptives*, 2 vols. Paris, 1844–89.

d'Avennes, É. P. *Atlas de l'art égyptien d'après les monuments, depuis les temps les plus reculés jusqu'à la domination romaine*. Paris, 1868–78; reprint Cairo, 1991.

Darnell, J. C. *Theban Desert Road Survey in the Egyptian Western Desert, Vol. 1: Gebel Tjauti Rock Inscriptions 1–45 and Wadi el-Hôl Rock Inscriptions 1–45*. OIP 119. Chicago, 2002.

Davies, N. de Garis, and A. H. Gardiner. *Ancient Egyptian Paintings*. Chicago, 1936.

De Buck, A. *The Egyptian Coffin Texts*, 7 vols. Chicago, 1935–61.

Der Manuelian, P. "Digital Epigraphy: An Approach to Streamlining Egyptological Epigraphic Method." *Journal of the American Research Center in Egypt* 35 (1998): 97–113.

–––––––. *Slab Stelae of the Giza Necropolis*. Publications of the Pennsylvania–Yale Expedition to Egypt 7. New Haven, CT, 2003.

Der Manuelian, P., and C. Loeben. "New Light on the Recarved Sarcophagus of Hatshepsut and Thutmose I in the Museum of Fine Arts, Boston." *Journal of Egyptian Archaeology* 79 (1993): 121–55.

Description de l'Égypte, ou recueil des observations et des recherches qui ont été faites en Égypte pendant l'expédition de l'armée française. Antiquités. 5 vols. Paris, 1809–22.

Desroches-Noblecourt, C., and C. Kuentz. *Le petit temple d'Abou Simbel*. 2 vols. Cairo, 1968.

Dorman, P. F. "The Proscription of Hatshepsut." In *Hatshepsut: From Queen to Pharaoh*, ed. C. Roehrig, with R. Dreyfus and C. A. Keller, 267–9. New York, New Haven, CT, and London, 2005.

Dreyer, G. *Umm el-Qaab I. Das prädynastische Königsgrab U-j und seine frühen Schriftzeugnisse*. Mainz, 1998.

Epigraphic Survey. *Medinet Habu 4: Festival Scenes of Ramesses III*. Oriental Institute Publications 51. Chicago, 1940.

Epigraphic Survey, *Reliefs and Inscriptions at Luxor Temple*, Vol. 1: *The Festival Procession of Opet in the Colonnade Hall*. Oriental Institute Publications 112. Chicago, 1994.

Fischer, H. G. "Archaeological Aspects of Epigraphy and Palaeography." In *Ancient Egyptian Epigraphy and Palaeography*, ed. H. G. Fischer, 29–50. New York, 1976.

Guilmant, F. *Le tombeau de Ramsès IX*. Mémoires publiés par les Membres de l'Institut francais d'Archéologie orientale 15. Cairo, 1907.

Hornung, E. *Das Buch von den Pforten des Jenseits*. Ägyptologische handlungen 7–8. Wiesbaden, 1979–90.

–––––––. *Texte zum Amduat*. Ägyptologische handlungen 13–14. Wiesbaden, 1987–92.

Hornung, Erik. *Das Buch der Anbetung des Re im Westens*. Ägyptologische handlungen 2–3. Wiesbaden, 1975–76.

Jacquet-Gordon, H. *Temple of Khonsu, Vol. 3: The Graffiti on the Khonsu Temple Roof at Karnak: A Manifestation of Personal Piety*. Oriental Institute Publications 123. Chicago, 2003.

Johnson, W. R. "À la recherche des décors perdus." *Dossiers histoire et archéologie* 101 (January 1986): 50–52.

Kahl, J. *Das System der ägyptischen Hieroglyphenschrift in der 0.–3. Dynastie*. Göttinger Orient Forschungen IV, Band 29. Wiesbaden, 1994.

–––––––. "Hieroglyphic Writing during the Fourth Millennium BC: An Analysis of Systems." *Archéo-Nil* 11 (2001): 103–34.

Lauffray, J. "Les «talatates» du IXe pylône et le *Teny-menou*," *Karnak* 6 (1978–80): 67–89.

Lepsius, R. *Denkmaeler aus Aegypten und Aethopien*, 5 vols. Berlin, 1849–1913.

Lesko, L. A. "Literacy." In *Oxford Encyclopedia of Ancient Egypt*, Vol. 2, ed. D. Redford, 297–9. Oxford, 2001.

Lipinska, J. "The Temple of Thutmose III at Deir el Bahri." In *Hatshepsut: From Queen to Pharaoh*, ed. C. Roehrig, with R. Dreyfus and C. A. Keller, 285–8. New York, New Haven, CT, and London, 2005.

Naville, É. *Das aegyptische Todtenbuch der XVIII. bis XX. Dynastie.* 3 vols. Berlin, 1886.

Parkinson, R. *Cracking Codes: The Rosetta Stone and Decipherment.* Berkeley, CA, 1999.

Parkinson, R., and S. Quirke. *Papyrus.* London, 1995.

Polz, D. "Excavation and Recording of a Theban Tomb: Some Remarks on Recording Methods." In *Problems and Priorities in Egyptian Archaeology*, ed. by J. Assmann, G. Burkard, and V. Davies, 134–8. London and New York, 1987.

Redford, D. *The Akhenaton Temple Project, Vol. 2: Rwd-Mnw, Foreigners, and Inscriptions.* Toronto, 1988.

Rosselini, I. *I Monumenti dell'Egitto et della Nubia.* 9 vols. Pisa, 1832–44.

Roth, A. M. "Erasing a Reign." In *Hatshepsut: From Queen to Pharaoh*, ed. by C. Roehrig, with R. Dreyfus and C. A. Keller, 277–81. New York, New Haven, CT, and London, 2005.

Seliger, F. "Vorstellung von zwei Computer-Programmen: II. Eine Grabungs-Dokumentation," *Göttingen Miscellen* 144 (1995): 85–99.

Sethe, K. *Die altägyptische Pyramidentexte*, 4 vols. Leipzig, 1908–22.

Smith, R. W., and D. Redford. *The Akhenaton Temple Project, Vol. 1: The Initial Discoveries.* Warminster, 1976.

Strudwick, N. *The Tombs of Amenhotep, Khnummose, and Amenmose (TT 294, 253, and 254).* Oxford, 1996.

Traunecker, C. "Les techniques d'épigraphie de terrain: principes et pratique." In *Problems and Priorities in Egyptian Archaeology*, ed. J. Assmann, G. Burkard, and V. Davies, 261–98. London and New York, 1987.

Wente, E. F. "The Scribes of Ancient Egypt." In *Civilizations of the Ancient Near East*, Vol. 4, ed. J. Sasson, 2211–22. New York, 1995.

Wilkinson, C. K., and M. Hill. *Egyptian Wall Paintings: The Metropolitan Museum of Art's Collection of Facsimiles.* New York, 1983.

Chapter 6: Monument and Site Conservation

Abdul-Qader, M. "Preliminary Report on the Excavations Carried Out in the Temple of Luxor, Seasons 1958–1959 & 1959–1960." *Annales du Service des Antiquités de l'Égypte* LX (1960): 228–79; pls. XL–XLI.

Abraham, G., and A. Bakr. "Comprehensive Development Plan for the City of Luxor, Egypt – Investment Project #1, Investment Portfolio for Proposed Grant of US $40 million to the Arab Republic of Egypt for the Restoration of the Avenue of Sphinxes." April 1999. http://www.abtassociates.com (1 December 2006).

Anthes, R. *Mit Rahineh 1956.* Philadelphia, 1965.

Agnew, N., and J. Bridgland, eds. *Of the Past, for the Future: Integrating Archaeology and Conservation: Proceedings of the Conservation Theme at the 5th World Archaeological Congress, Washington, D.C. June 2003.* Los Angeles, 2006.

Amin, N. "Capacity Building and Site Protection Needs in Egypt". In *Proceedings of the Ninth International Congress of Egyptologists, Grenoble, December 2004.* Leuven, forthcoming.

Avrami, E., R. Mason, and M. de la Torre, eds. *Values and Heritage Conservation. Research Report.* Los Angeles, 2000.

Cleere, H. "Introduction: The Rationale of Archaeological Heritage Management." In *Archaeological Heritage Management in the Modern World*, ed. H. Cleere. One World Archaeology 9. London and New York, 2000.

Cleere, H., P. O'Keefe, G. Trotzig, G. T. Wainwright, B. Startin, R. Elia, and R. Knoop. "Conservation and Site Management." *Antiquity* 67, No. 255 (June 1993): 400–45.

Corzo, M. A., and M. Afshar, eds. *Art and Eternity: The Nefertari Wall Paintings Conservation Project 1986–1992*. Los Angeles, 1993.

Davis, M. J., K. L. A. Gdaniec, M. Brice, and L. White, eds. *Mitigation of Construction Impact on Archaeological Remains*. Cambridge, 2004.

Description de l'Égypte, ou recueil des observations et des recherches qui ont été faites en Égypte pendant l'expédition de l'armée française. Antiquités. 5 vols. Paris, 1809.

El Amir, M. "The ΣΗΚΟΣ of Apis at Memphis." *Journal of Egyptian Archaeology* 34 (1948): 51–6; pls. XV–XVII.

El-Baz, F. "Finding a Pharaoh's Funeral Bark." *National Geographic* (April 1988): 512–33.

El-Iraqi, D. *Management of Cultural Heritage: A Goal Programming Approach*. Unpublished thesis submitted to the Department of Operations Research, Institute of Statistical Studies and Research, Cairo University, 2006.

Esmael, F. A, ed. *Proceedings of the First International Symposium on the Great Sphinx, Cairo, 29 February–3 March, 1992*. Cairo, 1992.

Feilden, B. M., and J. Jokilehto. *Management Guidelines for World Cultural Heritage Sites*. Rome, 1993.

Gamblin, S. "Thomas Cook en Égypte et à Louxor. L'invention du tourisme moderne au XIXe siecle." *Téoros* (Été, 2006): 19–25.

Hawass, Z. *The Secrets of the Sphinx: Restoration Past and Present*. Cairo, 1998.

———. "Site Management Plan at Giza Plateau: Master Plan for the Conservation of the Site." *International Journal of Cultural Property* 9, No. 1 (2000): 3–6.

———. *Egypt at the Dawn of the Twenty-first Century, Vol. 3: Conservation. Proceedings of the Eighth International Congress of Egyptologists, Cairo 2000*. Cairo and New York, 2003.

Jaritz, H., B. Dominicus, U. Minuth, W. Niederberger, and A. Seiler. *Mitteilungen des Deutschen Archäologischen Instituts, Abteilung Kairo* 52 (1996): 201–221.

Jeffreys, D. G. *The Survey of Memphis, Part I: The Archaeological Report*. London, 1985.

Jeffreys, D. G., J. Malek, and H. S. Smith. "The Survey of Memphis 1982." *Journal of Egyptian Archaeology* 70 (1984): 25–32; pl. VII.

Jones, M. "The Temple of Apis in Memphis." *Journal of Egyptian Archaeology* 76 (1990): 141–7; pls. VI and VII.

———. "The Work of the American Research Center in Egypt in the Tomb of Sety I in the Valley of the Kings, 1998–1999." In *Egypt at the Dawn of the Twenty-first Century, Vol. 1: Archaeology. Proceedings of the Eighth International Congress of Egyptologists, Cairo 2000*, ed. Z. Hawass, 252–61. Cairo and New York, 2003.

Lehner, M., M. Kamel and A. Tavares. *Giza Plateau Mapping Project. Season 2005 Preliminary Report*. Giza Occasional Papers 2. Boston, 2006.

Lipke, P. *The Royal Ship of Cheops*. National Maritime Museum, Greenwich, Archaeological Series No. 9. *British Archaeological Reports International Series* 225 (1984): 5–138.

Mahmud, S. A. *A New Temple for Hathor at Memphis*. Warminster, Wiltshire, 1978.

Mathers, C., T. Darvill, and B. J. Little, eds. *Heritage of Value, Archaeology of Renown. Reshaping Archaeological Assessment and Significance*. Gainesville, FL, 2005.

McKercher, B., and H. du Cros. *Cultural Tourism, the Partnership between Tourism and Cultural Heritage Management*. New York, 2002.

Norwich, J. J. "Tourism Pollution: The Future's Most Pervasive Problem." *Museum Management and Curatorship* 10 (1991): 45–52.

Orbashli, A. *Tourists in Historic Towns: Urban Conservation and Heritage Management.* London and New York, 2000.

Porter, B., and R. L. B. Moss. *Topographical Bibliography of Ancient Egyptian Hieroglyphic Texts, Reliefs, and Paintings,* Vol. II: *Theban Temples.* Oxford, 1972.

Pritchard, J. B. *Ancient Near Eastern Texts Relating to the Old Testament.* Princeton, NJ, 1950.

Rashed, A. Y. *Public Participation in the Conservation of Historical Environment: A Case Study of Luxor City, Egypt.* York, 1994.

Säve-Söderbergh, T., ed. *Temples and Tombs of Ancient Nubia. The International Rescue Campaign at Abu Simbel, Philae and Other Sites.* Paris and London, 1987.

Sedky, A. "The Politics of Area Conservation in Cairo." *International Journal of Heritage Studies* 11, No. 2 (May 2005): 113–30.

Seel, C. "A Gold Mine Worth LE 23 Billion (and Counting . . .)." *Egypt Today* (August 2006).

Sharpley, R., and D. J. Telfer, eds. *Tourism and Development: Concepts and Issues.* Aspects of Tourism 5. Clevedon, Somerset, 2002.

Sheehan, P. *Babylon of Egypt: The Making of Old Cairo.* Cairo, forthcoming.

Stanley-Price, N., and R. Burch, eds. *Conservation and Management of Archaeological Sites,* Vol. 6, Nos. 3 & 4. *Special Issue on Site Reburial.* London, 2004.

Teutonico, J. M., and G. Palumbo. *Management Planning for Archaeological Sites. An International Workshop Organized by the Getty Conservation Institute and Loyola Marymount University, May 2000, Corinth, Greece.* Los Angeles, 2002.

Thompson, M. W. *Ruins, Their Presentation and Display.* London, 1981.

Tung, A. M. *Preserving the World's Great Cities, the Destruction and Renewal of the Historic Metropolis.* New York, 2001.

Urry, J. *The Tourist Gaze.* 2nd ed. London, Thousand Oaks, CA, and New Delhi, 2002.

Vattenbyggnadsbyrån (VBB). *The Salvage of the Abu Simbel Temples.* Concluding report, December 1971. Örebro, 1976.

Von Beckerath, J. "'The Nile Level Records at Karnak and Their Importance for the History of the Libyan Period (Dynasties XXII and XXIII)." *Journal of the American Research Center in Egypt* 5 (1966): 43–55.

Weeks, K. R., and N. J. Hetherington. *The Valley of the Kings, Luxor, Egypt, Site Management Plan. The Theban Mapping Project,* Vol. V. Prepared for the World Monuments Fund. Cairo, 2006.

Chapter 7: Art of Ancient Egypt

Andreu, G., M.-H. Rutschowscaya, and C. Ziegler. *L'Égypte ancienne au Louvre.* Paris, 1997.

Claverly, A. M. *The Temple of King Sethos I at Abydos,* Vol. IV. London and Chicago, 1958.

Freed, R., Y. Markowitz, and S. D'Auria. *Pharaohs of the Sun: Akhenaten, Nefertiti, Tutankhamen.* Boston, 1999.

Klemm, R., and D. Klemm. *Steine und Steinbruche im Alten Agypten.* Berlin, 1993.

Quirke, S., and J. Spencer, eds. *The British Museum Book of Ancient Egypt.* London, 1992.

Roehrig, C., ed., with R. Dreyfus and C. A. Keller. *Hatshepsut from Queen to Pharaoh.* New Haven, CT, 2005.

Saleh, M., and H. Sourouzian. *Official Catalogue: The Egyptian Museum Cairo.* Mainz, 1987.

The Treasures of Ancient Egypt from the Egyptian Museum in Cairo. Vercelli, 2001.

Wenig, S. *Africa in Antiquity: The Catalogue.* Brooklyn, 1978.

Chapter 8: Ancient Egypt in Museums Today

Allen, J. P. *The Art of Medicine in Ancient Egypt.* New York, 2005.

Andreu, G. *Les artistes de Pharaon: Deir el-Médineh et la Vallée des Rois.* Paris, 2002.

Andrews, C. *Egyptian Mummies.* London, 1984.

Arnold, D., K. Grzymski, and C. Ziegler. *Egyptian Art in the Age of the Pyramids.* New York, 1999.

Arnold, D. *The Royal Women of Amarna.* New York, 1996.

Barrette, B. "Climate Control, Active and Passive." *Museum* 146 (1985): 81–4.

Berman, L. M. *Catalogue of the Egyptian Collection of the Cleveland Museum of Art.* Cleveland, 1999.

———. "Egypt Lost and Found in Boston." In *MFA Highlights: Arts of Ancient Egypt,* eds. L. M. Berman, R. E. Freed, and D. M. Doxey, 11–24. Boston, 2003.

Berman, L. M., and B. Letellier. *Pharaohs: Treasures of Egyptian Art from the Louvre.* Cleveland and Oxford, 1996.

Bongioanni, A., and M. S. Croce, eds. *The Illustrated Guide to the Egyptian Museum in Cairo.* Cairo, 2001.

Bothmer, B. V., and J. L. Keith. *Brief Guide to the Department of Ancient Art, The Brooklyn Museum.* Brooklyn, 1970.

Bovot, J. L. *Les serviteurs funéraires royaux et princiers de l'ancienne Égypte.* Paris, 2003.

Brovarski, E., S. Doll, and R. E. Freed. *Egypt's Golden Age: The Art of Living in the New Kingdom, 1558–1085 bc.* Boston, 1982.

Capel, A. K., and G. E. Markoe, eds. *Mistress of the House, Misress of Heaven: Women in Ancient Egypt.* New York, 1996.

Cooney, J. D. *Five Years of Collecting Egyptian Art at the Brooklyn Museum 1951–1956.* Brooklyn, 1956.

Cuno, J. "The Object of Art Museums." In *Whose Muse? Art Museums and the Public Trust,* ed. J. Cuno, 49–75. Princeton, NJ, and Cambridge, MA, 2004.

D'Auria, S. P. Lacovara, and C. Roehrig. *Mummies and Magic: The Funerary Arts of Ancient Egypt.* Boston, 1988.

Delange, E. *Catalogue des statues égyptiennes du Moyen Empire, 2060–1560 avant J.-C.* Paris, 1987.

Donadoni, A. M., et al. *Il Museo Egizio di Torino: Guida alla lettura di una civiltà.* Novara, 1988.

Dunand, F. *Terres cuites gréco-romaines d'Égypte.* Paris, 1990.

Dunham, D. *The Egyptian Department and Its Excavations.* Boston, 1958.

Edwards, I. E. S. *A General Introductory Guide to the Egyptian Collections of the British Museum.* London, 1969.

Eggebrecht, A., ed. *Ägyptens Aufstieg zur Weltmacht.* Mainz, 1987.

El-Aref, N. "New Law on the Way." *Al-Ahram,* No. 766 (27 October–2 November, 2005), p. 27.

El-Saddik, W. "The Egyptian Museum." *Museum* 57 (2005): 31–5.

El-Saghir, M. *The Discovery of the Statue Cachette at Luxor Temple.* Cairo, 1992.

Fay, B. *Egyptian Museum Berlin.* Berlin, 1982.

———. *Egyptian Museum Berlin.* Berlin, 1985.

Fazzini, R. *Images for Eternity: Egyptian Art from Berkeley and Brooklyn.* Brooklyn, 1975.

Fazzini, R., and R. S. Bianchi. *Cleopatra's Egypt: Age of the Ptolemies.* Brooklyn, 1988.

Fazzini, R. A., R. S. Bianchi, J. F. Romano, and D. B. Spanel. *Ancient Egyptian Art in the Brooklyn Museum.* Brooklyn, 1989.

Ferber, L. S.. *The Collector's Eye: The Ernest Erickson Collections at the Brooklyn Museum.* Brooklyn, 1987.

Freed, R. E., Y. Markowitz, and S. D'Auria. *Pharaohs of the Sun: Akhenaten, Nefertiti, Tutankhamen*. Boston, 1999.

Friedman, F. D. *Gifts of the Nile: Ancient Egyptian Faience*. Providence, 1998.

Friedman, R. *Egypt and Nubia: Gifts of the Desert*. London, 2002.

Hawass, Z. "A New Era for Museums in Egypt." *Museum* 57 (2005): 7–22.

Hayes, W. C. *The Scepter of Egypt*, Vols. I and II, 5th printing rev. New York, 1990.

Houlihan, P. "The Wilbour Library of Egyptology: A Vital Resource." *Ancient Egypt Magazine* 3, No. 6 (May/June 2003): 30–34.

Hoving, T. *Making the Mummies Dance: Inside the Metropolitan Museum of Art*. New York, 1993.

Ikram, S.. *American Contributions to Egyptian Archaeology*. Cairo, 2006.

James, T. G. H., and W. V. Davies. *Egyptian Sculpture*. London, 1983.

Jaritz, H. "The Museum of the Mortuary Temple of Merenptah." *Egyptian Archaeology* 19 (2001).

Jenkins, I. *Archaeologists and Aesthetes in the Sculpture Galleries of the British Museum, 1800–1939*. London, 1992.

Kennedy, R. "At Museums: Invasion of the Podcasts." *New York Times* (May 19, 2006): E1.

―――――. "Loss of Curators' Power Seen in Brooklyn Museum Plan." *New York Times* (June 22, 2006): E1.

Kozloff, A. P. "Egyptian Art." In *Miho Museum*, ed. T. Umehara, 10–40. Shigaraki, 1997.

Kozloff, A. P., and B. M. Bryan with L. M. Berman and E. Delange. *Egypt's Dazzling Sun: Amenhotep III and His World*. Cleveland, 1992.

Lewis, M. J. "Art for Sale." *Commentary* (March 2006): 36.

Lilyquist, C. "The Installation of the Egyptian Collection at the Metropolitan Museum of Art." *Museum* 142 (1984): 85–91.

MacGregor, N. "A Pentecost in Trafalgar Square." In *Whose Muse? Art Museums and the Public Trust*, ed. J. Cuno, 42–5. Princeton, NJ, and Cambridge, MA: 2004.

Mansour, Y. "The Grand Museum of Egypt Project: Architecture and Museography." *Museum* 57 (2005): 36–41.

Montembault, V. *Catalogue des chaussures de l'antiquité égyptienne*. Paris, 2000.

Newhouse, V. *Art and the Power of Placement*. New York, 2005.

Pearlstein, W. "Cultural Property, Congress, the Courts, and Customs: The Decline and Fall of the Antiquities Market?" In *Who Owns the Past? Cultural Policy, Cultural Property, and the Law*, ed. K. Fitz Gibbon, 21–4. New Brunswick, NJ, 2005.

Priese, K. H. *Ägyptisches Museum, Museumsinsel*. Berlin, 1991.

Quirke, S., ed. *The Temple in Ancient Egypt: New Discoveries and Recent Research*. London, 1997.

Radwan, A. "Highlights of Unknown Collections: Samples from the Site of Helwan." *Museum* 57 (2005): 87–90.

Roehrig, C. H., ed., with R. Dreyfus and C. A. Keller. *Hatshepsut: From Queen to Pharaoh*. New York, 2005.

Romano, J. F. *The Luxor Museum of Ancient Egyptian Art: Catalogue*. Cairo, 1979.

Russmann, E. R. *Eternal Egypt: Masterworks of Ancient Art from the British Museum*. London, 2001.

Saleh, M., and H. Sourouzian. *Official Catalogue: The Egyptian Museum Cairo*. Mainz, 1987.

Schneider, H. D. *Life and Death under the Pharaohs: Antiquities from the National Museum of Antiquities in Leiden, the Netherlands*. Leiden, 1996.

Schultz, R. "Museology, Egyptology, and Marketing Interests: A Contradiction?" In *Egyptology at the Dawn of the Twenty-First Century*, ed. Z. Hawass, 95–106. Cairo, 2002.

Seipel, W. *Gott, Mensch, Pharao: Viertausend Jahre Menschenbild in der Skulptur des alten Ägypten*. Vienna, 1992.

Silverman, D. P. *Searching for Ancient Egypt: Art, Architecture, and Artifacts from the University of Pennsylvania Museum of Archaeology and Anthropology*. Dallas, 1997.

Slayman, A. "The Mask of Ka-nefer-nefer." *Art+Auction* 29, No. 11 (July 2006): 20.

Staatliche Museen Preussicher Kulturbesitz. *Ägyptisches Museum, Berlin.* Charlottenburg, 1982.

Stille, A. *The Future of the Past.* New York, 2002.

Strudwick, N., and J. H. Taylor, eds. *The Theban Necropolis: Past, Present, and Future.* London, 2003.

Taylor, J. H., and N. C. Strudwick. *Mummies: Death and the Afterlife in Ancient Egypt: Treasures from the British Museum.* London, 2005.

Teeter, E. "The New Egyptian Gallery of the Oriental Institute, Chicago." *Egyptian Archaeology* 16 (Spring, 2000): 41–3.

Walsh, J. "Pictures, Tears, Lights, and Seats." In *Whose Muse? Art Museums and the Public Trust,* ed. J. Cuno, 77–101. Princeton, NJ and Cambridge, MA: 2004.

Welsby, D. A,. and J. R. Anderson, eds. *Sudan: Ancient Treasures.* London, 2004.

Whitehouse, H. "Dynastic Egypt in the Ashmolean Museum, Oxford." *Egyptian Archaeology* 24 (Spring 2004): 12–13

Wiese, A., and A. Brodbeck, eds. *Tutankhamun: The Golden Beyond, Tomb Treasures from the Valley of the Kings.* Basel, 2004.

Wildung, D. *Sudan: Antike Königreiche am Nil.* Munich, 1996.

Ziegler, C. *The Louvre: Egyptian Antiquities.* Paris, 1990.

————. *Les statues égyptiennes de l'ancien Empire.* Paris, 1997.

————, ed. *The Pharaohs.* Milan, 2002.

Chapter 9: Artifact Conservation and Egyptology

American Institute for Conservation. *Code of Ethics and Standards of Practice.* Washington, DC, 1994.

Beale, A. "Understanding, Restoring, and Conserving Ancient Bronzes with the Aid of Science." In *The Fire of Hephaistos: Large Classical Bronzes from North American Collections,* ed. Carol Mattusch, 65–80. Cambridge, MA, 1996.

Becker, L., L. Pilosi, and D. Schorsch. "An Egyptian Silver Statuette of the Saite Period – A Technical Study." *Metropolitan Museum Journal* 29 (1994): 37–56.

Blanchette, R. A., J. E. Haight, R. J. Koestler, P. B. Hatchfield, and D. Arnold. "Assessment of Deterioration in Archaeological Wood from Ancient Egypt." *Journal of the American Institute for Conservation of Historic and Artistic Works* 33 (1994): 50–70.

Bradley, S., and S. B. Hanna. "The Effect of Soluble Salt Movements on the Conservation of an Egyptian Limestone Standing Figure." In *Case Studies in the Conservation of Stone and Wall Paintings: Preprints of the Contributions to the Bologna Congress, 21–26 September 1986,* ed. N. S. Brommelle and P. Smith, 57–61. London, 1986.

Bradley, S., and A. P. Middleton. "A Study of the Deterioration of Egyptian Limestone Sculpture." *Journal of the American Institute for Conservation* 27 (1988): 64–86.

Brown, C. E., F. Macalister, and M. M. Wright, eds. *Conservation in Ancient Egyptian Collections.* London, 1995.

Chiotasso, L. M., and C. Sarnelli. "Preservation and Conservation of Archaeological Objects in Leather and Vegetal Fibres." In *Archaeological Conservation and Its Consequences: Preprints of the Contributions to the Copenhagen Congress, 26–30 August 1996,* 27–31. London, 1996.

Cronyn, J. *The Elements of Archaeological Conservation.* New York, 1990.

Drayman-Weisser, T. "A Perspective on the History of Conservation of Archeological Copper Alloys in the United States." *Journal of the American Institute for Conservation* 33 (1994): 141–52.

Ellis, L., and R. Newman. "The Analysis of Glazed Quartzite Sculpture from Kerma, Capital of Ancient Kush (Sudan)." In *Materials Issues in Art and Archaeology VII: Symposium Held November 30–December 3, 2004,*

Boston, Massachusetts, U.S.A.. Materials Research Society Symposium Proceedings, Vol. 852, eds. P. Vandiver, J. Mass, and A. Murray, 209–15. Warrendale, PA, 2005.

Farrell, E. F., C. Snow, and N. Vinogradskaya. "The Study and Treatment of Pa-Di-Mut's Cartonnage Mummy Case." *Journal of the American Institute for Conservation* 45 (2006): 1–14.

Frantz, J. H., and D. Schorsch. "Egyptian Red Gold." *Archeomaterials* 4 (1990): 133–52.

Gale, N., and Z. A. Stos-Gale. "Ancient Egyptian Silver." *Journal of Egyptian Archaeology* 67 (1981): 103–15.

Gänsicke, S., P. Hatchfield, A. Hykin, M. Szoboda, and C. Mei-An Tsu. "The Ancient Egyptian Collection at the MFA, Boston, Part 1: A Review of Treatments in the Field and Their Consequences and Part 2: A Review of Former Treatments at the MFA and Their Consequences." *Journal of the American Institute for Conservation* 42 (2003): 167–236.

Garland, K., and J. Rogers. "The Disassembly and Reassembly of an Egyptian Limestone Sculpture." *Studies in Conservation* 40 (1995): 1–9.

Gibson, L. T., B. J. Cooksey, D. Littlejohn, N. H. Tennent. "Characterisation of an Unusual Crystalline Efflorescence on an Egyptian Limestone Relief." *Analytica Chimica Acta* 337 (1997): 151–64.

Gilberg, M. "Alfred Lucas: Egypt's Sherlock Holmes." *Journal of the American Institute for Conservation* 36, No.1 (1998): 31–48.

Hatchfield, P. B. "Note on a Fill Material for Water Sensitive Objects." *Journal of the American Institute for Conservation* 25 (1986): 93–6.

Hatchfield, P. B., and R. Koestler. "Scanning Electron Microscopic Examination of Archaeological Wood Microstructure Altered by Conservation Treatments." *Scanning Microscopy* 1 (1987): 1059–69.

Hatchfield, P. *Pollutants in the Museum Environment: Practical Strategies for Problem Solving in Design, Exhibition and Storage*. London, 2002.

Jaeschke, R. L., and H. F. Jaeschke. "The Cleaning and Consolidation of Egyptian Encaustic Mummy Portraits." In *Cleaning, Retouching and Coatings: Technology and Practice for Easel Paintings and Polychrome Sculpture: Preprints of the Contributions to the Brussels Congress, 3–7 September 1990*, eds. J. S. Mills and P. Smith, 16–18. London, 1990.

La Niece, S., F. Shearman, J. Taylor, and A. Simpson. "Polychromy and Egyptian Bronze: New Evidence for Artificial Coloration." *Studies in Conservation* 47 (2002): 95–108.

Larkin, D. W. "Temple Gateway," Catalogue Entry 111. In *The American Discovery of Ancient Egypt*, ed. N. Thomas, 218–21. New York, 1995.

Lucas, A. *Antiquities: Their Restoration and Preservation*. 2nd ed. rev. London, 1932.

Maekawa, S., ed. *Oxygen-Free Museum Cases*. Los Angeles, 1998.

Muros, V., and J. Hirx. "The Use of Cyclododecane as a Temporary Barrier for Water-Sensitive Ink on Archaeological Ceramics During Desalination." *Journal of the American Institute for Conservation* 43 (2004): 75–89.

Newman, R. "Technical Examination of an Ancient Egyptian Pectoral." *Journal of the Museum of Fine Arts, Boston* 2 (1990): 31–7.

————. "Technical Report: Organic Residues from Egyptian Blue Anhydrite Duck Flasks and Other Anhydrite Vessels." *Metropolitan Museum Journal* 33 (1998): 49–53.

Nicholson, P., and I. Shaw, eds. *Ancient Egyptian Materials and Technologies*. Cambridge, 2000.

Nunberg, S., A. Heywood, and G. Wheeler. "Relative Humidity Control as an Alternative Approach to Preserving an Egyptian Limestone Relief." In *Le dessalement des matériaux poreux: 7èmes journées d'études de la SFIIC, Poitiers, 9–10 mai 1996*, 127–35. Champs-sur-Marne, 1996.

Petrie, W. M. F. *Methods and Aims in Archaeology*. London, 1904.

Pye, E. *Caring for the Past: Issues in Conservation for Archaeology and Museums*. London, 2001.

Rathgen, F. *The Preservation of Antiquities: A Handbook for Curators*. Cambridge, 1905.

Rodriguez-Navarro, C., E. Sebastian, E. Doehne, and W. S. Ginell. "The Role of Sepiolite–Palygorskite in the decay of Ancient Egyptian Limestone Sculptures." *Clays and Clay Minerals* 46 (1998): 414–22.

Schorsch, D. "Conservation in Egyptological Collections." In *The Oxford Handbook of Egyptology*, eds. I. Shaw and J. P. Allen. Oxford, forthcoming.

Scott, D. A., L. S. Dodd, J. Fuhrihata, S. Tanimoto, J. Keeney, M. R. Schilling, and E. Cowan. "An Ancient Egyptian Cartonnage Broad Collar: Technical Examination of Pigments and Binding Media." *Studies in Conservation* 49 (2004): 177–92.

Tétreault, J. *Airborne Pollutants in Museums, Galleries, and Archives: Risk Assessment, Control Strategies, and Preservation Management*. Ottawa, 2003.

Thickett, D., N. J. Lee, and S. M. Bradley. "Assessment of the Performance of Silane Treatments Applied to Egyptian Limestone Sculptures Displayed in a Museum Environment." In *Proceedings of the 9th International Congress on Deterioration and Conservation of Stone, Venice, June 19–24, 2000*, ed. V. Fassina, 503–11. Amsterdam, 2000.

Thompson, G. *The Museum Environment*. Oxford, 1994.

Tite, M. S. "Characterisation of Early Vitreous Materials." *Archaeometry* 29 (1987): 21–34.

Vergès, F. L. *Bleus égyptiens*. Leuven, 1992.

Watkins, S. C., and C. E. Brown, eds. *Conservation of Ancient Egyptian Materials*. London, 1988.

Wildung, D. "Einblicke-Zerstörungsfreie Untersuchungen an altägyptischen Objekten." *Jahrbuch Preussischer Kulturbesitz* 29 (1992 [1993]): 133–56.

Chapter 10: The Egyptian Language

Allen, J. P. *Middle Egyptian: An Introduction to the Language and Culture of Hieroglyphs*. Cambridge, 2000.

———. "Traits dialectaux dans les textes des pyramides du moyen empire." In *D'un monde à l'autre: Textes des pyramides et textes des sarcophages, Actes de la table ronde internationale "Textes des pyramides versus textes des sarcophages," IFAO, 24–26 septembre 2001*, eds. S. Bickel and B. Mathieu, 1–14. *Bibliothèque d'Etude* 139. Cairo, 2004.

Černý, J. and S. I. Groll. *A Late Egyptian Grammar*, 3rd ed. Studia Pohl: Series Maior 4. Rome, 1984.

Dreyer, G. "Frühe Schriftzeugnisse." In *Am Beginn der Zeit: Ägypten in der Vor- und Frühzeit*, eds. S. Schoske and A. Grimm, 12–15. Schriften aus der Ägyptischen Sammlung 9. Munich, 2000.

Edel, E.. *Altägyptische Grammatik*, 2 vols. Analecta Orientalia 34 and 39. Rome, 1955 and 1964.

Edgerton, W. F. "Stress, Vowel Quantity, and Syllable Division in Egyptian." *Journal of Near Eastern Studies* 6 (1947): 1–17.

———. "Early Egyptian Dialect Interrelationships." *Bulletin of the American Schools of Oriental Research* 122 (1951): 9–12.

Erman, A. *Neuägyptische Grammatik*, 2nd ed. Leipzig, 1933.

Gardiner, A. H. *Late Egyptian Stories*. Bibliotheca Aegyptiaca 1. Brussels, 1932.

———. *Egyptian Grammar, Being an Introduction to the Study of Hieroglyphs*, 3rd ed., rev. Oxford, 1964.

Gardiner, A. H., and K. Sethe. *Egyptian Letters to the Dead, Mainly from the Old and Middle Kingdoms*. London, 1928.

Goldwasser, O. *From Icon to Metaphor: Studies in the Semiotics of the Hieroglyphs*. Orbis Biblicus et Orientalis 142. Fribourg and Göttingen, 1995.

———. *Prophets, Lovers and Giraffes: Wor(l)d Classification in Ancient Egypt*. Göttinger Orientforschungen 38. Wiesbaden, 2002.

Hoch, J. E. *Semitic Words in Egyptian Texts of the New Kingdom and Third Intermediate Period*. Princeton, NJ, 1994.

Kahle, P. E. *Bala'izah: Coptic Texts from Deir el-Bala'izah in Upper Egypt.* Oxford, 1954.

Loprieno, A. *Ancient Egyptian: A Linguistic Introduction.* Cambridge, 1995.

Peust, C. *Egyptian Phonology.* Monographien zur Ägyptischen Sprache 2. Göttingen, 1999.

Polotsky, H. J. *Études de syntaxe copte.* Cairo, 1944.

Spiegelberg, W. *Demotische Grammatik.* Heidelberg, 1925.

Steindorff, G. *Lehrbuch der Koptischen Grammatik.* Chicago, 1951.

Vernus, P. *Future at Issue: Tense, Mood and Aspect in Middle Egyptian: Studies in Syntax and Semantics.* Yale Egyptological Studies 4. New Haven, CT, 1990.

Chapter 11: *Ancient Egyptian Literature*

Allen, J. P. *Middle Egyptian: An Introduction to the Language and Culture of Hieroglyphs.* Cambridge, 2000.

Assmann, J. *Ägyptische Hymnen und Gebete,* Orbis Biblicus et Orientalis. Freiburg and Göttingen, 1999.

———. "Egyptian Literature." In *The Anchor Bible Dictionary,* ed. D. N. Freedman, vol. 2, 378–90. New York, 1992.

Assmann, J., and E. Blumenthal, eds. *Literatur und Politik im pharaonischen und ptolemaischen Ägypten,* Bibliothèque d'Etude 127. Cairo, 1999.

Assmann, J., E. Feucht, and R. Grieshammer, eds. *Fragen an die altägyptische Literatur: Studien zum Gedenken an Eberhard Otto.* Wiesbaden, 1977.

Barucq, A., and F. Daumas. *Hymnes et prières de L'Égypte ancienne,* Littératures anciennes du Proche-Orient 10. Paris, 1979.

Berg, H. vanden and E. Aubourg. *MacScribe Hieroglyphic Text Processing,* PIREI II. Utrecht, 2000.

Bresciani, E. *Letteratura e poesia dell'antico Egitto.* Turin, 1969.

Brunner, H. *Altägyptische Weisheit: Lehren für das Leben.* Zürich and München, 1988.

———. *Grundzüge einer Geschichte der altägyptischen Literatur,* 4th rev. and expanded ed., Grundzüge 8. Darmstadt, 1986.

Brunner-Traut, E. *Altägyptische Märchen.* Düsseldorf and Köln, 1963.

———. *Lebensweisheit der alten Ägypter.* Freiburg, 1985.

———. "Altägyptische Literatur." In *Altorientalische Literaturen,* Neues Handbuch der Literatur Wissenschaft, ed. W. Röllig, 25–99. Wiesbaden, 1978.

Burkard, G. *Überlegungen zur Form der Ägyptschen Literatur: Die Geschichte des Schiffbrüchigen als literarisches Kunstwerk,* Ägypten und Altes Testament, Bd. 22. Wiesbaden, 1993.

———. "Der formale Afbau altägyptischer Literaturwerke: Zur Problematik der Erschließung seiner Grundstrukturen," *Studien zur Altägyptischen Kultur* 10 (1983): 79–118.

Burkard, G., and H. J. Thissen. *Einführung in die altägyptische Literaturgeschichte I: Altes und Mittleres Reich.* Einführungen und Quellentexte zur Ägyptologie. Münster, 2003.

Černý , J., and A. H. Gardiner, eds. *Hieratic Ostraca, I.* Oxford, 1957.

Erman, A. *The Ancient Egyptians: a sourcebook of their writings,* trans. by A. M. Blackman. New York, 1966.

Erman, A. and H. Grapow, eds. *Wörterbuch der Aegyptischen Sprache,* 7 vols. *Die Belegstellen,* 5 vols. Berlin, 1971.

Faulkner, R. O. *A Concise Dictionary of Middle Egyptian.* Oxford, 1981.

Fecht, G. "Die Form der altägyptischen Literatur: Metrische und stilistische Analyse," *Zeitschrift für ägyptische Sprache und Altertumskunde* 91 (1964): 11–63 and 92 (1965): 10–32.

Foster, J. L. *Ancient Egyptian Literature: An Anthology.* Austin, 2001.

———. *Hymns, Prayers, and Songs: An Anthology of Ancient Egyptian Lyric Poetry.* Writings from the Ancient World, vol. 8. Atlanta, 1995.

———. *Love Songs of the New Kingdom.* Austin, 1992.

————. "'The Shipwrecked Sailor': Prose or Verse? (Postponing Clauses and Tense-Neutral Clauses," *Studien zur Altägyptischen Kultur* 15 (1988): 69–109.

Fox, M. V. *The Song of Songs and the Ancient Egyptian Love Songs*. Madison, 1985.

Gardiner, Sir, A. H. *Egyptian Grammar*, 3rd rev. ed. Oxford, 1973.

Guess, A. *Catalogue des ostraca hiératiques littéraires de Deir el Medineh*, tôme IV, fasc. 1, Documents de Fouilles, tôme XXV. Cairo, 1990.

Hannig, R. *Großes Handwörterbuch Ägyptisch-Deutsch: die Sprache der Pharaonen (2800–950 v. Chr.)*, Kulturgeschichte der Antiken Welt, Bd. 64. Mainz, 1995.

Helck, W. *Die Lehre des Djedefhor und die Lehre eines Vaters an seinen Sohn*, Kleine Ägyptische Texte. Wiesbaden, 1984.

Helck, W., W. Westendorf, and E. Otto, eds. *Lexicon der Ägyptologie*, 7 vols. Wiesbaden, 1975–1992.

Hermann, A. *Altägyptische Liebesdichtung*. Wiesbaden, 1959.

Hollis, S. T. "Tales of Magic and Wonder from Ancient Egypt." In *Civilizations of the Ancient Near East*, ed. J. M. Sasson, Vol. IV, 2255–64. New York, 1995.

Hornung, E., and O. Keel, eds. *Studien zu Altägyptischen Lebenslehren*, Orbis Biblicus et Orientalis 28. Freiburg and Göttingen, 1979.

Leclant, J., ed. *La Sagesses du Proche-Orient ancien: Colloque de Strasbourg, 17–19 mai 1962*. Paris, 1963.

Lefebvre, G. *Romans et contes égyptiennes de l'époque pharaonique*. Paris, 1949.

Lichtheim, M. *Ancient Egyptian Literature*, 3 vols. Berkeley, CA, 1973–1980.

————. "Have the principles of ancient egyptian metrics been discovered?" *Journal of the American Research Center in Egypt* 9 (1971–2): 103–10.

Lopez, J. *Ostraca ieratici*, Catalogo del Museo Egizio di Torino, Serie Seconda – Collezioni, Vol. III, fascicoli 1–4. Milan, 1978–84.

Loprieno, A., ed. *Ancient Egyptian Literature: History and Forms*, Probleme der Ägyptologie 10. Leiden, 1996.

Mathieu, B. *La poesie amoureuse de l'Égypte ancienne: Recherches sur un genre littéraire au Nouvel Empire*, Bibliothèque d'Etude 115. Cairo, 1996.

————. "Études de metrique égyptienne I–IV," *Revue d'Égyptologie* 39 (1988): 63–82; *Revue d'Égyptologie* 41 (1990): 127–41; *Revue d'Égyptologie* 45 (1994): 139–54; and *Revue d'Égyptologie* 48 (1997): 109–163.

Möller, G. *Hieratische Paläographie*, reprint of 2nd rev. ed. (1927), 3 vols. in I. Osnabrück, 1965.

Moers, G., ed. *Definitely: Egyptian Literature: Proceedings of the Sympsion [sic] "Ancient Egyptian Literature: History and Forms," Los Angeles, March 24–26, 1995*, Lingua Aegyptia, Studia monographia Bd. 2. Göttingen, 1999.

Parkinson, R. B. *Poetry and Culture in Middle Kingdom Egypt: A Dark Side to Perfection*, London, 2002.

————. *The Tale of Sinuhe and Other Ancient Egyptian Poems 1940–1640 BC*. Oxford, 1997.

Plas, D. van der. *L'Hymne à la Crue du Nil*, 2 vols., Egyptologische Uitgaven IV. Leiden, 1986.

Posener, G. *Catalogue des ostraca hiératiques littéraires de Deir el Medineh*, tômes I–III, Documents de Fouilles, tômes I, XVIII, and XX. Cairo, 1938–80.

————. *Littérature et politique dans l'Égypte de la XIIe Dynastie*, Bibliothèque de l'École des Hautes Études, tôme 307. Paris, 1956.

————. "Literature." In *The Legacy of Egypt*, ed. J. R. Harris, 2nd ed., 220–256. Oxford, 1971.

————. "Les Richesses inconnues de la littérature égyptienne (Recherches littéraires I)," *Revue d'Égyptologie* 6 (1951): 27–48.

Preminger, A. and T. V. F. Brogan, eds. *The New Princeton Encyclopedia of Poetry and Poetics*. Princeton, 1993.

Redford, D. B., ed. *The Oxford Encyclopedia of Ancient Egypt*, 3 vols. New York, 2001.

Redford, D. B. "Ancient Egyptian Literature: An Overview." In *Civilizations of the Ancient Near East*, ed. J. M. Sasson, Vol. IV, 2223–41. New York, 1995.

Rocatti, A. *Sapienza egizia: La letteratura educativa in Egitto durante il II millennio a.C.* Brescia, 1994.

Schenkel, W. "Zur Relevanz der altägyptischen 'Metrik'," *Mitteilungen des Deutschen Archäologischen Instituts, Abteilung Kairo* 28 (1978): 103–7.

Schott, S. *Altägyptische Liebeslieder*, 2nd ed. Zurich, 1950.

Simpson, W. K., ed. *The Literature of Ancient Egypt: An Anthology of Stories, Instructions, Stelae, Autobiographies, and Poetry*, with trans. by R. K. Ritner, V. A. Tobin, and E. F. Wente, Jr., 3rd ed. New Haven, CT, 2003.

Spuler, B., ed. *Handbuch der Orientalistik, Bd. I, Ägyptologie, Abschnitt II, Literatur*. Leiden and Köln, 1970.

Vernus, P. *Chants d'amour de l'Égypte antique*. Paris, 1992.

Williams, R. J. "Egyptian Wisdom Literature." In *The Anchor Bible Dictionary*, ed. D. N. Freedman, vol. 2, 395–9. New York, 1992.

Chapter 12: Egyptian Religious Texts

Allen, J. P. "Funerary Texts and their Meaning." In *Mummies & Magic. The Funerary Arts of Ancient Egypt*, eds. Sue D'Auria, P. Lacovara, and C. H. Roehrig, 38–48. Boston, 1988.

———. "Reading a Pyramid." In *Hommages à Jean Leclant*, eds. C. Berger, G. Clerc, and N. Grimal, 5–28. *Bibliothèque d'Etude* 106/1. Cairo, 1994.

Allen, J. P., and P. Der Manuelian, eds. *The Ancient Egyptian Pyramid Texts*. Writings in the Ancient World 23. Atlanta, 2005.

Allen, J. P. *The Egyptian Coffin Texts, Vol. 8: Middle Kingdom Copies of Pyramid Texts*. Oriental Institute Publications, Vol. 132. Chicago, 2006.

Amenta, A. "Some Reflections on the 'Homosexual' Intercourse between Horus and Seth," *Göttinger Miscellen* 199 (2004): 7–21.

Assmann, J. "Die Verborgenheit des Mythos in Ägypten," *Göttinger Miscellen* 25 (1977): 7–43.

———. "Die Zeugung des Sohnes: Bild, Spiel, Erzählung und das Problem des ägyptischen Mythos." In *Funktionen und Leistungen des Mythos: Drei altorientalische Beispiele*, eds. J. Assmann, E. Frucht, and R. Grieshammer, 13–61. Orbis Biblicus et Orientalis 48. Freiburg, 1982.

———. *The Search for God in Ancient Egypt*. Trans. by David Lorton. Ithaca, NY, 2001.

———. *Altägyptische Totenliturgien. Totenliturgien in den Sargtexten*. Heidelberg, 2002.

Backes, B. *Das altägyptische 'Zweiwegebuch'. Studien zu den Sargtext-Sprüchen 1029–1130*. Ägyptologische Abhandlungen, 69. Wiesbaden, 2005a.

———. *Wortindex zum späten Totenbuch (pTurin 1791)*. Studien zum Altägyptischen Totenbuch 9. Wiesbaden, 2005b.

Baines, J. "Egyptian Myth and Discourse: Myth, Gods, and the Early Written and Iconographic Record," *Journal of Near Eastern Studies* 50 (1991): 81–105.

———. "Myth and Literature." In *Ancient Egyptian Literature. History and Forms*, ed. A. Loprieno, 361–77. Probleme der Ägyptologie 10. Leiden, 1996.

———. "Egyptian Letters of the New Kingdom as Evidence for Religious Practice," *Journal of Ancient Near Eastern Religions* 1 (2001): 1–31.

Barguet, P. "Les textes spécifiques des différents panneaux des sarcophages du Moyen Empire," *Revue d'Égyptologie* 23 (1971): 15–22.

Barré, J.-Y. *Pour la survie de pharaon. Les textes funéraires de l'Amdouat dans la tombe de Thoutmosis III*. Paris, 2003.

Barucq, A., and F. Daumas. *Hymnes et prières de l'Égypte ancienne*. Paris, 1980.

Beinlich, H. *Das Buch vom Ba*. Studien zum Altaegyptischen Totenbuch 4. Wiesbaden, 2000.

Beinlich, H., J. Hallof, H. Hussy, and C. von Pfeil. *Ägyptologische Tempeltagung (5.) Würzburg, 23.– 26. September 1999.* Ägypten und Altes Testament 33. Wiesbaden, 2002.

Bell, L. "The New Kingdom 'Divine' Temple: The Example of Luxor." In *Temples of Ancient Egypt,* ed. B. E. Shafer, 127–84. Ithaca, 1997.

Berger-el Naggar, C. "Des textes des pyramides sur papyrus dans les archives du temple funéraire de Pépy Ier." In *D'un Monde à l'autre. Textes des pyramides & textes des sarcophages. Actes de la table ronde internationale 'Textes des pyramides versus textes des sarcophages' Ifao, 24–26 septembre 2001,* ed. S. Bickel and B. Mathieu, 85–90. *Bibliothèque d'Etude*139. Cairo, 2004.

Bickel, S. *La cosmogonie égyptienne avant le Nouvel Empire.* Orbis Biblicus et Orientalis 134. Freiburg, 1994.

Bickel, S., and B. Mathieu, eds. *D'un monde à l'autre. Textes des pyramides & textes des sarcophages. Actes de la table ronde internationale 'Textes des pyramides versus textes des sarcophages' Ifao, 24–26 septembre 2001. Bibliothèque d'Etude* 139. Cairo, 2004.

Borghouts, J. F. *Ancient Egyptian Magical Texts.* Religious Texts Translation Series. Nisaba 9. Leiden, 1978.

Currid, J. D. *Ancient Egypt and the Old Testament.* Grand Rapids, 1997.

Darnell, J. C. *The Enigmatic Netherworld Books of the Solar–Osirian Unity. Cryptographic Compositions in the Tombs of Tutankhamun, Ramesses VI and Ramesses IX.* Orbis Biblicus et Orientalis 198. Freiburg, 2004.

Erman, A. *Life in Ancient Egypt.* Trans. by H. M. Tirard. Orig. ed., London, 1894; New York, 1971.

Eyre, C. *The Cannibal Hymn. A Cultural and Literary Study.* Liverpool Monographs in Archaeology and Oriental Studies, NS1. Liverpool, 2002.

Fairman, H. W. *The Triumph of Horus: An Ancient Egyptian Sacred Drama.* London, 1973.

Falck, M. von. *Das Totenbuch der Qeqa aus der Ptolemäerzeit (pBerlin P. 3003).* Handschriften des Altägyptischen Totenbuches 8. Wiesbaden, 2006.

Foster, J. L. *Hymns, Prayers, and Songs. An Anthology of Ancient Egyptian Lyric Poetry.* Writings in the Ancient World 8. Atlanta, 1995a.

_____. "The *Hymn to Aten*: Akhenaten Worships the Sole God." In *Civilizations of the Ancient Near East,* ed. J. M. Sasson, vol. 3, 1751–61. New York, 1995b.

Franke, D. "The Middle Kingdom Offering Formulas – A Challenge." *Journal of Egyptian Archaeology* 89 (2003): 39–57.

Frankfort, H., and H. A. Frankfort. *Before Philosophy. The Intellectual Adventure of Ancient Man. An Essay on Speculative Thought in the Ancient Near East.* Orig. ed. Chicago 1946; Baltimore, 1971.

Gardiner, A. H. "Hymns to Sobk in a Ramesseum Papyrus." *Revue d'Égyptologie* 11 (1957): 43–56.

Geisen, C. *Die Totentexte des verschollenen Sarges der Königin Mentuhotep aus der 13. Dynastie. Ein Textzeuge aus der Übergangszeit von den Sargtexten zum Totenbuch.* Studien zum Altägyptischen Totenbuch 8. Wiesbaden, 2004.

Gestermann, L. *Die Überlieferung ausgewählter Texte altägyptischer Totenliteratur ("Sargtexte") in spätzeitlichen Grabanlagen.* Ägyptologische Abhandlungen 68. Wiesbaden, 2005.

Gillam, R. A. *Performance and Drama in Ancient Egypt.* London, 2005.

Goebs, K. "A Functional Approach to Egyptian Myth and Mythemes," *Journal of Ancient Near Eastern Religions* 2 (2002): 27–59.

_____. "The Cannibal Spell: Continuity and Change in the Pyramid Text and Coffin Text Versions." In *D'un monde à l'autre. Textes des pyramides & textes des sarcophages. Actes de la table ronde internationale 'Textes des pyramides versus textes des sarcophages' Ifao, 24–26 septembre 2001,* eds. S. Bickel and B. Mathieu, 143–73. *Bibliothèque d'Etude*139. Cairo, 2004.

Goyon, J.-C. *Le rituel du sHtp sxmt au changement de cycle annuel. Bibliothèque d'Etude* 141. Cairo, 2006.

Grajetski, W. *Burial Customs in Ancient Egypt: Life and Death for Rich and Poor.* London, 2003.

Guglielmi, W., and J. Dittmar. "Anrufungen der persönlichen Frömmigkeit auf Gans- und Widder-Darstellungen des Amun." In *Gegengabe. Festschrift für Emma Brunner-Traut,* eds. I. Gamer-Wallert and W. Helck, 119–42. Tübingen, 1992.

Guilhou, N. "Un texte de guérison." *Chronique d'Egypte* 70 (1995): 52–64.

Gülden, S. A. *Die hieratischen Texte des P. Berlin 3049*. Kleine ägyptische Texte 13. Wiesbaden, 2001.

Gülden, S., and I. Munro. *Bibliographie zum Altägyptischen Totenbuch*. Studien zum Altägyptischen Totenbuch 1. Wiesbaden, 1998.

Hegenbarth-Reichardt, I. *Der Raum der Zeit. Eine Untersuchung zu den altägyptischen Vorstellungen und Konzeptionen von Zeit und Raum anhand des Unterweltbuches Amduat*. Ägypten und altes Testament 64. Wiesbaden, 2006.

Hornung, E. *Conceptions of God in Ancient Egypt: The One and the Many*. Trans. by J. Baines. London, 1982.

———. *Akhenaten and the Religion of Light*. Trans. by D. Lorton. Ithaca, 1999a.

———. *The Ancient Egyptian Books of the Afterlife*. Trans. by D. Lorton. Ithaca, 1999b.

Jacquet-Gordon, H. *Temple of Khonsu, Vol. 3: The Graffiti on the Khonsu Temple Roof at Karnak: A Manifestation of Personal Piety*. Oriental Institute Publications 123. Chicago, 2003.

Kemp, B. J. "How Religious Were the Ancient Egyptians?" *Cambridge Archaeological Journal* 5 (1995): 25–54.

Knigge, C. *Das Lob der Schöpfung. Die Entwicklung ägyptischer Sonnen- und Schöpfungshymnen nach dem Neuen Reich*. Orbis Biblicus et Orientalis 219. Freiburg, 2006.

Köthen-Welpot, S. *Theogonie und Genealogie im Pantheon der Pyramidentexte*. Habelts Dissertationsdrucke. Reihe Ägyptologie 6. Bonn, 2003.

Kruchten, J.-M. "Oracles." In *The Oxford Encyclopedia of Ancient Egypt*, ed. D. B. Redford, vol. 2, 609–612. New York, 2001.

Lapp, G. *Totenbuch Spruch 17*. Totenbuchtexte 1. Synoptische Textausgabe nach Quellen des Neuen Reiches. Basel, 2006.

Leitz, C. *Quellentexte zur ägyptischen Religion. 1. Die Tempelinschriften der griechisch-römischen Zeit*. Einführungen und Quellentexte zur Ägyptologie, 2. Münster, 2004.

———. *Kurzbibliographie zu den übersetzten Tempeltexten der griechisch-römischen Zeit*. Bibliothèque d'Etude 136. Cairo, 2005.

Lichtheim, M. *Ancient Egyptian Literature, Vol. 3: The Late Period*. Berkeley, CA, 1980.

Loprieno, A. "Defining Egyptian Literature: Ancient Texts and Modern Theories." In *Ancient Egyptian Literature. History and Forms*, ed. A. Loprieno, 39–58. Probleme der Ägyptologie 10. Leiden, 1996.

Luiselli, M. M. *Der Amun-Re Hymnus des P. Boulaq 17 (P.Kairo CG 58038)*. Kleine ägyptische Texte 14. Wiesbaden, 2004.

Lüscher, B. *Untersuchungen zu Totenbuch Spruch 151*. Studien zum Altägyptischen Totenbuch 2. Wiesbaden, 1998.

———. *Das Totenbuch pBerlin P. 10477 aus Achmim (mit Photographien des verwandten pHildesheim 5248)*. Handschriften des Altägyptischen Totenbuches 6. Wiesbaden, 2000.

———. *Die Verwandlungssprüche (Tb 76 – 88)*. Synoptische Textausgabe nach Quellen des Neuen Reiches. Totenbuchtexte 2. Basel, 2006.

Mathieu, B. "Études de métrique égyptienne. II: Contraintes métriques et production textuelle dans l'Hymne à la crue du Nil," *Revue d'Égyptologie* 41 (1990): 127–41.

———. "Études de métrique égyptienne, III. Une innovation métrique dans une 'litanie' thébaine du Nouvel Empire," *Revue d'Égyptologie* 45 (1994): 139–54.

———. "Études de métrique égyptienne, IV. Le tristique ennéamétrique dans l'hymne à Amon de Leyde," *Revue d'Égyptologie* 48 (1997a): 109–63.

———. "La signification du serdab dans la pyramide d'Ounas. L'architecture des appartements funéraires royaux à la lumière des Textes des Pyramides." In *Études sur l'ancien empire et la nécropole de Saqqâra dédiées à Jean-Philippe Lauer*, eds. C. Berger and B. Mathieu, 289–304. Orientalia Monspeliensia, 9/1–2. Montpellier, 1997b.

_____. "La distinction entre textes des pyramides et textes de sarcophages est-elle légitime?" In *D'un monde à l'autre. Textes des pyramides & textes des sarcophages. Actes de la table ronde internationale 'Textes des pyramides versus textes des sarcophages' Ifao, 24–26 septembre 2001*, ed. S. Bickel and B. Mathieu, 247–62. *Bibliothèque d'Etude* 139. Cairo, 2004.

Mendel, D. *Die kosmogonischen Inschriften in der Barkenkapelle des Chonstempels von Karnak*. Monographie Reine Élisabeth 9. Turnhouts, 2003.

Meurer, G. *Die Feinde des Königs in den Pyramidentexten*. Orbis Biblicus et Orientalis 189. Freiburg, 2003.

Meyer-Dietrich, E. *Senebi und Selbst: Personenkinstituentien zur rituellen Wiedergeburt in einem Frauensarg des Mittleren Reiches*. Orbis Biblicus et Orientalis 216. Freiburg, 2006.

Mohamed, Z. S. *Festvorbereitungen: Die administrativen und ökonomischen Grundlagen altägyptischer Feste*. Orbis Biblicus et Orientalis 202. Freiburg, 2004.

Molen, R. van der. *A Hieroglyphic Dictionary of Egyptian Coffin Texts*. Probleme der Ägyptologie, 15. Leiden, 2000.

_____. *An Analytical Concordance of the Verb, the Negation and the Syntax in Egyptian Coffin Texts*. Handbuch der Orientalistik, Section One. The Near and Middle East 77. Leiden, 2005.

Morenz, L. D. *Beiträge zur Schriftlichkeitskultur im Mittleren Reich und in der 2. Zwischenzeit*. Ägypten und Altes Testament 29. Wiesbaden, 1996.

Morenz, S. *Egyptian Religion*. Trans. by A. E. Keep. London, 1973.

Morgan, E. E. *Untersuchungen zu den Ohrenstelen aus Deir el Medine*. Ägypten und Altes Testament 61. Wiesbaden, 2004.

Munro, I. *Das Totenbuch des Bak-su (pKM 1970.37(pBrocklehurst) aus der Zeit Amenophis' II*. Handschriften des Altägyptischen Totenbuches 2. Wiesbaden, 1995a.

_____. *Das Totenbuch des Jah-mes (pLouvre E. 11085) aus der frühen 18. Dynastie*. Handschriften des Altägyptischen Totenbuches 1. Wiesbaden, 1995b.

_____. *Der Totenbuch-Papyrus des Hohenpriesters Pa-nedjem II. (pLondon BM 10793(pCampbell)*. Handschriften des Altägyptischen Totenbuches 3. Wiesbaden, 1996.

_____. *Das Totenbuch des Nacht-Amun aus der Ramessidenzeit (pBerlin P. 3002)*. Handschriften des Altäyptischen Totenbuches 4. Wiesbaden, 1997.

_____. *Das Totenbuch des Pa-en-nesti-taui aus der Regierungszeit des Amenemope (pLondon BM 10064)*. Handschriften des Altägyptischen Totenbuches 7. Wiesbaden, 2001a.

_____. *Spruchvorkommen auf Totenbuch-Textzeugen der dritten Zwischenzeit*. Studien zum altägyptischen Totenbuch 5. Wiesbaden, 2001b.

_____. *Ein Ritualbuch für Goldamulette und Totenbuch des Month-em-hat*. Studien zum Altaegyptischen Totenbuch 7. Wiesbaden, 2004.

_____. *Der Totenbuch-Papyrus des Hor aus der frühen Ptolemäerzeit (pCologny Bodmer CV + pCincinnati 1947.369 + pDenver 1954.61)*. Handschriften des Altägyptischen Totenbuches 9. Wiesbaden, 2006.

Murnane, W. J. *Texts from the Amarna Period in Egypt*. Writings from the Ancient World 5. Atlanta, 1995.

O'Rourke, P. F. "Drama." In *The Oxford Encyclopedia of Ancient Egypt*, ed. D. B. Redford, Vol. 1, 407–410. New York, 2001.

Parkinson, R. B. "'Homosexual' Desire and Middle Kingdom Literature." *Journal of Egyptian Archaeology* 81 (1995): 57–76.

Patanè, M. "La structure poétique de la stèle C 30 du Musée du Louvre." *Bulletin de la Société d'Égyptologie Genève* 6 (1982): 77–82.

_____. "À propos de la structure rythmique des litanies d'Esna." *Göttingen Miscellen* 62 (1983a): 63–66.

_____. "Analyse métrique des litanies égyptiennes." *Göttingen Miscellen* 64 (1983b): 61–5.

_____. "La structure de l'hymne à Sesostris III." *Bulletin de la Société d'Égyptologie Genève* 8 (1983c): 61–5.

Pierre-Croisiau, I. "Nouvelles identifications de textes des sarcophages parmi les "nouveaux" textes des pyramides de Pépy Ier et de Mérenrê." In *D'un monde à l'autre. Textes des pyramides & textes des sarcophages. Actes de la table ronde internationale 'Textes des pyramides versus textes des sarcophages' Ifao, 24–26 septembre 2001*, ed. S. Bickel and B. Mathieu, 263–78. *Bibliothèque d'Etude* 139. Cairo, 2004.

Pinch, G. *Votive Offerings to Hathor*. Oxford, 1993.

———. *Magic in Ancient Egypt*. London, 1994.

Plas, D. van der, and J. F. Borghouts. *Coffin Texts Word Index*. Publications interuniversitaires de recherches Égyptologiques informatisées, 6. Utrecht-Paris, 1998.

Podemann Sørensen, J. "Divine Access: The So-called Democratization of Egyptian Funerary Literature as a Socio-cultural Process." In *The Religion of the Ancient Egyptians. Cognitive Structures and Popular Expressions. Proceedings of Symposia in Uppsala and Bergen 1987 and 1988*, ed. G. Englund, 109–25. Acta Universitas Upsaliensis. Uppsala Studies in Ancient Mediterranean and Near Eastern Civilizations 20. Uppsala, 1987.

Quack, J. F. "Zur Lesung und Deutung des Dramatischen Ramesseumpapyrus." *Zeitschrift für ägyptische Sprache und Altertumskunde* 133 (2006): 72–89.

Quirke, S. *Ancient Egyptian Religion*. London, 1992.

Ritner, R. K. "Horus on the Crocodiles: A Juncture of Religion and Magic in Late Dynastic Egypt." In *Religion and Philosophy in Ancient Egypt*, ed. W. K. Simpson, 103–16. Yale Egyptological Studies 3. New Haven, CT, 1989.

———. "Daily Ritual of the Temple of Amun-Re at Karnak. P. Berlin 3055. A Selection." In *The Context of Scriptures. 1. Canonical Compositions from the Biblical World*, ed. W. W. Hallo, 55–57. Leiden, 1997.

———. "Magic: An Overview." In *The Oxford Encyclopedia of Ancient Egypt*, ed. D. B. Redford, Vol. 2, 321–6. New York, 2001.

Robinson, P. "'As for Them Who Know Them, They Shall Find Their Paths': Speculations on Ritual Landscape in the 'Book of Two Ways.'" In *Mysterious Lands*, eds. D. O'Connor and S. Quirke, 139–59. London, 2003.

Rochholz, M. *Schöpfung, Feindvernichtung, Regeneration. Untersuchung zum Symbolgehalt der machtgeladenen Zahl 7 im alten Ägypten*. Ägypten und Altes Testament 56. Wiesbaden, 2002.

Rößler-Köhler, U. *Zur Tradierungsgeschichte des Totenbuches zwischen der 17. und 22. Dynastie (Tb 17)*. Studien zum Altägyptischen Totenbuch 3. Wiesbaden, 1999.

Roth, A. M., and C. H. Roehrig. "Magical Bricks and the Bricks of Birth," *Journal of Egyptian Archaeology* 88 (2002): 121–39.

Sadek, A. I. *Popular Religion in Egypt during the New Kingdom*. Hildesheimer Ägyptologische Beiträge 27. Hildesheim, 1987.

Sauneron, S. *The Priests of Ancient Egypt*. Trans. by A. Morrisett. New York, 1969.

Schlögl, H. A. *Der Gott Tatenen. Nach Texten und Bildern des neuen Reiches*. Orbis Biblicus et Orientalis 29. Freiburg, 1980.

Schmidt, B. B. "Flood Narratives of Ancient Western Asia." In *Civilizations of the Ancient Near East*, ed. J. M. Sasson, Vol. 4, 2337–51. New York, 1995.

Schott, S. *Bemerkungen zum ägyptischen Pyramidenkult*. Beiträge zur ägyptischen Bauforschung und Altertumskunde 5, Part 2, 135–224. Cairo, 1950.

Servajean, F. *Les formules des transformations du livre des morts: à la lumière d'une théorie de la performativité, XVIIIe–XXe dynasties. Bibliothèque d'Etude* 137. Cairo, 2004.

Sethe, K. *Amun und die Acht Urgötter von Hermopolis. Eine Untersuchung über Ursprung und Wesen des ägyptischen Götterkönigs*. Abhandlungen der Preussischen Akademie der Wissenschaften 4. Berlin, 1929.

Shalomi-Hen, R. *Classifying the Divine: Determinatives and Categorization in CT 335 and BD 17*. Göttinger Orientforschungen IV. Reihe Ägypten 38. Wiesbaden, 2000.

Shubert, S. B. *You Who (Still) Live on Earth: A Study of the Egyptian Appeal to the Living Texts.* Ph.D. dissertation, University of Toronto, 2006.

Spalinger, A. J. "Festival Calendars." In *The Oxford Encyclopedia of Ancient Egypt*, ed. D. B. Redford, Vol. 1, 519–20. New York, 2001.

Stadler, M. A. *Der Totenpapyrus des Pa-Month (P. Bibl. nat. 149).* Studien zum Altaegyptischen Totenbuch 6. Wiesbaden, 2003.

Teeter, E. *The Presentation of Maat: Ritual and Legitimacy in Ancient Egypt.* Studies in Ancient Oriental Civilization 57. Chicago, 1997.

Topmann, D. *Die "Abscheu"-Sprüche der altägyptische Sargtexte. Untersuchungen zu Textermen und Dialogstrukturen.* Göttinger Orientforschungen. IV. Reihe: Aegypten 39. Wiesbaden, 2002.

Ullmann, M. *König für die Ewigkeit. Die Haüser der Millionen von Jahren. Eine Untersuchung zu Königskult und Tempeltypologie in Ägypten.* Ägypten und Altes Testament 51. Wiesbaden, 2002.

Valloggia, M. *Le mastaba de Medou-Nefer.* Balat 1. Fouilles de l'Institut Français d'Archéologie Orientale du Caire, 31/1–2. Cairo, 1986.

Verhoeven, U. *Das Totenbuch Monthpriesters Nespasefy aus der Zeit Psammetichs I. pKairo JE95714 + pAlbany 1900.3.1 pKairo JE 95649 pMarseille 91/2/1 (ehem. Slg. Brunner) + pMar.* Handschriften des Altägyptischen Totenbuches 5. Wiesbaden, 2001.

Vischak, D. "Common Ground between Pyramid Texts and Old Kingdom Tomb Design: The Case of Ankhmahor." *Journal of the American Research Center in Egypt* 40 (2003): 133–57.

Wallin, P. *Celestial Cycles. Astronomical Concepts of Regeneration in the Ancient Egyptian Coffin Texts.* Uppsala Studies in Egyptology 1. Uppsala, 2002.

Walls, N. "On the Couch with Horus and Seth: A Freudian Analysis (Or, the Case of Pharaoh's Mommy)." In *Desire, Discord and Death: Approaches to Ancient Near Eastern Myth*, N. Walls, 93–125. American Schools of Oriental ResearchBooks 8. Boston, 2001.

Wegner, J. "A Decorated Birth-Brick from South Abydos." *Egyptian Archaeology* 21 (2002): 3–4.

———. "Echoes of Power. The Mayor's House of Ancient *Wah-Sut.*" *Expedition* 48 (2006): 31–6.

Wiebach-Koepke, S. *Phaenomenologie der Bewegungsablaeufe im Jenseitskonzept der Unterweltbuecher Amduat und Pfortenbuch und der liturgischen "Sonnenlitanei."* Ägypten und Altes Testament 55. Wiesbaden, 2003.

Wilkinson, R. H. *The Complete Temples of Ancient Egypt.* London and New York, 2000.

Willems, H. *The Coffin of Heqata (Cairo JdE 36418): A Case Study of Egyptian Funerary Culture of the Early Middle Kingdom.* Orientalia Lovaniensia Analecta 70. Leuven, 1996.

Zeidler, Jürgen. "Zur Frage der Spätentstehung des Mythos in Ägypten." *Göttingen Miscellen* 132 (1993): 85–109.

INDEX

Abu Simbel, 100, 138, 150
academia, 19
academics, 33
aesthetics, 23
Africa, 27, 31, 124
Afro-Asiatic languages, 193
air pollution, 103
Akhenaten, xii, 34n19, 68, 98, 99, 134–137, 214, 238–239, 247n23
Akhenaton Museum, 147
Akhenaton Temple Project, 94
Akkadian, 189, 194, 198, 199
Alabama-Birmingham, University of, xi
Alexandria, 8, 44, 62, 81, 99, 101, 149, 164
Al-Idrisi, 7, 8
Allen, J. P., xii, 242
Amarna, vii, 21, 57, 60, 62, 65, 66, 68, 72, 74, 92, 136–137, 140, 147, 150, 154, 196, 240
Amenemhat III, 131
Amenhotep I, 132
Amenhotep III, viii, xii, 96n15, 110, 133, 134, 135, 138, 146, 149, 159
Amenhotep IV, 134, 135, 136, 146
American Research Center in Egypt, v, xi, xii, 21, 110, 112, 117, 148
American University in Cairo, v, xi, 21
Amunhotep III, 99
Ankhaf, 127
Annales du Service, 11, 258
anthropologists, 15, 27, 54
anthropology, 23, 26, 30, 46

antiquarians, 99
antiquities, 3, 7, 20, 76, 81–82, 88, 99, 145, 147, 148, 152, 153, 163, 164, 172
  market, 150, 151
  repatriation of, 3, 152
Arabic, 8, 20, 36, 189, 194, 197, 198, 199, 204n3, 228
ARCE. *See* American Research Center in Egypt
archaeologists, 10, 12, 13, 18–20, 59–60, 61, 62, 63, 65, 74, 75, 76n5, 99, 110, 119, 163, 164, 172
archaeology, 2, 3, 7–21
  father of modern, 12
  focus of, 74
  methods, 12, 20
  reports, 21
  settlement, 57, 74
  sponsors of projects, 20
  teams in, 13, 15, 18–20
  theory of, 20
archaeozoologists, 16
architects, 15, 60, 99, 154, 155, 175
Arizona, University of, i
art historians, 15
art history, 2, 123–142
art market, 163
art, Egyptian
  hallmarks of, 125
  monumental, 123
  styles and forms, 124
  use of stone, 123
  use of wood, 124
  viewpoint of, 125

277